Windows® 10

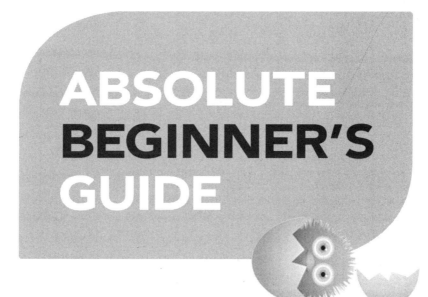

ABSOLUTE BEGINNER'S GUIDE

Alan Wright

800 East 96th Street,
Indianapolis, Indiana 46240

Absolute Beginner's Guide to Windows 10

ISBN-13: 978-0-7897-5456-1
ISBN-10: 0-7897-5456-8

Library of Congress Control Number: 2015932056

Printed in the United States of America

First Printing: September 2015

Trademarks

All terms mentioned in this book that are known to be trademarks or service marks have been appropriately capitalized. Que Publishing cannot attest to the accuracy of this information. Use of a term in this book should not be regarded as affecting the validity of any trademark or service mark.

Windows is a registered trademark of Microsoft Corporation.

Warning and Disclaimer

Every effort has been made to make this book as complete and as accurate as possible, but no warranty or fitness is implied. The information provided is on an "as is" basis. The author and the publisher shall have neither liability nor responsibility to any person or entity with respect to any loss or damages arising from the information contained in this book.

Special Sales

For information about buying this title in bulk quantities, or for special sales opportunities (which may include electronic versions; custom cover designs; and content particular to your business, training goals, marketing focus, or branding interests), please contact our corporate sales department at corpsales@pearsoned.com or (800) 382-3419.

For government sales inquiries, please contact governmentsales@pearsoned.com.

For questions about sales outside the U.S., please contact international@pearsoned.com.

Editor-in-Chief
Greg Wiegand

Executive Editor
Rick Kughen

Development Editor
William Abner

Managing Editor
Sandra Schroeder

Project Editor
Seth Kerney

Copy Editor
Megan Wade-Taxter

Indexer
Erika Millen

Proofreader
Gill Editorial Services

Technical Editor
Karen Weinstein

Publishing Coordinator
Kristen Watterson

Interior Designer
Mark Shirar

Cover Designer
Matt Coleman

Compositor
Bumpy Design

Contents at a Glance

Table of Contents

About the Author

Alan Wright has worked professionally in and around IT for more than 10 years. He has provided enterprise-level support in the Detroit, Michigan, area and now focuses on developing training materials for computer users while continuing to provide software and hardware support for small business and residential users. He holds several certifications from CompTIA and Microsoft and enjoys working with technology and teaching others how they can make technology work for them as computers and tablets continue to evolve. Alan has been the technical editor on other books from Que Publishing, including *Using Windows 8*, and co-authored *Windows 8.1 Absolute Beginner's Guide*.

Dedication

This book is dedicated to my patient and loving wife Pam, as well as our sons Joshua and Jonathan. They certainly had to share my attention with Windows 10 for several months while this book was in development.

Acknowledgments

I want to acknowledge the hard work of the many Microsoft engineers who have worked miracles to get the initial Windows 10 technical preview to where it is today. The millions of Windows Insiders form another group that has undeniably influenced how Windows looks today, and I hope they continue to shape Windows in the years to come. The growing group of developers of apps for Windows deserve some love. Windows is only as good as the apps that we use each day. It has been exciting to see the changes and improvements that developers are bringing to the Windows ecosystem.

Finally, I would be remiss if I did not thank some of the great editors that have helped bring this book to completion. Bill, Karen, and Megan are just some of the extra hands that have helped shape this book. Their comments and suggestions have helped to create a publication that I am pretty happy with. Rick Kughen has been a great executive editor to work with; he has helped keep things in perspective even when deadlines and changes have created anxiety.

We Want to Hear from You!

As the reader of this book, *you* are our most important critic and commentator. We value your opinion and want to know what we're doing right, what we could do better, what areas you'd like to see us publish in, and any other words of wisdom you're willing to pass our way.

We welcome your comments. You can email or write to let us know what you did or didn't like about this book—as well as what we can do to make our books better.

Please note that we cannot help you with technical problems related to the topic of this book.

When you write, please be sure to include this book's title and author as well as your name and email address. We will carefully review your comments and share them with the author and editors who worked on the book.

Email: feedback@quepublishing.com

Mail: Que Publishing
      ATTN: Reader Feedback
      800 East 96th Street
      Indianapolis, IN 46240 USA

Reader Services

Visit our website and register this book at quepublishing.com/register for convenient access to any updates, downloads, or errata that might be available for this book.

INTRODUCTION

I am delighted you are reading this introduction, whether you're considering buying this book or because you already own it. I know you'll find value reading it while you wrestle with this beast called Windows 10.

Windows 10 is just a few years removed from the Windows 8 operating system that really shook things up by introducing a modern, touch-oriented interface. Although Windows 8.1 improved on that design by adding features that improved the desktop experience, you will find Windows 10 to be a blend of the best features from its predecessors, including Windows 7.

Windows 10 is unique in that it has been designed and refined during a lengthy testing phase that benefited from feedback from millions of Windows Insiders who installed early versions of Windows 10 on an estimated 1.5 billion desktops, laptops, tablets, as well as virtual computers. This has resulted in new features and enhancements to existing apps and tools as well as improvements to the overall look and feel of the operating system. Microsoft has certainly encouraged and responded to this outsider input to ensure that the final product will be met with the welcome it deserves.

Microsoft has indicated that the reason this latest release of Windows skipped the expected "Windows 9" moniker is to emphasize the differences that set this operating system apart from its predecessors.

Windows 10 will power and unify computers, phones, gaming systems, and even new products such as the Surface Hub and Microsoft HoloLens. The user interface (UI) blends the Microsoft Modern design introduced in Windows 8 that features a minimal, consistent design and menus that are hidden until needed with familiar elements that have been a constant feature of Windows throughout its many iterations, like the start button and title bar.

Standard applications can be installed in Windows 10, or you can install apps made available through the Windows Store that are developed to leverage the Modern UI, making them attractive, engaging, and fast. Speed has been a priority that makes the Windows 10 start-up process much quicker; you might even wonder whether you really clicked Restart or you just imagined doing so.

Yep, for you beginners, that means there's a lot to learn about the new Windows environments. Good thing there's a book out there for the absolute beginner—am I right?

This book is intended to help you—whether you're new to Windows or just new to Windows 10—accomplish whatever it is you need or want to do during your personal or professional day. If you walk into the office and find your computer has been upgraded to Windows 10, you can read how to run (and where to find) your old programs. You can learn how to move around the system and how to work with your old files. You can also learn how to do those seemingly difficult administrative functions, such as setting up a printer or a second monitor.

If you have taken advantage of the opportunity to upgrade to Windows 10 from an older version of Windows or you find Windows 10 is loaded on a new computer you acquire for use at home, you can learn how to connect to all those social media networks, such as Facebook and Twitter. You can discover how to have fun with the photos you take and those that are shared with you. You can read how to buy and enjoy movies, music, and games. And for those times when work follows you home or your personal time is overrun by home business tasks, such as homework or creating a budget, you can learn how to be productive and efficient.

Microsoft has made a big deal about how Windows 10 can run on laptops, workstations, tablets, and many other devices. Allowing for form-factor differences, the user interface is essentially identical on all devices with the exception of how you interact with it: mouse, keyboard, stylus, speech, or touch. This book will focus on the Windows for PCs experience regardless of the computer and tablet hardware you use. Although this book doesn't cover the unique capabilities of certain models, such as the Lenovo Yoga Tablet 2, you can follow along with the lessons, how-tos, and explanations using whatever hardware you have.

The screenshots shown in this book come from a wide range of devices—some from small laptops, others from gigantic servers, and a few from tablets. Odds are you won't see a difference between them.

What Is an Absolute Beginner?

The book is respectful of your level of expertise. You are probably either new to Windows or, especially, new to Windows 10. You probably can handle a mouse and a keyboard, but the book guides you from the moment your computer or tablet starts through all the most common functions you're likely to demand from it.

How This Book Is Organized

The book follows a logical path, starting with the most basic information and getting into more specific topics in later chapters. Chapter names describe the type of information you will find, which will help you if you need to jump around in the book. For example, Chapter 13, "Connecting to Networks and the Internet," might be useful right away if you have a new device and cannot figure out why things are not connecting to the Internet. Feel free to read chapters and parts in any order you like. You might notice in the table of contents that there are four parts that group chapters according to broad categories:

- Part 1: Getting Started

- Part 2: Customizing Your Windows 10 Computer

- Part 3: Being Productive

- Part 4: Having Fun

If you are brand new to Windows, you will benefit from taking your time with the chapters composing the first part of this book. A detailed index is found in the back will be very useful if you're looking for content related to a specific command or feature.

Each chapter follows a standard format, but diversions from the format occur here and there. The first section in each chapter is a short list describing the things you can learn and do, along with a brief description and why the chapter is important. This short section also alerts you to any techniques you need to know to complete the tasks described in the chapter, as well as where in the book to find that guidance.

Special Bonus Content Online

I am also pleased to let you know that registered owners of this book have access to five additional bonus chapters online, with more than 100 pages of additional information related to recommended apps, consideration of many default applications included with Windows 10, and additional information related to File Explorer, as well as two chapters aimed at keeping your computer healthy and resolving problems that might occur. Be sure to register your book and check out this additional online content!

Conventions Used in This Book

This book is designed to be easy to understand. Even though Windows 10 might seem hard to learn, to help make your task of learning Windows simpler, instructions are formatted or written in a specific way to keep them consistent.

You will find numbered steps that you can follow to accomplish specific tasks. Useful illustrations and screenshots are carefully selected to help you recognize features or confirm that you are following steps correctly.

Selects and Selecting

Windows asks you to do lots of things. You're asked to click here, choose that, press this, and enter those. Given that you might use a touch-driven tablet or a mouse and keyboard, some of the instructions in the book are streamlined to reduce confusion by settling, as often as possible, on using the word *select*. When you see *select*, you complete the most natural action for the thing you are asked to select, whether that's a click of the mouse or a finger tap of the screen.

Many references are made throughout the book to specific keyboard, mouse, or touch techniques that would be used to accomplish the same task. This is done to expose you to the various methods that are built in to Windows 10 and to make you aware of these alternative techniques that you might need if you are suddenly faced with a different device than you are used to. Touchscreen users can find countless sets of specific instructions to interact with Windows via touch whenever the gesture for doing so with a touchscreen device is not obvious or is notably different from doing so with a mouse.

Finally, although you can accomplish most tasks in Windows with a mouse or via touch, you can still do a lot with a keyboard that enables you to work faster than with a mouse or touch. With that in mind, I try to present keyboard shortcuts here and there throughout the book to expose you to time-saving techniques that can make you look like a computer guru with your friends.

Special Elements

A few special tools employed in this book series emphasize certain points and concepts that might not be directly related to the topic discussed but are important enough to mention. These elements come in the form of Tips, Cautions, Notes, and Sidebars.

 NOTE   A Note is a useful piece of information that is not quite part of the core topic of the chapter or the section of the chapter where the note appears.

 TIP   A Tip is a useful piece of information that should help you get your work done a bit faster or a bit better in Windows 10.

 CAUTION   A Caution appears if there is a particular pitfall you must avoid or if there's a chance of losing your data executing one of the procedures in the book.

SIDEBAR

Sidebars will point out additional information that might be slightly off-topic. It can be additional background information or other details that are good to know.

Let Me Know What You Think

It is always nice to hear from readers, and I invite you to email me at alanlwright@outlook.com. I can't promise to respond to each email; however, I do promise to read each one. Your feedback and comments are welcome.

1

MEET WINDOWS 10

Windows 10 brings several new and exciting features that are covered in detail throughout this book. A few of these features are mentioned here in the first chapter, and I'll point you to chapters that discuss these in more detail. Whether you're a new computer user or a veteran, this chapter is all part of getting to know Windows 10.

If you just brought home a new computer with Windows 10 preinstalled, or if your computer has been upgraded to Windows 10, maybe you're thinking, "Now what?" The obvious answer is to power up your computer and sign in. If you're making the jump to Windows 10 from Windows 7 or an even older version of Windows, you'll notice this process is quite a bit different from what you're used to. If you have been stuck with Windows 8 and are worried whether Windows 10 will be a good experience, stop worrying; Windows 10 will make you wonder why you stayed with Windows 8 as long as you did.

If you haven't used Windows before, the start-up process can seem even more complicated. For these reasons, this chapter walks you through the steps necessary to start your computer and then sign in to Windows.

What's New in Windows 10

Windows 10 improves on and introduces numerous features to make your computing life easier and more productive. Following is a list of important new features and the chapters where these are covered in greater detail:

- **Start menu**—The Start screen was introduced in Windows 8, and it quickly polarized long-time Windows users with its new-fangled navigation interface. Windows 10 has created a more flexible interface with the Start menu that still has colorful live tiles and a highly customizable layout. The Start menu is first shown later in this chapter and then examined in detail in Chapter 3, "Optimizing the Start Menu."

- **Cortana**—Cortana is the personal assistant that is integrated into Windows 10. You can interact with Cortana using voice or keyboard commands. Use Cortana when searching for data on your device or out on the Web. Cortana is designed to learn about you so it can be an efficient personal assistant. Cortana is considered in detail in Chapter 9, "Using Search and Cortana."

- **Microsoft Edge**—Microsoft has re-created the web browser to create a faster and more stable browser that works well with modern websites and adds new capabilities to the browsing experience. Microsoft Edge is covered in detail in Chapter 14, "Browsing the Web."

- **Action Center**—Notifications are an important feature in today's interconnected world. Windows uses the new Action Center, shown in Figure 1.1, to keep notifications and other tools highly available in one place. The Action Center is discussed in Chapter 6, "Finding Your Way Around the Windows Desktop."

- **Continuum**—Continuum is the name Microsoft uses to refer to the dynamic ability that allows a device to automatically switch between desktop and tablet mode. The layout is altered to make touch or mouse interaction more efficient. This enables devices like tablets with keyboards to jump from one mode to the other when a keyboard is removed or deactivated. This feature is examined in Chapter 2, "Interacting with Windows."

FIGURE 1.1

The Action Center is a one-stop location for notifications and important system tools.

- **Task View**—Task View is a new feature to Windows 10. It allows a computer user to organize virtual desktops that fit different tasks. For example, one desktop might have applications running for business tasks while another has email and news apps running. You can jump between these desktops easily without wishing you had a bigger display. Task View is covered in Chapter 6.

- **OneDrive**—OneDrive is by no means a new feature. It was integrated into Windows 8 (with the name SkyDrive at the time), and it is even available to Apple and Android devices. However, its integration might be new to many Windows users moving from older systems, and its value is hard to overemphasize. OneDrive is covered in Chapter 22, "Working with OneDrive."

There are of course more new features that are less visible and many updates to apps that might get you excited or make you feel a bit lost. In either case, we'll consider these throughout this book as you continue to get familiar with Windows 10.

Starting Up Windows

Before you start up Windows 10 for the first time, there are a few things you should keep in mind:

- If someone other than you installed Windows 10, check with that person for the user ID and password you should use. Be sure to ask whether a *local account* or a *Microsoft account* was used. You'll learn more about these two account types and how to set them up in Chapter 19, "Sharing Your Windows Computer with Others."

- If you sign in to Windows 10 for the first time at your place of business, check with a person from your IT or support organization for your user ID and password, and if required, your domain. The domain identifies what part of the corporate network you log in to. If your computer has been upgraded to Windows 10, your user ID, password, and domain are probably the same as you used previously.

- If you are upgrading or starting up a new personal Windows 10 device for the first time, you will be asked to set up the device and sign in with an existing Microsoft account as the recommended sign-in option. A Microsoft account is an email address and a password that Microsoft can authenticate. You can choose to create a local account as well, although this option is not immediately offered. While creating these accounts is considered in this chapter, Chapter 19 discusses the use of these two account types in more detail. Keep in mind that an Internet connection will be needed to log in with a Microsoft account for the first time.

When you boot up your device, you either will be prompted to sign in with an existing account that has been set up previously or will be creating a new account for the first time on a new computer. Both possible situations are considered in the following sections. With these login options in mind, go ahead and boot up your Windows 10 computer.

 NOTE   If you're wondering if "signing in" is the same as "logging in," you are correct. Microsoft has adopted the term "signing in" to describe that process to identify one's self to Windows.

Signing In with an Existing Microsoft or Local Account

When you sign in to a Windows 10 device that has been set up previously, you will need to know the password or sign-in method that was set up for you. If you already have an existing Microsoft account, you should already have a password in place and be able to log right in. However, if you're working with an existing local account or one that someone else has set up for you, be sure to ask the person who did set up Windows what kind of password your account uses.

Beside a traditional password, Windows 10 allows for a few alternative sign-in methods depending on security settings and the device hardware. For example, some devices can now use biometrics by scanning fingerprints or a camera equipped for facial recognition; this is part of a new feature called Windows Hello. Two common alternative sign-in options can be later specified for sign-in: PIN and Picture Password. Besides saving you the repetitive stress of entering your password, these two options offer a lot of flexibility to determine how to access your user account:

- **PIN**—A *PIN* is a four-digit number you use to identify yourself when you sign in to Windows. A PIN is particularly useful to tablet users who normally do not have a physical keyboard.

- **Picture Password**—A *picture password* is a combination of a picture and touch gestures. To define a picture password, choose a picture from your Pictures folder and then make three gestures: you can choose to tap or draw lines or circles. Windows records the position of the gestures, their length, and the order in which you make them.

For information on setting up one of these two options, refer to Chapter 19. Examples of these two options are shown in this section.

With your account name and password in hand, follow these steps to sign in to Windows:

1. You can sign in to Windows by opening the Lock screen, sometimes referred to as the Welcome screen, as shown in Figure 1.2. The picture in your Lock screen might be different from the one shown here, but you can tell you're in the right place if you see the time and date superimposed on your picture. You actually can choose your Lock screen or allow Microsoft Spotlight to update your Lock screen images (default). Microsoft Spotlight will also provide additional tips that will appear now and then right on the Lock screen. To set up your Lock screen, see Chapter 8, "Tweaking Windows to Reflect Your Personality."

FIGURE 1.2

The Lock screen appears when Windows is locked, which automatically occurs if you do not enter your user ID and password promptly or have a period of inactivity.

2. From the Lock screen, swipe up, tap the spacebar, or click once on the screen. Any of these three gestures reveals the sign-in screen.

3. Select your account and username if more than one account appears (see Figure 1.3). If your portrait is the only portrait on the screen, skip this step and continue with step 4.

FIGURE 1.3

Select your account to sign in.

4. Your account should appear alone on the screen. From there, how you sign in depends on the type of password protection you have and the last method that was used. If more than one method is available, you can change options by selecting from the **Sign-in Options** icons shown below the password field. Alternative options are represented by icons. Select an alternative to use that method:

   • To sign in with a conventional password, enter it into the Password box and press Enter. If you want to verify you entered your password correctly, tap and hold or click and hold the eye-shaped icon near the end of the Password box, as shown in Figure 1.4.

FIGURE 1.4

You can check that you entered your password accurately.

- To sign in with your PIN, enter its four digits. Note that you will be signed in immediately after correctly entering the last digit of your PIN.

- If you used your picture password the last time you signed in, a screen like the one shown in Figure 1.5 appears. (Your picture will be different from the one shown here.) Make your three gestures on the picture. If you successfully make the three gestures, you are signed in.

5. If this is the first time this account is logging in to the device, you will be met with a series of colored status screens as Windows creates a new profile on the device for your account.

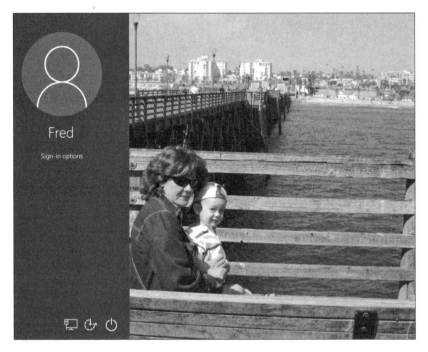

FIGURE 1.5

The Picture Password screen appears if you last signed in using your picture password.

 NOTE   If you made a mistake signing in with a picture password, Windows 10 prompts you to try again. Select OK and (more accurately) make your three touch gestures on the picture. To redo the gestures before Windows prompts you, select Start Over.

Signing In to a New Windows 10 Device

When you sign in to a Windows 10 device that has never been set up, you will be guided through the setup process with a series of screens that offer you options. During this setup process you either will sign in with an existing online account (such as a Microsoft account) that has been set up previously or will be creating a new account. Both scenarios are considered in this section.

When purchasing a new device, you will need to create a user account the first time you sign in. I recommend that you create a Microsoft account if you do not already have one. There are several advantages that you will enjoy when connected to the Internet. It is also possible that you need or prefer a local account. For details on these two account types, see Chapter 19. Both of these account types can be created easily when signing in by following these steps:

1. When first powering up a new device, you are greeted with a "Hi There" and prompted to set up the device with regional settings as shown in Figure 1.6. Indicate your choices and select **Next**.

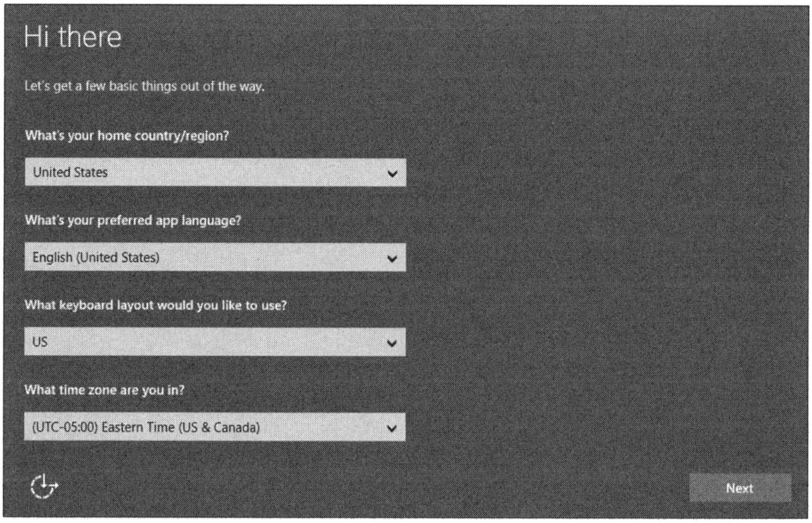

FIGURE 1.6

Set up a new device by first selecting your regional and language preferences.

2. Accept the Microsoft license terms to proceed.

3. As shown in Figure 1.7, Windows offers you a choice of Express settings or you may select Custom Settings to go through the default settings. (I recommend that you at least look through the Custom settings.) To proceed with

the defaults, select **Use Express Settings**. Express settings are set to do the following:

- Send speech, typing, and ink input data to Microsoft to improve the response of input methods

- Send data to improve input recognition and suggestions

- Allow apps to use your advertising ID for more targeted advertising

- Allow apps to access location information and location history

- Enable SmartScreen for safer web browsing (this is a good option to keep enabled)

- Send browsing history to Microsoft to enable page prediction

- Automatically connect to suggested hot spots

- Automatically connect to networks shared by contacts

- Send problem reports to Microsoft

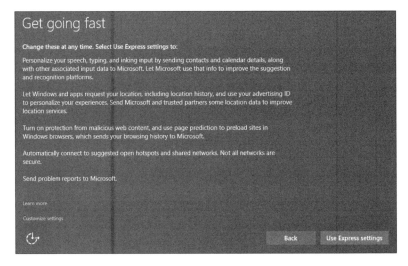

FIGURE 1.7

Start setting up your computer quickly with express settings, or feel free to look through the custom settings.

4. You are next asked if this is your PC or if it belongs to your organization as shown in Figure 1.8. Because organizations can enable certain features and they might use their own cloud account for improved security, be sure to check with your IT department for direction here. If this is your PC, go ahead and select **I Do** and then select **Next**.

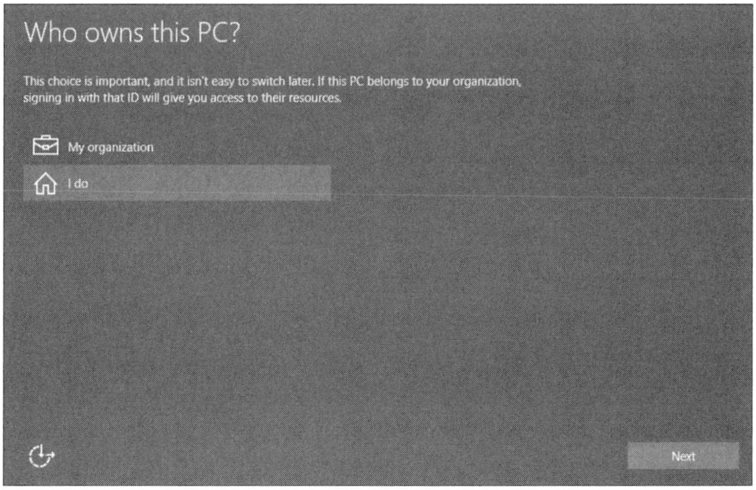

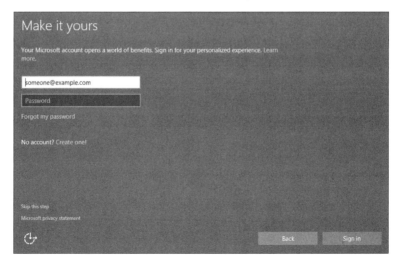

FIGURE 1.8

You might need to check with your IT department for instructions when first signing in to a PC owned by your organization.

5. You will be prompted to sign in to the device, as shown in Figure 1.9. If you have a Microsoft account, sign in with the current password. You must be connected to the Internet to verify the password and finish setting things up. Enter your credentials, select **Sign In**, and skip to step 6. To create a Microsoft account, select **Create One** and follow the directions given. Creating a Microsoft account is also detailed in Chapter 19.

FIGURE 1.9

Select from different options when signing in for the first time, use an existing Microsoft account, create one, or create a local account by skipping this screen.

6. To create a local account, select **Skip This Step**. You will proceed to the next screen where you will create a local account, as shown in Figure 1.10. Select a username and enter a password twice to confirm spelling; you will be required to provide a password hint. When finished, select **Next**.

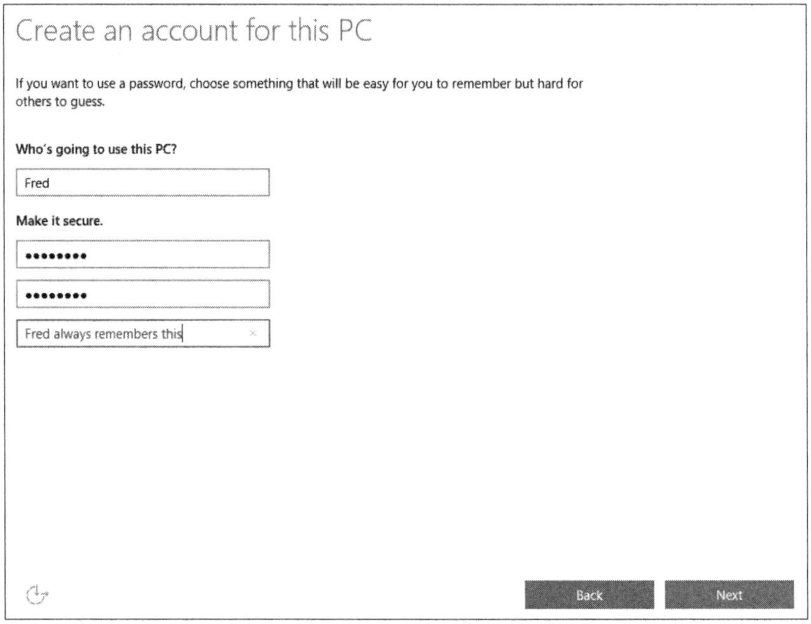

Create an account for this PC

If you want to use a password, choose something that will be easy for you to remember but hard for others to guess.

Who's going to use this PC?

Fred

Make it secure.

••••••••

••••••••

Fred always remembers this

Back   Next

FIGURE 1.10

Create a local account if you prefer not to use a Microsoft account.

7. Windows will proceed to create a new account profile on this device starting with a friendly "Hi" followed by a series of colorful status updates. When this steps finishes, you will be looking at your Desktop.

8. You will likely see some notifications regarding optional Windows features such as OneDrive or other Windows apps that are already installed on your device. You will be prompted to classify the network to which you are currently connected, as shown in Figure 1.11. Select **Yes** to let Windows know that this is a private trusted network or **No** to indicate that this is a public network such as a coffee shop.

After you have signed in, you will be able to start exploring and personalizing how Windows 10 looks and acts. The first thing you will need to learn about is the Start menu.

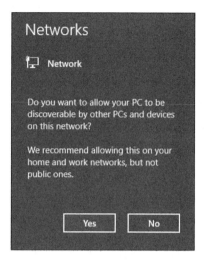

FIGURE 1.11

Let Windows know whether it is connected to a secure private network or an unsecure public one.

Introducing the Start Menu

After signing in to Windows, you are dropped off at the Desktop. In Windows 10 the newly designed Desktop and Start menu introduce a few changes compared to previous versions of Windows. Select the Start button to show the Start menu, as shown in Figure 1.12. The Start menu shows your most used apps as well as tiles that have been pinned. The Start menu is highly customizable and can be resized, or it can fill the screen.

To start, here's a short review of some of the key items you can see on the Start menu:

- **Tiles**—A tile is the representation of an application whether it is a desktop application or a Windows app. Tiles can be resized. Most tiles can be static, or they can be animated *Live Tiles*, displaying useful updated information from the app, such as new email alerts, weather details, news, or recent social network status updates. Live tiles may not display anything until you begin to use them, and they certainly grab your attention. Chapter 3 provides plenty of information about using, organizing, and manipulating tiles. To open the application, select the tile.

Live tile   Start menu

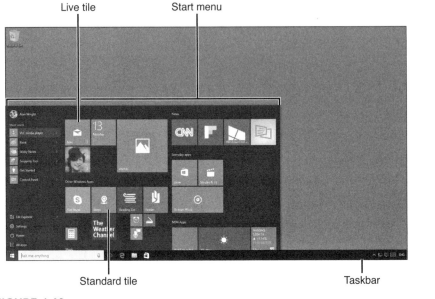

Standard tile   Taskbar

FIGURE 1.12

The Start menu is your gateway to everything Windows has to offer.

- **Start button**—The Start button is more than simply a way to invoke the Start menu. Right-click (or tap and hold using a touchscreen) the Start button to reveal a context menu with many advanced features and tools that power users will love, as shown in Figure 1.13.

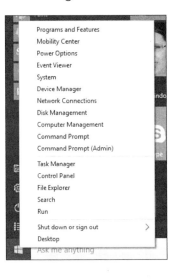

FIGURE 1.13

The Start button hides a lot of power user goodies when opening the context menu.

- **Account menu**—Touching or selecting the account that is currently signed in will reveal a drop-down menu with tools for signing out, locking the computer, and changing account settings.

When using some apps, the taskbar might autohide to allow more screen space for the app that is running. Because most of your work in Windows initiates from the Start menu, it is important to know how to quickly return here. Based on the device you use, follow one of these methods to return to the Start menu:

 Swipe up from the bottom of the screen to reveal the taskbar, and select the Start button. Many Windows tablets have a Start button that is always available, generally near the bottom of the display.

 Press the Windows key.

Bring the mouse cursor to the bottom of the screen to reveal the taskbar, and select the Start button.

Displaying All Apps

Unpinned apps and apps you use less often will not be immediately visible on the Start menu. To view everything installed on your device, select All Apps from where it appears above the Start button. The list of desktop applications and apps installed on your device appears as an alphabetical listing through which you can scroll, as shown in Figure 1.14. In some cases a folder is displayed that contains multiple applications. Select the folder to reveal its contents in a drop-down list. To return to the initial Start menu view, select the back arrow that appears above the Start button.

Browsing apps installed on your device by scrolling through the alphabetical list of applications can become rather tedious if you have installed a lot of applications. You can select a letter from the All Apps list to quickly jump to another letter in the list, as shown in Figure 1.15.

 TIP One of my favorite features in Windows 10 is the ability to start typing the name of an app or a desktop application from a physical keyboard anytime the Start button has been pressed or selected. The cursor automatically appears in the search field, and you just start typing the name of an application to quickly locate it. Windows will display desktop applications and apps that are installed on your device (among other things); you can just select the item to launch the app from there. This can be much faster than navigating All Apps or even looking for a tile. This ability has other uses also— for example, Chapter 9 takes a more detailed look at how to search using this technique.

FIGURE 1.14

You can easily see all the apps installed in Windows by selecting All Apps from the Start menu.

FIGURE 1.15

Jump to a letter when viewing the alphabetical All Apps list.

Pinning an Application to the Start Menu

Pinning an app to the Start menu is an important skill to learn right away. Pinned apps are easy to find, and with Windows apps, you can benefit from Live tile updates.

Follow these steps to pin an app to the Start menu:

1. From the Start menu, locate an application from the **Most Used** list or from the **All Apps** list.

2. Right-click (or tap and hold on a touchscreen) the application, as shown in Figure 1.16, to reveal the context menu. Select **Pin to Start**.

3. The application will be added to the bottom of your Start menu with other pinned applications.

FIGURE 1.16

Pin applications to the Start menu so you can easily find them.

Seeing Tiles That Are Offscreen

It doesn't take long for new tiles to add up and overflow on the Start menu. When you pin new apps, pictures, and shortcuts to the Start menu, your display of tiles starts to grow. The collection of tiles won't fit on a single screen, so you need to scroll down to see the rest of them; then you scroll back up to see the tiles you passed.

To see tiles off the screen, follow these steps based on the device you use:

- Scroll up and down by placing your finger on the screen in the area of the tiles and then swiping up or down in one smooth motion. If your attempt to swipe is mistaken as a tap, try to swipe on an empty spot on the Start menu, avoiding tiles.

- Use your arrow keys to navigate the Start menu. You will need to use the right arrow first to move into the tile area before the up and down arrows will allow you to select tiles and scroll through the Start menu tiles.

- Use the scroll wheel if your mouse is so equipped, or use the vertical scroll-bars to the right of the start menu.

Using the Getting Started App

Microsoft knows that a lot of new features are included in Windows 10, and they have included a Get Started app to help. You will find this pinned to the Start menu by default. If you do not see it, search for *Get Started*. The app contains screenshots, videos, and links to Microsoft websites that are designed to briefly answer questions and show how to accomplish basic tasks using the new Windows features and apps. The Get Started app is shown in Figure 1.17.

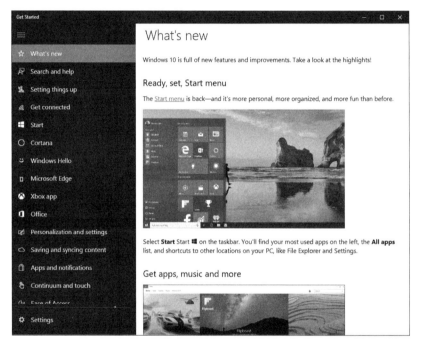

FIGURE 1.17

The Get Started app will also help answer questions about new Windows 10 features.

Exiting Windows

When you need to take a break from your computer—perhaps to shop for computer books—you should consider how long you will be away and in what state you should leave your computer. For example, if you are sharing your computer and are finished, then signing out of your account and letting the next person sign in is the best option. If you are going to be away from your computer for only a short period of time but are working on sensitive information, you should lock your computer.

Locking your computer immediately displays the Lock screen without affecting the programs running or the files that are open. This enables you to get back to work quickly as soon as you sign back in. With the sleep option, four choices are available to manage your computer while you take a break. You can also completely power down your computer if you think you're going to be away for a longer period of time.

Signing Out of Windows 10

Signing out is a good idea on shared computers. You leave no trail behind when you sign out of Windows. Any programs running when you signed out are shut down, and any connections you had open are closed. To sign out, follow these steps:

1. On the Start menu, select your account portrait to reveal the drop-down menu shown in Figure 1.18.

FIGURE 1.18

Sign out using the account drop-down menu located in the Start menu.

2. Select **Sign Out**.

3. If you attempted to sign out with unsaved work in either a Desktop or Windows app, Windows prompts you to save the work, as shown in Figure 1.19.

Signing out leaves your computer powered on but available for other users to sign in with their own accounts.

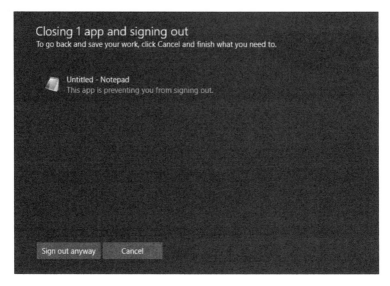

FIGURE 1.19

You see a warning on the Start menu if you try to sign out with unsaved work.

Locking Windows 10

Locking Windows 10 is useful if you are going to be away from your computer but want to resume your work or play when you return. Locking also prevents others from accessing the information on your computer.

To lock Windows, do one of the following:

- On the Start menu, select your account portrait and then select **Lock**.

- From a keyboard, press Windows+L.

Putting Windows 10 to Sleep

If you don't intend to use your computer for a longer period of time (for example, a few hours or even a full day), it makes sense to put the computer to sleep. When a computer is asleep, it is still running, although in a low-power mode. Because you can leave your applications and documents open when you put your computer to sleep, it usually takes far less time to start work again by awakening a computer than to power it up from scratch and reopen whatever program you were working on.

To put Windows to sleep, do one of the following:

- From the Start menu, select **Power**, and then select **Sleep**.

- Press Ctrl+Alt+Delete. Then, click or press the power button in the lower right and select **Sleep**.

To wake your computer from sleep mode, moving the mouse, typing, or pressing and releasing the power button typically wakes it. Do not press and hold the power button; doing so will typically shut down your computer.

Shutting Down Your Windows 10 Computer

If you're going to be away from your computer for an extended period of time and don't want it sucking away even the minimal amount of power that sleep mode uses, you can shut it all the way down. If you do not close any running programs or apps, Windows will attempt to do this before shutting down for you, but you must save any unsaved work. Otherwise, you will lose your changes since the last time you saved.

To shut down Windows, do one of the following:

- From the Start menu, select **Power**, and then select **Shut Down**.

- Press Ctrl+Alt+Delete. Then, click or press the power button in the lower right and select **Shut Down**.

THE ABSOLUTE MINIMUM

- Sign in to Windows with a Microsoft account if possible.

- You can use a PIN or a picture password instead of a password to sign in to Windows 10. These password types are particularly useful if you use a Windows 10 tablet.

- Get comfortable with using the Start menu; you will be using it frequently.

- Pin apps to the Start menu to quickly locate them when you need them.

- You have a wide choice of options when you want to pause your work and protect your files. Be sure to make the right choice—sleep, sign out, lock, or shut down—based on how long you will be away from your computer, whether you are sharing your computer, and where your computer is located.

INTERACTING WITH WINDOWS

Although this chapter's title suggests a broad presentation about working with Windows and does not identify a specific version, the focus of this chapter is relatively narrow. Windows 10 enables new methods to control what happens on the screen while continuing to support more traditional techniques. The methods you employ will make your experience more satisfying, which is why this book devotes an entire chapter—this one—to helping you learn how to interact with the various switches, dials, knobs, buttons, and pulleys that enable you to control what Windows does.

One of the notable features in Windows 10 is the support for mobile devices. Microsoft has made much of the fact that Windows 10 can run on laptops, desktops, tablets, smartphones, game consoles, as well as new devices like HoloLens. Allowing for form factor differences, the user interface (the part of the software that you touch, look at, and respond to) is consistent across all these devices, even if the method you use to interact with each is different.

In this chapter we focus on the ways in which you will interact with Windows on desktop, laptop, and tablet form factors. There are some things the mouse can't do that the finger or stylus can, and the keyboard can bring 100 keys to the party, whereas the mouse brings just 2 or 3.

Getting to Know the Windows 10 Interfaces

Because Windows 10 has to work across a range of hundreds of different models of desktops, laptops, and tablets, Microsoft dictated specific guidelines as to how all these hardware devices should work with it. These guidelines apply to traditional personal computers as well as tablets. So, the product of all this consistency is a batch of techniques (for example, "Click like this," "Swipe like that") that work across all kinds of devices.

In this section of the chapter, you can review how to interact with Windows 10 computers using the four main interfaces: touch, the mouse, the keyboard, and the Touch keyboard.

Working with Continuum and Tablet Mode

Windows 10 has introduced a new feature called Continuum that allows your device to be smart about the best interface based on the current hardware available. If you have a tablet, you will likely be using touch to interact with Windows. Your device can work in Tablet mode to make things more spaced out on the screen, allowing for an improved touch experience and fewer mistakes because things are too crowded together. Your Start menu can be full screen rather than just occupying a portion of the screen, and the taskbar can hide app icons. If a keyboard and mouse are connected, Windows can exit Tablet mode to allow for more precise mouse input. Continuum makes these changes happen automatically. You can override the way Tablet mode is engaged or which actions are taken.

To make changes to Tablet mode, follow these steps:

1. From the Desktop, type **tablet mode** in the search box.

2. Select **Tablet Mode Settings** from the search results. The Settings app will open to Tablet mode, as shown in Figure 2.1.

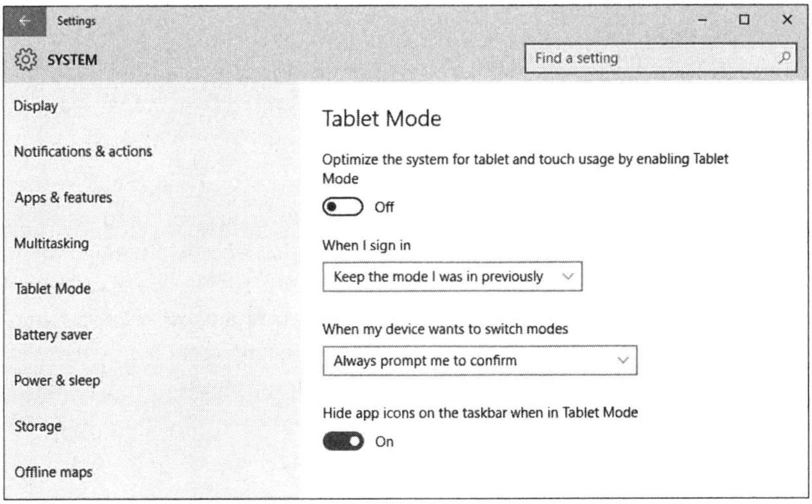

FIGURE 2.1

Windows lets you control just how automatically Tablet mode will work on your device.

3. You can manually switch Tablet mode **Off** or **On** for the device using the first switch. (This task can also be accomplished much easier from the Action Center.)

4. Change whether Tablet mode is automatically selected when starting your device by using the drop-down list **When I Sign In**:

- **Immediately Enter Tablet Mode**—This will start your device in Tablet mode regardless of your hardware configuration. The Start menu will be open full screen and ready to use.

- **Take Me to the Desktop**—This will open to the Desktop, and the Start menu will be minimized. Tablet mode will not be enabled.

- **Keep the Mode I Was in Previously**—This choice allows the device to remember which mode was in use last time, and it will return to that.

5. Change how Continuum reacts to hardware changes by using the drop-down list **When My Device Wants to Switch Modes**. The choices are

- Never Prompt Me and Always Stay in My Current Mode

- Always Prompt Me to Confirm

- Never Prompt Me and Always Switch Modes

6. The last switch, **Hide App Icons on the Taskbar When in Tablet Mode** is **On** by default. You can turn this **Off** if you prefer to see icons for apps that are open while in Tablet mode.

 TIP You can manually change modes at any time using the Action Center. An example is presented later in this chapter in the section "Using the Touch Keyboard."

 NOTE Windows 10 includes stylus support, and many tablets include this accessory. The stylus input is discussed briefly in relation to the new web browser Microsoft Edge in Chapter 14, "Browsing the Web." Voice has become another important way to interact with Windows. Voice interaction is covered in Chapter 9, "Using Search and Share."

Using the Mouse in Windows 10

The mouse is a great choice for any device when precision is a factor, although touch is more efficient and easier to use with a tablet. Following are the commands you see associated with use of the mouse:

- **Point**—Unless you have a special version of Windows that can read your mind, you use a mouse to *point* to the item on the screen with which you want to work. The mouse pointer is usually in the shape of an arrow, but you can always change it to another shape, as explained in Chapter 10, "Configuring Input Device Settings." You can also download Windows *themes* that bring together a new color scheme and fun graphics, including cool, new mouse pointers, to give Windows a different look and feel.

- **Click**—Besides picking up dust, the most common action you take with the mouse is *click*. You *click* to select items, to start and stop actions in Windows, to indicate where text you write should be inserted, and more. To *click* with your mouse, just tap the primary mouse button.

- **Double-click**—The *double-click* mouse action traditionally has been used in Windows to start a program or launch a task. In Windows 10 most of those *double-clicks* have been changed to single-clicks, mainly to make things more consistent for all users. Any of the programs you ran in previous versions of Windows that required a *double-click* have the same requirements if you run the same programs on the Desktop.

- **Right-click**—The right-click traditionally is used to display a context menu of commands related to the item you *right-click*. For example, *right-clicking* a photo might present commands to open your photo editing application and to add the picture to a slide show. This convention still works on the Desktop but not on the Start screen. On the Start screen, *right-clicking* displays the Apps bar, and in Windows 10 apps, right-clicking displays the Command bar. The App bar and Command bar are described in Chapter 5, "Working with Windows Apps."

 NOTE   When you see the command to select or click, this always refers to the primary mouse button, as described in this section. Any task that requires you to click the secondary mouse button clearly says to use the secondary or right-click mouse button. You also can specify which button on your mouse is the primary button. Refer to Chapter 10 for help with configuring the mouse.

- **Click and drag**—The *click-and-drag* action is used to select and move files, folders, or any other item from one place to another in Windows 10. You can always use the cut-and-paste menu convention (when available) to move things, but you can save time and look smarter by using *click and drag*. *Click and drag* is also known as *drag and drop*. One of the most prominent areas in which you can employ *click and drag* on the Windows 10 Start screen is where you can drag a tile to a new location on the Start screen. *Click and drag* can also be used to select a group of items that are next to one another.

 TIP   Windows always treats click and drag as a move action. This means the item you were dragging will no longer be in the location from which you dragged it. To use click and drag as a copy action, press and hold down the Ctrl key before you release the mouse key to drop the file in its new location. Windows will copy the file rather than move it.

- **Right-click and drag**—A cousin to the click and drag is the *right-click and drag*. Just as the right-click displays a menu with commands specific to the item you click, so does the *right-click and drag*. Windows recognizes the item you are dragging and pops up a menu relevant to the item and the destination of your drag. *Right-click and drag* can also be used to select a group of items that are next to one another.

Using the Keyboard in Windows 10

Windows 10 includes an onscreen keyboard that appears when you need it. This section is dedicated to the physical keyboard. You can read about the Touch keyboard in a bit, in the section "Using the Touch Keyboard."

The keyboard is an important tool for interacting with Windows 10, but its role is for more than entering text and punctuation. You can use a large number of key shortcuts to issue commands to Windows 10. A keyboard shortcut (or key combination) refers to two keys (or more) pressed simultaneously to issue a specific command, such as Windows Key+F to use the Search tool. Some of the newer key combinations in Windows 10 use the Windows key as the first key in the combination. Keep in mind when using keyboard shortcuts that you should always press the Windows key slightly before pressing the second key.

Table 2.1 lists some useful key combinations you can use with Windows 10.

TABLE 2.1   Windows Keyboard Shortcuts

Press This	To Do This
Windows (alone)	Open or close the Start menu
Windows+D	Shows the Desktop; open apps are minimized
Windows+E	Opens File Explorer
Windows+F	Jumps cursor to the Search field on the taskbar (Cortana if enabled)
Windows+H	Opens the Share pane; likely you will be sharing a screenshot of the current desktop
Windows+I	Opens the Settings app
Windows+K	Opens the Media Connect pane
Windows+M	Minimizes all windows on the Desktop
Windows+P	Opens the Project pane to connect to a projector or second display device
Windows+Q	Opens the Search app (Cortana if enabled)
Windows+T	Goes to taskbar on the Desktop where you can cycle through running apps
Windows+X	Opens the Start button context menu
Windows+Z	Opens the App Commands bar when working with a modern app with this feature
Windows+Comma	Peeks at the Desktop
Windows+Tab	Activates Task View allowing you to jump between open Desktops and applications
Windows+PrtScn	Takes a picture of a screen and places the picture in the Photos folder in Screenshots

There are of course dozens—if not hundreds—of keyboard shortcuts you can use to simplify your life. Many software makers integrate keyboard shortcuts into their interfaces; therefore, a key combination can differ from one application to another. Certain combinations have become standard, and a quick Internet search will present a very long list of results. Rather than try to memorize all of them, try to learn a few that really help you. They will quickly become second nature. Once you get those down, you can add more gradually.

In Table 2.2 I offer my top 10 keyboard shortcuts.

TABLE 2.2   Favorite Keyboard Shortcuts

Press This	To Do This
Ctrl+C	Copy.
Ctrl+V	Paste.
Alt+Tab	Jump between open applications; similar to the Windows+Tab.
PrintScrn	Capture whatever is on the screen to your Windows clipboard. This is useful when helping someone troubleshoot a problem that you cannot see.
Alt+PrintScrn	Capture the currently selected window to your Windows clipboard.
Ctrl+Z	Undo. This is a standard shortcut for most applications.
Tab	Jump to the next field. I am surprised how often I watch people fill out an online form or work in Excel who do not know that Tab allows them to jump from field to field.
Shift+Tab	Jump to previous field.
Ctrl+A	Select All.
Ctrl+F	Find. This will generally open a search tool, and I use this often when looking for something specific on a web page.

Using Touch in Windows 10

The touch interface was introduced in Windows 8, and its implementation has become more polished in Windows 10. In previous versions of Windows, you could use a stylus, a mouse, and the keyboard to work with Windows, such as to sketch and trace. With Windows 10, you can use your finger or another touch device to completely interact with Windows and issue commands. A number of hardware manufacturers have brought mobile devices to market to take advantage of the new Windows touch interfaces, including Microsoft with its own popular

Surface brand of tablets. Here are some of the devices that leverage the new touch capabilities:

- Tablets

- Laptops with touchscreens

- Touch-sensitive displays

- Phones

Whereas you use the word *click* to specify the action you take with a mouse to interact with Windows, touch-specific commands generally use the word *gesture* because it's a word that describes just about any action you take with your touch device. Here is a list of the gestures used with Windows 10, including some tidbits on how the gesture works:

- **Swipe**—The swipe is a short movement with your finger or fingers across the screen of the device. The fingers are on the screen only for a short period of time. A direction is usually given when you are instructed to swipe, such as Swipe Down from the top of the screen.

- **Tap**—It doesn't get any easier than this gesture. To tap, just touch your finger to the screen.

- **Tap and hold**—The tap-and-hold action is the touch equivalent of the mouse right-click. You usually press and hold a specific item, such as a file or folder. This action is used predominantly to display a special menu that contains commands relevant to the item you pressed and held. You can tell you pressed long enough by the appearance of the small square symbol at the point on the screen where you held.

- **Pinch and stretch**—Use the pinch gesture and the stretch gesture to zoom into an image (stretch) or to shrink an image (pinch). To pinch, place two fingers on the display separated a bit over the image you want to change. While keeping contact with the screen, slowly draw both fingers together as if you were softly pinching a baby's cheek. You can stop drawing your fingers together when you are happy with the results of the pinch, such as reducing the size of an image.

  To stretch, place two fingers on the display slightly touching one another over the image you want to affect. While keeping contact with the screen, slowly draw both fingers apart. You can stop drawing your fingers apart when you are happy with the new size of the image.

Using the Touch Keyboard

Windows 10 displays an onscreen touch-friendly keyboard when it detects that one is necessary, as shown in Figure 2.2. As you type letters, predictive text will present words you can select rather than typing the entire word. The keyboard can display letters, numbers, symbols, and emoticons. To toggle these keyboards, use the &123 key and the emoticon key. Windows 10 includes a deep emoticon library, as shown in Figure 2.3.

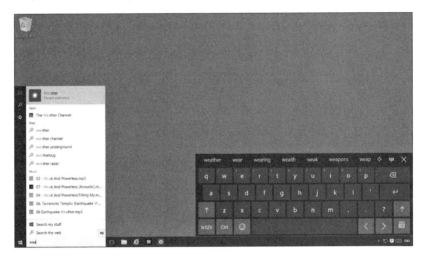

FIGURE 2.2

Windows displays the Touch keyboard automatically when it believes you need it.

FIGURE 2.3

The Touch keyboard offers an extensive library of emoticons.

There are two conditions that, together, let Windows 10 know that a touch keyboard is needed:

- You use a touch device, such as a tablet or a touch screen. (Windows 10 can detect it.)

- You are on a screen requiring text input and no physical keyboard is detected.

You can choose between three keyboard layout modes. To choose the keyboard mode, tap the main language key at the bottom-right corner of the Touch keyboard (refer to Figure 2.2), and then tap the tile for the keyboard mode you need (see Figure 2.4):

- Regular Keyboard

- Split Keyboard (sometimes referred to as a thumb keyboard)

- Handwriting Recognition

FIGURE 2.4

Change the layout modes for the Touch keyboard.

While the Touch keyboard normally appears when needed, you occasionally might find that the keyboard does not display automatically. If you do not see the Touch keyboard while using a touchscreen device, follow these steps:

1. Select the keyboard icon on the taskbar to manually invoke the Touch keyboard (refer to Figure 2.2).

2. If you do not see a keyboard icon on the taskbar, select and hold the taskbar until the context menu appears as shown in Figure 2.5. Make sure that the option Show Touch Keyboard Button is checked.

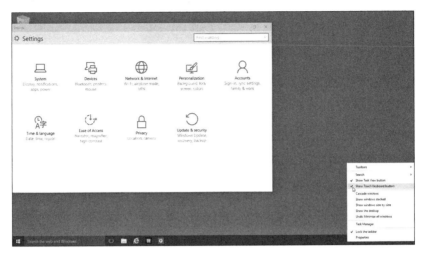

FIGURE 2.5

The Touch keyboard icon will not appear on the Taskbar if it's not enabled.

3. Enable Tablet mode by swiping in from the right on your touchscreen (or by selecting the Action Center icon on the taskbar) to reveal the Action Center. Locate the **Tablet Mode** tile in the bottom section of the Action Center pane (see Figure 2.6). Select it to enable Tablet mode. Windows will now expect touch interaction rather than keyboard and mouse input. (For more information about the Action Center, see Chapter 6, "Finding Your Way Around the Windows Desktop.")

 NOTE The Touch keyboard should not be confused with the On-screen keyboard that can be enabled using Ease of Access tools. To learn more about setting up and using Ease of Access tools, see Chapter 12, "Configuring Notifications and Advanced Settings."

FIGURE 2.6

Make sure your touchscreen device is in Tablet mode when looking for the Touch keyboard.

Using Controls

If you have experience with Windows 7 or an earlier version of Windows, you can probably skip this section unless you would like a refresher. If you are a beginner to Windows or are new to computers in general, this section helps you get comfortable with the tools and objects you use on the Desktop.

Window

A window is the control that organizes and stores other controls. It is the main organization unit in all Windows software that powers millions of computers and devices around the world. It might help you to think of a window as a container that allows you to see or interact with an app or a Desktop application. The window is so important that Microsoft named its operating system after it. Software programs present their options and settings in a window, you supply information to those programs in a window, and the messages the program reports back to you are presented in a window.

Figure 2.7 shows a window and points out a few key parts. You can find a lot of information about windows in Chapter 6.

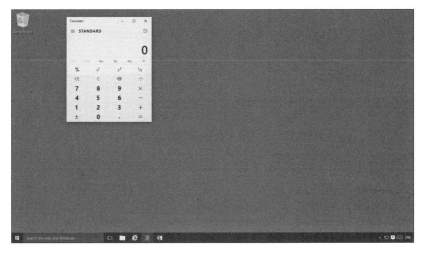

FIGURE 2.7

A typical window found on the Desktop.

Button

A button's use is fairly obvious. You click a button to execute the command indicated by the text on the button. In many cases, a button that is labeled OK means *proceed as planned* or *I am through making choices—go ahead and finish the job.* A button with the label Cancel usually indicates *forget it, I changed my mind* or *don't finish what you started.* Sometimes a picture or an image is used as a button. You click the picture to execute the command portrayed by the picture. Figure 2.8 shows examples of different buttons, including both traditional buttons and new tile buttons used in Windows 10.

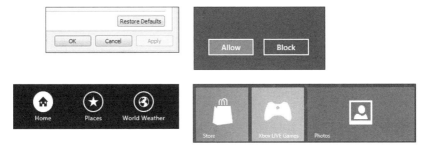

FIGURE 2.8

Buttons in Windows come in a variety of shapes and sizes.

Text Box

If you have ever entered your name or address to register a new program or to identify yourself to a website, you have used a text box. If the program you use requires more information from you than just a single line of information, you will see a much larger text box.

 TIP Most text boxes work properly with the Windows cut/copy/paste mechanism. This means you can copy information from a document or an email message and then paste it into a text box (Ctrl+C is the keyboard shortcut to copy selected text). Sometimes you can't access a menu when entering information into a text box, and sometimes you can't choose Paste. In these cases you can usually use the keyboard command to paste by pressing Ctrl+V while the cursor is inside the text box.

Check Box

You might see a check box when you must select whether some state or condition is on or off. The presence of a check in the box generally indicates an option or choice is enabled, or *on*. In most uses, a check box actually isn't checked. Rather, an "x" symbol fills the box part of the control. Figure 2.9 shows examples of check boxes used both to enable options and to select items.

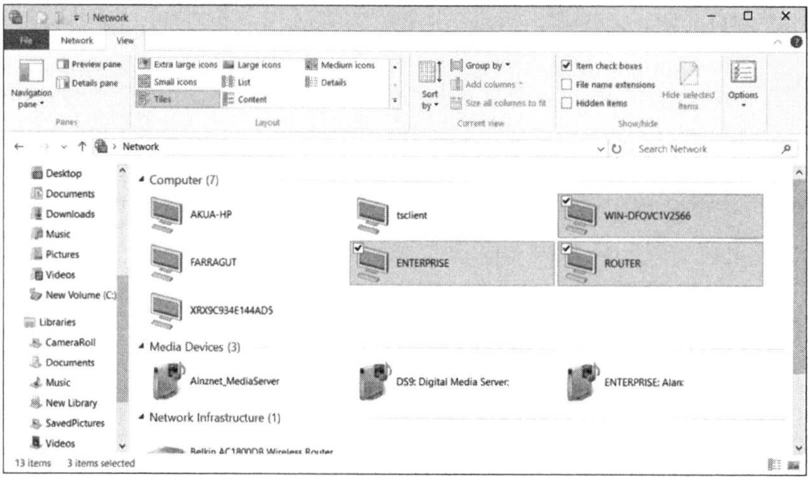

FIGURE 2.9

A check box indicates an on or off condition.

To check or uncheck a check box, do one of the following:

- Click in the check box or on the text to change it.

- Tap in the check box or on the text to change it.

Switch

Windows 10 introduces the toggle switch control. Like the check box control, the switch presents an on or off condition. The label next to the switch tells you what setting is controlled. It's easy to toggle the switch to on or off with the mouse or touch, as shown in Figure 2.10.

To switch a Windows 10 toggle, do one of the following:

- Click and drag the bar to the other end of the toggle.

- Press and hold on the bar, and then drag it to the far end of the toggle.

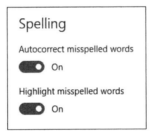

FIGURE 2.10

The switch is used to turn some setting on or off.

Drop-Down List

A drop-down list, also called a *drop-down menu*, presents a list of items from which you can choose. The items in the list appear to drop when you select the text or the arrow button on the right side of the control, as shown in Figure 2.11. The currently selected item in the list is always shown in the visible portion of the drop-down list when it is minimized, and it appears highlighted within the drop-down list. Long lists enable you to scroll to browse the entire list.

To select an item from a list in a drop-down control, do one of the following:

- Select the arrow at the end of the control or the visible text of the current selection. Then scroll through the list to find your item. Select your item when you find it.

- Tap the arrow beside the control to drop down the list of choices. Scroll through the list until you find your item. When you do, tap it.

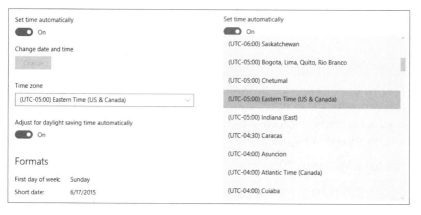

FIGURE 2.11

A drop-down list takes up less room, but it can contain many choices.

Combo Drop-Down List

A combo drop-down list is similar to the drop-down list control described earlier. The only difference is you can enter the name of the item you want to select in the part of the control that displays the selected item with the combo drop-down list.

The list automatically selects the first item in the list whose name matches the text you type. This control is used when it is believed you might not know whether the item you're interested in is actually in the list. It's quicker to verify that the item you want is listed by entering its name rather than scrolling through the list. Examples include typing letters into a search box and the way website suggestions appear when you manually type in a URL address.

Hamburger Menus

Hamburger menus have invaded Windows with Windows 10. Called *hamburger menus* due to a resemblance to a hamburger patty with a top and bottom bun, this type of menu has been a common feature in other operating systems and has gained wide acceptance. The hamburger menu in Windows generally is used to reveal important controls that do not need to always be visible in a modern app. The hamburger menu can expand a vertical list of icons to reveal their purpose, or it can reveal a hidden list of controls, as shown in Figure 2.12.

To expand the contents of a hamburger menu, simply select the menu icon. To hide the menu, either select the icon again or make a selection inside or outside of the menu.

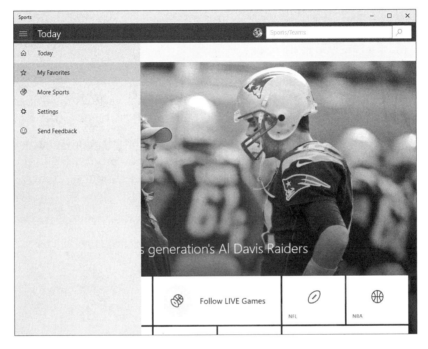

FIGURE 2.12

Hamburger menus reveal important controls when needed.

THE ABSOLUTE MINIMUM

- There are four primary interfaces you can use to interact with Windows 10: mouse, keyboard, Touch keyboard, and touch.

- Windows 10 appears and operates almost identically on different devices.

- Make sure you recognize and know how to use the tools to interact with Windows 10, such as the On/Off toggle switch and drop-down menus.

- Although the keyboard alone does not have the capability to access all the buttons, lists, and switches that a mouse or your finger does, keyboard shortcuts are available that automate many of the important tasks in Windows.

3

OPTIMIZING THE START MENU

Because the Start menu serves as your dashboard to access the many features and applications contained within Windows 10, you should spend some time organizing and customizing how it looks. There are endless possibilities of tile arrangements using different tile sizes. You can also name organized groups of tiles, or applications, using logical labels.

Organizing All Those Tiles

In Chapter 1, "Meet Windows 10," you had a quick introduction to the Start menu and became familiar with some basic features. By now you have no doubt begun to pin applications to your Start menu, and you might notice that it can become a free-for-all very quickly, as shown in Figure 3.1.

In this section you will find out how to change the look and feel of the Start menu while maintaining some order. The key to the Start menu is to make things easy to find without pinning so many applications that you are frustrated when hunting for an application.

FIGURE 3.1

The Start menu can begin to look like a random mess.

 NOTE   Refer to Chapter 1 for steps on how to pin applications to the Start menu.

Accessing the Context Menu of a Tile

Before you change any tile's appearance or function, you need to open the context menu for that tile. This is different from selecting the tile and opening the application.

The context menu will vary a bit between Desktop applications and Windows apps such as the one shown in Figure 3.2. To open the context menu, do one of the following based on the device you use:

 Touch and hold a tile for a second or two until an ellipsis appears in the lower-right corner of the tile. Select the ellipsis to reveal the touch-friendly context menu.

Use your left- and right- or up- and down-arrow keys to move across the Start menu. As you do so, a checkered border appears around tiles as you pass over them. Press the menu key when you have moved to the tile you want to select.

Right-click the tile.

FIGURE 3.2

The context menu provides a few tools for organizing your tiles.

Making a Tile Bigger or Smaller

With the context menu you can select the size for any tile. There are four sizes for Windows apps: large, wide, medium, and small (refer to Figure 3.2). Desktop applications that are pinned to the Start menu will offer only two size choices: small and medium. You might prefer smaller tiles to fit more tiles on the screen. Other tiles that have live tile capabilities will work better when a larger size is used. You also can use size to indicate priority or importance to your routine. For example, apps you use often, such as Calendar and Mail, might be represented by large tiles, and apps you use to pass the time, such as a social media app, could be represented with small tiles. The size of the tiles can be changed to suit your individual preference—there is no right or wrong tile size.

To change a tile's size, follow these steps:

1. Open the context menu for the tile using the methods outlined in the previous section.

2. Select **Resize**. Choose from the size options indicated.

3. As you make changes to tile sizes, the surrounding tiles will move to accommodate the new size. Figure 3.3 shows a mosaic composed of four different sizes.

FIGURE 3.3

Use different tile sizes to make certain tiles more prominent.

Controlling Live Tiles

Many Windows apps are designed to provide updates, images, and information through the use of Live tiles. This can be distracting in some cases, and you can even feel that your Start menu has become too busy with so many tiles morphing and changing constantly.

Live tiles can be disabled very easily by following these steps:

1. Open the context menu for the tile using the methods outlined earlier in this chapter.

2. Select **Turn Live Tile Off** (refer to Figure 3.2).

Live tiles are generally designed to display more content with larger sizes and usually will not function when set to the smallest size. Some Windows apps also include Live tile options within the app that can provide settings for transparency, images, or which information from the app will appear in the Live tile.

Moving a Tile

You can reorganize the tiles on the Start menu as you like. No rules dictate where certain tiles should appear, so you can move a tile to whatever position you like.

To move a tile, do one of the following based on the device you use:

- Touch and hold on the tile to be moved, and immediately drag it to its new location.

- Click and drag the tile to its new location. Notice when you click and hold the tile that the other tiles dim and shrink slightly. Also notice how the other tiles on the Start menu seem to move out of the way and open an empty spot as you drag a tile across the screen (see Figure 3.4).

FIGURE 3.4

Moving a tile.

Show More Tiles

One result of pinning more tiles to your Start menu is that your screen can only display so many tiles at a time before you need to scroll down to see additional tiles you have pinned. This is especially noticeable on devices with smaller screens. For this reason, devices like tablets running in Tablet mode will display the Start menu full screen, and the navigation menu will be reduced to a hamburger menu icon.

Having larger screens, desktop and laptop computers will run in Desktop mode by default with a Start menu that takes up just a portion of the screen and an expanded navigation menu. You actually can manually change the size of the Start menu or make it full screen.

To show more tiles, follow these steps:

1. From the Start menu, hover your mouse cursor over one of the two edges of the Start menu. The cursor will turn into a two-sided adjustment arrow. Select the edge and drag it to reposition the size of the Start menu. The horizontal adjustment will depend on your screen resolution. Release the edge when it is in the correct position.

2. From the Start menu, select **Settings** to open the Settings app.

3. Select **Personalization** and then **Start** from the navigation pane.

4. Under Start, slide the switch to On for **Use Start Full Screen**, as shown in Figure 3.5. The Start menu will now be full screen with a condensed navigation menu similar to Tablet mode.

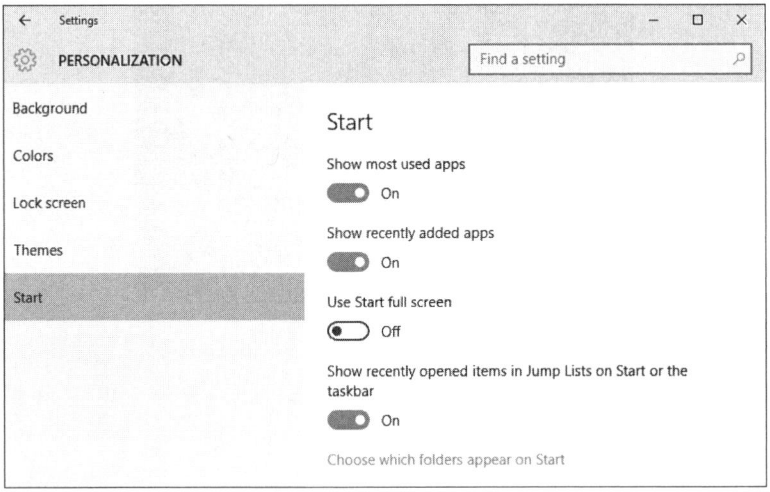

FIGURE 3.5

You can use a full-screen Start menu while in Desktop mode if that is what you want.

Personalizing Tile Groups

Your collection of tiles is bound to grow as you install new programs and apps. You also can pin documents and web pages to the Start menu, so it's likely you will add many, many tiles to the Start menu in a short period of time. To help keep track of tiles and easily locate them, you can organize tiles into groups of your own design.

For example, you might create a group of tiles of all your photo-related applications. The groups are organized into columns on the Start menu. A wider margin separates one group from another. You can move your tile groups when you like, and you can place a name above each group. An example of a number of tile groups appears in Figure 3.6.

FIGURE 3.6

You can organize the tiles on the Start menu into groups.

Creating a Tile Group

Tile groups, as the name implies, are tiles grouped into a collection where there isn't any separation by margins or blank space. Within these groups you can adjust tile size and where they appear within the group. Sometimes it is easier to break out particular tiles into a separate group so they are easier to find or to where they make more sense from an organizational standpoint. Windows puts its default tiles into somewhat logical groups, but they might not appeal to you.

To create a tile group, follow these steps:

1. From the Start menu, select a tile and drag it to an area below a group or between two groups. Tiles will move and shift to allow you to add the tile to an existing group; however, you will drop it into a new group when you see a horizontal title bar appear for the new group name, as shown in Figure 3.7. Release the tile to create the group.

2. Drag additional tiles to the group.

Figure 3.8 shows that you have created a new group with several tiles separated by margins on either side.

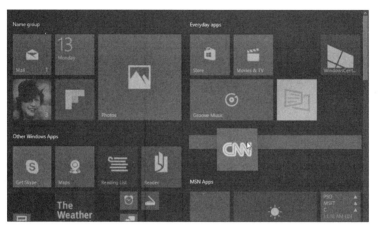

FIGURE 3.7

Dragging a tile to create a new group.

FIGURE 3.8

A newly created group.

Moving Tile Groups

You might want to change the order of your groups so that frequently accessed tiles require less scrolling or if you have changed your organizational structure.

To move a tile group, follow these steps:

1. From the Start menu, locate a tile group you would like to move.

2. Select the title bar, which currently might be an empty space above the group, and drag it to a new location in the Start menu. The group will condense to just the title bar for the group.

3. As shown in Figure 3.9, groups will shift to make space for the group and a space holder will appear to indicate possible locations for the group. Release the group when you are satisfied.

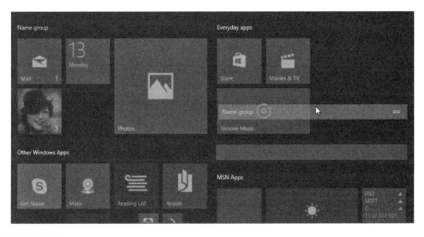

FIGURE 3.9

By dragging the title bar of a group, you can easily rearrange tile groups.

Naming a Tile Group

It might make sense for you to name your groups so you can easily locate your tiles, rather than trying to remember into which group you put a tile.

To label a tile group, follow these directions based on the device you use:

 Select the title bar for a group you want to name. Your cursor will appear in a text field with the current name. If no name has yet been provided, it will simply say Name Group. Type the name of the group in the box that appears, as shown in Figure 3.10.

👆 Tap and hold the title bar for a group you want to name. Your cursor will appear in a text field with the current name. If no name has yet been provided, it will simply say Name Group. Just like the step for using a mouse, type the name of the group in the box that appears, as shown in Figure 3.10.

You can repeat these steps for another group or click or tap anywhere on the screen to return to the normal Start menu.

FIGURE 3.10

You enter the name of the tile group in the text box that appears when you select the title bar for the group.

Organizing the Navigation Menu of the Start Menu

The Start menu includes a customizable navigation menu that features your most frequently used apps by default. In turn, jump lists will appear for many apps in this list showing recent files or web pages accessed by the application. Some will appreciate the ability to remove items that appear in these lists. To remove an application from the Most Used list or from a jump list, simply right-click the item you want to remove and select **Remove from This List**, as shown in Figure 3.11. Notice that you can pin an item to a jump list as well.

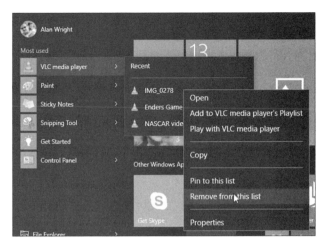

FIGURE 3.11

You can remove items from lists that appear in the Start menu.

Some important settings are available that you can use to customize the navigation menu of the Start menu. They will influence what appears here.

To customize the navigation menu, follow these steps:

1. From the Start menu, select **Settings** to open the Settings app.

2. Select **Personalization** and then **Start** from the vertical navigation menu of the Settings app (refer to Figure 3.5).

3. Under Start there are three switches that determine what can appear in the navigation menu:

   • **Show Most Used Apps**—This switch enables the Most Used list. Apps will appear and disappear from this list based on your usage. Turn this switch to **Off** to prevent this.

   • **Show Recently Added Apps**—This list will appear occasionally when you have installed new applications on your device.

   • **Show Recently Opened Items in Jump Lists on Start or the Taskbar**— This allows Windows to use jump lists that will list the most recently files that have been opened by an application. (Figure 3.11 shows an example of a Jump List for the VLC Media Player application.) If you want to disable the jump list feature for some reason, slide the switch Store and Display Recently Opened Items in Start and the Taskbar to **Off**. Notice that this will also prevent jump lists from working on the taskbar for pinned applications such as File Explorer.

4. Select the text **Choose Which Folders Appear on Start** to see a list of additional features that can be added to the navigation menu. The Settings app will shift its focus to the list shown in Figure 3.12. Permanently add shortcuts to the navigation menu immediately above the Start button using switches. Switch anything that you would like to see when opening the Start menu to **On**. (In Tablet mode you will still need to expand the hamburger menu, so you might prefer to pin these to the Start menu as a tile instead.) To see these changes take effect, you may need to sign out and then sign back in to your device.

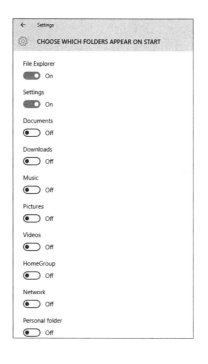

FIGURE 3.12

You can permanently add key shortcuts to the Start menu from the Settings app.

THE ABSOLUTE MINIMUM

- You can customize the appearance of the tiles on the Start menu by changing their sizes and moving them around.

- Leverage the ability to pin apps so that applications are easy to locate on your Start menu.

- Change the size of your Start menu when in Desktop mode to show more apps and prevent the need to scroll when hunting for a tile.

- You can create new groups for tiles, add names to groups, or rearrange groups of tiles.

- Pin documents or websites within jump lists to keep them handy.

- Customize the navigation menu by adding folders that you often access.

IN THIS CHAPTER

- Learning About Windows Apps
- Finding and Installing Windows Apps in the Windows Store
- Managing Windows Apps Purchases
- Uninstalling Windows Apps

4

INTRODUCING WINDOWS APPS

Windows apps are certainly one of the features that set Windows 10 apart from older versions that required a person to have an installation disk or download an application and then laboriously guide that installation by making several choices regarding download destination, features, add-ons, and so forth. Windows apps are applications that are installed through the Windows Store. They are simple to install, manage, and uninstall.

Much of the new look—colors, appearance, layout, and even placement of buttons and menus—in the new Windows comes from a set of design principles introduced with Windows 8 that have been refined in Windows 10. Microsoft has provided guidelines and standards to developers to ensure their apps have consistent features and behavior and that your Windows 10 device is not compromised by a Windows app that has been installed to your device.

This new design standard developed by Microsoft is currently named Microsoft Design Language, although it is still common to hear it referred to as Metro, Modern, Windows 8 style, and Universal. All the applications and tools that Microsoft and other companies build for Windows 10 using Microsoft Design principles are known as Windows Apps.

The goal of Chapters 4 and 5 is to bring you up to speed as quickly and clearly as possible on these new software applications, covering everything from finding an app to install to understanding the special menus and features that set them apart.

This chapter also introduces you to the Windows Store and the process of installing and uninstalling Windows apps on your device. In the following chapter, you will take a closer look at some of the features that characterize a Windows app as well as a number of new concepts and techniques, all intended to help you manage the kinds of apps you'll find in the Windows Store. Many of these techniques build on some of the skills presented earlier in the book. Be sure to review Chapter 2, "Interacting with Windows," if you are confused while reading the step-by-step procedures.

Learning About Windows Apps

Windows apps are software applications that have been developed by Microsoft and other software companies specifically for use in Windows 8 and Windows 10. The design principles that govern the development of these apps enable them to run on many devices and form factors; Windows apps that truly meet these criteria are referred to as *universal apps*. This term first appeared with reference to Windows 8 because some apps were being developed that could also run on the mobile Windows Phone 8 operating system. Windows 10 has taken this concept to a new level by employing the Windows 10 operating system core to power smartphones, Xbox gaming systems, as well as new devices.

The same Windows app can be installed on a Windows 10 PC, a Windows 10 phone, an Xbox, a Microsoft HoloLens, or numerous other devices that use Windows 10. This is certainly not the case with Windows desktop applications, which are very limited by the hardware specifications of a particular device. (See the sidebar "The Difference Between Windows Apps and Desktop Applications" in this section.)

Although a majority of the desktop applications used in previous versions of Windows, especially Windows 7, can run in Windows 10 on a PC, the opposite does not hold true—Windows apps cannot run on older versions of Windows. Here is more basic information you need to know about Windows apps:

- Windows apps can run full screen or in windows on the Desktop. This also is influenced by running your device in Tablet or Desktop mode.

- Windows apps are available only through the Windows Store, which is built in to Windows 10. The Windows Store is covered later in this chapter.

- Windows apps are designed to be more secure, allowing you greater control over whether an app has permission to access or control things like a camera or access your contacts.

- Windows apps can be updated automatically without requiring a reboot.

- The Windows Store also handles the installation of Windows apps in the background, saving you the hassle of selecting options and clicking a series of Next buttons when installing new software.

- Windows apps hide menus and tools. This is not done to trick you! This is done to keep the content front and center. These menus and toolbars are easily revealed when you need them, and you will soon find this to be a practical design that keeps things clean and uncluttered.

- Windows apps leverage features and devices that are installed on your computer in a consistent way for sharing, printing, configuration, and searching. This integration might require a bit of a change in thinking on your part because we traditionally would look *inside* an app for important tools, such as for sharing to a social media website or when searching for content. Now, it is important to understand that the app will hand these tasks off to the operating system.

 NOTE Windows 10 leverages the flexibility of Windows apps to care for many common tasks such as playing music, looking at photos, or getting the news. This means that changes to layout and function for apps and other aspects of Windows 10 itself can be handled easily by means of updates without any disruptions or major upgrades just to add functionality to a couple of key system applications. As a result, the appearance of apps and even Windows 10 will continue to evolve and shift as improvements continue to be realized and pushed out to devices by means of updates.

Although the design of a Windows app is generally quite different from a Windows Desktop application, Windows 10 does much to provide a consistent experience when using many standard features that you have grown accustomed to when working with Windows in the past. Some of these include

- Resizing windows in Desktop mode

- Haphazardly arranging multiple windows on the screen while in Desktop mode

- Minimizing windows

This consistency makes it easy to use both types of applications without even thinking about the differences, as shown in Figure 4.1. In the rest of this chapter, you can find enough hands-on instruction to make you a near-expert with Windows apps before you charge off on your own working with them.

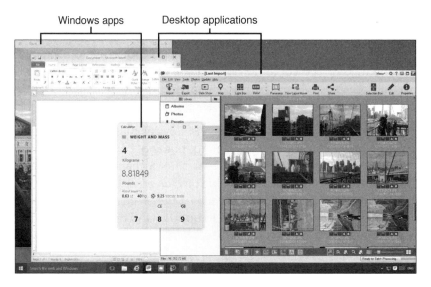

FIGURE 4.1

Windows apps and Desktop applications can run side by side in Windows 10. Can you spot the differences?

THE DIFFERENCE BETWEEN WINDOWS APPS AND DESKTOP APPLICATIONS

In this book you might notice Windows apps and Desktop applications referred to as distinct types of software. What is the difference? Generally, they are both *applications*, code that has been written and assembled to make things happen on your device. The reason for the distinction has to do with how these applications are *installed* on your device.

A *Windows app* is installed through the Windows Store. It is *sandboxed*, which is a technical term referring to a way of running an application that prevents it from making changes to the operating system—Windows 10 in this case. Permission is granted to use system resources and data, and this permission can be revoked if you choose. Windows 10 can recover system resources that an app might be trying to use when performance is affected.

A *Desktop application* uses a traditional installation disc or downloaded program to install the application. Desktop applications are also generally referred to as *Win32 applications*. Desktop applications will make changes to the registry and other parts of the operating system so that Windows knows they are on the device. Desktop applications can overload system resources, causing a device to run slowly; a reboot may be required to recover performance. Uninstalling a Desktop application can leave bits and pieces behind, and those bits and pieces can present a higher security risk due to the way they interact with the operating system. Desktop applications are considered in Chapter 7, "Working with Windows Desktop Applications."

Microsoft has made tools available to developers that enable them to "easily" update Win32 applications and convert them to Windows apps. The process lets Windows create virtual registry changes and directories, allowing the application to work as expected, while still allowing for a secure sandboxed experience for the device that can be easily and cleanly uninstalled. If developers feel this conversion is worth the extra effort, you might soon see long-time favorite Desktop applications appearing in the Windows Store as Windows apps.

Shopping at the Windows Store

The Windows Store is an online marketplace integrated into Windows 10 that sells Windows apps developed by Microsoft and other companies. (You will also find music, movies, and TV shows to purchase or rent.) You buy the apps at the store, and then Windows installs the apps to your device, usually without a single additional step on your part. Using the Windows Store requires an Internet connection—the faster the connection, the faster your apps will be downloaded and installed.

The Windows Store organizes and provides automatic updates to the apps you acquire from the store. This means when the developer for a Windows app releases an update to an app that you own, Windows will install the updates automatically when you have an Internet connection that permits updates to be downloaded.

The Windows Store is also a Windows app, so you should be as comfortable shopping in the store as you are writing and reading email in the Mail app or creating a slide show in the Photo app. The Windows app has been updated to provide a better interface and easier navigation for Windows 10. You open the store by selecting the store's tile on the Start screen, as shown in Figure 4.2.

FIGURE 4.2

Enter the store by selecting its tile on the Start screen.

With the store open, you can browse through categories to look at all the apps available or use the Search tool shown in the upper-right corner of Figure 4.3. The home screen in the store presents a handful of currently featured apps as well as a list of picks for you and the current top sellers and free apps. Ratings are provided for apps, and you can see the price. Scroll up and down, and select arrows or swipe to scroll right or left in each list of apps on the Home screen.

By selecting an app, you can read more detailed overviews and specifications of the app to help you determine whether you want the app. More information is provided regarding ratings, and reviews help you understand the reason for the rating, as shown in Figure 4.4. Scroll down to view screenshots, features, and related apps. Finally, important information is provided regarding device support, the app size, and permissions the app requires, as shown in Figure 4.5.

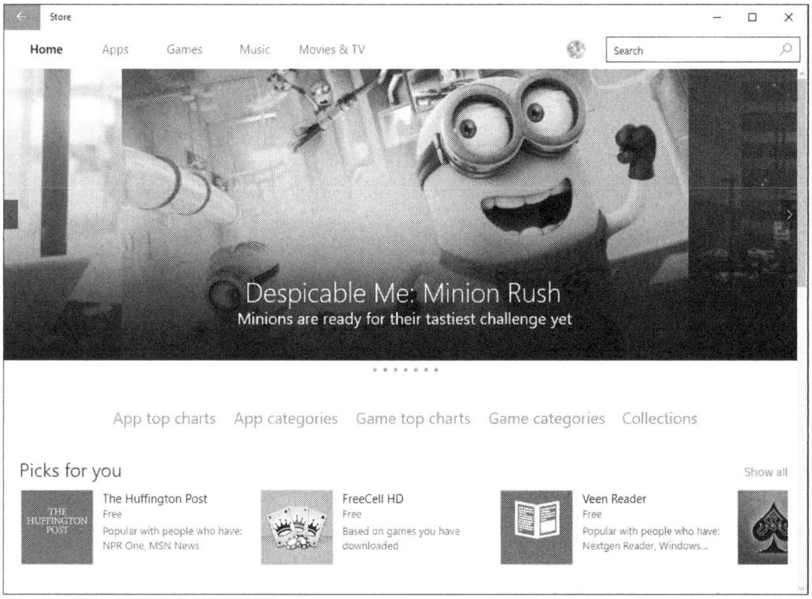

FIGURE 4.3

The Home screen offers featured apps as well as popular choices in a variety of categories.

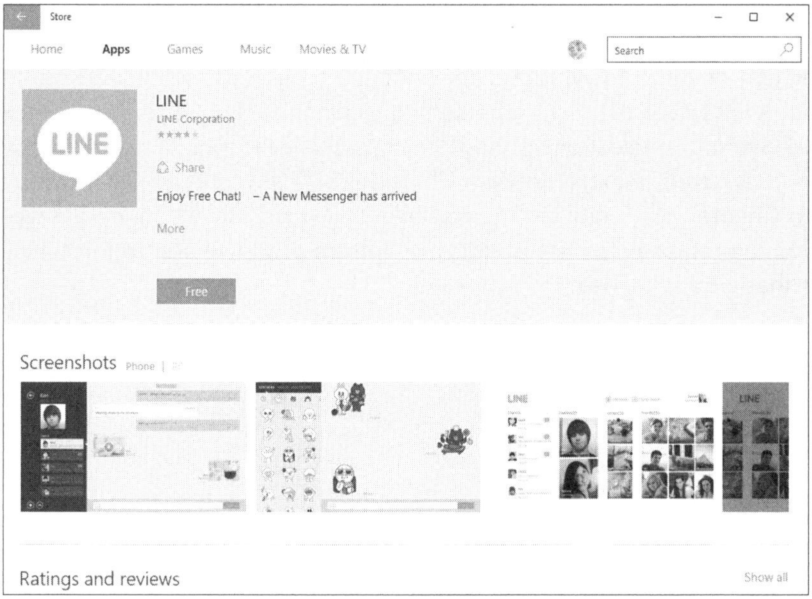

FIGURE 4.4

Select an app in the Windows Store app to learn more about it and look over reviews.

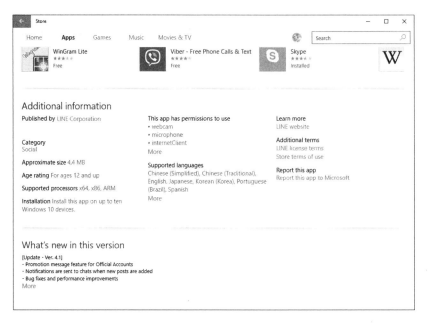

FIGURE 4.5

Checking the app size and permissions in the Windows Store app can help you determine whether you want to install an app.

The Windows Store is divided into types of media, with two types—apps and games—devoted to Windows apps. At any time in the store, you can use the navigation links near the top of the screen to jump back to Home or to look at Apps and Games. The sections of the Windows Store labeled Music and Movies & TV are considered in more detail in Chapter 25, "Having Fun with Movies and Video," and Chapter 26, "Enjoying Music." While viewing any of the media types in the app, you can scroll all the way to the bottom of the screen to jump to categories for that type, as shown in Figure 4.6.

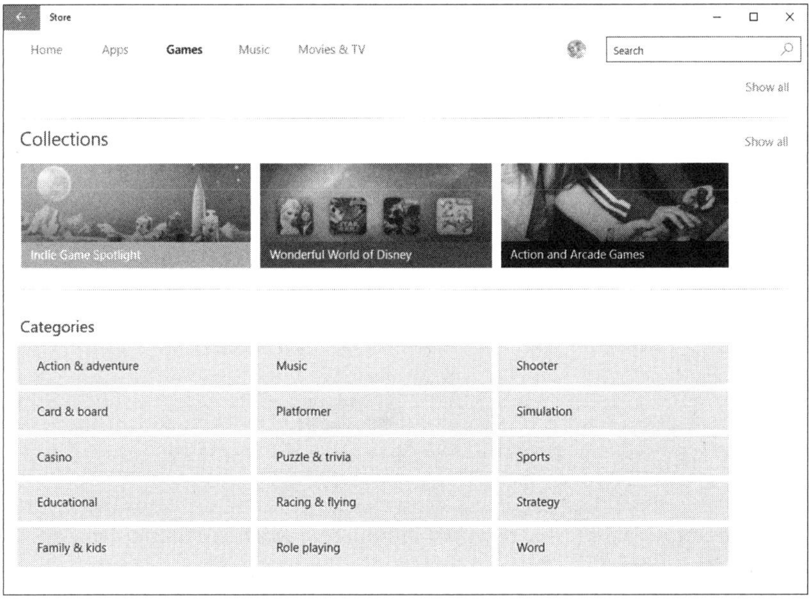

FIGURE 4.6

When viewing a media type in the Windows Store app, you can jump to categories within that type from the bottom of the screen.

Purchasing an App

Purchasing an app should take no more than two clicks and possibly a password entry, provided you have set up your account information (see the next section, "Managing Your Windows Store Purchases," and Chapter 24, "Using Your Microsoft Account for Purchases"). To purchase an app, follow these steps:

1. Select an app within the Windows Store that you would like to install on your device. If this is an app that you already own, the install button will be labeled Install; otherwise, a price is indicated, which in some cases will be Free. Select the **Install** button.

2. If a price was indicated, you will be prompted to provide your Microsoft account password to confirm your identity. Select **OK**.

3. You will be prompted to review the purchase information, as shown in Figure 4.7. Select **Buy** to pay for the purchase or **Cancel** to return to the app information.

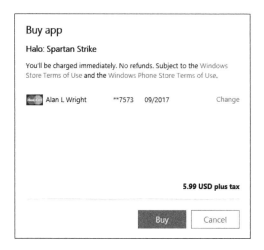

FIGURE 4.7

You will need to confirm your payment information when purchasing an app in the Windows Store app.

4. The Install button will be replaced with progress updates as the app is installed. Above the app information to the left of your account badge will be a downward pointing arrow with the number of current downloads, as shown in Figure 4.8.

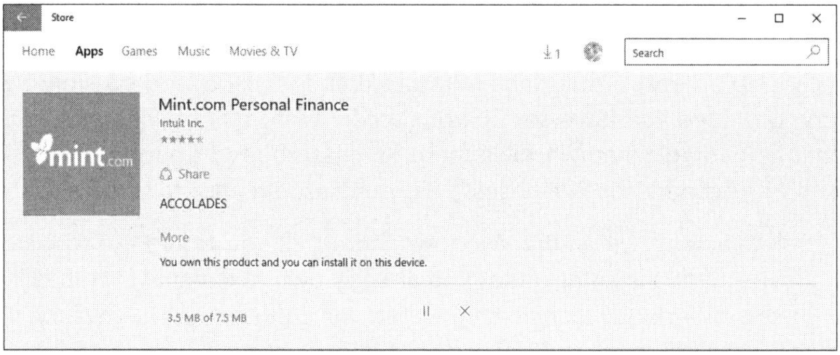

FIGURE 4.8

After selecting Install, an app will begin downloading to your device.

5. Select the Downloads indicator to see details of any pending installs in the queue, as shown in Figure 4.9. Apps that are being downloaded or installed will display their progress; they can be paused or canceled from the Downloads and Installs screen. Once finished, the app will remain briefly in the queue showing as Completed.

FIGURE 4.9

You can check the progress as apps are installed.

Newly installed apps will appear in the Start menu with the tag New on their icon to alert you to apps you have not yet opened.

Managing Your Windows Store Purchases

Managing your app purchases includes a few in-app and online tools that can be launched from the Windows Store app. Select your account badge in the Windows Store app to reveal the account tools shown in Figure 4.10. Although some apps in the Window Store are free, most aren't. Your Microsoft account must include payment information to purchase apps and other media through the Windows Store. You can enter credit card information or a PayPal account number. In addition to setting up your payment option, you also can specify whether a password should be entered each time you purchase an app.

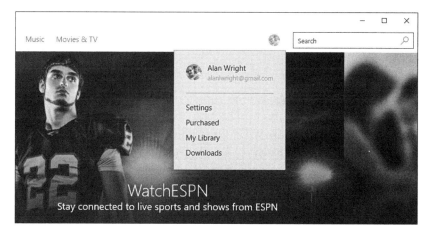

FIGURE 4.10

Manage your activity and apps with your Microsoft account, which can be accessed from the Windows Store app.

To manage your account in the Windows Store, follow these steps:

1. Select your account badge in the Windows Store app to reveal the account tools.

2. Select **Settings**. The Settings pane for the Windows Store app appears, as shown in Figure 4.11. Windows apps are updated automatically by default. You can disable this option by sliding the switch to Off.

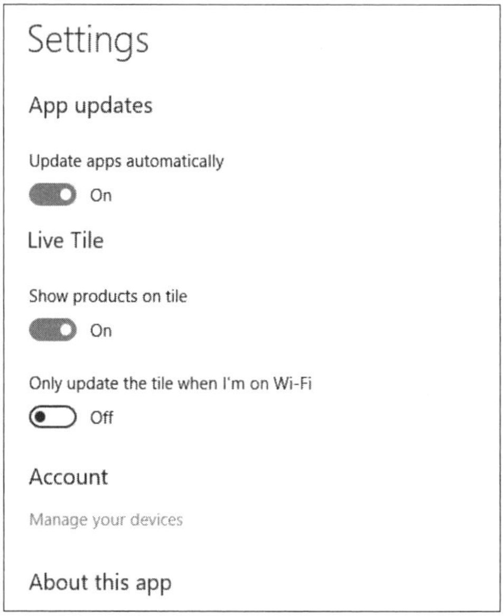

Settings

App updates

Update apps automatically

⬤ On

Live Tile

Show products on tile

⬤ On

Only update the tile when I'm on Wi-Fi

◯ Off

Account

Manage your devices

About this app

FIGURE 4.11

You manage account information, app updates, and other preferences for the Windows Store in Settings.

3. Reopen the account tools from step 1 and Select **Purchased**. Your web browser will open to your online Microsoft account Payment and Billing overview, as shown in Figure 4.12. From here, you can see a history of the most recent purchases made using your Microsoft account. Select options such as Purchase History to see a more detailed breakdown of purchases by year. You can also update payment methods and review other aspects of your Microsoft account from here.

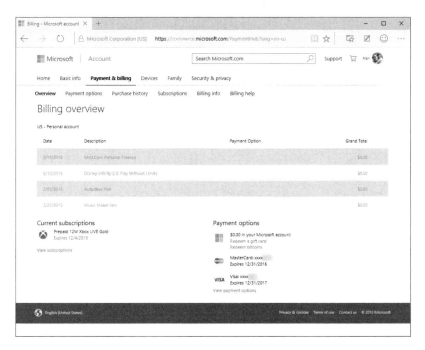

FIGURE 4.12

Jump to your online Microsoft account to manage payment and billing information.

4. Reopen the account tools from step 1 and select **My Library**. The Windows Store app will display the apps and games you own. Select the download arrow to download that app to the current device, as shown in Figure 4.13.

5. Finally, from the account tools, you can select **Downloads** to jump to the Downloads and Installs screen. This can be useful if you are not always able to get updates. Select the Check for Updates button to initiate a manual check for updates to your apps.

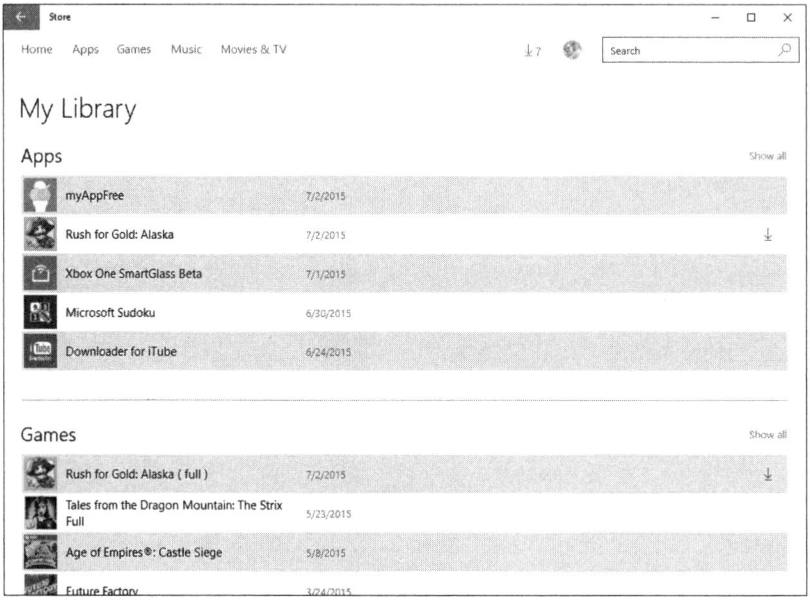

FIGURE 4.13

Download and install apps you already own from your Library in the Windows Store app.

Uninstalling Apps

Uninstalling apps is very straight forward—with the exception of some apps that are considered part of the Windows operating system and cannot be uninstalled. An example of a system app that cannot be uninstalled is the Calculator app. You will no doubt install many apps to try over the life of your device, and new apps might replace old favorites. Uninstalling apps that are no longer used is important to recover storage space on your device, if nothing else.

Follow these steps to uninstall Windows apps:

1. From the Start menu, locate the tile for an app you want to uninstall. Tap and hold or right-click to reveal the options for that app. Swipe up or right-click to select an app you want to uninstall. (It may be easier to select the down arrow and work from the Apps screen.) A check mark appears on the app's tile, and the App bar appears at the bottom of the Start screen.

2. Select **Uninstall**, as shown in Figure 4.14.

    If you do not see that option, select the ellipsis or **More Options** to see Uninstall. If you still do not see this option, you might have selected a system app that cannot be uninstalled.

FIGURE 4.14

You can uninstall Window Store apps directly from the Start menu.

3. You will be prompted for confirmation, as shown in Figure 4.15. Select **Uninstall**.

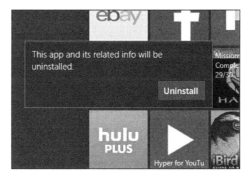

FIGURE 4.15

To help you avoid unpleasant accidents, you will be asked to confirm your decision to uninstall an app.

Windows apps uninstall remarkably quickly. In the event that you select an app that cannot be uninstalled, you will simply not see the uninstall option. Additionally, if you select an app that is a Desktop application, Windows will open a window to guide you through the process of uninstalling the Desktop application. Uninstalling Desktop applications is considered in more detail in Chapter 7.

THE ABSOLUTE MINIMUM

- Windows apps are applications developed by Microsoft and other software developers that are designed to run in Windows 10. This is different from traditional Windows desktop applications.

- Windows apps are purchased through the Windows Store. You can browse for apps by category, or you can search for apps using keywords.

- The Windows Store provides feedback and reviews to help developers improve their products and to alert users to good and bad features. Most developers appreciate feedback and will work to improve their apps.

- Windows apps are available for purchase from the Windows Store. Sometimes, apps are available at no charge or on a trial basis. You enter payment methods, such as a credit card and PayPal information, to pay for app purchases in the Windows store.

- Uninstall Windows apps quickly right from the Start menu.

5

WORKING WITH WINDOWS APPS

If you are a long-time user of Windows, you might have developed some basic expectations when it comes to running applications. If you are new to Windows, you might have had experience with running applications in other operating systems. Windows 10 has improved the way that modern apps, Windows apps, run on a device.

In this chapter, we look at some of the characteristics of Windows apps. We also learn about settings for storage, app management, and system defaults related to Windows apps.

This chapter builds on some key points that were covered in the previous chapter, "Introducing Windows Apps." Additionally, be sure to review Chapter 2, "Interacting with Windows," if you are confused while reading the step-by-step procedures.

Running Windows Store Apps

Starting an app probably seems like a basic topic, perhaps one that doesn't merit its own section in a book. But Windows apps are still a relatively new creation that most Windows users have never used. Although you might not readily notice much difference between a Win32 Desktop application and a Windows app, differences do exist. This section explains what happens when a Windows Store app starts, what happens when a Windows app is running, as well as how to close a running app.

 NOTE Much has been done to ensure that Windows apps perform well on Windows 10. Microsoft has provided more tools to developers for Windows 10 than were previously available for Windows 8. This enables developers to create snappier apps with more ways to leverage the hardware on your device.

Starting a Windows Store App

To start a Windows Store app, select the tile from the Start menu that represents the app you want to start. Figure 5.1 shows a representative set of Windows Store app tiles. Immediately after you select a tile, you see a bit of fancy animation that quickly transitions to the open app.

FIGURE 5.1

Windows apps are started by selecting a tile from the Start menu. The tiles can be simple in design using static colors and graphics, or they can include live tile updates and animation.

Depending on whether your device is in Tablet mode or Desktop mode, the app will open full screen or as a window. You'll notice Windows apps appear flat, borderless, and broad. There are no buttons, sliders, or other controls that appear to be raised off the screen, as shown in Figure 5.2, which features the popular Flipboard app.

FIGURE 5.2

Notice how Windows apps, like Flipboard, appear flat with no raised buttons or ribbon menus.

Because Windows apps are designed to keep the focus on content and to keep distracting menus and controls off the screen until needed, you might initially feel that settings are missing or that an app is too simple. Just remember that most controls are hidden or minimized until selecting icons like the hamburger menu or visual cues such as an ellipsis that the app developer might use to let you know additional controls or options are hidden. Some Windows apps even hide the title bar when they are in full screen. To reveal a title bar that has hidden on you, swipe down from the top of the screen with a touchscreen or position your mouse cursor near the top of the screen, as shown in Figure 5.3.

FIGURE 5.3

Windows apps can hide title bars until needed; you can reveal them with a simple swipe or by using your mouse cursor.

TIP   When your device is in Tablet mode, apps open to full screen by default, hiding any other apps that might be open. To further complicate this situation, your taskbar does not show open apps by default while in Tablet mode. How do you return to other apps that are open? The easiest way is to simply swipe in from the left side of the screen to reveal open apps in Task View. You could also select the Start menu and reselect the app or minimize the current app from its title bar.

Stopping a Windows 10 App

Closing a Windows 10 app is pretty straightforward compared to Windows 8. Closing a Windows 10 app truly closes and immediately releases any memory or CPU resources that were being allocated for that app. If you are instructed to close an app, perhaps for troubleshooting purposes—or you simply want to impress your friends—here are a few ways to close an app (these methods work for Desktop applications as well):

- Be sure you are in the app you want to close. Slowly drag your finger on the screen down from the top of the screen. By the time you reach the bottom of the screen, the app will shrink and should disappear from view. When you start this gesture, be sure your finger is close to the edge of the screen that borders the rest of your device.

- Press Alt+F4.

- From the title bar, close the app by selecting X.

- From Task View, select the X to close an app even if it is on a different desktop. (Task View is covered in detail in Chapter 6, "Finding Your Way Around the Windows Desktop.")

Using Common Windows App Menu Tools

Almost all Windows apps have at least one setting that you can adjust. Accessing and locating the menus and settings can vary a bit between Windows apps because the placement and implementation is left to the app developer, although consistency is encouraged. For example, the Adobe Reader app enables you to input a name that will be used to tag any annotations made on a PDF file using the app. Settings for the Adobe Reader app are accessed from the hamburger menu located on the title bar, as shown in Figure 5.4.

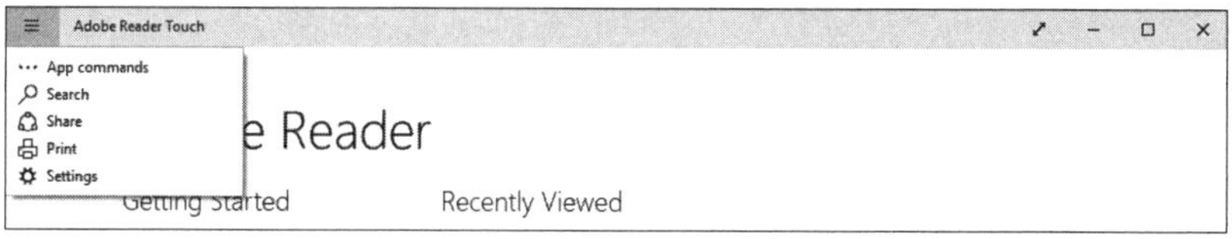

FIGURE 5.4

Many hidden controls can be accessed from the title bar of apps, like the Adobe Reader app.

Other apps might locate a hamburger menu below the title bar to keep it visible at all times, as shown in the Sports app in Figure 5.5. Select the hamburger menu icon to reveal the menu. The contents of a hamburger menu will vary according to the app and what the developer of the app has decided to include there. Options such as Settings or Favorites are commonly found in a hamburger menu.

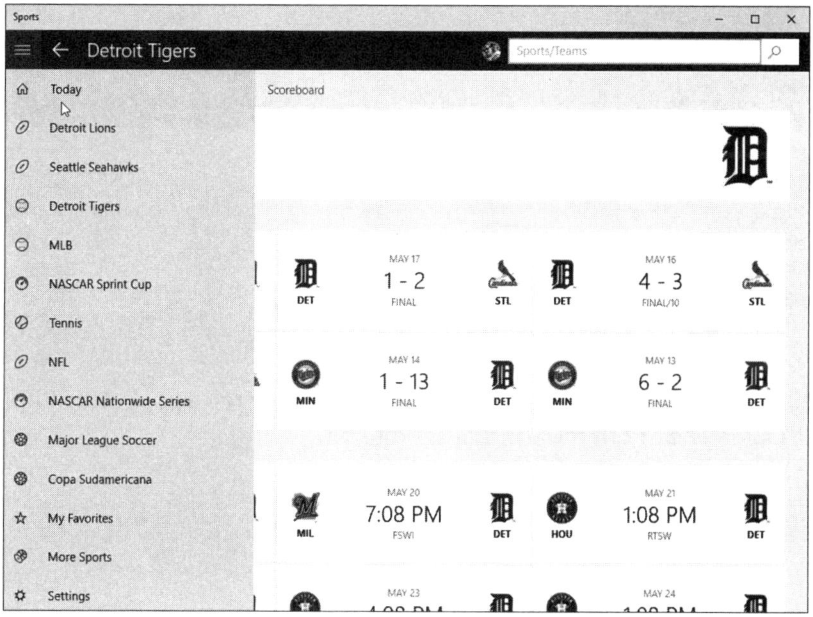

FIGURE 5.5

Hamburger menus can be used to contain many tools, including the settings for that app as shown here in the Sports app.

Many apps use upper or lower App Command bars to contain additional tools or options. Shown in Figure 5.6, the Adobe Reader app reveals tools for printing or annotating.

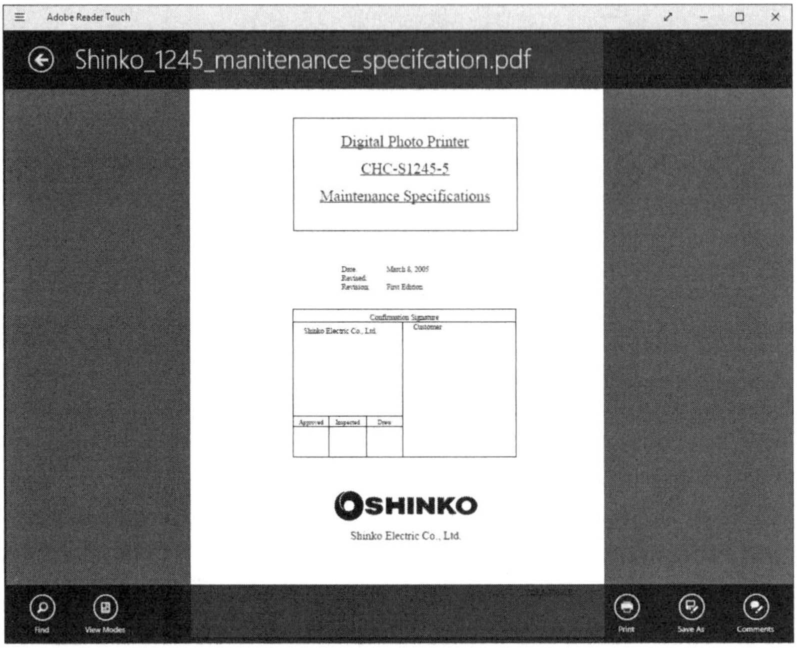

FIGURE 5.6

Some apps, like the Adobe Reader app, hide tools in the App Command bar until you need them.

To open an App Command bar, try one of the following based on the device you use:

- Look for a hamburger menu on the title bar of the app. Select App Commands from the hamburger menu.

- Press Windows+Z.

- Right-click any empty area of the Start screen.

Managing Windows Apps

Windows 10 offers a few additional ways to manage your Windows apps. File types and tasks are associated with Microsoft recommended defaults, which coincidentally tend to be Windows apps. Another area where Windows 10 enables you to manage apps is storage. Both of these areas are discussed in this section.

Choosing Default Apps

When you need to send an email, perhaps using the Share feature in another app, Windows will check to see which app is your default for handling this task and then open the designated app. The same thing determines which app is used to play music, look at pictures, or open a web page when you open a file or short-cut. Although the default choices are good, you might have reasons to use a different app. This determination is actually something you can change with a few simple clicks.

To modify the current Windows default apps, follow these steps:

1. From the Start menu, select **Settings** to open the Settings app.

2. Select **System** and then select **Default apps** from the vertical menu to the left. The app will display Choose Default Apps with a list of common apps, as shown in Figure 5.7.

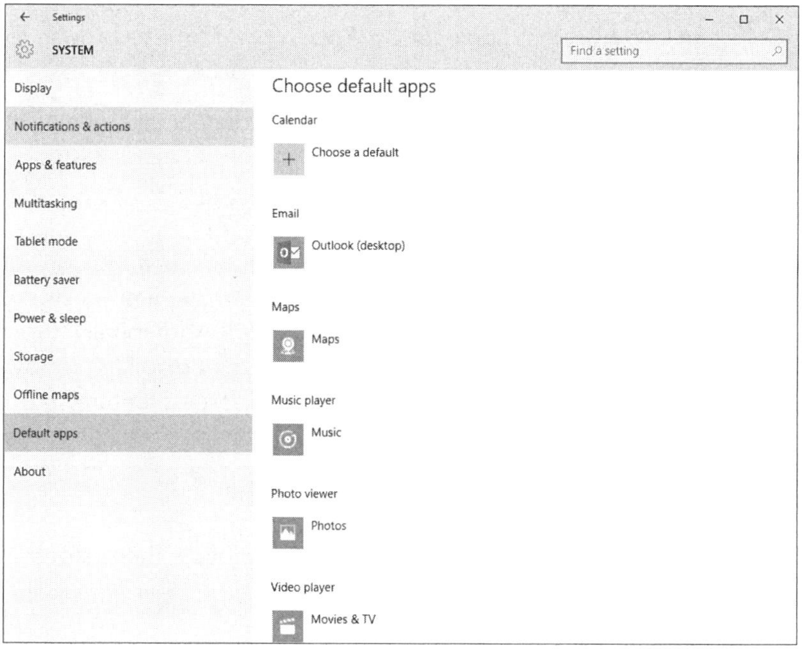

FIGURE 5.7

Windows keeps track of preferred apps to handle common tasks in the Settings app.

3. Select the current app for the task, and a menu will appear with other apps (including Desktop applications) that can handle this task, as shown in Figure 5.8.

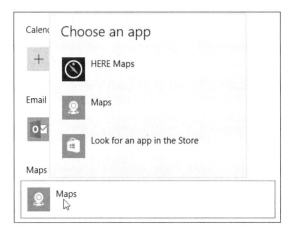

FIGURE 5.8

Change which app is used for a task by selecting it from a list.

4. Select an app or select **Look for an App in the Store** to browse for Windows apps in the Windows Store to install to your device.

5. Close the Settings app. Your choice will immediately take effect.

Managing Storage Options for Windows Apps

Managing how your device uses attached storage such as a memory card is an issue that is more likely to concern tablet users who have limited storage space than a desktop user with a large-capacity hard drive. Additionally, there are some large apps out there and more to come, so the flexibility to move apps around and manage your storage options is an important feature to be aware of. Windows includes tools that allow you to see which apps are consuming the most storage space and uninstall apps. In some cases you can even move an app to a different drive.

To view and make changes to your installed apps, follow these steps:

1. From the Start menu, select **Settings** to open the Settings app.

2. Select **System** and then select **Apps & Features** from the vertical menu to the left. Windows will capture current information about the Windows apps and Desktop applications installed on your device; then this information will be displayed under Apps and Features, as shown in Figure 5.9.

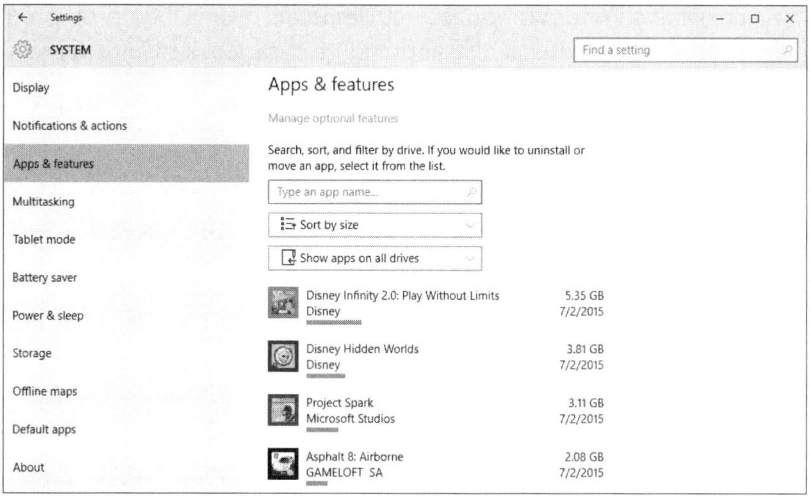

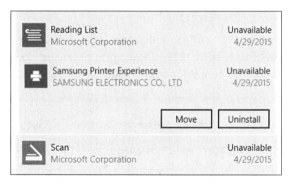

FIGURE 5.9

Open the Installed Apps pane in the Settings app to check which apps are taking up the most storage space.

3. Use the filters to target the information. For example, you can sort the apps by size, name, or install date. You can also select which drive you want to look at.

4. Select an app from the list. The buttons Move and Uninstall will be displayed for the selected app, as shown in Figure 5.10. (An additional drive must be available or the Move button will be grayed out.)

FIGURE 5.10

You can choose to uninstall or move apps from the Settings app.

5. To uninstall a Windows app, select **Uninstall**. You will be prompted to confirm your decision to uninstall the app and its data. Select **Uninstall** to confirm.

6. To move an app to a different drive, select **Move**. You will be prompted to select a drive, as shown in Figure 5.11.

7. Windows will move the app to the selected drive, which can take some time depending on the size of the app you are moving.

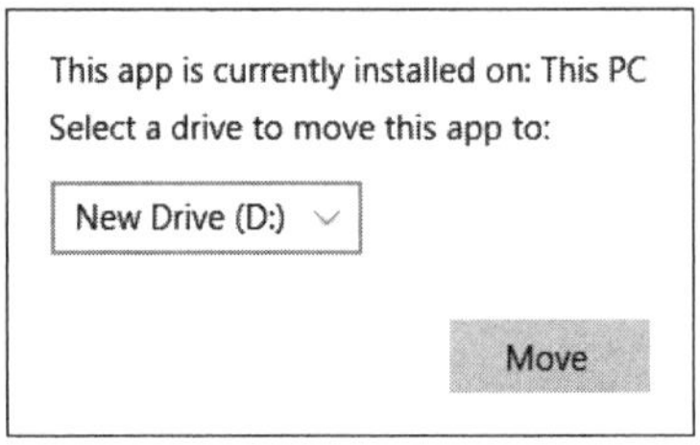

This app is currently installed on: This PC
Select a drive to move this app to:

New Drive (D:) ⌄

Move

FIGURE 5.11

To recover some space, you can move a large app to a different drive.

 NOTE   Even though Desktop applications are listed in the Installed apps list, they cannot be moved in this manner. The only option you will see is to Uninstall a Desktop application. Desktop applications are covered in detail in Chapter 7, "Working with Windows Desktop Applications."

Managing Default Save Locations

Another way that storage can be managed is by indicating a default save location for a specific task, such as installing new apps or saving certain file types. Windows 10 enables you to modify the locations used by default.

Follow these steps to manage default save locations on your device:

1. From the Start menu, select **Settings** to open the Settings app.

2. Select **System** and then select **Storage** from the vertical menu to the left. The Storage pane of the Settings app will appear, as shown in Figure 5.12.

3. To change the default location used when installing new apps, select the drop-down menu below Save New Apps and Games To. From the drop-down menu, select a new drive location. When installing apps in the future, Windows will save them to this new location.

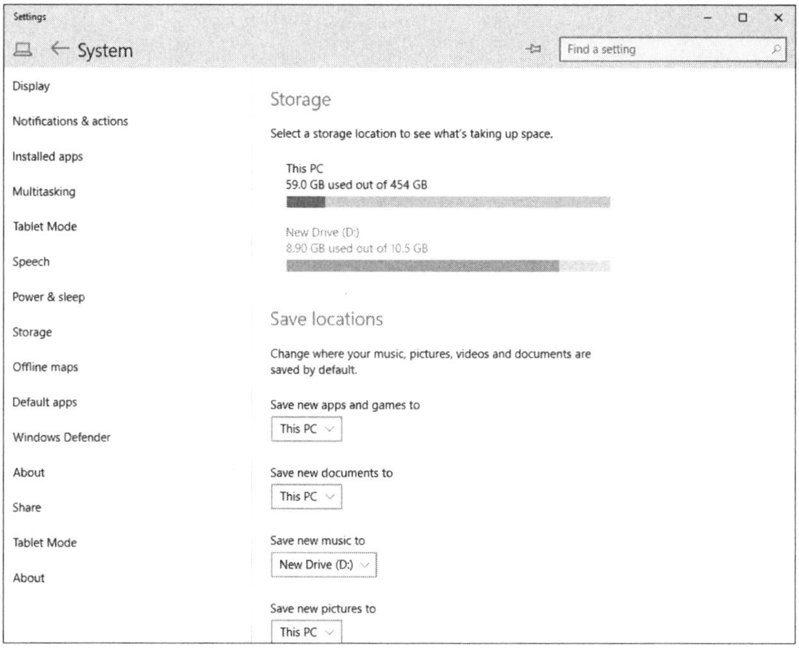

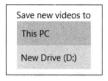

FIGURE 5.12

Use the Storage pane in the Settings app to manage default save locations.

4. Notice that other default locations are indicated here. Select from the drop-down menus to change the default location for any of these, as shown in Figure 5.13.

FIGURE 5.13

Select a different drive location for saving apps or other types of media that can consume a lot of space.

 CAUTION Changing your default save location for apps could make things overly complicated on most devices from a support standpoint and should be a last resort if you are dealing with low space issues on your main drive. Saving things like videos, pictures, and music to a different drive, however, is a much more practical way to use this feature. If space is not an issue, I recommend leaving your save locations at their defaults.

THE ABSOLUTE MINIMUM

- Windows apps are software programs developed by Microsoft and other software developers that are designed to run in Windows 10. They are designed to run efficiently without overtaxing your system resources, and most will run across a variety of form factors.

- The hamburger menu is a common design feature in Windows apps. Look to this menu for settings and other important tools when using an app.

- Rather than using the default apps that Microsoft has chosen for tasks, select the apps you prefer in the Default Apps pane of the Settings app.

- If you are running out of space in your main drive, you can move large apps that are space hogs.

- Default save locations can be modified in Windows 10 for media and for installing new apps.

6

FINDING YOUR WAY AROUND THE WINDOWS DESKTOP

Change is never easy to get used to, especially when it involves a device we use and rely on day in and day out. Microsoft has done an admirable job in bringing changes and updates to the Windows platform without sacrificing many of the familiar features that have made Windows the go-to computer operating system for businesses and consumers.

Windows 8 had relegated the Desktop to such an extent that many people were uncomfortable with the drastic departure from previous versions. Many popular features have been reintroduced into Windows 10, so whether you're a long-time user or a newbie, this chapter is sure to be useful in familiarizing yourself with the Windows 10 Desktop.

Introducing the Desktop

One of the goals Microsoft pursued in designing Windows 10 was to combine the media-driven computer user experience that was the focus of Windows 8 with the Desktop-centric experience familiar to the productivity-oriented user from previous versions of Windows. Modern apps and Desktop applications can be used together without fighting for screen space.

The Desktop, shown in Figure 6.1, provides an environment where apps can be positioned strategically on your display or can be full screen. Folders and documents can be saved on the Desktop. The taskbar that runs along the bottom of the Desktop can be customized, and it is home to many important tools.

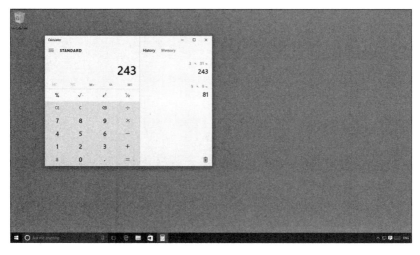

FIGURE 6.1

The Windows 10 Desktop is similar to the Desktop of previous versions of Windows.

The desktop will behave differently depending on whether you are in Tablet mode or Desktop mode. You can quickly change modes by opening the Action Center and selecting Tablet mode to enable or disable Tablet mode. (Tablet mode is covered in more detail in Chapter 2, "Interacting with Windows.") In Desktop mode, applications run in resizable windows by default, and several open windows can be accommodated and positioned at whim. While in Tablet mode, applications run full screen by default. Several applications can be open and "snapped" to portions of the screen if your screen size accommodates this. The differences are highlighted in the following two sections.

Using the Desktop in Desktop Mode

While your device is in Desktop mode, open applications can be resized and positioned with few restrictions. Applications or apps that are open appear on the taskbar (refer to Figure 6.1). Windows makes some tasks easy by using *snap* to quickly locate and resize an application. Snapping an application takes place when you drag the title bar of the application's window to an edge of the display. As shown in Figure 6.2, Windows offers an outline on the screen to show you where the application will appear when snapped.

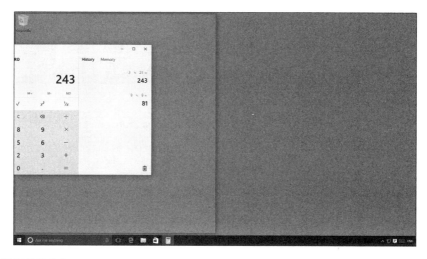

FIGURE 6.2

Snap applications to edges of the display to quickly locate and resize them.

To snap an application in Desktop mode, follow these steps:

1. Open an application or an app while in Desktop mode.

2. Select the title bar of the application or app, and drag it to the left or right edge of the screen. Windows will show an outline for the resized application. Release the application to snap it to this location.

3. After an application has been snapped, Windows will offer to snap another open app to fill the rest of the screen. As shown in Figure 6.3, select one of the very large thumbnails to fill the rest of the screen.

FIGURE 6.3

When snapping applications to the screen, Windows will proactively offer to fill the rest of the screen with other open applications.

4. Select the title bar again and drag away from the edge of the display. The app will resume its normal size and can be released to position it.

5. Select the title bar again and drag to the top edge of the display. The outline will swell to fill the entire screen. Release and the application will be full screen. (You also can accomplish this by double-clicking the title bar.) Other applications will remain open and running behind the full screen application.

6. Select and drag the title bar again and drag to an edge in one of the corners of the display. If your screen resolution allows for it, the application will fill a quarter of the screen. Lower resolution settings will allow you to snap to only half of the screen.

When running multiple applications on the Desktop, the taskbar becomes very important for keeping track of what is open. All open applications appear on the taskbar with a line under their icon. Whichever application is currently selected will also show its icon highlighted (refer to Figure 6.1).

A desktop can quickly become cluttered after several applications are open and overlapping. While in Desktop mode, the taskbar has a useful tool that was first introduced in Windows 7 and that allows you to temporarily become Superman. Bring your cursor to the far right end of the taskbar, and hover it over the Peek tool—also called the Show Desktop button—for a second or two. (The Show Desktop button appears as a narrow vertical piece of the taskbar to the right of the notification area.)

As shown in Figure 6.4, when Peek is activated all open windows become transparent, and you can see through them with your x-ray vison to the desktop. The Peek tool can do more; simply select it to minimize everything revealing your Desktop.

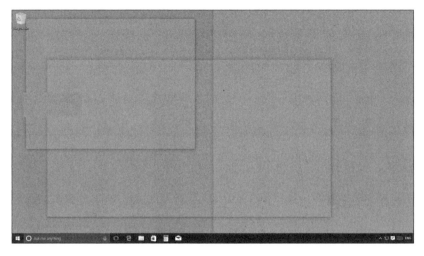

FIGURE 6.4

The Show Desktop button is a handy way to see and access your Desktop when you have many applications open in Desktop mode.

Using the Desktop in Tablet Mode

While you are in Tablet mode, you will see and use the Desktop less as a work space. The focus will remain on the Start menu and applications, while the Desktop is rarely if ever seen. Documents and folders that are on the desktop are hidden by default, and tools like Peek are not available. Snap behaves differently while in Tablet mode as well.

To snap an application in Tablet mode, follow these steps:

1. Open an application or an app while in Tablet mode. The application will open full screen.

2. Swipe down from the top of the display, and drag the application to the left or right edge of the screen. Windows will show an outline for the resized application. Release the application to snap it to this location. A wide vertical border will appear at the center of the screen on the edge of the application that was just snapped.

3. After an application has been snapped, Windows will offer to snap another open app to fill the rest of the screen (refer to Figure 6.3). If no other applications are open, the next application you open will snap into the remainder of the screen.

4. Use the vertical border between two applications to adjust how much screen space each one gets. As shown in Figure 6.5, drag the bar to the left or right to establish the shared border. Both applications will snap to this new size when the border is released.

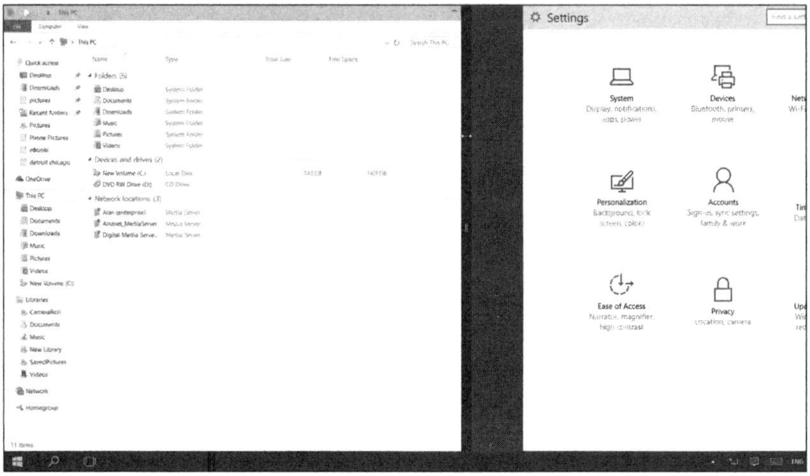

FIGURE 6.5

Snapped applications can be nudged into sharing more or less screen space while in Tablet mode.

Using Task View

Today we tend to multitask when using a computer or tablet. A great solution to this is having several displays that we can use to spread all of our applications out so that no application obscures any other. This is not very realistic in many situations, however. Beside the cost, we certainly wouldn't want to sit on an airplane next to someone that had two or three monitors connected to his laptop.

Task View is a new feature that has been built in to Windows 10 to address this very issue, allowing you to improve your Desktop experience on a single display by creating virtual Desktops. As shown in Figure 6.6, you can have multiple Desktops open with different application running on each one. Rather than minimizing applications or moving things around when you need to switch tasks throughout the day, you can just jump between Desktops. Applications can even be taken from one Desktop and placed into a different one. Task View works with Desktop mode and Tablet mode with subtle differences and has been referred to as a poor man's cheat for having multiple displays.

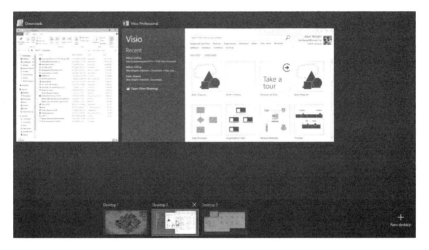

FIGURE 6.6

Task View enables you to get around the hassle of working with a single display when multitasking.

To use Task View, follow these steps in Desktop mode:

1. Open an application or two, including the Settings app, and arrange them on your Desktop.

2. Select the **Task View** icon on the taskbar. Your open applications will appear as large thumbnails.

3. Select the **New Desktop** button that appears in the lower-right corner of the screen.

4. As shown in Figure 6.7, a new Desktop named Desktop 2 will appear above the taskbar, while your original Desktop will be named Desktop 1. No application thumbnails will be visible.

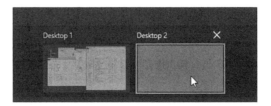

FIGURE 6.7

Add and remove Desktops on-the-fly with Task View.

5. Hover your cursor over **Desktop 1** until the open applications from Step 2 are again visible. Select the **Settings** app and drag it to Desktop 2, as shown in Figure 6.8. Release the app. The app will no longer have a thumbnail on Desktop 1, and Desktop 2 will now show that the Settings app is on that desktop.

FIGURE 6.8

Move applications between Desktops while using Task View.

6. Select **Desktop 2**. You will jump to a desktop that has only the Settings app open. Select the **Start** menu and open another application.

7. Select the **Task View** icon again on the taskbar. Notice that both Desktops accurately reflect the open applications on each desktop. Select **Desktop 1**. You will now be back to where you started in step 1 minus the Settings app.

8. Select the **Task View** icon again on the taskbar. Hover over Desktop 2 and select the **X** to close Desktop 2. You will now be looking at thumbnails for all of the open applications that had been on Desktop 1 and Desktop 2. They are both open in the original Desktop.

Virtual desktops are not a new concept; there have been third-party versions available in the past for Windows. However, this is the first time they are integrated into Windows. Also, you should recognize that multiple desktops and open applications will still need to share the same hardware resources. If your device has a slower CPU and less RAM, it will impact how many items can be open. Take some time to experiment with creating Desktops for different tasks. The Windows+Tab keyboard shortcut, which activates Task view, can become your best friend if you start using Task View regularly.

TIP When using a touchscreen, whether in Desktop mode or Tablet mode, you can swipe in from the left to enter Task View.

Working with the Taskbar

An important element of the Desktop is the taskbar. Although the taskbar (shown in Figure 6.9) takes up little space, it performs a number of important tasks. Here is the full list of the taskbar's capabilities:

- Provides the Start button to invoke the Start menu

- Lists the programs currently running on the Desktop, even if a program is obscured from view

- Enables you to switch to a running program by selecting the program's icon on the taskbar

- Includes the notification area, which is home to the Action Center, as well as other icons that provide you status alerts and messages from applications that might be running or system resources

- Displays the current time and date

- Displays various toolbars you can choose to show or hide

- Enables you to quickly enter text for searching locally or across the Internet or just enter a website address

- Allows you to pin shortcuts for applications

- Includes a shortcut to File Explorer

- Provides a shortcut to Task View and additional virtual desktops

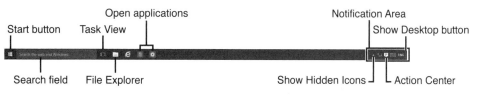

FIGURE 6.9

The taskbar is a critical part of the Desktop.

The taskbar can be resized, be moved to a different part of the screen, and be hidden when not needed. Toolbars can be added or removed, and shortcuts to applications can be pinned to the taskbar. All these options are considered in this section.

Using the Action Center

The Action Center is an important feature of the taskbar. Located in the notification area, the Action Center is home to settings you are most likely to access on a routine basis. Notifications from modern apps and from Windows will appear here as well. While many apps show a brief toast notification that you might or might not have time to read, you can look for notifications you may have missed in the Action Center.

As shown in Figure 6.10, settings such as Wi-Fi, screen brightness, Bluetooth, and Tablet mode are found right here. All Settings is a shortcut to open the Settings app. The exact settings that appear here will depend on your device. Remember that on a touch screen the Action Center can be opened by simply swiping in from the right side of the screen.

FIGURE 6.10

The settings and notifications feature found in the Action Center is one of the best features in Windows 10.

Notifications will continue to collect until you reboot your computer or take some action. To act on a notification, follow these steps:

1. Open the Action Center, selecting its icon in the notification area or swiping in from the right edge of a touchscreen.

2. Hover your cursor over a notification in the Action Center. The notification will appear highlighted, as shown in Figure 6.11.

3. Select the notification to launch the app that originated the notification. The notification will disappear from the Action Center.

4. To disregard a notification and remove it from the Action Center, hover your cursor over the notification and select the X. You also can clear all notifications for a specific app at once by selecting the X next to the app name in the Action Center.

FIGURE 6.11

Select notifications from the Action Center.

 NOTE Microsoft has indicated that it intends notifications to become more interactive in the future, enabling a person to take action on a notification without ever opening the app that sent the notification.

Modern apps tend to be enabled by default to send notifications. If you would like to limit which apps have this permission, these can be managed in the Settings app. This subject is covered in more detail in Chapter 12, "Configuring Notifications and Advanced Settings."

Customizing the Taskbar

Many features of the taskbar can be customized. The notification area, previously referred to as the system tray, already might include additional tools such as language or the Touch keyboard. Other items on the taskbar may not be used and seem like a waste of space. You might have other preferences, like relocating the taskbar or having it hide when not needed. Features such as these can be tweaked, added, or removed by customizing the properties for the taskbar.

To customize the taskbar, follow these steps:

1. Right-click the taskbar (or tap and hold on a touchscreen) to reveal the taskbar context menu (shown in Figure 6.12).

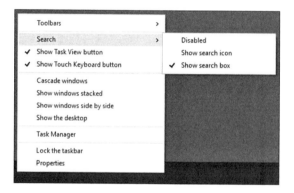

FIGURE 6.12

Customizing the taskbar starts with the taskbar context menu.

2. Select **Toolbars** to show a list of toolbars available on this device. Select a toolbar to enable it; a checkmark will appear when enabled. Select it again to disable it.

3. Select **Search** to reveal three choices regarding the Search field. (Search is replaced with *Cortana* when enabled.) **Show Search Box** is enabled by default; you can replace the text field with an icon or disable it altogether.

4. The **Show Task View Button** can be disabled by selecting it to remove the checkmark.

5. The **Show Touch Keyboard Button** can be enabled or disabled. It will appear in the notification area when enabled.

6. The option **Lock the Taskbar** prevents changes to the shape, position, and size when enabled. The taskbar can be relocated by simply selecting it and dragging it to another edge of the display.

7. Select **Properties** to open the Taskbar and Start Menu Properties dialog box shown in Figure 6.13.

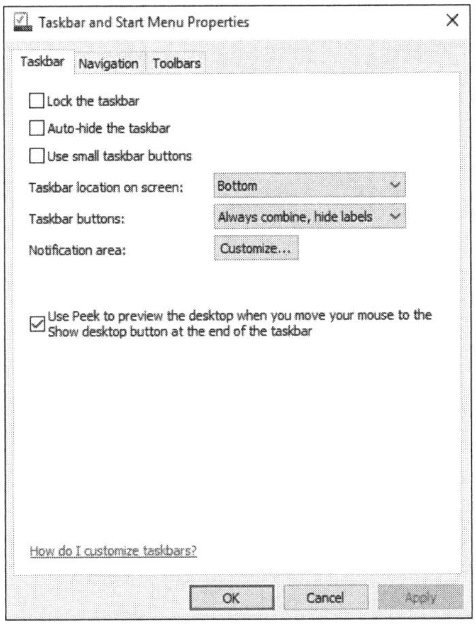

FIGURE 6.13

Some taskbar features are tweaked from the Taskbar and Start Menu Properties dialog box.

8. Use checkboxes to enable **Lock the Taskbar**, **Auto-Hide the Taskbar**, or **Use Small Taskbar Buttons**.

9. The **Taskbar Location On Screen** drop-down list enables you to relocate the taskbar to the bottom, left, right, or top of the display.

10. The **Taskbar Buttons** drop-down list refers to how separate windows for the same application are displayed on the taskbar. Multiple Word documents or web pages, for example, can appear as separate labeled buttons on the taskbar or can be stacked under a single icon to conserve space. The default is set to **Always Combine, Hide Labels**.

11. The last checkbox is enabled by default to enable the Show Desktop button, which allows the Peek tool to reveal the Desktop in Desktop mode.

12. Select **Customize** for **Notification Area** to open the Settings app to the Notifications & Actions pane, as shown in Figure 6.14.

13. Select a Quick Action button to choose from a list of settings buttons that can be included in the Action Center. Under Notifications you can make changes to some of the types of notifications that appear in the Action Center and elsewhere.

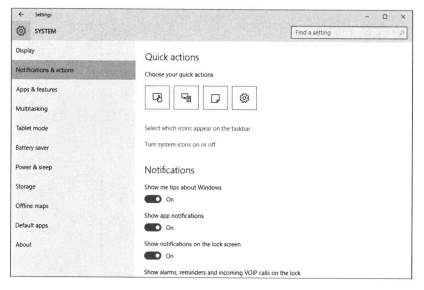

FIGURE 6.14

Further customize the taskbar from the Settings app.

14. Below the Quick Actions settings buttons, select the link **Select Which Icons Appear on the Taskbar**. You will see a list of icons for system resources such as Network and Volume. There might be other notification icons unique to your device for printers or touchpads. Slide the switch to **On** to make the icon always visible in the notification area of the taskbar. When the switch is Off, the icon will be hidden until accessed from the taskbar by selecting the **Show Hidden Icons** button (shaped like a triangle).

15. Select the back arrow to return to the Notifications & Actions pane from step 12.

16. Select **Turn System Icons On or Off**. A list of system icons will be displayed for essential systems, including Clock, Volume, Network, Power, Input Indicator, Location, and Action Center. Slide the switch to On or Off to completely remove the notification icon from the notification area of the taskbar. When set to Off, these icons are also removed from the hidden icons mentioned in step 14. Some icons might be grayed out depending on your device's hardware.

17. Close the Settings app and select **OK** or **Apply** to save changes in the Taskbar and Start Menu Properties dialog box before closing it.

Working with Applications from the Taskbar

When in Desktop mode, the taskbar is an important tool for keeping track of applications that are open or that we use often. As shown in Figure 6.15, applications that are currently open, even when there may be multiple instances, can be easily identified from the taskbar. Open applications appear with a solid line below their icon on the taskbar. Additionally, shortcuts to applications can be pinned to the taskbar to keep them highly available. Use restraint because real estate is limited when pinning applications to the taskbar. You can also pin folders to make them easy to open from the taskbar.

FIGURE 6.15

You can manage applications from the taskbar while in Desktop mode.

To pin items to the taskbar, follow these steps:

1. Open the Start menu and locate an application you want to pin to the taskbar.

2. Right-click the application, as shown in Figure 6.16.

FIGURE 6.16

Pin applications to the taskbar to make it even easier to find them.

3. Select **Pin to Taskbar**. The application will now appear as an icon on the taskbar.

4. To pin a folder to the taskbar, open **File Explorer** and navigate to a folder you want to make highly available.

5. Select and drag the folder to the File Explorer icon on the taskbar. You will see the action **Pin to File Explorer** indicated. Release the folder.

6. Right-click the File Explorer icon to reveal the context menu shown in Figure 6.17. Your folder will appear under Pinned. A list of folders may appear under Frequent. Hover the cursor over a folder in the Frequent list and select the thumbtack **Pin to This List**. The folder will also appear under Pinned.

 TIP To remove a pinned application, right-click the icon on the taskbar. Select **Unpin This Program from Taskbar**. The icon will disappear from the taskbar. To remove a folder from the Pinned list, hover over the folder with your cursor or right-click the folder and select **Unpin from This List**. The folder will no longer appear here.

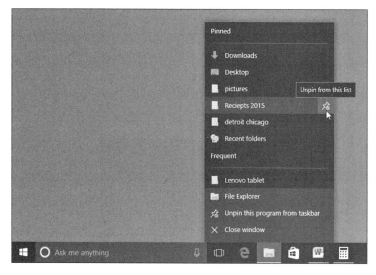

FIGURE 6.17

Pin folders to File Explorer on the taskbar to make it even easier to find them.

People have used the Desktop as a place to save shortcuts for decades, resulting in cluttered Desktops that become their own challenge to navigate. Pinning a few well-chosen items to the taskbar is a much better way to keep them visible while working with other applications that can cover the Desktop. It also reduces the clutter you might otherwise have to deal with at some point in the future. Having said that….

Keeping the Desktop Organized

You can use the area of the Desktop above the taskbar much as you use your desktop in your office or at home. You can keep the files associated with a project you are working on anywhere on the Desktop. You can organize the files into folders, and the folders also can be kept on the Desktop; however, I don't necessarily recommend this because it clutters the Desktop. Back at home or in the office, when you acquire new files or folders or other items, you might temporarily drop them onto your desk to file away or store later. In Windows, when you download content from the Internet or create a new document, you can just as easily drop the content onto the Desktop.

With all the files potentially moving on and off of the Desktop, even organized users might find their Desktop in a state of disorder and mess from time to time. Fortunately, it's not hard to keep the Desktop clutter under control with a few built-in tools.

CAUTION It is good to remember that the Desktop is actually a special folder that is unique for each person who can sign in to the same device. Contents of the Desktop are kept out of sight of other users inside of your Users folder. Documents and pictures saved to the Desktop will not appear automatically appear in the Documents and Pictures libraries. Many people have forgotten to copy files from the desktop and subsequently lost data that was saved to their Desktop when moving to a new computer.

CAUTION Files and folders saved to the desktop will be hidden when your device is in Tablet mode. Consider saving documents to other locations, and pin folders to File Explorer on the taskbar to avoid this issue.

Arranging the Desktop

The Desktop has an invisible grid that keeps every item positioned in uniform columns and rows. When you save, move, download, or copy a file to the Desktop, or if a program you use saves a file to the Desktop, Windows immediately snaps the file into an empty cell in the grid. Windows normally fills the grid from left to right and from the top down, but you can turn this option off. Turning this option off enables you to place an item anywhere on the Desktop, although it's still lined up in one of the invisible rows and columns. This is just one of the ways you can control how things are arranged on your Desktop.

To configure how Windows arranges the Desktop, follow these steps:

1. Right-click or tap and hold an unused spot on the Desktop; then select **View** (see Figure 6.18).

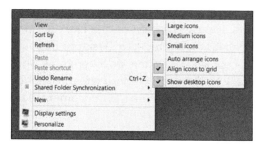

FIGURE 6.18

Use tools like Auto Arrange Icons and Align Icons to Grid to keep the Desktop organized.

2. If Align Icons to Grid is checked, the invisible grid is in use. If **Align Icons to Grid** is not checked, select it to turn the grid on.

3. To allow Windows to arrange the Desktop, select **Auto Arrange Icons**. To keep icons anywhere you like on the Desktop (but still lined up), select **Auto Arrange Icons** to clear the check mark and leave **Align Icons** enabled.

4. Other options you can select here include indicating the icon size that Windows will display on the Desktop and the option Show Desktop Icons. Disabling Show Desktop Icons will hide everything on the Desktop. Select the option again to make everything visible again. Besides being a great way to scare someone, this can make it easy to quickly tidy up if someone else will need to access your computer.

5. Right-click or tap and hold an unused spot on the Desktop; then select to **Sort By**.

6. Sort categories include **Name, Size, Item Type**, and **Date Modified**. Select a criteria to immediately rearrange the icons on the Desktop based on that category.

THE ABSOLUTE MINIMUM

- The way you use the Desktop is determined by the mode your device is using. Use the Action Center to manually switch between Tablet mode and Desktop mode.

- Use Task View to add virtual desktops when using a single display to let you easily jump between tasks without rearranging open applications.

- The Action Center hosts important settings buttons such as Brightness or Tablet mode and maintains a history of notifications.

- You can customize the taskbar by opting to show and hide icons as well as pin applications and folders to the taskbar.

- The notification area of the taskbar allows icons to provide alerts and status information. You can select which icons appear here.

7

WORKING WITH WINDOWS DESKTOP APPLICATIONS

This chapter continues the teaching about how applications work in Windows first touched on in Chapter 1, "Meet Windows 10," and then expanded on in Chapter 6, "Finding Your Way Around the Windows Desktop." As you learned in Chapter 4, "Introducing Windows Apps," modern Windows apps are distinct from Windows Desktop applications for a few reasons. Windows apps are acquired only through the Windows Store and are installed and can even be updated automatically in the background without the need to get your hands dirty picking directories and making decisions about install options.

This chapter will teach you how to work with and then manage Desktop applications. You'll learn how to install and remove Desktop applications. If you are comfortable working with programs in Windows 7 or earlier versions of Windows, you might have less to learn in this chapter than others; however, it pays to review the steps in this chapter because Windows 10 has introduced a new way to manage Desktop applications.

Introducing Desktop Applications

For many Windows 10 users, the Desktop remains the core of their experience. Sure, there has been a host of new software applications built specifically for Windows 10, known as Windows apps, but applications specific to the Desktop—ranging from Microsoft Office to financial software such as Quicken, to iTunes, to a host of games—all install and run on Windows just as they always have. Windows 10 does not go out of its way to distinguish between the two application types, which contributes to a uniform experience overall, as shown in Figure 7.1.

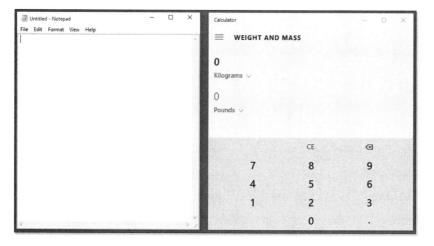

FIGURE 7.1

Notepad is a Desktop application, while the Calculator is a modern Windows app.

You do not need to lose sleep trying to keep track of which applications are which. However, understanding the differences can help you recognize why the experience varies a bit between the two types.

NOTE In this book, the term *applications* is often used as a general description of any software designed to run on Windows, which includes modern apps as well as Desktop applications. *Desktop applications* refers to Win32 applications (as well as other code frameworks that developers have used over the years) that can be installed from discs or downloaded from a website. They require a traditional installer and lack some of the features that modern Windows apps bring to the table.

 NOTE Microsoft announced to developers early in 2015 that Desktop applications will be allowed into the Windows Store. This will make it possible for developers to offer existing games, productivity, and line-of-business software side-by-side with Windows apps all in one place. Developers will be required to prepare their Desktop applications using App-V to list them in the Windows Store as a "desktop app." Although this means the developer will need to do some work, it is a lot less work than re-creating existing applications with a different code language. It also means that these Desktop apps will behave as Windows apps in most respects that matter: fast installs, clean uninstalls, secure apps, updates through the Windows Store, and easier resource management by Windows.

Working with Desktop Applications

Desktop applications are not going away anytime soon. You might have licenses for expensive applications purchased in the past that are compatible with Windows 10, or you might have favorites that have yet to make their way into the Windows Store as modern Windows apps. Whatever the reason, this section helps you understand how Desktop applications run in Windows 10.

A Desktop application might appear similar to a Windows app, but there are a few noteworthy differences:

- Tasks such as printing and sharing to other apps will be limited to what has been anticipated by the developer of that application. For example, printing will be handled within the application, as shown in Figure 7.2.

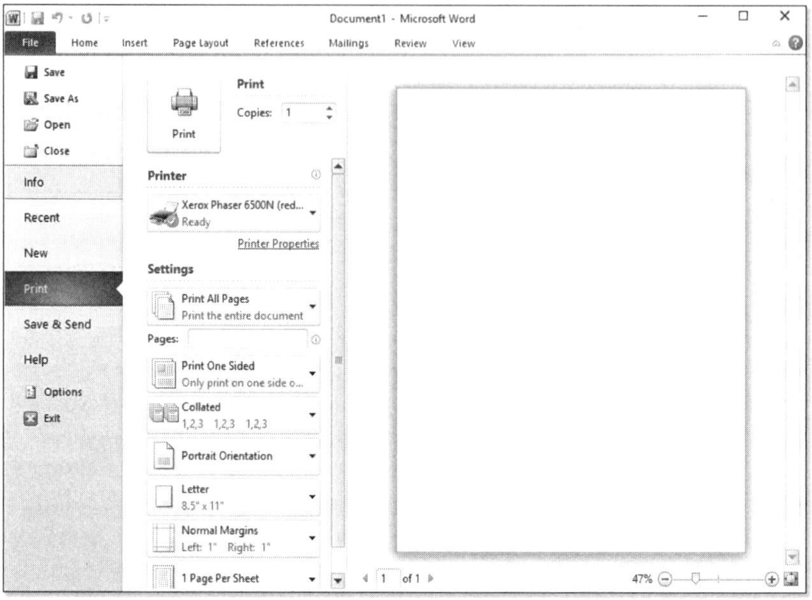

FIGURE 7.2

Desktop applications such as Word 2010 will not hand off tasks like printing to Windows the way a modern Windows app would.

- Menus and toolbars are not guided by Microsoft Design language, so they can appear anywhere, stay visible all the time, and have a hard time displaying on smaller screens.

- Desktop applications cannot automatically adjust the spacing for menus to provide a better touchscreen experience when using Tablet mode.

- Desktop applications can be installed for all users on a device, whereas a Windows app is installed only for the current user.

- Desktop applications will install multiple files—sometimes in multiple locations on a device—make changes to the registry, install drivers and toolbars, and make any other system changes to ensure they work as intended. Uninstalling a Desktop application seldom undoes and removes all of this, and this can negatively impact a device after many applications have been installed and uninstalled over time.

- Desktop applications often allow you to run multiple instances of the same application, whereas Windows apps will run only a single instance.

- A Desktop application can occasionally start to use more resources than it should, which will cause a computer to become less responsive or even seem to freeze up altogether. A reboot of the device can be necessary to recover. (Bonus Chapter 5, "Resolving Common Problems," considers some trouble-shooting steps.) On the other hand, a Windows app will simply crash without bringing the entire device to a halt.

This is not to say that everything about Desktop applications is bad; there are many well-written Desktop applications that run light, perform well, and never cause any issues. It is important to understand that by their nature the user experience relies on the developer and his ability to anticipate the wide range of devices and form factors that will run Windows 10. Windows can control an unruly Windows app, but an unruly Desktop application could disrupt Windows 10.

CAUTION Desktop applications should be downloaded and installed only from reputable sources because they can increase the exposure of Windows to viruses and exploitation. Generally a company will offer links on its intranet to trusted downloads that have been tested and are compatible with its systems. Reviews might be another tool to help you determine whether other users have had problems after downloading and installing an application.

Starting Desktop Applications

Desktop applications can be started just like a Windows app by selecting them. They appear in the Start menu in the alphabetical All Apps list. In some cases, you might find a folder containing several Desktop applications. Select the folder to reveal its contents, as shown in Figure 7.3; select it again to collapse the folder.

FIGURE 7.3

Desktop applications can appear within a folder in the Start menu.

NOTE You might find that some Desktop applications that appear here are actually installers or trial versions that have been included on a device to encourage you to try an application or purchase a productivity suite or utility in order to use it.

By now you have noticed that after starting up an application, an icon representing the program appears on the taskbar. After starting a number of applications, the taskbar soon starts to fill up with an array of colorful icons. (If your device is working in Tablet mode, you might not see this happen because the taskbar is not set to show icons for open applications by default.) Hovering your cursor over an icon displays a small thumbnail or portrait of the open application.

It is not too unusual to have several instances of the same Desktop application running at the same time. For example, you can have one document open in Microsoft Word and then open another document, which will open a new instance of Microsoft Word. In this case, the taskbar will show only a single icon for the Desktop application; however, when you move the cursor over the application icon, a row of portraits—one for each document—appear above the main portrait (see Figure 7.4). To jump to a specific document, select the portrait with which you want to work.

FIGURE 7.4

Use the Desktop taskbar to jump between several instances of a Desktop application running at the same time.

 TIP A quick way to switch to a program or document without moving the cursor is to use a keyboard shortcut. Press and hold the Alt key, and then press the Tab key. A screen appears showing portraits of each program or app window open in Windows 10. While holding down the Alt key, tap the Tab key repeatedly to move the highlight to the next window on the screen. Release both keys when you have selected the window to which you want to switch.

Using Run as Administrator

Sometimes you might need to run a Desktop application with elevated privileges as an administrator for it to work correctly. This is because Windows might not allow certain actions to execute to protect your device. It is not recommended that you do this unless directed to do so by someone you trust.

To run a Desktop application with administrator privileges, follow these steps:

1. From the Start menu, locate a Desktop application. It can be a tile or could appear in the list of apps.

2. Right-click the application icon to view the context menu, as shown in Figure 7.5.

FIGURE 7.5

Desktop applications have slightly different context menus that include Run as Administrator.

3. Select **Run as Administrator**.

4. If you are not logged in with an administrator account, you will be prompted by User Account Control (UAC) to provide credentials from an account that is an administrator, as shown in Figure 7.6.

FIGURE 7.6

UAC will require administrator credentials when using Run as Administrator.

Pinning Desktop Applications to the Taskbar

You can save trips to the Start screen to start your favorite or most-used Desktop applications by pinning an icon of each of your favorite applications on the taskbar.

Chapter 6 includes steps for pinning an application to the taskbar. To start one of your pinned applications, select its icon on the taskbar.

 TIP A pinned application will also be able to show jump lists, which makes it a good way to jump straight into a recently used or pinned document.

Saving Shortcuts for Desktop Applications to the Desktop

The Desktop has long been a favorite place for saving documents and keeping shortcuts for applications. In Windows 10 you can still pin shortcuts for Desktop applications—this process also works for creating shortcuts to Windows apps.

TIP   Shortcuts for applications that have been saved to the Desktop are just that: shortcuts. If you delete the shortcut at a later time, this has no effect on the application.

 NOTE   Items that are saved to the Desktop are not visible while your device is in Tablet mode.

To create a shortcut on the Desktop for a Desktop application, follow these steps:

1. From the Start menu, locate a Desktop application. It can be a tile or could appear in the list of apps.

2. Select the application and drag it to the desktop, as shown in Figure 7.7. The icon will change, and you will see the test Link indicating that it is prepared to create a link.

FIGURE 7.7

Drag applications from the Start menu to the Desktop to create shortcuts.

3. Position and release the application to create a shortcut on the Desktop in that spot.

The Desktop shortcut can be moved or renamed, and the original link will remain in the Start menu.

Exiting Desktop Programs

Windows does not require you to shut down a program when you finish working with it. But there are a few reasons you should consider routinely closing Desktop applications when you finish with them. If you have a number of applications running concurrently, your computer's speed can be negatively impacted. If your computer seems to be running more slowly than normal, consider shutting down some applications—especially if you have several instances running.

To close a Desktop application, follow these steps. (Save any changes before closing an application.)

1. On the taskbar, locate the icon for the program you want to close.

2. Right-click the icon.

3. From the menu that appears, select **Close Window** (or **Close All Windows** if you have multiple windows open).

4. If you have unsaved work, you will be prompted to save your work, as shown in Figure 7.8.

FIGURE 7.8

When closing a Desktop application, you will be prompted to act on any unsaved changes.

The application will close, and the application's icon will disappear from the task-bar. Note that an application that you have pinned to the taskbar remains pinned even after you have closed all its document windows.

Working with Windows

You don't necessarily need to be a Windows expert to work with multiple programs at once with several windows open on the Desktop. You might be working in an Office program, such as Microsoft Word or Excel; you might have Microsoft Edge open to check in at some of your favorite social media sites; and you might have a File Explorer window open to organize a folder. So, innocently, you can have three windows fighting for screen real estate. It's easy, though, to arrange, move, and resize windows to leverage all the room on the Desktop. Figure 7.9

shows the basic controls at the top of a typical window with the important parts pointed out. When you select the icon from the title bar, you will reveal additional options from a system menu as shown.

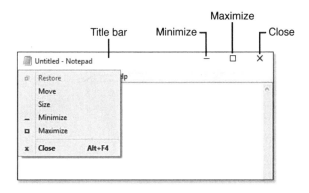

FIGURE 7.9

These controls are common to virtually all Desktop app windows.

The following list summarizes the various methods available to manage windows on the Desktop:

- You can easily resize and reshape a window. You can't change the window's shape from rectangular to circular, but you can make the window short and wide, narrow and tall, perfectly square, or anything in between. To resize a window using a mouse, point to any border of the window you want to resize. When the pointer becomes a double-headed arrow, click-and-drag the pointer to move the border.

- You can enlarge a window so it fills up your entire screen space (known as maximize), obscuring every other window you have open. To do so, click the **Maximize** button on the window's title bar.

- You can also remove a window from view without closing the program. Select the **Minimize** button (-) to hide the window.

- You can minimize all open windows simultaneously, exposing the Desktop. To do so, click the taskbar between the time and date and the edge of the screen. You can also right-click the taskbar and select **Show the Desktop**.

- To return a window to its most previous state, select the **Restore** button. You also can restore the window by choosing **Restore** from the Control menu on the upper-left corner of the window. The Restore command works only when the window is in a maximized state.

- You can move a window around your Desktop by dragging the window by its title bar.

- When you start multiple programs on the Desktop, or if you open several documents, it can become difficult to arrange and size the windows so that you can work efficiently. You can move and resize the windows manually, but Windows provides a few quick commands to arrange the windows on the Desktop. Right-click the taskbar to find these choices:

  - Cascade Windows

  - Show Windows Stacked

  - Show Windows Side by Side

Installing and Removing Programs

Windows Desktop applications are not installed from the Windows Store, like Windows apps are. Desktop applications are often purchased and downloaded from reliable sources, and many people still like to purchase installation discs. Desktop applications that you choose to install come with their own installation utility. Desktop applications are removed the same way, although you kick off the uninstall process from a central location in Windows that was referred to earlier in Chapter 4.

Installing Programs

The installation process for new programs has lots of variations. Keep in mind that the setup process is designed by the company that developed the software you are installing, meaning anything can happen:

- For software installed from a CD or DVD, the installation program usually starts as soon as the disc is inserted into the drive. If a program does not start, you should navigate to the disc using File Explorer. Look for a program named install.exe, autoplay.exe, or setup.exe. Double-click the file to start the installation program.

- Setup programs are not perfect. You might need to uninstall a program if the setup stops unexpectedly so you can try to run the setup program again.

- Setup programs sometimes require that the person installing the software have administrator rights. To run the setup program as an administrator, locate the setup program (possible names are setup.exe and install.exe), right-click the program, and select **Run as Administrator**.

You will generally be prompted by User Account Control to confirm your intention to install an application. You might be prompted to accept license terms; provide an activation key, a serial number, or registration details; indicate an installation location; and indicate which components are installed. If you have trouble with the installation, you may need to do some investigating and contact the company that has created the software for support.

CAUTION   Watch for adware and toolbars that are often packaged with software. If you see the option to use a custom install, use this and carefully check what is being installed at each step before selecting Next. Many "free" applications gain revenue by including these extra nuisance applications and toolbars that at best are not likely to be used and can actually introduce malware at worst.

Removing Windows Programs

You might need to remove an installed program for a number of reasons, including the following:

- You are running out of free disk space.

- There seems to be a problem with the software, and you need to reinstall it.

- You no longer use or plan to use the software.

- The application is bloatware that was preloaded onto your system by the device manufacturer. You have no intention of using it, and it might actually slow down your system when starting up.

- You plan to install new software that is incompatible with an installed application.

There is no harm in leaving a program installed if you have enough free disk space and if the application does not interfere with another application. If you need to remove an application, however, follow these steps:

1. Save any unsaved work—some applications require a reboot to finish uninstalling.

2. From the Start menu, select **Settings** to open the Settings app.

3. Click **System**, and then select **Apps & Features** from the navigation menu of the Settings app. Windows will generate a list of all applications currently installed on the device. Scroll down to find the application you want to uninstall, and select it.

4. Select the **Uninstall** button. A warning will pop up letting you know that the app and its related info will be uninstalled, as shown in Figure 7.10. Select **Uninstall** to continue.

5. Windows will initiate the uninstall program that is associated with that Desktop application. Follow the steps indicated by the uninstaller. You might be prompted to restart Windows to complete the uninstall process.

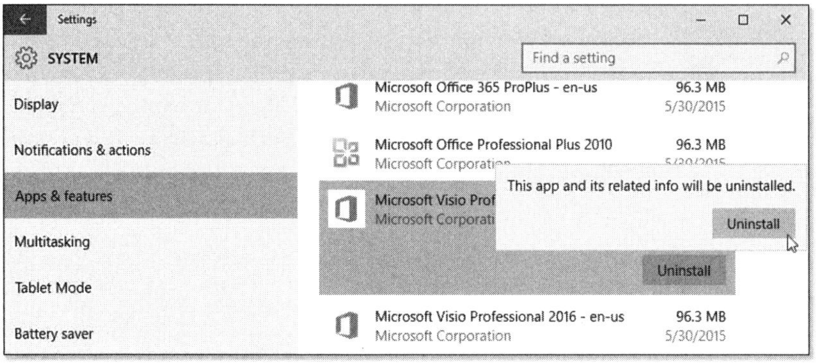

![Settings window showing Apps & features with uninstall confirmation dialog](settings-window)

FIGURE 7.10

Uninstall a Windows Desktop application through the Settings app.

TIP Uninstall can also be selected when you right-click to view the context menu for a desktop application in the Start menu. Windows will guide you through the process for uninstalling the application.

NOTE Some applications are part of Windows 10 and cannot be uninstalled. They will not appear in the list, and no uninstall option will be offered when looking at their context menu in the Start menu.

THE ABSOLUTE MINIMUM

- Windows Desktop applications and Windows apps can run side-by-side and are often hard to distinguish from one another.

- Create desktop shortcuts by dragging applications from the Start menu to the Desktop.

- To switch to a different program, click the icon representing the program on the taskbar. Alternatively, press and hold the Alt key and then press the Tab key. A screen appears showing portraits of each program or app window open in Windows 10. While holding down the Alt key, tap the Tab key repeatedly to move the highlight to the next window on the screen. Release both keys when you have selected the window to which you want to switch.

- To arrange the open windows on the Desktop, right-click the taskbar to reveal a menu. Select Cascade Windows or one of the two Show Windows commands to arrange the open windows.

- Windows Desktop applications can be uninstalled in the Settings app or by using the context menu.

8

TWEAKING WINDOWS TO REFLECT YOUR PERSONALITY

This chapter is all about eye candy. Short of playing games, shopping online, and keeping up with Twitter and Facebook, there probably is no greater distraction from real work than tweaking and adjusting all those preferences that make Windows your own. You wouldn't be the first person to neglect working in favor of picking colors and pictures for your Windows background.

This chapter takes you through the various personalization settings, as well as points out a few other settings you will want to check out, such as synching all your Windows devices to reflect these new settings.

Personalizing Windows to your liking requires you to work with the Settings app and File Explorer. Many of the procedures and skills necessary to set these personal options are described in Chapter 2, "Interacting with Windows," and Chapter 21, "File and Folder Basics."

Personalize Windows

When you first install Windows, you start with a preselected wallpaper and a neutral color scheme that may have been determined by the manufacturer of your Windows 10 device. You will find that an assortment of icons has been added to your Start menu. Although the choices might be appealing, you certainly are not obligated to stick with them!

In this section, you will see how you can modify those choices and use colors and photos to personalize various visual properties of Windows. Don't like the account picture that appears next to your name? You can use any photo you like for your account picture. You also can select from a palette of color themes and choose from a selection of background patterns to personalize Windows. The color and photo choices you make will impact the overall appearance of Windows, including the Start menu, as shown in Figure 8.1.

FIGURE 8.1

The Desktop and Start menu are all about personalizing.

After you spend a little time with these settings, you can drastically alter the appearance of Windows 10 to truly reflect your personality—be it subtle or zany. You might also want to look at Chapter 3, "Optimizing the Start Menu," which focuses on ways to customize the Start menu and includes settings related to the Start menu found in the Personalization section of the Settings app.

TIP   If you are using a Microsoft account, your personalization settings can be synchronized to any Windows 10 devices that you log in to using your Microsoft account. By default, synchronization is enabled so you have the same appearance on any device without the need to repeat these steps. To learn more about this feature and how to enable or disable it, see the section "Syncing Your Account Settings" later in this chapter.

NOTE   In some business environments, Personalization settings might be disabled or there may be a company policy regarding changes to the Desktop background or wallpaper. You might find it to be prudent to check first before turning your company computer into an homage to *Star Wars*.

Personalizing the Desktop Background

One of the most enjoyable tasks in the computer world is to make Windows feel like home. The best place to start is the Desktop background. The background can be a picture or color, or you can easily set up a slideshow of images you control. I like to think that the Desktop provides you with a window to an image that inspires you. For images, you can select from stock images that come with Windows, download wallpaper images from the Internet, or choose pictures you have saved to your computer from a camera or email. To change the Desktop background, follow these steps:

1. Open the Settings app by selecting **Settings** from the Start menu; then select **Personalization**.

2. Select **Background** from the vertical menu off to the left. The Desktop Background preview appears showing the currently selected background, as shown in Figure 8.2.

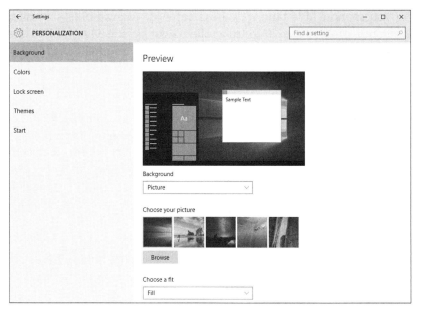

FIGURE 8.2

A number of options are available to format the Desktop background.

3. Using the drop-down menu under Background, select **Picture**, **Solid Color**, or **Slide Show**. The options presented below will alter depending on the background type you have selected. If you select **Solid Color**, skip to step 7. If you select **Slide Show**, skip to step 8.

4. If you have selected **Picture**, you can either choose from recent images that appear under Choose Your Picture or select **Browse** to navigate using File Explorer to a folder on your computer where you have saved images. Select an image.

5. After you have selected an image file, it will appear in the preview and the Desktop background will be replaced with your choice.

6. Under **Choose a Fit**, you can use the drop-down menu to fine-tune how your selected image will appear on the desktop. **Fill** or **Center** are usually safe options; other options can distort the image or leave undesirable solid colors to fill in around an image that does not fill the screen. You can experiment and choose the option you like best using the handy Preview tool. Figure 8.3 shows an image that has been centered on the desktop. The final results may be influenced by the image quality.

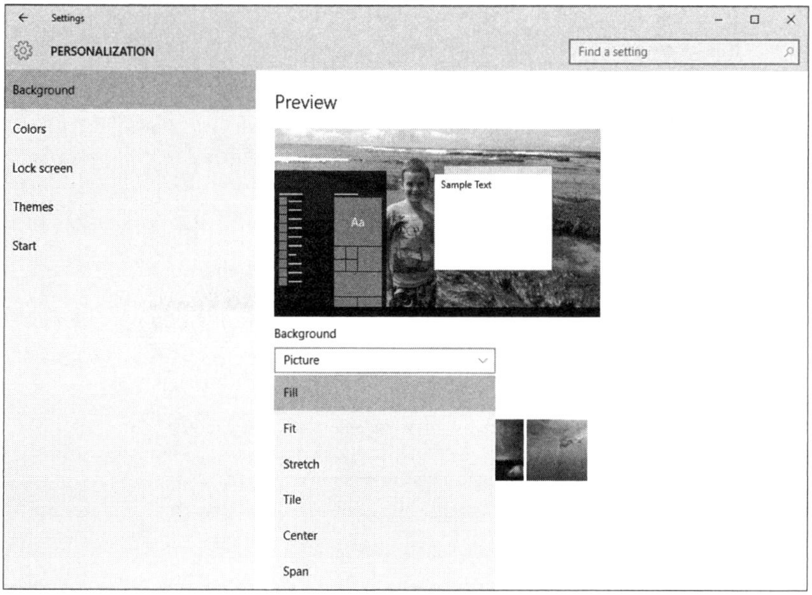

FIGURE 8.3

Tweak how a picture is displayed on the Desktop background using choices under Choose a Fit.

7. If you selected **Solid Color** in step 3, you will have the option to select from a palette of Standard Colors. Select a color, and you will see the Preview and Desktop change to reflect your choice.

8. If you selected **Slide Show** in step 3, the background will change to an image that is currently in your Pictures folder. You can create a folder that contains images you want to use for your desktop. Select **Browse** and navigate to the folder using File Explorer. Select the folder and select **Choose This Folder**. Figure 8.4 shows that the folder Phone Pictures has been selected, and the first picture in that folder is shown in the Preview.

9. By default, your background will change every 30 minutes. To change the time, select the drop-down under Change Picture Every and select a time increment. Choices range from 1 minute to 1 day.

10. Close the Settings app and enjoy your new background.

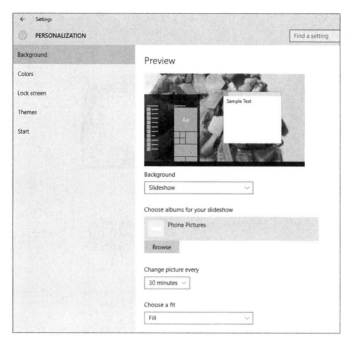

FIGURE 8.4

Selecting a folder to turn your Desktop background into a slideshow is easy in Windows 10.

Changing the Color Scheme

You can change the accent color used in the Start menu, taskbar, Action Center, and window borders. By default, Windows 10 uses a nice feature to select a color automatically that complements the current background. You can tweak this effect and even override it altogether to lock in your color preferences. To change the Windows color scheme, follow these steps:

1. Open the Settings app by selecting **Settings** from the Start menu; then select **Personalization**.

2. Select **Colors** from the vertical menu off to the left. A preview is provided to display the current color choices, as shown in Figure 8.5.

3. To select your own color, slide the switch to **Off** under Automatically Pick an Accent Color from My Background. Select a color from the list under **Choose Your Accent Color**. This new color choice will be applied to Windows, and the Preview window will give you an idea of how this would look with your background.

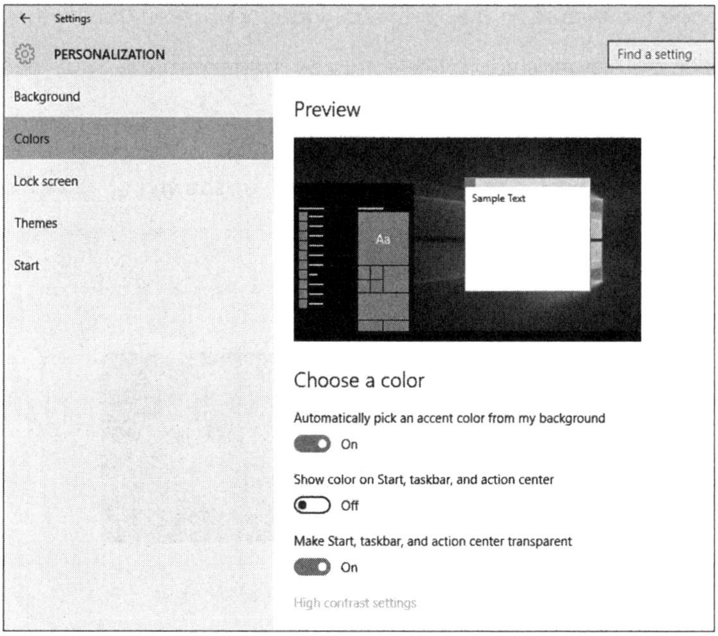

FIGURE 8.5

Allow Windows to automatically select a color that complements your background, or manually set a color scheme in Personalization.

4. To apply the current color choice to your taskbar, Start menu, and Action Center backgrounds, slide the switch to **On** under **Show Color on Start, Taskbar and Action Center**.

5. To turn off the transparency effect that is enabled by default, slide the switch to **Off** under **Make Start, Taskbar, and Action Center Transparent**.

6. Close the Settings app.

> **NOTE** There is also a link to use High Contrast color settings at the bottom of the Colors menu. This will take you to the Ease of Access settings within the Settings app. Ease of Access is considered in more detail in Chapter 12, "Configuring Notifications and Advanced Settings."

Customizing the Lock Screen

The Lock screen appears when you have signed out of Windows or you haven't used Windows for a period of time and your current settings trigger the Lock screen. The Lock screen can be personalized in several different ways.

To change the picture that appears on your Lock screen, follow these steps:

1. Open the Settings app by selecting **Settings** from the Start menu; then select **Personalization**.

2. Select the **Lock Screen** from the vertical menu off to the left. A preview is provided to display the current selection, as shown in Figure 8.6.

FIGURE 8.6

The Settings app enables you to allow Windows to present Lock screen images, or you can use your own.

3. Select the drop-down menu under Background to change the source image for the Lock screen. Choose from **Picture** or **Slideshow**. The Slideshow option is discussed in the following section.

4. If you select **Picture** in step 3, you can then do one of the following:

   - To use one of the pictures that ships with Windows, select the picture you like displayed under **Choose Your Picture**. The picture you choose replaces the current Lock screen picture on the screen.

   - If you want to use one of your pictures as the Lock screen background, select **Browse** to navigate to a file using File Explorer. Select your picture and then select **Choose Picture** to apply it as your Lock screen image.

Setting a Lock Screen Slideshow

A nice feature in Windows 10 is the capability to turn your Windows device into a digital picture frame. By default, Windows pulls pictures from your Pictures library on the device. You can add more folder locations as well.

To set up a slideshow on your Lock screen, follow these steps:

1. Open the Settings app by selecting **Settings** from the Start menu; then select **Personalization**.

2. Select **Lock Screen** from the vertical menu off to the left. A preview is provided to show the current selection.

3. Select the drop-down menu under **Background**, and select **Slideshow**.

4. Windows will play a slideshow based on the source folders that are selected. If you want to stick with the default Pictures folder, then skip to the next step. If you would like to specify different or additional folders, select **Add a Folder** under Choose Albums for Your Slide Show to point Windows to additional sources of pictures for the slideshow. To remove a source folder, select it and then click the **Remove** button that appears.

5. To change the behavior of the slideshow, select **Advanced Slideshow Settings**; it appears below the source folders. The Settings app will display Advanced Slide Show Settings, as shown in Figure 8.7.

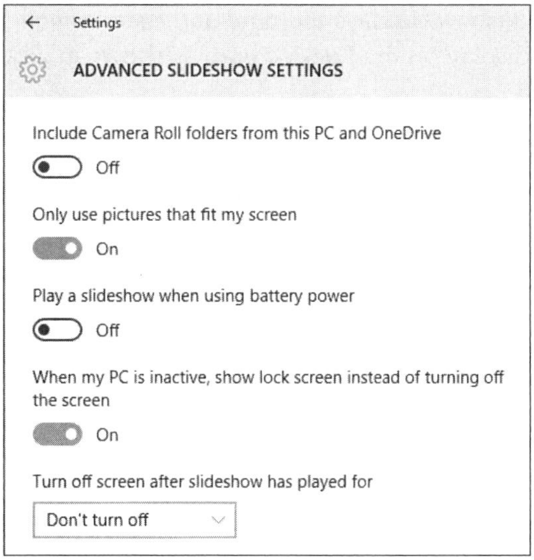

FIGURE 8.7

Control how long a slideshow will play and other behaviors while the Lock screen is enabled by using the Advanced Slide Show Settings.

6. Use the sliding switches to enable or disable settings that affect the quality of the slideshow:

   • When enabled, Include Camera Roll Folders from This PC and OneDrive will try to use an Internet connection to present the local and Internet-based OneDrive camera rolls. This can be better to leave disabled in most circumstances.

   • It is best to leave the switch to **On** for Only Use the Pictures That Fit Best on My Screen.

   • It is generally a good idea to leave the setting **Off** for Play a Slide Show When Using Battery Power.

   • The last slider is On by default if you have enabled the slideshow for the Lock screen. Rather than going to a black screen immediately, this switch needs to be **On** to display the Lock screen and overrule settings that might be configured under screen timeout settings elsewhere.

7. Select the drop-down list under **Turn Off the Screen After Slide Show Has Played for** to establish a time limit. **Don't Turn Off** is enabled in Figure 8.7, which means the slideshow will play until the computer is unlocked. You can shorten this to **3 hours**, **1 hour**, or **30 minutes**, after which the screen will go dark.

The slideshow that plays shows individual pictures as well as mosaics with panning effects. Your slideshow displays the time and date as well as any notifications that are allowed to display on the Lock screen, as shown in Figure 8.8.

FIGURE 8.8

The Lock screen can play a slideshow from selected picture folders on your device.

Lock Screen Apps

When you are not using your computer, you can still receive notifications from apps on the Lock screen. This lets you know that emails have arrived, calendar appointments need attention, or chat messages perhaps need a reply.

To allow an app to send notifications to your Lock screen, follow these steps:

1. Open the Settings app by selecting **Settings** from the Start menu; then select **Personalization**.

2. Select **Lock Screen** from the vertical menu off to the left. A preview is provided to show the current selection. Scroll down to the two controls related to app notifications (refer to Figure 8.6).

3. By default, the Calendar app is selected to display detailed status notifications. Select the current app under **Choose an App to Display Detailed Status**, and select an alternative app from the list that appears if you desire to give preference to a different app.

4. A group of apps is shown under Choose Apps to Show Quick Status. If you want to add another app, select the last icon (a large plus sign) to add an app. As shown in Figure 8.9, you can select an app from the available list to add it to your Lock screen.

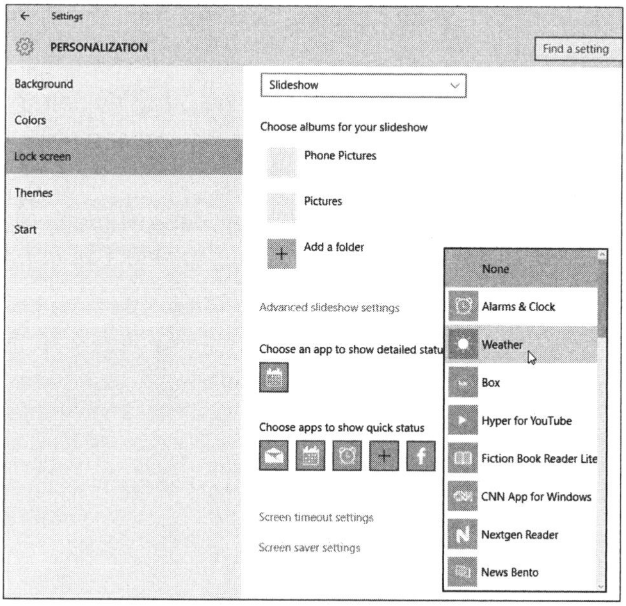

FIGURE 8.9

Select an app from the list of installed apps to allow notifications to appear on the Lock screen.

5. Select any additional apps that appear on the list to allow notifications to appear from the Lock screen.

6. To prevent an app from giving notifications on the Lock screen, select its icon and select **None** from the top of the drop-down list.

TIP If you are bothered by chimes and other sounds that notifications might make, they can be silenced. To learn more about additional settings that control notifications, look over information in Chapter 12.

Changing Timeout Settings

You might want to change how much time is required before your screen will darken after no input is recognized. There are two settings: one when on battery power and the other for when your device is plugged in. This is not the same as what happens when your device goes into a low-powered sleep state. Your screen simply is turned off to conserve power when not in use. During this period any input will turn the screen back on and your Lock screen will appear. These settings are ignored if you have configured a slideshow to display on your device.

To change the amount of time required to turn off the screen, follow these steps:

1. Open the Settings app by selecting **Settings** from the Start menu; then select **Personalization**.

2. Select **Lock Screen** from the vertical menu off to the left. A preview is provided to show the current selection. Scroll down and select the text **Screen Timeout Settings** (refer to Figure 8.6).

3. You will be taken to the Power and Sleep pane of the Settings app, as shown in Figure 8.10. Use the drop-down menus to select an appropriate time for battery or plugged-in power states.

4. Close the Settings app. Your settings are immediately applied.

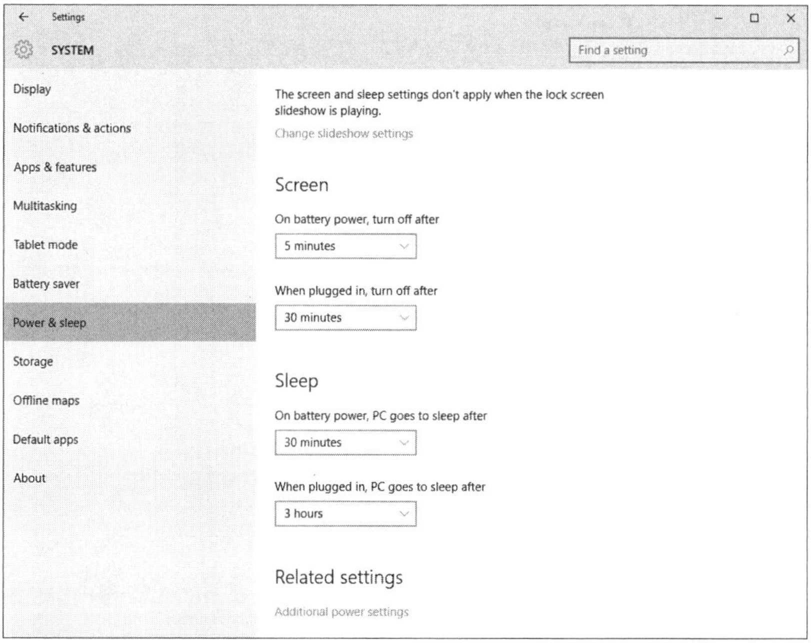

The screen and sleep settings don't apply when the lock screen slideshow is playing.

FIGURE 8.10

You can specify how much time is required before turning off your device's screen.

Setting Up a Desktop Screensaver

Screensaver programs became popular with the introduction of Windows as a means to prevent images from the new-at-the-time highly graphical software applications from creating a ghosted image on the display. This action came to be known as burning in. Display technology has advanced, and the risk of burning in is negligible for modern displays, yet screensavers remain popular. If you want to use one, you can always find a screensaver that reflects your mood and personality.

Follow these steps to configure a screensaver in Windows 10:

1. Open the Settings app by selecting **Settings** from the Start menu; then select **Personalization**.

2. Select **Lock Screen** from the vertical menu off to the left. Select **Screen Saver Settings** from the bottom of the Lock screen settings. The Screen Saver Settings appears (see Figure 8.11).

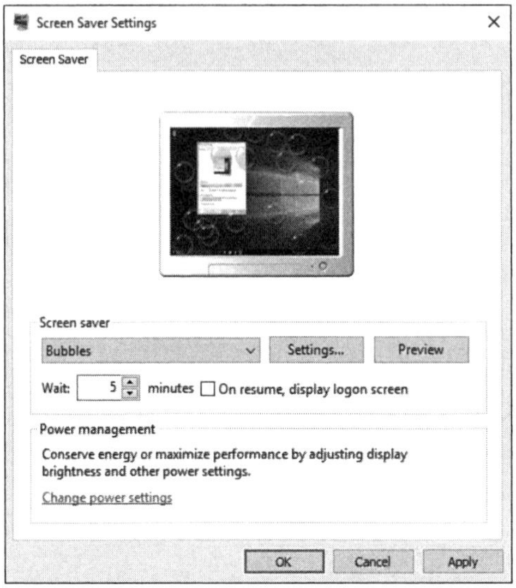

FIGURE 8.11

You can choose from six screensavers that come with Windows.

3. Select the **Screen Saver** list to display the drop-down list of screensavers installed on your computer.

4. In the Screen Saver list, choose the screensaver you want to use. Notice that the monitor image at the top of the dialog box shows you a preview of the screensaver you selected.

5. Depending on the screen saver you selected, there may be options for you to set. For example, the 3D Text screensaver has a number of options. Select the **Settings** button to customize the screensaver. Select OK when complete.

6. Select **Preview** to review your screensaver as it will appear in use. Select anywhere on the screen to close the preview.

7. In the **Wait** box, enter the amount of time during which there is no activity on your computer before the screensaver starts.

8. If your computer is in a location where there are people that you would prefer not to potentially access your computer, enable the **On Resume, Display Logon Screen** check box. This requires a user to sign in to clear the screensaver after it starts.

9. Select **OK**.

10. Close the Screen Saver Settings windows and the Settings app.

Modifying the Theme

Over the years, Windows has included many ways to personalize the user expe-
riences over the years that have become associated with a *theme*. Themes are
simply personalized choices for the appearance and sounds that we see and hear
when interacting with Windows. Many users will be happy with the visual choices
already outlined in this chapter, while others might prefer the more granular controls that were available in previous versions of Windows. The Themes pane of
the Settings app provides you with links to some of the Control Panel applets that
allow you to download and select packaged themes, as well as control sounds,
icons, and pointers. Most prepackaged themes include a few wallpapers that will
play as a slideshow. Some themes might update icons and sound effects, too.

To work with packaged themes, follow these steps:

1. Open the Settings app by selecting **Settings** from the Start menu; then select
   Personalization.

2. Select **Themes** from the vertical menu off to the left. The Themes pane
   appears, as shown in Figure 8.12.

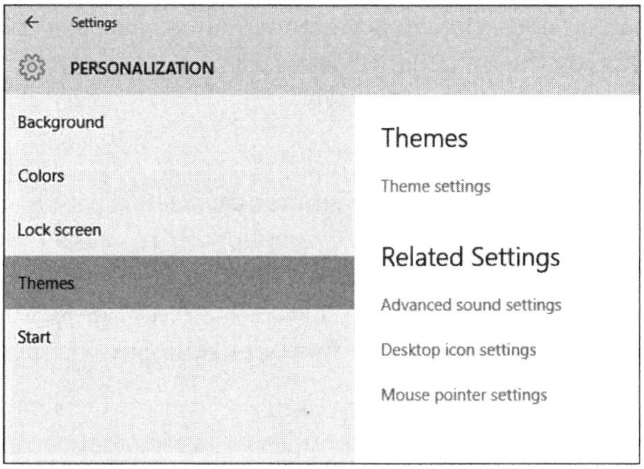

FIGURE 8.12

The Settings app includes links that allow you to customize the appearance and sounds of Windows.

3. Under Themes select **Theme Settings**. The Personalization window opens,
   shown in Figure 8.13.

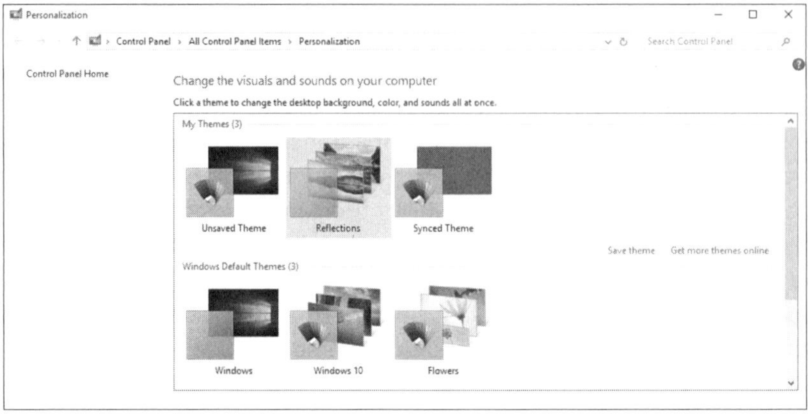

FIGURE 8.13

Select from packaged themes included with Windows or go online to look for others.

4. Scroll down to select from default themes that are already installed on your device or select **Get More Themes Online** to open a web browser that allows you to browse prepackaged themes from Microsoft's download library. Downloading and opening a theme will automatically replace the current settings, and your new theme will appear under My Themes.

Changing Sound Settings

Windows allows you to modify the sounds associated with events, such as a blocked pop-up window or a device connection. To make changes to the defaults sounds Windows uses for these events, open the Settings app to Personalization and then the Themes pane (refer to Figure 8.12). Under Related Settings, select **Advanced Sound Settings**. This opens the Sound dialog box shown in Figure 8.14.

Under Program Events, there is a long list of events that can trigger an assigned sound file to play. Select an event and select **Test** to get a preview of the sound. You can replace the current sound by selecting **Browse** and locating a sound file of your own choosing. If you decide that you would prefer to undo changes, select the drop-down under Sound Scheme and select **Windows Default** to reset all changes.

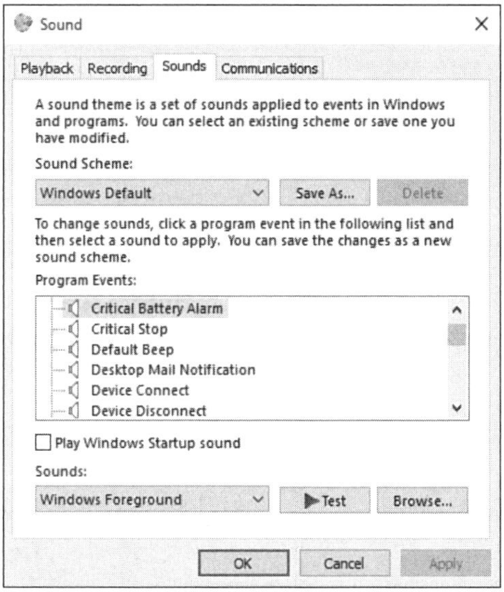

FIGURE 8.14

Choose different sounds for events that occur when working in Windows.

Changing Desktop Icons

Windows allows you some control over which icons appear by default on your Desktop. Of course, Desktop icons only appear when your device is in Desktop mode, and they are hidden by default when your device is in Tablet mode. To make changes to the default icons that appear on your Desktop, open the **Settings** app to **Personalization** and then select **Themes** (refer to Figure 8.12). Under Related Settings select the link **Desktop Icon Settings**. This will open the Sound dialog box shown in Figure 8.15.

Under Desktop Icons there are five icons that can be activated by selecting them. The Recycle Bin is selected by default. The appearance of the icons is displayed below in a preview, and these icons can be replaced with other choices by selecting **Change Icon**. Select from available icons or select **Browse** to navigate using File Explorer to a different icon that you have perhaps downloaded. Applying a theme can update your icon choices unless you deselect the checkbox at the bottom of this dialog box. To revert changes and return to defaults select the icon to restore and then select the **Restore Default** button.

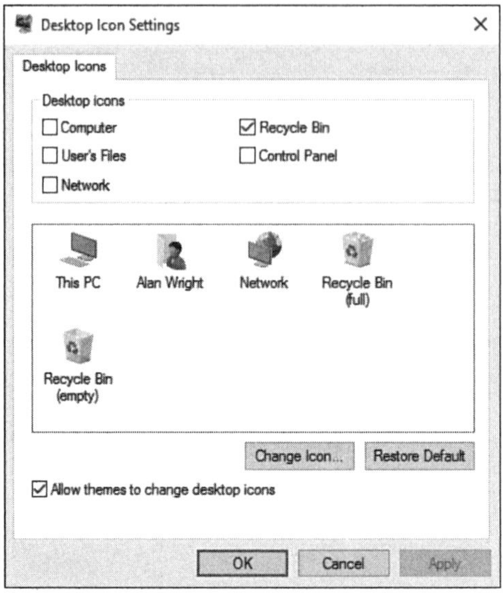

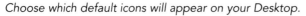

FIGURE 8.15

Choose which default icons will appear on your Desktop.

Changing the Mouse Pointers

You may want to customize the mouse pointers you use in Windows. You can adjust the pointers to reflect your personality and taste, or you might need to switch to pointers that are larger than normal to make it easier to see them. There are 15 pointers you can customize, such as the selection pointer and the double-arrow pointer. You can customize one or more of the pointers individually, or you can switch to a full set of 15 pointers.

To change the mouse pointers, follow these steps:

1. Open the Settings app by selecting **Settings** from the Start menu; then select **Personalization**.

2. Select **Themes** from the vertical menu off to the left. The Themes pane will appear (refer to Figure 8.12).

3. Under Related Settings select **Mouse Pointer Settings**. The Mouse Properties dialog box appears, as shown in Figure 8.16.

4. To use a predefined set of pointers, scroll through the schemes at the top of the dialog box. Select a scheme to inspect the pointers. If you find a scheme you like, select **OK**. Select **OK** again to close the Mouse Properties window.

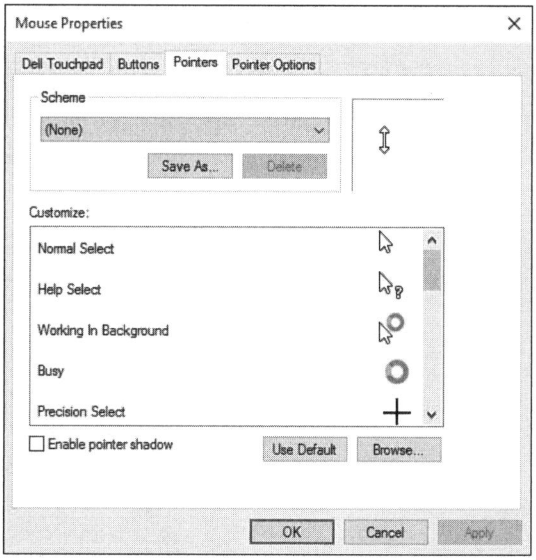

FIGURE 8.16

You can change many aspects of the mouse, including the pointer appearance, how fast the pointer moves across the screen as you move the mouse, and more.

5. To customize a pointer, select it in the **Customize** list.

6. Select **Browse** to open the Cursors folder, which contains a complete list of pointers available in Windows.

7. Select the pointer you want to use from the list; then select **Open**. You should be returned to the Mouse Properties dialog box.

8. Select the next pointer you want to customize, and then repeat steps 6 and 7.

9. Select **OK** to close the Mouse Properties dialog box.

10. Close the Settings app.

Personalizing Your Account Picture

You can select one of your personal photos to use as your account picture. Your account picture appears not only on the screen where you sign in, but also on the upper-left corner of the Start menu. Some apps with permission to access your Account info might display it as well.

To change your account picture, follow these steps:

1. Open the Start menu and select your name at the top.

2. Select **Change Account Settings** from the list that appears (see Figure 8.17). The Settings app opens to Accounts. Your Account is selected on the left, and Your Picture is displayed on the right.

FIGURE 8.17

Update your account picture from the current account information displayed on the Start menu.

3. To replace the current image with an image you already have saved on your device, scroll down a little and select **Browse**. File Explorer will open to the Pictures folder. Navigate to the image file, select the image, and then select **Choose Picture**. Your account picture will be updated, as shown in Figure 8.18.

4. To take a picture using a camera connected to your computer, select **Camera** under Create Your Picture. When the Camera app starts, snap the photo, set the crop marks, and select **OK**.

FIGURE 8.18

You can select a photo to use as your account picture or shoot a new photo to use.

5. The image you chose appears in the portrait back on the Account Picture screen. Close the Settings app. Your new picture now will display next to your name on the Start menu.

Syncing Your Account Settings

If you are using a Microsoft account, all your account choices can synchronize with other Windows 10 devices. This option is enabled by default, and it is certainly a nice feature that helps to maintain a consistent look and feel if you juggle multiple devices in your routine. You might want to disable this option or select which aspects of your account information are synced.

To make changes to your Microsoft account sync settings, follow these steps:

1. Open the Settings app by selecting **Settings** from the Start menu; then select **Accounts**.

2. Select **Sync Your Settings** from the vertical menu off to the left. A list of switches appears to the right, as shown in Figure 8.19.

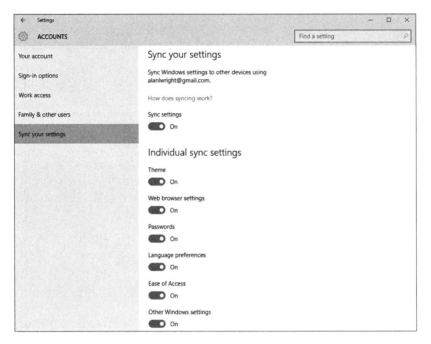

FIGURE 8.19

You can control which settings are synchronized between Windows 10 devices while using a Microsoft account.

3. To disable all syncing, slide the switch to **Off** under Sync Settings.

4. To disable syncing of choices for colors and background images outlined in this chapter, slide the switch to **Off** for Theme under Individual Sync Settings.

You can choose to stop synchronization of many aspects of your Windows settings. Besides Theme, you can also disable apps, web browser settings, passwords, language preferences, Ease of Access, and other Windows settings.

THE ABSOLUTE MINIMUM

Here are the key points to remember from this chapter:

- You can change a number of preferences and options in Windows 10 to suit your personality and mood. You can apply these preferences to any computer you sign in to with your Microsoft account.

- Nothing says "This computer is mine" more than a custom color choice and personal photos used in various places. You can specify the color scheme to use throughout Windows, as well as the pictures that appear on the sign-in screen and Lock screen. The pictures can be anonymous, such as a setting sun or another landscape or view. Or the pictures can be personal, showing you, family, friends, pets, or whatever.

- You can use your device as a digital picture frame when not in use. Enable the slideshow option for your Lock screen and select folders with an image you want to have displayed.

- Many applications offer the option to display information periodically without your having to open them. These messages, known as *notifications*, can be included in your Lock screen. For example, if you want to see the new email notification, just make sure this app is included in your apps that appear on the Lock screen.

USING SEARCH AND CORTANA

Search is important to all of us, whether we are looking for a picture, a song, or a document we know we saved…somewhere. With Windows 10, Search leverages Bing, and your search now extends far beyond your device, making it easy to look for things both near and far, right from the taskbar. Windows 10 brings search to a new level by introducing Cortana as a personal assistant that will try to anticipate your needs and personalize search results as she gets to know you. Cortana has many features, and her integration into Windows extends to the web browser. In this chapter you will learn about the settings that affect searching as well as how to set up and manage Cortana.

Using Windows Search

You have no doubt used some brand of search in the past. You might have opened a web browser to search for a restaurant or prices for a new flat-screen TV. Perhaps you have opened File Explorer and then searched on your computer for a resume you used a couple years ago or a manual you downloaded, and now you don't know where you saved it. Perhaps you have fallen into the habit of saying "Google it" when someone asks a question you don't know the answer to. With Windows 10, these common tasks (and more) are all rolled into the Search box located prominently on the Windows taskbar with the text Search the Web and Windows. Select this box to open the search pane, as shown in Figure 9.1

FIGURE 9.1

Select the search box on the taskbar to open the Search pane.

 TIP   The easiest way to search for something in Windows 10 is to press the Windows key and start typing when using an attached keyboard. Your cursor is automatically active in the search box on the taskbar, and you will begin to see proposed search results as you type. If you are using an app that obscures the taskbar, you can still open the Search pane by pressing Windows+S.

To initiate a search in Windows 10, follow these steps:

1. Select the search text box located on the Windows taskbar. The Search pane will open (refer to Figure 9.1). If you're using a touchscreen device, select the search box again to invoke the Touch keyboard.

2. Begin typing a word or phrase for your search. Figure 9.2 shows the word "weather" used as a search query.

FIGURE 9.2

Type in a search query to get immediate results that are refined as you type.

Search result categories will include

- **Apps**—Apps list both Windows apps and Desktop applications installed on your device that match your query.

- **Folders**—Folders or files that match the search query are displayed. Find pictures and documents quickly using search.

- **Web**—Web search variations using your typed query are offered under Web. Select one to open a web browser with that search query.

- **Store**—Store results shows apps in the Windows Store that match your search query.

- **Settings**—Settings are shown that match your search query. Select the indicated setting to open the Settings app or a Windows system settings applet, and jump directly to that particular setting.

> **TIP** Results will vary a bit depending on the query. In some cases, such as the one shown here, Windows apps installed on the device match the query and are shown at the top of the list. This can be a quick way to find an app without even looking at the Start menu.

3. If your result is not already shown, select a category to broaden the scope within that category. For example, select the category **Apps** to see all applications on your device that match the search query, as shown in Figure 9.3. Use sort options to list by **Most Relevant** or **Most Recent**.

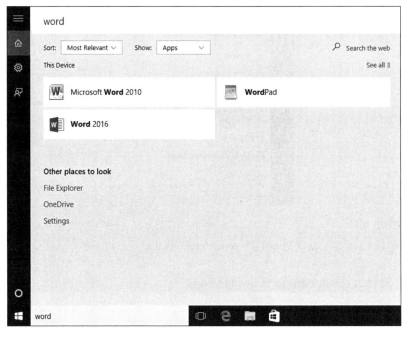

FIGURE 9.3

Target search results by selecting category headings that match a search query.

4. Another way to refine your search is to select **My Stuff** in step 2. This will limit your search to your device and your OneDrive. As shown in Figure 9.4, search results are again grouped into categories and can be sorted or filtered.

Categories include Documents, Folders, Apps, Settings, Photos, Videos, and Music. File paths are indicated, and you will see whether a result is on This Device or OneDrive. Document contents and tags for photos also show up in this search. Select a file from the search results to open it.

FIGURE 9.4

Use filters when viewing search results.

5. Finally, you can direct your search outward by selecting **Web** in step 2. This will open your web browser to continue your search on the Internet.

   TIP   Search is a powerful tool that can be used to jump to specific settings for your device without the need to dig through menus in the Settings app. For example, typing the word "video" in the Windows search text box will show settings to assign a default video player, enable audio description for video in Ease of Access settings, as well as view the name of the video card on the device.

Configuring Search

Search does not offer too many settings that can be managed from your device. Although this book focuses on features and settings included with Windows 10, some settings will affect web results, and you should be aware of them.

To configure how web results are gathered, follow these steps:

1. Select the search text box located on the Windows taskbar to open the search pane.

2. Select **Settings** from the search pane to open Settings, as shown in Figure 9.5.

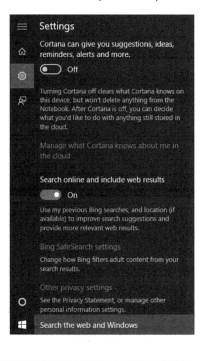

FIGURE 9.5

Settings for search are focused on web content or enabling Cortana.

3. Under Search, select **Bing SafeSearch Settings** to open a web page for Bing search settings, as shown in Figure 9.6. Update current choices related to filtering adult content, location, language, and whether Bing can offer suggestions as you type a search query. Select **Save** when finished.

4. Return to Settings in the search pane from step 2, and select **Other Privacy Settings**. The Settings app will open to Privacy settings, as shown in Figure 9.7.

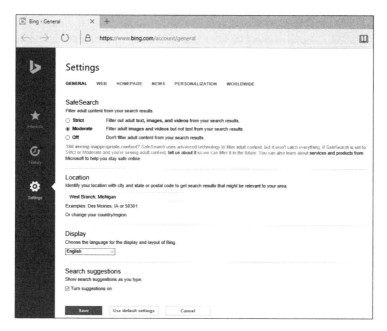

FIGURE 9.6

Update how Bing presents web search results to your device from online Bing settings.

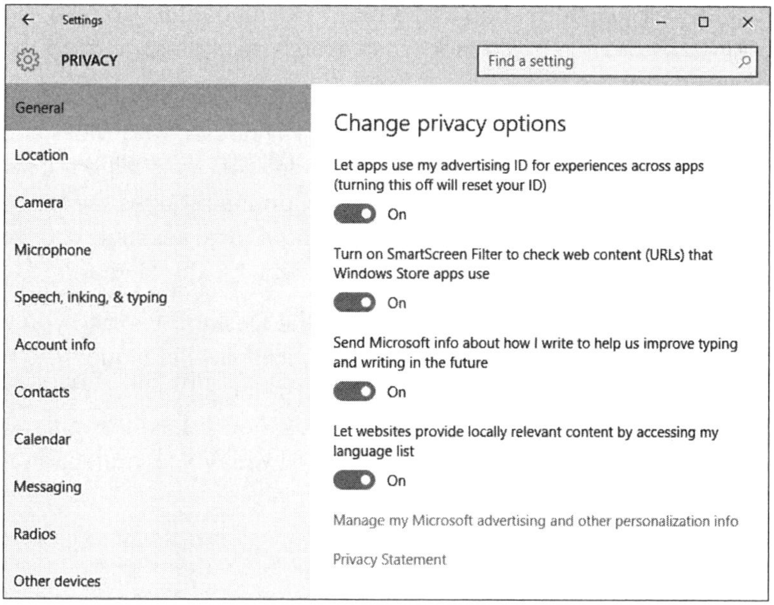

FIGURE 9.7

Jump into the Settings app to ensure your privacy is protected when using search.

TIP Look over your current settings. These settings are not so much related to search results as to how search queries might be used by Microsoft.

You can configure many additional settings from the online Bing settings shown in Figure 9.6. Several Bing search settings are designed to provide targeted advertising and targeted search results. Search for a restaurant, and it is reasonable and beneficial to expect local results.

Some people feel uncomfortable with their search information being saved and used to provide targeted advertising. Privacy is certainly something we should value. Some of these settings allow you to protect your privacy at the cost of getting generic search results. Others like getting results that reflect an awareness of brands and product preferences. The setting you select here influences the results Bing provides for Internet searches.

Getting to Know Cortana

No doubt one of the features you have heard about in Windows 10 is the new personal assistant named Cortana. The name *Cortana* originated in the Halo action games that were designed for Xbox by Bungie. Cortana was the "female" artificial intelligence that guided the player as gameplay progressed with a combination of helpful information and a bit of playful banter. Cortana in Windows 10 is designed to provide much more than search results—something that she does quite well in most cases.

Cortana is a feature that is integrated into all Windows 10 devices and will soon be available as an app for iOS and Android devices, so it will not be surprising to find that multiple devices can use Cortana. Cortana requires the use of a Microsoft account. If you are signed in to a device using a local account, you will need to convert it to a Microsoft account to use Cortana.

The first time you select the search box on the Desktop taskbar, you will see an invitation to activate your personal assistant, as shown in Figure 9.8. After learning your name, Cortana is designed to keep a growing journal of information reflecting your interests and contacts that will enable her to take the initiative in offering relevant news and information. She works well with voice interaction and can even reply to many search queries.

 NOTE Cortana will continue to improve—she will continue to be updated with new features through Windows Update, and her ability to work with you will improve over time as she learns about your interests.

FIGURE 9.8

Take search to the next level by activating Cortana, your new personal assistant.

 NOTE Cortana's integration into Windows extends into the new Microsoft Edge web browser. To learn more about Cortana and Microsoft Edge, see Chapter 14, "Browsing the Web."

Setting Up Cortana

Setting up Cortana initially is painless, and if you later decide you do not like having Cortana, you also can easily disable this feature. I recommend you give her a try.

To set up Cortana, follow these steps:

1. Select the search text box located on the Windows taskbar. You will likely see an invitation (refer to Figure 9.8). Select **Next** to start the setup process. If you do not see the invitation, you can also select **Settings** within the search pane and under Cortana slide the switch to **On**.

2. You will need to grant Cortana some pretty broad access initially to set her up. Figure 9.9 show the types of information Cortana will need to access. Location, email and text messages, browser history, search history, calendar details, and more are all required to get started. You can tweak some of these later. Select **I Agree** to continue. Depending on other settings you have already enabled, you may be asked to allow Cortana permission to turn on some input features such as speech, inking, and typing personalization.

FIGURE 9.9

You will need to grant Cortana access to a lot of personal information during setup.

3. You might be asked whether you would like to turn on the feature "Hey Cortana," which allows Cortana to monitor ambient sound through your microphone. When you say, "Hey Cortana," Cortana is triggered and will actively listen to the following words. Select **Yes, Please** to enable or **Skip** to leave this off for now.

4. Cortana asks you to type in a name or nickname. Type in the name you would like Cortana to use when addressing you. Cortana might offer to pronounce the name, and you can work with her to get the pronunciation right. Select **Use That** once you are satisfied with the name.

Cortana is now ready to go. The search box on the taskbar will now show "Ask Me Anything" rather than the text "Search the Web and Windows." The next time you select the search box on the Windows taskbar, you will be greeted by name and Cortana will already have some personalized information to share, as shown in Figure 9.10.

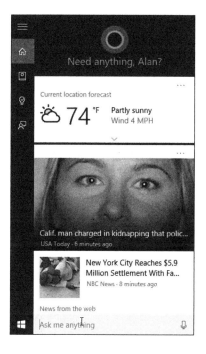

FIGURE 9.10

Cortana starts working right away and offers information based on settings you might have made in other Windows apps.

Using Cortana

Cortana can be used for frivolous and whimsical purposes, or you can use her to handle productivity-related tasks. Although interaction can be by voice or keyboard, voice has a definite cool factor and is certainly much easier. If you're unable to use voice interaction, you can start providing input through the search box by typing in a task. As shown in Figure 9.11, you can also select Reminders from the hamburger menu within Cortana to review existing reminders or create a new one.

FIGURE 9.11

Cortana is designed to remind you about events as well as assist with many daily tasks.

Some high-level tasks that Cortana can handle using voice commands include

- **Calendar**—Add appointments or check calendar information without opening the Calendar app.

- **Reminders**—Create reminders based on conditions such as time or location.

- **Note**—Add a recorded note to the OneNote app.

- **Alarm**—Add or enable an alarm to the Alarms app.

- **Music**—Identify songs playing and then purchase them, and play songs on your device using a variety of filters such as artist or title.

- **Places**—Pull up maps, get directions, search for nearby attractions, and check traffic.

You will find experimentation to be a valuable way to get a feel for how Cortana responds to queries. Ask Cortana for information on movie times, and she will offer up website links to help answer your question. Ask a math question, and she will often answer you. Ask Cortana to open an application, and she will do so. Ask Cortana "What can you do?" to get suggestions for basic queries and tasks that you can ask Cortana to get started.

 TIP   Cortana is designed to be entertaining and display her personality. Try asking Cortana to sing to you or to tell you a joke. Ask Cortana "Who is Siri?", "What is Halo?", or "Open the pod bay doors" to get some tongue-in-cheek replies.

To illustrate how easily you can add a reminder with Cortana using voice commands, follow these steps:

1. If Hey Cortana is enabled and your device has a microphone, simply say, "Hey Cortana." Cortana will open a small listening pane, as shown in Figure 9.12. If Hey Cortana is not enabled, press **Windows+Q** on your keyboard or select the search text box located on the Windows taskbar; then select the microphone icon to the right of Ask Me Anything.

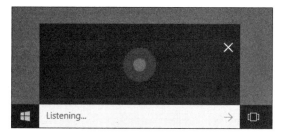

FIGURE 9.12

Cortana will listen for voice input when triggered.

2. Speaking clearly, state a reminder. Figure 9.13 shows a reminder being set up after speaking the words, "Hey Cortana, remind me to pick up milk at Walgreens." Cortana will ask clarifying questions such as when to do this. The answer can be a place or a time.

3. Once the scope of the reminder is clear, Cortana will state and show what the reminder consists of, and you will be asked if this is correct. If you say yes, the reminder is added.

FIGURE 9.13

Cortana will understand key words associated with tasks and prompt for additional information as needed to understand the scope of a task.

4. Select **Reminders** from Cortana's hamburger menu to see active reminders, as shown in Figure 9.14. Select the reminder you just created in step 2.

5. Select **Complete** and the reminder will be removed from the list of reminders.

FIGURE 9.14

Select Reminders within Cortana to review or update the status of pending reminders.

Managing Cortana

Compared to the default Windows search covered earlier in this chapter, Cortana has many more settings available to manage how she can use the personal information to which she has access. You can manage settings related to your interests that Cortana tracks, settings related to privacy, and how Cortana interacts with you. If you decide at some point that Cortana is too intrusive, or you are concerned about your privacy, you can disable her at any time.

Managing Cortana's Notebook

Cortana uses a notebook to track things that are of interest to you. You will find entries have been added by default and others that were added automatically by Cortana. This notebook can have interests manually added, and you can remove information you would rather Cortana did not track.

To manage Cortana's notebook, follow these steps:

1. Select the search text box located on the Windows taskbar to access the hamburger menu within Cortana.

2. Select **Notebook** from the hamburger menu. The list of current interests Cortana tracks will be displayed, as shown in Figure 9.15. You might recognize some categories from MSN apps and, indeed, Cortana picks up on some interests by checking these apps for searches and favorites you have indicated.

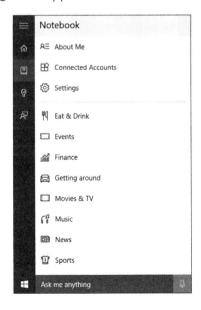

FIGURE 9.15

Cortana's notebook can be modified to let her know about which interests you want her to track.

3. Select the "+" to manually add an entry into the notebook. You will be prompted to select a category. Select **News**, for example. You can then select an existing news interest or select **Add a Category** and type in a news topic of your own. News stories that Cortana can find using Bing news services to match your new interest will now appear on the Cortana home view (refer to Figure 9.10).

4. Select an entry in the notebook to view options for that interest. The specific options will vary depending on the category. As shown in Figure 9.16, switches allow you to tweak what information Cortana tracks for you and whether notification should be used. Make changes if warranted, and select **Save**. You can select **Delete** to remove this from the notebook, and Cortana will no longer track it.

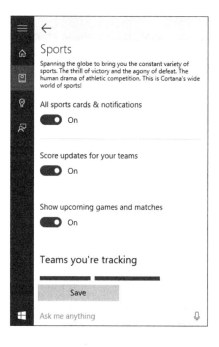

FIGURE 9.16

Interests listed in Cortana's notebook can be tweaked to indicate which details you want to know about, or they can be removed altogether.

Tweaking Cortana's Settings

If you want greater control over how much Cortana knows about you, then you need to tweak some of Cortana's settings. You can update the name or nickname that was provided during setup, help Cortana to know your voice, disable

Cortana's ability to read your email and text messages, and jump up to the cloud to manage even more settings for Cortana that will affect all the devices you use.

To manage Cortana's settings, follow these steps:

1. Select the search text box located on the Windows taskbar to open Cortana, and then select **Notebook** from the hamburger menu (refer to Figure 9.15).

2. Select **About Me**. Update the name Cortana uses for you by selecting **Change My Name**, and follow the cues to update the name Cortana will use to refer to you. Under Favorite Places, you can update locations that have been saved in the Maps app.

3. From the hamburger menu, again select **Notebook** and now select **Settings**. Settings will appear, as shown in Figure 9.17.

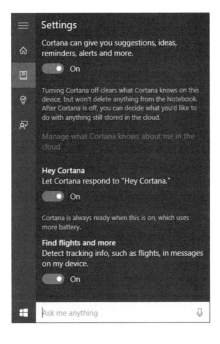

FIGURE 9.17

Cortana has a few important settings you can use to control voice and privacy settings.

4. Under Hey Cortana, you can turn this feature on or off using a switch. Below this is a good warning to take note of—the Hey Cortana feature will consume more battery life.

5. Scroll down further to Find Flights and More. This switch enables Cortana to look for keywords that might appear in emails and texts related to time, dates, tracking information, and flight information. This information can let Cortana

proactively alert you to appointments, flight delays, and tracking information. This can be useful, but it can make some people uncomfortable. Set the switch to **Off** if you want to disable this feature.

6. Scroll down to **Taskbar Tidbits**. Cortana is designed to be proactive and will volunteer information that seems to fit with your interests. If you find this to be disturbing or unwanted behavior, disable Taskbar Tidbits by sliding the switch to Off.

7. Scroll down and select the link **Other Privacy Settings** to open the Settings app to general privacy settings. Look over your current settings (refer to Figure 9.7). These settings are not so much related to search results as to how search queries might be used by Microsoft.

8. Under Search you will see a link, **Bing SafeSearch Settings**, that opens your web browser to the online Bing account general settings (refer to Figure 9.6). Update current choices related to filtering adult content, location, language, and whether Bing can offer suggestions as you type a search query. Select **Save** when finished.

Cortana is designed to bring a consistent experience across all your devices. To accomplish this, some of her settings are maintained online in the cloud. Changes there will affect all the devices you use that rely on Cortana. Although it is not recommended if you plan to continue using Cortana, it is a good idea to clear this if you decide to no longer use her.

To make changes to online Cortana settings, follow these steps:

1. Select the search text box located on the Windows taskbar to open Cortana; then select **Notebook** and then **Settings** from the hamburger menu (refer to Figure 9.17).

2. Select the link **Manage What Cortana Knows About Me in the Cloud**. Your web browser will open to the online Bing account personalization settings, as shown in Figure 9.18.

3. Under Interests, you can select **Clear** to remove all interests that Cortana has been tracking on your behalf. You will be asked to confirm that you are sure you want to clear your saved interests. Select **Clear** again.

4. Under Other Cortana Data and Personalized Speech, Inking, and Typing, you can select **Clear** to remove data that Cortana has uploaded up until this moment. Select **Clear** again when asked whether you are sure you want to clear your recommendations.

After you have cleared the online data Cortana has been using, Cortana will start fresh to accumulate data unless you have also disabled Cortana on your devices.

FIGURE 9.18

Cortana keeps some information about you in the cloud. This information should be cleared if you no longer plan to use Cortana.

Disabling Cortana

If you ever decide that Cortana is not a good fit or you would rather not have Cortana enabled on a particular device, you can flip the switch to turn her off.

To disable Cortana, follow these steps:

1. Select the search text box located on the Windows taskbar to open Cortana; then select **Settings** from the hamburger menu (refer to Figure 9.17).

2. Slide the first switch under Cortana to **Off**. That's it.

 TIP If you decide that you want to disable Cortana on all of your devices, you should also consider clearing online data that she has accumulated. Steps to do so are covered in the previous section, "Tweaking Cortana's Settings."

THE ABSOLUTE MINIMUM

- The Search box is capable of much more than Internet searches. Spend some time experimenting with search results, and notice the difference between local file, app, settings, and web-based results.

- You can configure settings to control how web search works and whether your searches are saved by Bing.

- Enable and try using Cortana. You will find Cortana to be much more robust than search by itself.

- Take time to experiment with commands and queries to get a feel for what Cortana can and cannot do.

- If you disable and stop using Cortana, you should also clear any personal data that Cortana might have saved to the cloud.

10

CONFIGURING INPUT DEVICE SETTINGS

Basic hardware setup is essential to getting the most out of Windows. Windows 10 does a very good job in sensing what hardware is attached and automatically configuring your settings based on common preferences. In this chapter, you learn about setting up your mouse, touchpad, keyboard, and language settings. Setting up some aspects of your hardware might require you to consult instructions from a manufacturer, especially where third-party drivers or software need to be installed.

The Control Panel or PC Settings?

Windows 10 uses two basic avenues to reach the settings you will work with. If you occasionally wonder which method of changing your settings is the correct one to use, just remember that both make changes to the same operating system settings. Many common configuration settings are able to be performed from the modern Settings app, and you will find it to be much easier to use with a touch device. Although some settings and configuration options are duplicated and can be accessed from either Settings or the Control Panel, the Control Panel, shown in Figure 10.1, often has a deeper set of configuration options to work with.

The *Control Panel* is the Windows interface to all the settings for Windows and its many devices such as mouse and keyboard, display, language, and so on. You can make configuration changes by selecting icons in the Control Panel; these are often referred to as *applets*. Applets are small programs that open as small windows referred to as *dialog boxes*. These are designed to make specific changes to settings that Windows references so that it knows how to display information on the screen or how to make sense of input from connected devices. You will be referred to both the Settings app and the Control Panel often in this chapter as you explore the basic configuration choices available to you. The Control Panel on your device will have the same basic set of applets, and it will likely include applets unique to your device depending on the hardware or software your device uses.

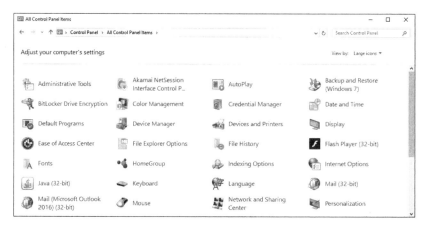

FIGURE 10.1

The Control Panel is the comprehensive center for changing how Windows and your devices operate.

To open the Control Panel follow these steps:

1. From the taskbar, select the search box. Enter the text **Control** in the search field, and select **Control Panel** from the results. This will open the Control Panel on the Desktop.

2. In the upper-right corner of the Control Panel, select the drop-down arrow to change **View by** from **Category** to **Large Icons** to get the view shown in Figure 10.1. This will make it easier to locate specific tools rather than trying to guess in which category they might be found.

TIP   A faster way to locate a specific tool when you know its name is to simply use the Search tool. If you were to search for **Date and Time**, which is an applet in the Control Panel, you would see results that point to the Control Panel applet. Other searches for settings may point to the modern Settings app (which uses a gear as the icon in the search results). Changes in either the Settings app or the Control Panel applet will accomplish the same thing. You will find yourself using the Settings app more often; however, if you are hunting for a missing feature or looking for more detailed choices, the Control Panel applet is a good tool to know about.

Setting Up Your Mouse or Touchpad

A number of available settings enable you to customize exactly how your mouse operates. Some of these settings control basic functions, such as determining which of the buttons on the mouse is the primary button, and some permit you to express your personality with your mouse.

Although basic settings can be configured from the PC Settings pane using the Settings charm, we will focus primarily on the more robust settings available through the Desktop's Control Panel.

Mouse Settings

Here is a list of the settings you can change for your mouse:

- **Primary button**—Mice are shipped typically with the left button configured as the primary button. You can change this configuration to make the right button the primary button.

- **Double-click speed**—Several Windows commands require you to double-click. You can slow the double-click speed to give you more time to make the second-click.

- **ClickLock**—If you have difficulty dragging items in Windows, the ClickLock option can help you. This option enables you to drag an item without holding down the mouse button while you drag the item. Instead, you click the item to be moved, hold down the mouse button over the item for a few seconds, and then release the button. To drop the object you're dragging, just click again after you have positioned the item.

- **Motion**—You can configure your mouse pointer to keep pace with you, moving swiftly across the screen as you work. This setting is known as *pointer speed*. However, when you move the mouse, if you find that the pointer tends to fly out of control across the screen, forcing you to search for the pointer after you stopped moving the mouse, you might want to slow down the pointer.

- **Snap to**—Windows does a good job of asking you to confirm actions that have permanent consequences, such as deleting a file or saving a document with the same name as an existing file. Windows confirms your actions with a small window, usually with some text (Are You Sure?) and two buttons (OK and Cancel). Windows can move the pointer to the button it expects you to answer with, making it faster to either click it or select the other button.

- **Visibility**—You can add some excitement to your screen by using pointer trails. This option resembles a snake trailing behind the mouse pointer as you move it across the screen and enhances its visibility. Figure 10.2 shows you an example of pointer trails in use.

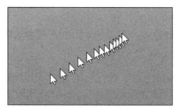

FIGURE 10.2

Mouse trails add pizzazz and serve a practical purpose by allowing you to more easily locate your mouse pointer.

- **Hide pointer while typing**—You might find you are distracted by the mouse pointer when you stop scrolling to type. Windows provides an option to hide the pointer while you type.

- **Show location of pointer when I press the CTRL key**—Some users have difficulty locating the mouse pointer on the screen, especially when they use large monitors. By enabling the Show Location of Pointer option, you can flash an easy-to-spot signal locating the pointer by pressing the Ctrl key, as shown in Figure 10.3.

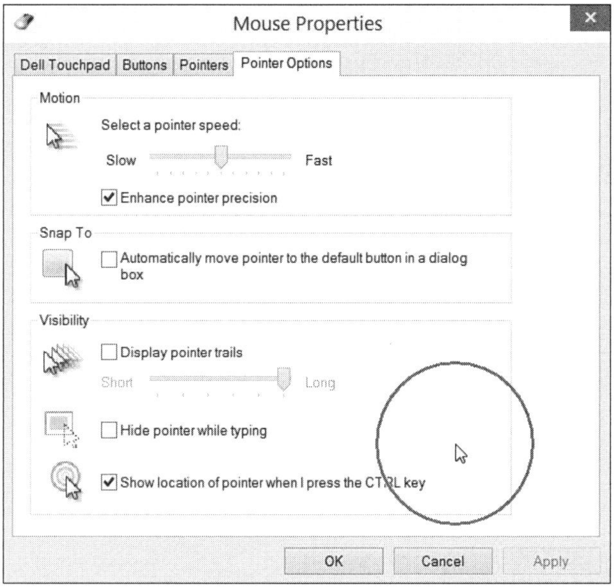

FIGURE 10.3

The Show Location of Pointer option helps you locate the pointer simply by pressing the Ctrl key.

- **Scroll wheel**—Most mice come with a scroll wheel or some form of touch-enabled strip that is positioned near the front of the mouse, enabling you to access it as easily as you can the mouse buttons. You turn the wheel (or drag your finger) when you need to scroll up or scroll down. The vertical scrolling setting controls the sensitivity of the wheel. The setting is measured in the number of lines scrolled for every notch you spin in the wheel. Some mice even provide a horizontal setting for the wheel, enabling you to move from left to right and vice versa simply by applying pressure to the side of the wheel.

TIP   Basic mouse settings can be taken care of from the Settings app. Search for Mouse & Touchpad to jump straight to the Mouse settings. Under Related Settings (refer to Figure 10.5) you will find a link labeled Additional Mouse Options, which will open the Mouse Properties applet.

To change any of the preceding settings, follow these steps:

1. Open the **Control Panel** and select **Mouse**. This opens the Mouse Properties window, as shown in Figure 10.4.

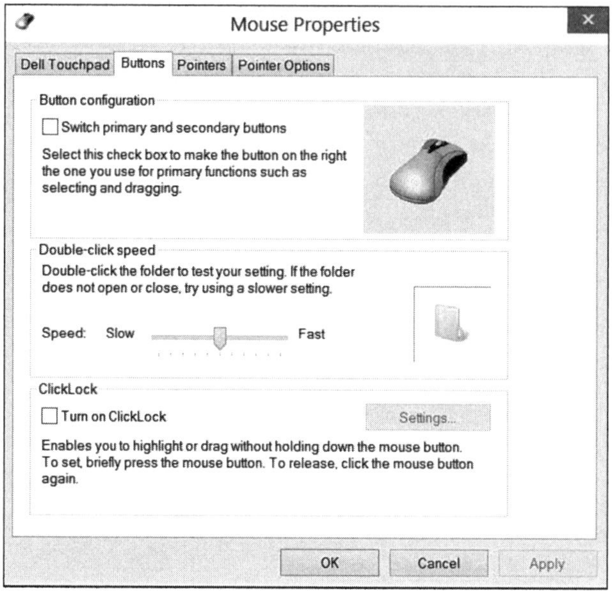

FIGURE 10.4

Change many settings controlling how your mouse works in the Mouse Properties dialog box.

2. Choose the mouse control you want to change. There are two tabs that include all the options just described: **Buttons** and **Pointer Options**. The tab **Pointer Options** includes settings related to how the pointer appears on the screen.

3. When you're done making changes, click **OK** to close the dialog box and save the various changes you made to the mouse settings. Click **Cancel** to discard the changes, or click **Apply** to save the changes without closing the dialog box.

You might want to customize the mouse pointers you use in Windows. You can adjust the pointers to reflect your personality and taste, or you might need to switch to pointers that are larger than normal to make it easier to see them. See Chapter 8, "Tweaking Windows to Reflect Your Personality," to learn how you can customize your mouse pointers.

Touchpad Settings

Your Windows device, especially if it's a laptop, may have a touchpad. Touchpad settings are often configured using software provided by the hardware manufacturer; therefore, you might see software on your device that has been included for this purpose. Windows also includes some general settings for touchpads. These can be grayed out or missing if you have touchpad controls available to the Desktop that override these settings; in that case you should consult the instructions your device manufacturer provided. Often these settings are located in the Mouse applet of the Control Panel as a tab (refer to Figure 10.4).

To adjust these settings, follow these steps:

1. Select the **Start** button, and then select **Settings** to open the Settings app.

2. Select **Devices**.

3. Select **Mouse & Touchpad**, as shown in Figure 10.5.

4. From the Touchpad settings, you may see settings related to adjusting tap sensitivity, swiping gestures, reverse scrolling, and even enabling or disabling the touchpad itself.

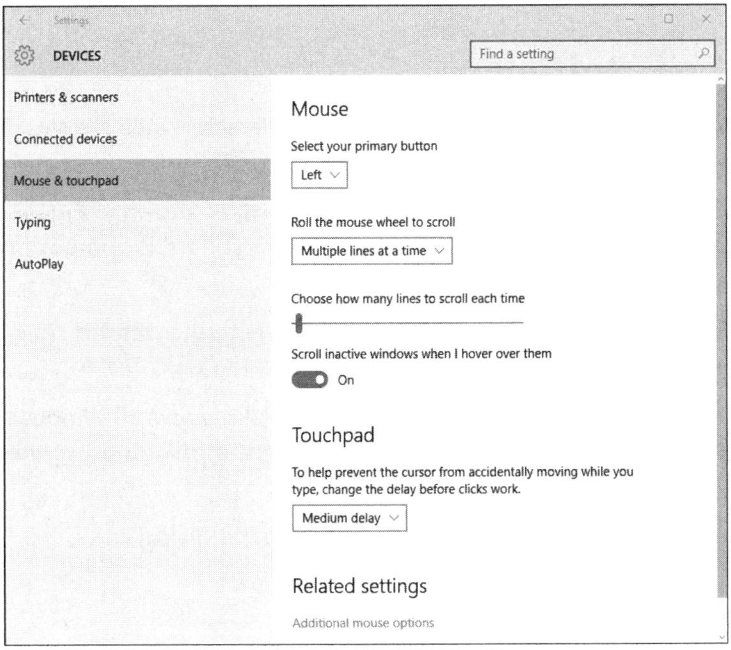

FIGURE 10.5

You can adjust basic settings for your mouse and touchpad from the Settings charm.

Setting Up Your Keyboard

Although the keyboard is an important part of your computer, there are only a few settings you can change:

- Setting how rapidly characters repeat across the screen

- Setting when a character starts repeating across the screen

- Setting the cursor blink rate

Two settings control what occurs when you depress a key on the keyboard to repeat the key's character on the page. These settings might not be useful for your everyday work unless you design a form or document that includes underlines to enter information or characters to create a border. The settings are

- **How long a key is depressed before the character begins repeating**—If this setting is too short, the slightest delay in moving your finger off of a key causes the character to begin repeating across the screen (depending on the program you use).

- **How rapidly the character repeats**—This rate can span from a steady pulse to a staccato spray of the character across the screen.

Changing Keyboard Settings

To access the screens where the repeating character rates are set, do the following:

1. Use the Search tool to search for **keyboard**, as shown in Figure 10.6. Select **Keyboard** (Control Panel) to display the Keyboard Properties dialog box, as shown in Figure 10.7.

2. Drag the pointer on each of the two sliders to the desired speed. Try your settings in the box in the middle of the dialog box.

3. You also can adjust the rate the cursor blinks across all Windows 10 apps in the Keyboard Properties dialog box. Drag the pointer along the **Cursor Blink Rate** slider to the desired speed.

4. Select OK to save your settings and close the dialog box.

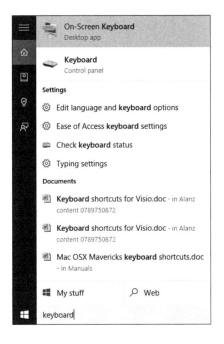

FIGURE 10.6

Use the Search tool to quickly locate specific settings for your devices.

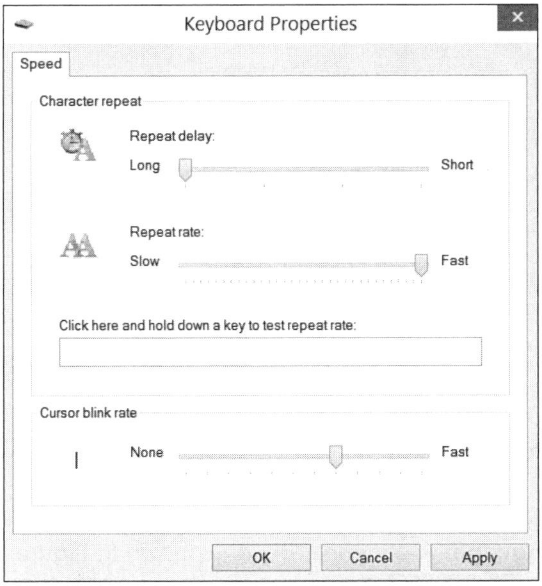

FIGURE 10.7

Set the character repeating rate in the Keyboard Properties dialog box.

Personalize Language, Keyboard, and Date Formats

One of the most personal aspects of Windows 10 is your language and other locale settings. You can customize the number, currency, time, and date formats to match your nationality and cultural preferences.

The first phase is to set your language in Windows:

1. Open the **Settings** app by selecting it from the **Start** menu. You also can open it by swiping in from the right on a touch screen device, selecting the **All Settings** button in the Notification Center.

2. Select **Time & Language** from the list of settings, and then select **Region & Language**. The languages currently added to this device are indicated, as shown in Figure 10.8.

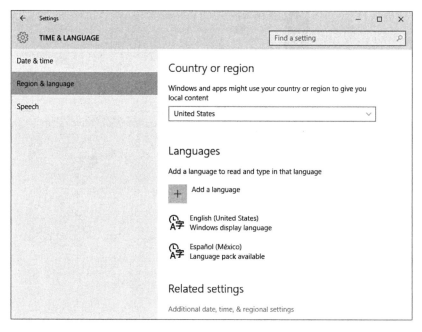

FIGURE 10.8

You can select language and other aspects of your locale from the Region and Language pane.

3. If the language you want to switch to is shown, skip to step 6. If not, select **Add a Language**. A pane like the one shown in Figure 10.9 should appear, displaying a list of languages.

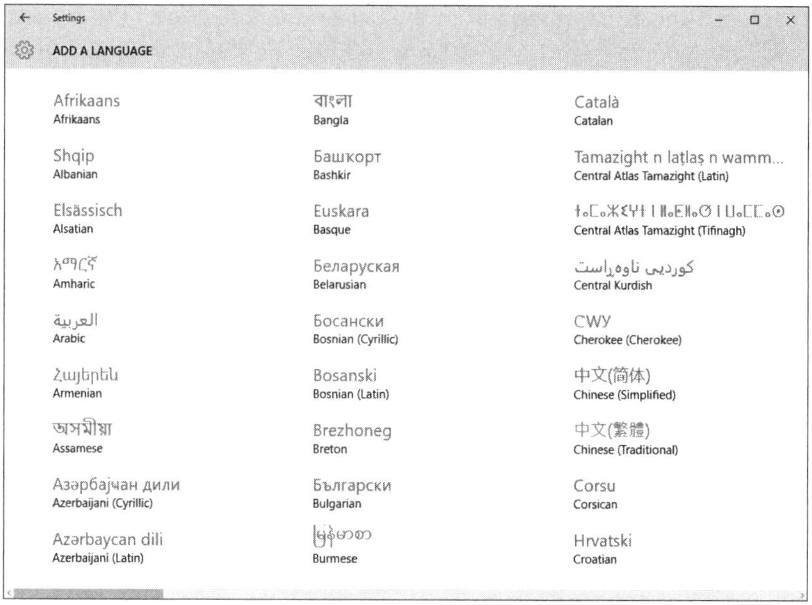

FIGURE 10.9

You can select from a long list of base languages, as well as select a dialect.

4. Scroll down the list and locate the base language you want to select. For example, if you want to select Mexican Spanish, for now, locate Spanish and select it.

5. A list of the regional variants of the language you chose should be on the screen. Select the dialect you want, and it will be added.

6. You should be back to the Time & Language pane, shown previously in Figure 10.8. If there is more than one language in the list, the first language in the list is the one used. Select the language you want to use to reveal additional buttons; then select **Set as Primary**. You also might see **Options** for a language. Select **Options** to review possible spell-checking and keyboard options.

If you need to adjust your locale's time and date formats, follow these steps:

1. Open the **Settings** app by selecting it from the **Start** menu. You also can open it by swiping in from the right on a touch screen device, selecting the **All Settings** button in the Notification Center.

2. Select **Time & Language** from the list on the left side of the screen; then you will see your current **Date & Time** settings, as shown in Figure 10.10.

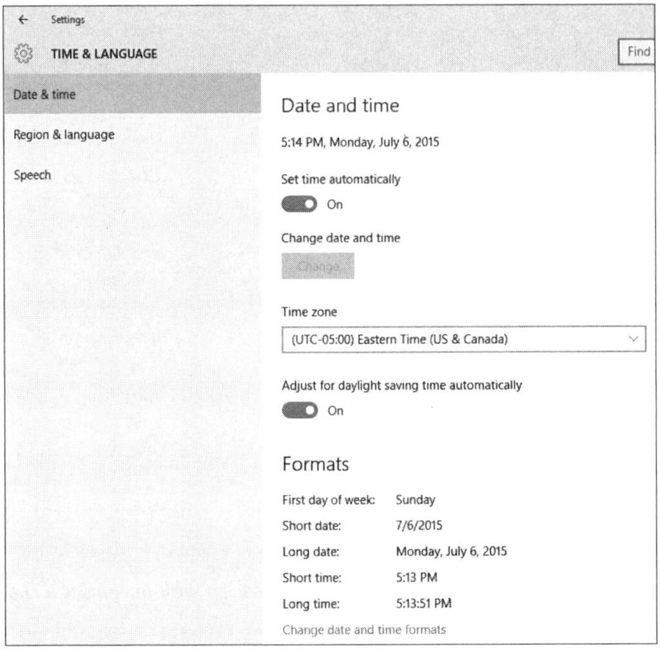

FIGURE 10.10

You can change time zone, set the time, and adjust for daylight saving time with a couple of quick selections.

3. Under **Formats**, you see examples that show you how the different date fields, such as long date, short date, and so on, will appear throughout Windows (based on the language you selected). If you want to change any of the fields, select **Change Date and Time Formats**. A new view opens that enables you to select from format choices any of the date and time fields listed using drop-down menus; just select the desired format from the list (see Figure 10.11).

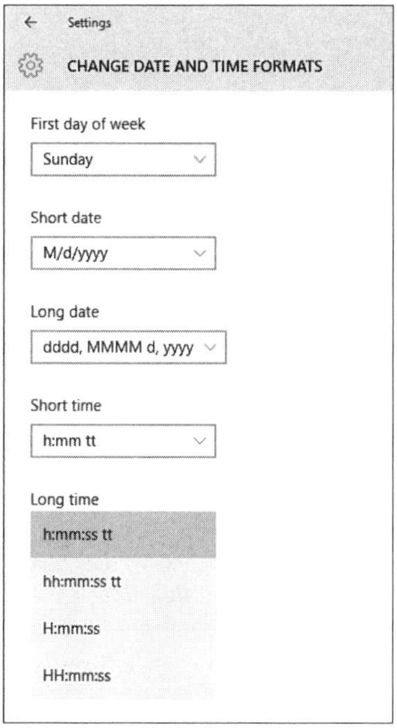

FIGURE 10.11

You can modify how dates and time appear in Windows by selecting from available formats.

4. Make your format changes, and then use the back arrow to return to **Time & Language**. The changes you made are now shown in the **Formats** summary below the **Date & Time** information.

THE ABSOLUTE MINIMUM

- Use the Control Panel to access configuration settings that are not available in the PC settings app. Consider pinning the Control Panel to Start or even to your Desktop taskbar for easy access. (Chapter 3, "Optimizing the Start Menu," considers pinning applications to the Start menu.)

- Use the Control Panel Mouse and Keyboard applets to find more options when configuring how these peripherals work with Windows.

- Use the Settings app to add languages or to change language and date settings.

IN THIS CHAPTER

- Optimizing Your Display
- Working with Multiple Monitors
- Adjusting Brightness
- Setting Up Speakers
- Managing Notification Sounds

11

CONFIGURING DISPLAY AND SOUND SETTINGS

If you have ever shopped for a quality office chair, you know that the offerings range from very simple designs to very complex ones—with what appear to be dozens of levers and knobs that can mystify you with all the levels of adjustment offered. Windows 10 is naturally designed to be visually appealing and greener than any previous version of Windows with a simple and intuitive interface. From the first time you power up your device, many settings will be automatically configured and optimized to get the best usage out of your device without requiring you to consider every possible display or power option available. But make no mistake, all those levers and knobs are there, just out of sight. Although you should not feel that you *need* to make changes to enjoy your Windows 10 device, there are quite a few settings that you can control that can heighten your user experience.

In this chapter, you learn about settings included in Windows that you can easily adjust to control the display and sound features of your Windows 10 device. Setting up some aspects of your hardware might require you to consult instructions from a manufacturer, especially where third-party drivers or software need to be installed.

Setting Up Your Display

The computer component you work with the most is the display. The display interfaces with one of the most delicate parts of your body: your eyes. For this reason, you should set up the display to be easy for your eyes to use. Although Windows usually sets it correctly by default, Resolution is the key setting for a comfortable but efficient setup with your computer. In addition, Windows 10 has improved the way it works with multiple displays, which can make your work (and play) experience a more productive one. In this section, you learn how to set your resolution and how to set up a second monitor.

Understanding Resolution

The *resolution* of your display determines the level of detail or *sharpness* of the image you see on a computer screen. Other hardware on your computer will also contribute to the quality of the images. For instance, video cards and having the correct drivers affect quality settings such as the richness of colors and luminance.

Here is what you need to know about resolution:

- Displays on the screen are composed of pixels. Each pixel has the same size and shape (usually square or rectangular, but it can be any shape). Generally, we enjoy images that have very high pixel counts because they enable sharper images and are easier on the eyes. Lower pixel counts give rise to descriptive terms like *pixelated—Minecraft* is an example of a game that uses a low resolution to give it a pixelated appearance.

- Resolution is measured using a count of columns and rows of pixels to indicate how many pixels are actually in the display. Thus, you will see screens described with common resolutions such as 1024×768, 1366×768, and 1920×1080. The first number indicates the columns, and the second provides the number of rows of pixels.

- Screen resolution is often adjustable. You typically can lower or even raise the resolution used on a display using settings in Windows. Often video games offer the option to alter the resolution to improve game play when playing a video game on the computer.

- The greater the resolution, the more detailed images onscreen will appear to the eye. Two similar laptops might both offer 15.6" screens, yet the amount of pixels squeezed into that screen space by the manufacturer might differ. Watch out for hot sales that offer very cheap prices for a laptop. One of the reasons they can afford to sell that device for so little is often due to the low-resolution screen!

- There is a trade-off when choosing a high resolution. Some screens are just not large enough when used at the highest resolutions to be practical for normal computer use. Text can be very sharp rendered, but it might be too small to read comfortably—especially if you already use reading glasses!

- An LCD monitor has a native resolution—that is, a resolution at which it's designed to operate. Although LCD monitors can operate at different resolutions, using a nonnative setting incurs a considerable hit to image quality. So, if you're planning to buy a new LCD monitor, you should note the resolution you prefer to work with and make sure the one you pick is designed to operate at that resolution. A typical 23" LCD monitor operates at 1920×1080, which is a full HD display.

RESOLUTION AND ASPECT RATIO

You also might see other references when considering displays that are commonly used for comparison. Numbers such as 1080p, 1080i, or 720p refer to the vertical count of pixels in each row on the screen; this is another way of referring to resolution. 720 and 1080 are both considered high definition (HD), and they are very easy on the eyes. The letters *i* and *p* refer to the way the display refreshes. Interlaced (i) screens are not as preferred as progressive (p) scan. You might even encounter larger numbers like 2160p, 4320p, and 8640p, which are considered ultra high definition (UHD).

Numbers such as 4:3 and 16:9 refer to the shape of the screen. The aspect ratio 4:3 simply lets you know that for every four horizontal pixels there are three vertical ones—and this was the standard square-ish computer monitor shape for a long time. 16:9 is also called *widescreen* and is common in larger flat screens and laptops.

If you ever need to change the screen resolution on your Windows 10 device, just follow these steps:

1. Open the **Settings** app by selecting it from the **Start** menu. On a touchscreen, swipe in from the right, and select **All Settings** from the Action Center.

2. Select **System** and then select **Display** from the navigation bar to the left. The **Customize Your Display** pane shown in Figure 11.1 appears. If you have more than one screen attached to your computer, you see each of them represented and numbered (refer to Figure 11.2 in the following section). Be sure to select the monitor you want to work with in the **Display** field (or click its representation on this screen). If you aren't sure which monitor is identified in the list, select **Identify** to prompt Windows to flash a large number on your screens, making it easy to identify each display.

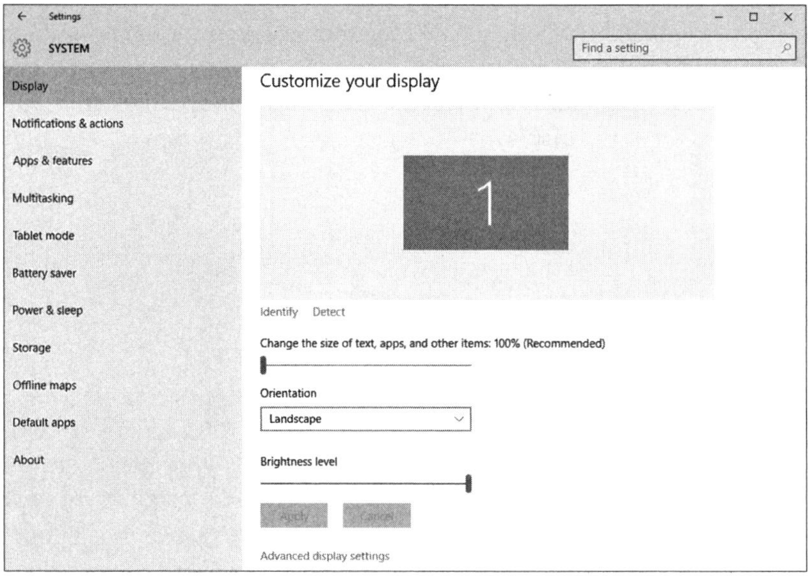

FIGURE 11.1

You can control your screen resolution through the PC settings app.

3. Select Advanced Display Settings to adjust your resolution. Select the current resolution to display a drop-down menu for each display; select the new resolution from the available choices. You typically will see a recommended resolution, which will probably already be selected as the default.

4. Select **Apply** to see immediately the resolution you chose at work. The screen updates to the resolution you selected.

5. If you are happy with the new resolution, select **Keep Changes**. If you want to select another resolution or stick with the original resolution, select **Revert**.

6. To select a different resolution, repeat steps 3–5.

 TIP   You can potentially select a resolution your display doesn't support, resulting in a blank screen when you attempt to change it. If this happens, just sit tight for a few seconds. If you don't select **Keep Changes** in the confirmation dialog box, Windows reverts to the previous resolution in 15 seconds.

Setting Up Multiple Monitors

You can set up a second monitor if your computer has the capability. (Consult your computer's documentation to verify whether it's possible.)

There are a number of advantages to having a second monitor. If you use a tablet or laptop for mobility, you can use a larger display with higher resolution when working at your desk. You can extend your screen horizontally so you have more room across Windows. You also can extend your screen vertically to have more room top to bottom. You can open several programs at the same time and arrange them on your extended display. You can even have the same image generated on both displays (duplicate), something that can come in handy for presentation purposes. If you're using a desktop computer, you can look at the back of your computer near where your monitor is plugged in. You might be able to recognize a second unused port equal or similar to the one the first monitor is using. It is not uncommon to see two different types of connectors for video on modern desktop computers. Some common port types are DVI, VGA, HDMI, and DisplayPort. Virtually all laptops manufactured in the last few years have an external monitor port that can work at the same time as your laptop's built-in display. Even many Windows tablets, such as the Microsoft Surface, have a video out port you can use for attaching a second display.

When you add a second screen to your computer, you can configure it for use with Windows by following these steps:

1. Open the **Settings** app by selecting it from the **Start** menu. On a touchscreen, swipe in from the right, and select **All Settings** from the Action Center.

2. Select **System** and then select **Display** from the list to the left. Under **Customize Your Display**, look for the **Multiple Displays** setting shown in Figure 11.2. Use the drop-down arrow to choose from duplicating or extending your display. You can also select to display on only one display screen.

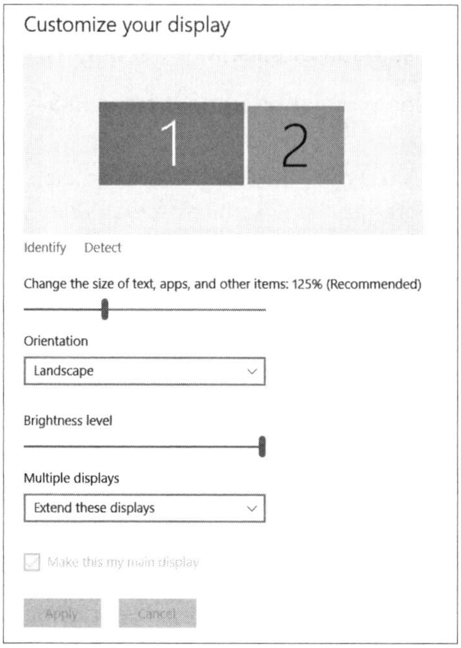

FIGURE 11.2

In Windows 10 you can change the behavior of multiple displays in the PC settings app.

3. If you need to change the position of your displays relative to one another, you can select and drag a screen placing it to the right, left, above, or below (see Figure 11.3). This will determine how your mouse cursor moves between extended displays and affects panoramic wallpaper choices.

4. Click **Apply** to make changes.

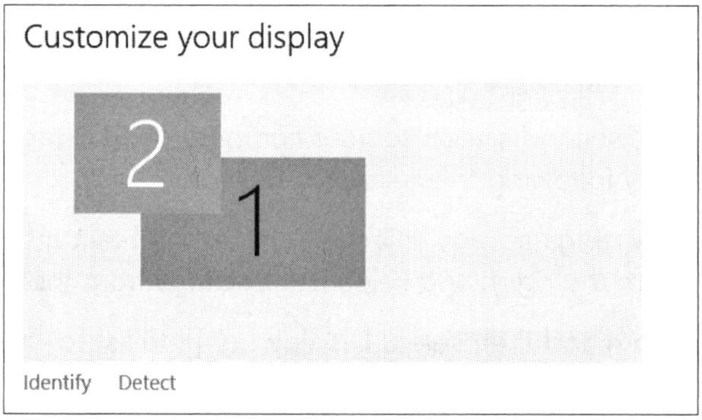

FIGURE 11.3

Select and drag a display to change the orientation of your displays to match their physical orientations.

NOTE Another way to quickly change how your Windows 10 device uses a second display is through the Commands menu that appears on the title bar in PC Settings. Select **Project** from the list; then choose from **PC Screen Only**, **Duplicate**, **Extend**, or **Second Screen Only**. This can be especially useful when working with a projector for a meeting.

Additionally, most laptops will have a function key designed to trigger this same option.

Windows 10 has other settings related to multiple displays that enhance the user experience in diverse situations. Consider some of these enhancements:

- Show different backgrounds on each display or extend the same background across several displays.

- Have taskbars set to display just the applications that are on each screen (see Figure 11.4).

- Dots per inch (DPI) scaling can optimize how apps are displayed on ultra-high-resolution screens. This can be set the same for all displays, or a unique setting can be used for each display. (See the next section for more information.)

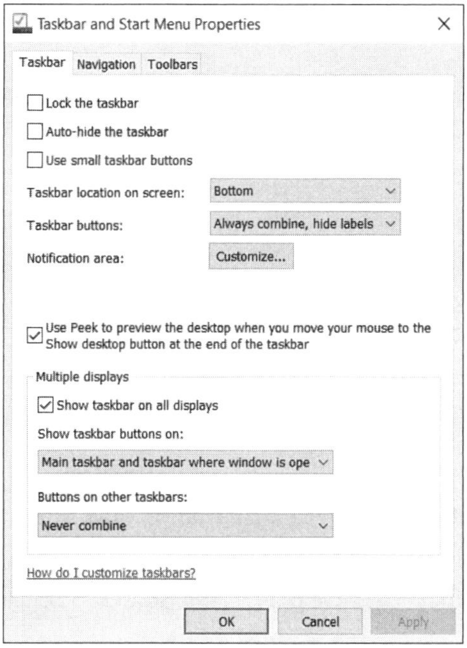

FIGURE 11.4

Control how the taskbar behaves across multiple displays.

Make Things Bigger on Your Display

If you find yourself squinting or reaching for glasses just to make out the text on your screen, why not try to just make things bigger on the screen? Unfortunately, some people opt to use a lower resolution so that items are rendered larger on the display. Although this seems like a good strategy, it leaves you with a less sharp image as a result. Windows 10 makes it much easier to scale items so that they are larger without taking a hit on the resolution and sharpness!

Follow these steps to use DPI scaling to change the size of apps and text:

1. Open the **Settings** app by selecting it from the **Start** menu. On a touchscreen, swipe in from the right; select **All Settings** from the Action Center.

2. Select **System** and then select **Display** from the navigation bar to the left. The **Customize Your Display** pane appears (refer to Figure 11.1).

3. Under **Change the Size of Text, Apps, and Other Items**, you can select the slider to make everything appear larger (or smaller). If your display allows, you might have a few choices on the slider, as shown in Figure 11.5.

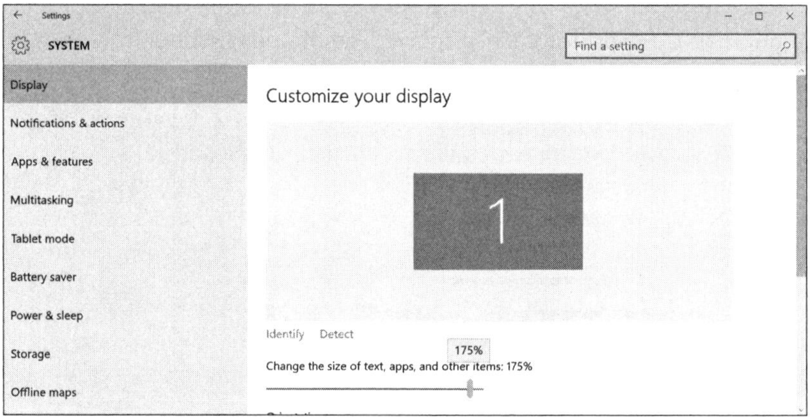

FIGURE 11.5

Change the scaling on your display from the Settings app to make everything appear larger without losing resolution.

You may not want *everything* to be larger. Follow these steps to use DPI scaling to change the size of text:

1. From the taskbar, type **Display** in the Search box. Select the **Display** applet.

2. Under **Change Only the Text Size**, you can select the drop-down menu to select which types of text you would like to change to make everything appear

larger (or smaller). If your display allows, you might have a few choices on the slider, as shown in Figure 11.6. If you want to apply this scale to all displays when using multiple displays, select the box **Let Me Choose One Scaling Level for All My Displays**.

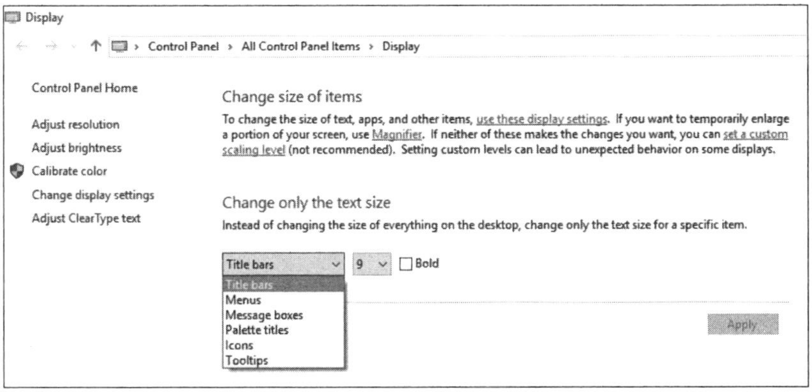

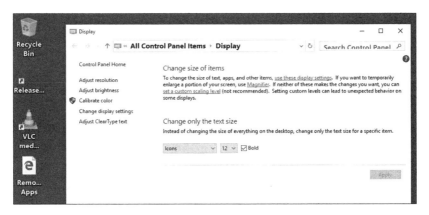

FIGURE 11.6

The Control Panel Display applet provides additional DPI scaling options.

3. If you want to change only the size of text, leave the scaling setting at the recommended level in step 2 and look to the section **Change Only the Text Size**. Use the drop-down menu to select types of text to scale and select the font size. You can even select **Bold** as a text effect, as shown in Figure 11.7.

4. Click **Apply** to make changes.

FIGURE 11.7

Scale the size of just specific types of text, such as Icons, to make navigation easier on the eyes.

NOTE You can also change the DPI scaling by selecting Set a Custom Scaling Level from the Display applet. This can cause unexpected results, and the preferred method is to use the Settings app or target just text, as shown here.

Adjusting Brightness

Brightness is often taken for granted. Windows devices that rely on batteries benefit from settings that dim the display while on battery power, thus extending how much time the battery can power your device. Not only can this add hours of life to your device between charges, but it is also better for the environment. An increasingly common feature found on portable devices adjusts screen brightness using a setting called adaptive brightness, which is intended to adjust display brightness based on ambient light using a light sensor.

Basic adjustments to display brightness can be made on most laptops using the keyboard to adjust screen brightness. Alternatively, you can search for brightness in the Search Everything tool, select Change Screen Brightness (with a touch-screen device you can swipe in from the right and select Settings), and then select Screen (or Brightness on some devices) to reveal a slider you can use to manually change the current display brightness.

If you find your tablet or laptop is inexplicably changing between a dim setting and bright setting, it is likely caused by an adaptive brightness sensor. This can become quite distracting at times. If you want to disable this feature, follow these steps:

1. Open the **Settings** app by selecting it from the **Start** menu.

2. Select **System**, and then select **Display** from the list to the left. If your device has adaptive brightness, you will see a switch below the Brightness level labeled **Adjust My Screen Brightness Automatically** (see Figure 11.8).

3. Slide the toggle to **Off** and disable this feature. Then close the Settings app.

TIP On a touchscreen, swipe in from the right and select the **Brightness** button from the Action Center. Each tap will adjust the brightness level by 25%. Tap and hold the brightness button to reveal and select **Go to Settings** to jump into the System > Display pane referred to in this section.

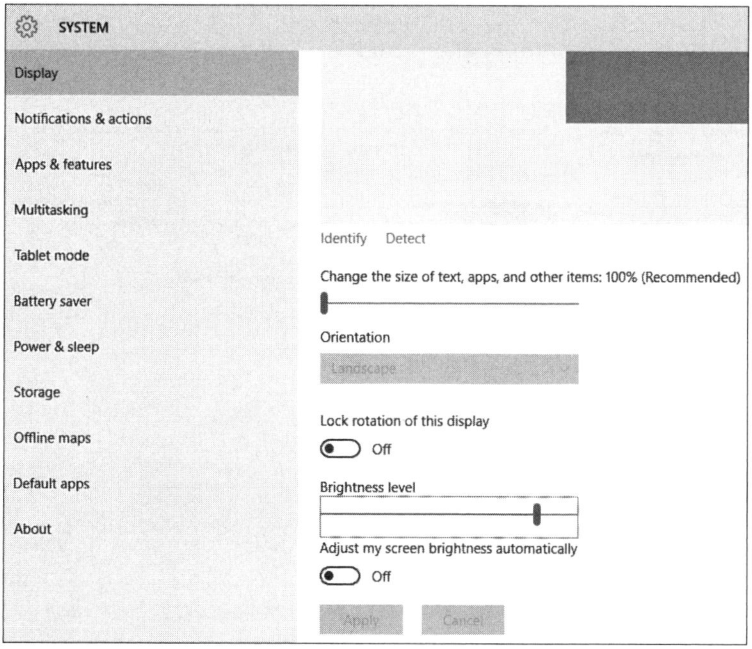

FIGURE 11.8

You can disable the adaptive brightness feature if it becomes too distracting.

Although the next chapter deals with power plans in more detail, you might want to have more control over screen brightness, especially if you find yourself routinely changing screen brightness settings. You can find more granular control settings buried in your current power plan.

To make permanent changes to the brightness on your screen, you need to follow these steps:

1. From the taskbar type **power** into the Search box. Select the **Power Options** applet.

2. The Power Options window opens. Under **Choose or Customize a Power Plan**, your current power plan will be indicated—**Balanced** is the default. More than one possible plan might be listed with your current plan enabled, as shown in Figure 11.9. Select **Change Plan Settings** (to the right of your current plan).

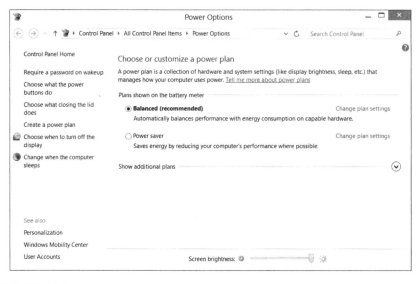

FIGURE 11.9

Brightness settings are part of your power plan.

3. The Edit Plan Settings window appears. Select **Change Advanced Power Settings** (at the bottom of the window). The Power Options dialog box appears, as shown in Figure 11.10.

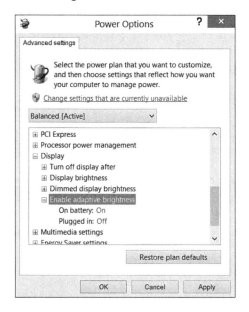

FIGURE 11.10

Tweak display settings from the Power Options dialog box.

4. Scroll down in the list of settings to find **Display**. Expand the menu by selecting the plus sign, and scroll down to find **Display Brightness**. Select the
   plus sign to see the current settings for **On Battery** and **Plugged In**. Adjust
   the setting if needed by selecting the current number and using the up and
   down arrows to change the number. **100%** when plugged in is normal; if you
   want the brightest display even while using battery power, change this to
   100% also.

5. Expand the **Enable Adaptive Brightness** settings. This is generally **On** by
   default. You can disable this feature when on battery or when plugged in.
   Disable this feature here by selecting **On** and then selecting **Off** from the
   drop-down list.

6. Click **OK** to apply the settings and close this window. Close all other windows
   if you are done changing your settings.

CAUTION   Balanced power plan settings are meant to give
you the best performance while on battery with the longest time
possible. Changes to these settings can significantly cut your battery time. Also, the Adaptive Brightness is a great feature when it is
working correctly. You might need to update your drivers if you are
experiencing problems with this feature. Make changes here with
caution. After making changes to these settings, you can always
go back by selecting **Restore Default Settings for This Plan** in the
Edit Plan Settings window in step 3 from the steps just outlined.

Setting Up Sound

Setting up how sound works in Windows might seem like a task that should not be
required. Shouldn't your computer play your music and beep and chime at all the
appropriate occasions without your having to do anything? The answer, of course,
is yes. In this section you learn a few handy tricks such as how to get the best
sound from the speakers you just purchased and how to specify when sounds can
be heard as certain computer events occur.

Setting Up Your Speakers

If you play videos or music on your computer, having a set of speakers, or at least
headphones, is a given. Most computers today can produce amazing surround
sound for movies and games with the right set of high-end speakers. Even if you
are content with a couple of inexpensive desktop speakers, you might be able to
achieve better sound quality.

These days, plugging in speakers is easy. On a desktop computer each of the plugs from your speakers is colored, and the jacks in the back of your computer also are colored. Just match the colors and you're good to go. Follow the instructions provided with your hardware to be sure your speakers are set up correctly. After everything is plugged in correctly, follow these steps to set up the sound quality and configuration:

1. From the taskbar, type **sound** into the Search box. Select the **Sound** applet. The Sound dialog box appears on the Desktop.

2. Select the **Playback** tab.

3. Select **Speakers** and then select **Configure**. The Speaker Setup dialog box appears, as shown in Figure 11.11.

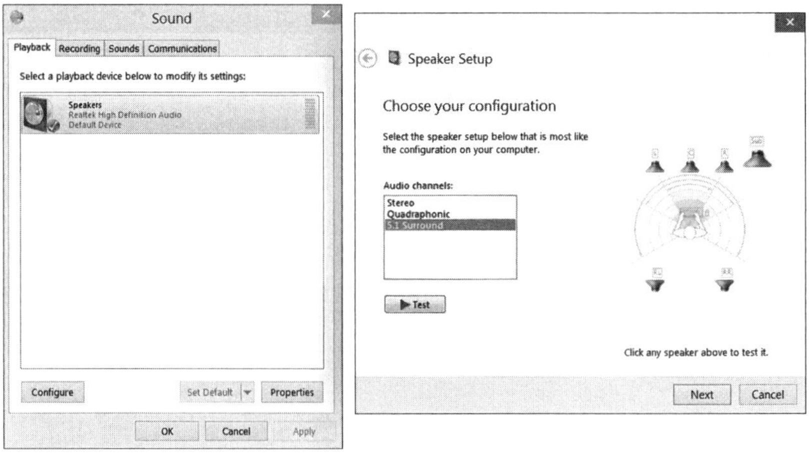

FIGURE 11.11

You can troubleshoot settings and test sound quality using the Sound applet.

4. Select your speaker setup from the list. The diagram shows you the configuration. Select **Test** to hear a test sound rotate through each of the speakers, or click a speaker to hear just one. Click **Next**.

5. On the **Customize Your Configuration** screen, you can confirm which speakers should be used by selecting them. Again, you can test individual speakers to ensure that they are producing sound as expected. Click **Next**.

6. You might have the option to select full-range speakers. You may need to consult the documentation for your speakers if in doubt. Click **Next**.

7. Click **Finish**.

8. Try your configuration with music, videos, and DVDs. Feel free to run through the steps again to fine-tune the setup. Finally, don't be afraid to select a configuration that sounds great even if it doesn't match your real setup. You're the boss!

Managing Sound for Windows Events

Windows is set up to play certain sounds when various events occur. These can alert you to take some action, or they can be associated with a notification such as when an email message arrives, an app is installed or updated, and so on. Even though these sounds can be useful, sometimes they can be inappropriate. In this section we focus on notification settings you should know about that enable you to control whether notifications will use sounds.

To determine whether sounds can be used with notifications and to establish quiet time, follow these steps:

1. From the taskbar, type **notifications** into the Search box. Select **Notification & Action Settings** from the search results. The Settings app will open.

2. Scroll down to the section **Show Notifications From These Apps**, as shown in Figure 11.12. As you can see, most apps are enabled to provide sound notifications.

FIGURE 11.12

The Settings app provides you with a few tools to manage how apps alert you to updates under Notification settings.

3. Select an app that you do not want to generate audible notifications. The pane will focus to that app and display a few switches for notification options.

4. Locate the switch labeled **Play a Sound When a Notification Arrives** and slide the toggle to **Off**, as shown in Figure 11.13. This will prevent sounds from accompanying notifications for this app at all times.

FIGURE 11.13

You can control whether your device makes sounds at the wrong time using Notification settings.

Windows includes a feature called Quiet Hours. It is designed to establish a quiet time to prevent sounds from disturbing you or others at 2 a.m. While the details of this tool are still in flux, you can manually use it to silence your notifications for meetings and other occasions. To enable Quiet Hours open the Action Center and select the button Quiet Hours. When you are ready to return to normal activity, use the same button to disable Quiet Hours.

THE ABSOLUTE MINIMUM

- To change the resolution of your display, you can access the Display settings through the Settings app.

- Use DPI scaling to make items and text larger on your display.

- Windows can accommodate multiple monitors if your computer has the capability. You can specify whether the image from the computer appears on one screen, appears on both screens, or extends across the screens—in effect, doubling your screen real estate.

- You can disable Adaptive Brightness if you prefer to keep a steady brightness on your tablet or laptop.

- Use settings associated with Notifications to prevent sounds from disturbing others.

12

CONFIGURING NOTIFICATIONS AND ADVANCED SETTINGS

HAL 9000, the artificial intelligence antagonist in the classic 1968 film *2001: A Space Odyssey*, was pure science fiction. Although the idea of a talking computer seemed plausible, the concept was more than a little unnerving. Fast forward nearly 50 years, and we have become accustomed to our devices communicating and, yes, even talking to us. Hello Cortana! On our Windows 10 device this communication principally occurs in the form of notifications. In this chapter you see how to manage those notifications.

You also explore how a group of settings labeled Ease of Access can make interacting with a Windows 10 device much easier for you or others you might know. Finally, you learn about some of the power settings that control how your device behaves and how you can manage these settings when necessary.

Managing Notifications You Receive

Notifications can enhance your experience with apps you have installed, or they can be a nuisance. These can be updates that appear briefly on the screen regarding new emails, game updates, messaging, and much more. You can disable notifications globally, or you can be selective about which apps can push notifications to you. You can even establish quiet times that respect your sleep or work schedule.

In Windows 10 you can see banner notifications, sometimes called *toast notifications*, which are small notifications that appear for a few seconds on your screen. While these generally disappear automatically, some may stay onscreen longer, allowing you to take some action as shown in Figure 12.1. You can take a closer look at notifications by selecting the Notifications icon on the taskbar, as shown in Figure 12.2. This enables you to review notifications you might have missed when they appeared as banner notifications. You can select individual notifications to clear them from this list, clear all notifications from an app, or select Clear All to start fresh.

FIGURE 12.1

Banner notifications can appear onscreen for a variety of reasons, such as alerting you to emails received, app updates, or reminders about appointments.

FIGURE 12.2

You can check for missed notifications right from the taskbar.

Most apps are enabled by default to send banner notifications. They can alert you to promotions or appointments or simply to make you aware of updates that have occurred since you last used an app. You might decide that some of these are unwelcome or frivolous. You can disable banner notifications globally or just disable the feature for specific apps.

To modify your settings for notifications, follow these steps:

1. From the taskbar, start typing **notifications** in the Search field.

2. Select **Notifications & Action Settings**. The Settings app will open with Notifications & Actions selected in the left navigation bar, as shown in Figure 12.3.

3. Under Notifications, you can make changes to the way notifications behave in general. For example, you can turn **Show App Notifications** to **Off** from here. This will prevent all notifications from being created and might be a bit extreme.

FIGURE 12.3

You can change settings globally for notifications.

4. Under **Show Notifications from These Apps**, you can scroll down and turn off apps individually to prevent notifications from select apps (see Figure 12.4).

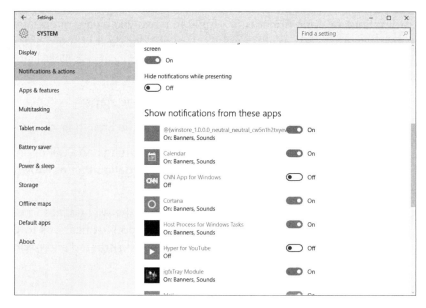

FIGURE 12.4

Suppress notifications for individual apps.

5. Select an app to reveal specific types of notifications that can be switched on or off to suite your preferences, as shown in Figure 12.5.

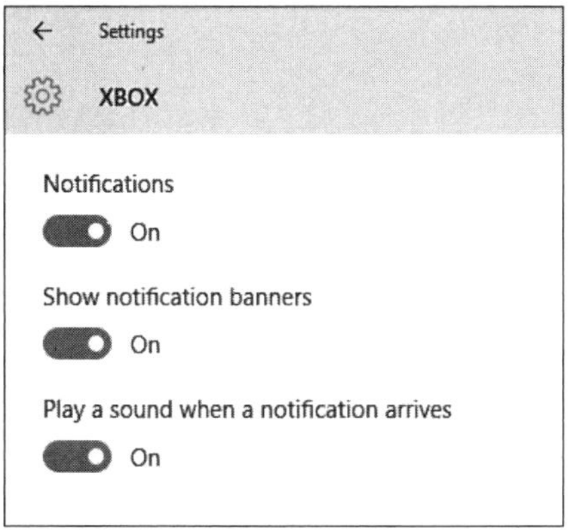

FIGURE 12.5

Very specific types of notifications can be disabled.

Notifications can also be audible. To learn more about enabling or disabling audible notifications, see the "Managing Sound for Windows Events" section in Chapter 11 on page 197.

Yet another way that you can manage notifications is by enabling a temporary suppression of all notifications. This is great if you will be doing a presentation or need to avoid distractions for a period of time. You can easily do this from the Action Center.

To temporarily suspend all notifications, follow these steps:

1. Open the Action Center by selecting the Notifications icon on the taskbar or by swiping in from the right with a touchscreen device (see Figure 12.6).

2. Select **Quiet Hours**. All notifications will be suppressed.

3. Select **Quiet Hours** again to allow notifications to resume.

Finally, notifications can have unique settings that are best controlled from within the app itself. The Facebook app has individual notification settings for all types of events. To access the notification settings, open the app and then select **Settings** from the Commands menu. Select **Notifications** from the Settings pane, and then disable any events for which you do not need to receive notifications.

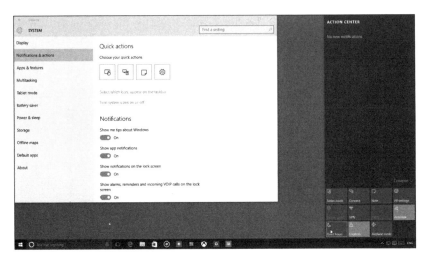

FIGURE 12.6

Notifications can be suppressed temporarily when needed using the Action Center.

Twitter is another good example of this feature. Select **Settings** from the Command menu, and then select **Options** from the Settings pane. As shown in Figure 12.7, you can select types of notifications and even the source of the event. Notice also that toast notifications can be disabled from here, as can live tile updates.

FIGURE 12.7

Some apps have their own settings to manage notifications, like the Twitter app shown here.

Ease of Access

With Windows 10, the accessibility options, known as Ease of Access, provide you with powerful options. Accessibility options are of use both to individuals with disabilities and individuals without. You might find it easier to work with the display configured in a high-contrast format; hearing a voice confirmation of commands also can be helpful. Larger mouse pointers or thicker cursor lines are other settings you can modify here to make things easier to find on the display.

Ease of Access settings that can be enabled include

- **Narrator**—Use the Narrator settings to provide vocalization for text that is on the screen as well as controls and options you can select. You can select the voice and tweak the voice quality as well as how voice interacts with onscreen content.

- **Magnifier**—The Magnifier can be enabled to make a portion of the screen larger (see Figure 12.8).

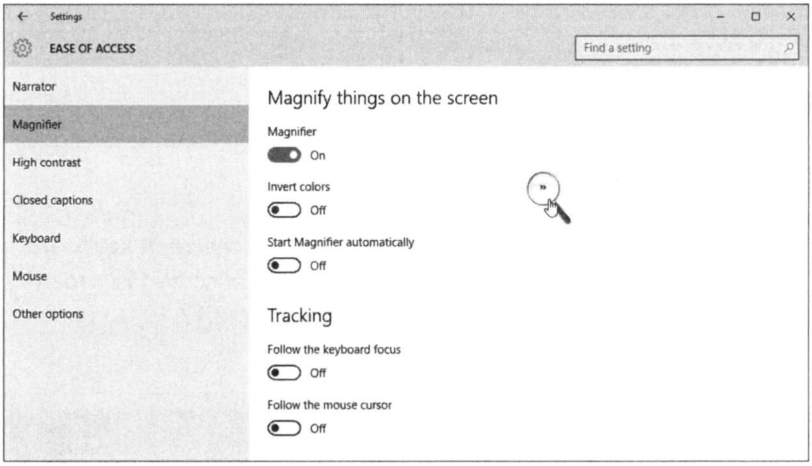

FIGURE 12.8

This image shows the Ease of Access settings screen enlarged with the Magnifier option turned on.

- **High Contrast**—High contrast includes a few predefined themes that are combined to make text stand out on the screen, as shown in Figure 12.9.

FIGURE 12.9

The image shows the Ease of Access screen with the High Contrast setting turned on using the High Contrast White theme.

- **Keyboard**—Although it might look like the touchscreen keyboard, enable the Ease of Access keyboard to have access to an onscreen keyboard you can use with a mouse. Select Options, as shown in Figure 12.10, to enable or disable features like predictive text.

FIGURE 12.10

The onscreen keyboard is part of the Ease of Access tools and is different from the touch keyboard that appears when using a touchscreen device.

- **Mouse**—Use Mouse settings to control variables such as the mouse pointer size and color.

- **Other Options**—Other options include Visual Options such as leaving toast notifications onscreen for a longer period, up to five minutes. Also, if using a touchscreen device, you might find Touch Feedback settings to be useful (see Figure 12.11).

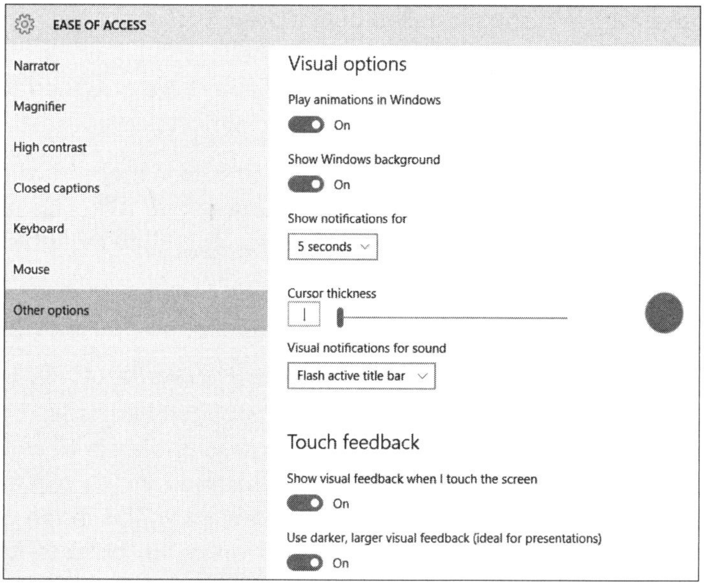

FIGURE 12.11

Especially useful when sharing your screen, enable the visual Touch Feedback for touchscreen devices. The dark circle shown here indicates where the screen is currently being touched.

To use the Ease of Access settings, follow these steps:

1. From the **Start** menu, select **Settings** to open the Settings app.

2. Select **Ease of Access**.

3. To use one or more of the following options, select from the categories to the left, such as **Magnifier**.

4. Enable the feature, as shown previously in Figure 12.8, by moving the slider to the right to the **On** position. Scroll through the options and turn on additional options as needed.

5. Select other options from the left to enhance readability and usability by using the **Narrator**, **High Contrast**, **Keyboard**, **Mouse**, or **Other** options.

Managing Power Options

Windows 10 is designed to help you be efficient and control power consumption, but these options are helpful beyond wanting to be a good citizen of the environment. You might be interested in options to automatically reduce the brightness of your screen after a period of nonuse, as well as other options to reduce wear on your computer.

If you travel with Windows installed on a laptop, you might be interested in putting the computer to sleep when you close the laptop lid, which makes restarting your computer easy and quick. Desktop computers are designed to be left on all the time with the ability to power down to an almost powerless state.

Windows enables you to customize how power is managed on your computer in extreme detail. More than 20 settings can be tweaked. Although the most basic settings can be accessed using the PC Settings app, the Power Options applet in the Control Panel offers the greatest range of settings.

Before diving into the details, there are a couple terms you should know:

- **Sleep mode**—When your computer goes to sleep, Windows saves any unsaved work and reduces power to the monitor, hard drives, fan, and network connections. Windows takes notice of your system when it goes to sleep, and it uses enough power to retain your settings and data in a memory where the settings can be accessed and applied quickly. This mode protects your work while the computer sleeps but returns the computer to full power in the same state that you left it in just a few seconds.

- **Hibernate mode**—Hibernate mode is much like Sleep mode. Hibernate mode also captures the state of your computer so that it can restore it on request, but in Hibernate mode, your computer is fully powered down. This means restoring a computer from Hibernate takes a bit longer than recovering from Sleep mode because data and settings have to be restored to the memory from where they were saved on your computer's hard drive.

A Simple Approach to Using Power Plans

If you are nervous about changing something on your computer that could cause unexpected damage, you can relax. Often you are well served by simply choosing one of a group of power plans. A *power plan* is a prebuilt set of approximately 14 options, each of which manages some aspect of power or energy consumption, such as preventing a slideshow from running when the computer is low on battery life. Windows includes one or more power plans, and the company that built your computer might have loaded a plan onto the computer. You can even create a plan from scratch, change one and give it a new name, or delete one.

Here are some sample power plans:

- **Balanced**—Conserves energy when the computer is not used but employs full power when you are actively working at the computer, perhaps using multiple applications.

- **High Performance**—Uses full power all the time and will drain power quickly for laptop computers running on a battery.

- **Power Saver**—Reduces power consumption as much as possible, which causes applications to run a bit more slowly, reduces the display's brightness setting, and more.

Follow these steps to select a power plan:

1. From the **Start** menu search for **power**.

2. Select **Power Options** from the list of results. The Power Options dialog box opens, as shown in Figure 12.12.

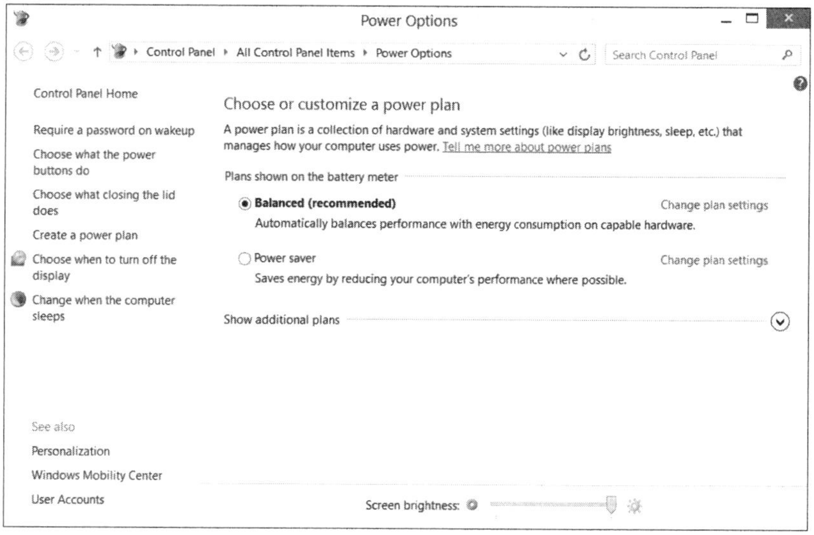

FIGURE 12.12

You change from a balance power plan to one that is more energy efficient.

3. Select the plan you want to use from the list of plans. To review the settings for a plan, select the corresponding **Change Plan Settings**. Click **Cancel** when you have finished reviewing the plan's settings.

4. Close the Power Options dialog box. The power settings in the plan you selected will now be active.

Common Options Related to Power

You can tweak several options that determine when your computer goes to sleep and what happens when it awakes:

- Specify whether a password is required to unlock your computer after it has been awakened.

- Choose what happens when you press the Power button on your computer.

- Specify the length of time during which you're not at your computer before the display turns off.

- Specify the length of time during which you're not at your computer before the computer goes to sleep.

These options probably give you all the control you need over power use. For example, to have your laptop shut down automatically when closing the lid on battery power, follow these steps:

1. Open the Power Options dialog box. To do so, from the **Start** menu search for a setting named **power**, and then select **Power Options** from the list of results (refer to Figure 12.12).

2. Select **Choose What Closing the Lid Does** from the list on the left.

3. Under the choices labeled **On Battery**, expand the drop-down menu labeled **When I Close the Lid**.

4. Select **Shut Down** from the list, as shown in Figure 12.13.

5. Click **Save Changes**.

6. To make additional changes, return to the Power Options dialog box and then select the option you are interested in from the list on the left. The options are self-explanatory.

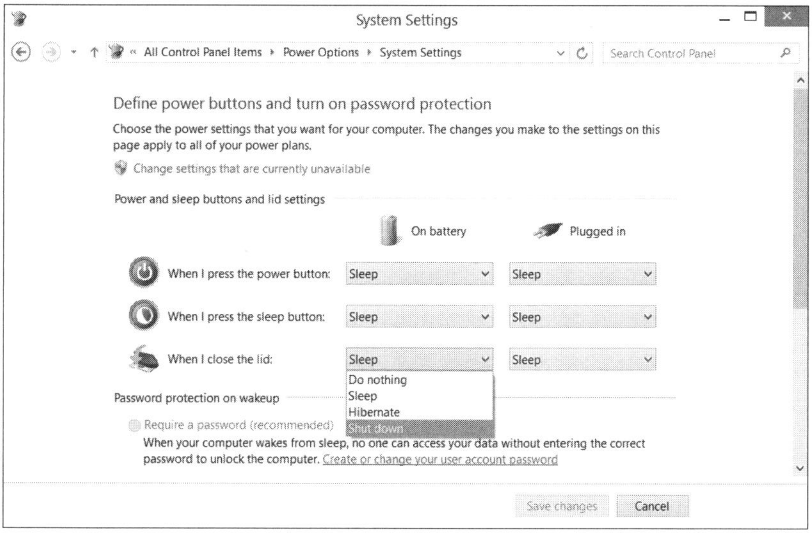

FIGURE 12.13

Select from options in the Power Options applet of the Control Panel to control what happens when you close the lid on your laptop.

The Manual Method to Manage Power Options

While not for the faint of heart, you can also dive into the power plan settings and manually tweak the advanced settings for a customized power plan. I do not recommend doing this unless you have a clear objective in mind and are familiar with the settings you are modifying. Changing the power settings so that your hard drive never powers down, for example, can actually shorten the life of a hard drive. On the other hand, some settings, such as the default behavior when your device is on low battery power or whether your laptop fan runs to cool the processor while on battery, need to be addressed here.

The manual method calls for you to specify a value for each of the 14 or so setting types. It takes time to do so, but the payoff is a power plan configured to your exact requirements. To do so, select a plan, as previously described in step 3 under "A Simple Approach to Using Power Plans." Before you close the Power Options dialog box, as instructed in step 4, select **Change Plan Settings** and then **Change Advanced Power Settings**. Change the settings as needed, click **OK**, and then click **Save Changes**. This updates the plan you selected. Review the steps in the "Adjusting Brightness" section of Chapter 11, "Configuring Display and Sound Settings," for an example of this manual method. Use Restore Plan Defaults to undo changes and restore a power plan to its original state.

CAUTION Changing advanced settings in the power plan can improve performance; however, doing so can also have a negative impact on hardware if set incorrectly. Change an advanced setting only if you are familiar with the setting and know what the effect will be on your hardware.

THE ABSOLUTE MINIMUM

- Disable unwanted notifications from applications that you do not need updates or alerts from.

- Temporarily hide notifications when you need to work without interruption or will be sharing your screen.

- Use Ease of Access settings to enhance your Windows experience by enabling visual and audible features or by modifying how your mouse and keyboard work with Windows.

- You can apply a few built-in, ready-to-use power schemes. You can also build your own power scheme that leverages up to 60 individual settings.

- Use Power Options to assign actions to the use of power buttons, closing the lid on a laptop, or sleep times.

13

CONNECTING TO NETWORKS AND THE INTERNET

Although Windows has plenty of cool and fun features, most of its power comes from the ability to work with other devices and connect us to the Internet. For example, your personal contacts are developed and maintained through social media, email, and messaging on the Internet. These contacts are the fuel that powers the sharing capabilities throughout Windows. And the information you work with every day is a combination of content you have stored on your computer merged with content Windows finds on the Internet. It's fair to say that Windows has limited functionality without a connection to the Internet. Fortunately, Windows makes connecting to the Internet easy regardless of your location.

This chapter provides several step-by-step lists of instructions to help you connect wherever you are.

Reviewing Important Internet Connection Basics

Connecting to the Internet from your desktop, laptop, or tablet usually runs smoothly after everything is set up properly. But there are lots of moving parts in the process, any of which can stop working or become dated as new capabilities are developed. One way to anticipate problems, as well as to be on the lookout for faster and better ways to connect, is to know the basics of connecting to the Internet. You won't necessarily become an Internet engineer after reading this section, but you can certainly gain a better understanding of what happens when you fire it up.

Learning About Internet Service Providers

The devices you use today to browse the Web, send and receive email, play videos, and more cannot connect to the Internet on their own. Whether you are at home, in an office, on a plane, in a coffee shop, or even at the grocery store, you need a way to connect to the Internet. This connection is provided by an *Internet service provider (ISP)*. The ISP provides access to the Internet for a fee. Even large companies that provide their employees fast Internet access do so by working with an ISP. Figure 13.1 illustrates how your computer works with the ISP.

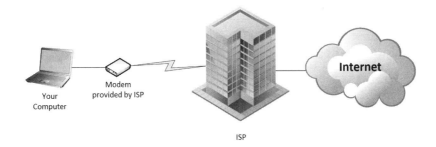

FIGURE 13.1

The ISP provides access to the Internet. Your connection does not run through your ISP's headquarters. The picture shows your ISP managing your connection.

NOTE   You can compare the service provided by an ISP to the way you access electricity, water, or natural gas. In fact, access to the Internet might one day be regulated as another utility.

Checking the Hardware Required to Connect

Although Windows is powerful, connecting to the Internet usually requires some hardware. The hardware usually (but not always) is provided by the ISPs and includes the following:

- **Modem**—The modem is a device that bridges the Internet to your computer or home/office network. Each type of Internet connection—cable, DSL, and such—uses a different type of modem. If you'd prefer not to lease or purchase a modem from your provider, you can usually purchase one compatible with most providers from your preferred home electronics retailer. Many newer modems include Wi-Fi capability and can also double as a router.

- **Ethernet cable**—Except for dial-up and mobile broadband connections, you need an Ethernet cable to connect your computer to the modem or to connect the modem to a router and your computer to the router. If an Ethernet cable was not provided by your ISP, you can purchase one at any store that sells electronics, especially computer equipment.

- **Wireless antennae**—If you want to connect wirelessly but your device does not have a wireless network adapter already built in, you can purchase and connect one easily.

 NOTE   Another common device you might have is called a *router*, which is discussed in this chapter in the section "Understanding Routers for Internet Connection Sharing." Routers are essential if you want to share your connection across multiple devices.

Learning the Internet Connection Services Typically Available

Each ISP uses a specific technology to connect your computer to the Internet. The technology the ISP provides, plus the price the ISP charges, the availability of the service, how to use and configure the technology, and how convenient and reliable the technology is, all combine to define a service offered by the ISP. It might be that you have a number of services available at your home. If that is the case, review each option carefully to make a decision. Price is important, but be sure to research the reliability of the service. Reliability is defined by how often the service is down and whether the connection you pay for is provided at the speed advertised. There might be just one ISP doing business in your neighborhood, and that ISP might provide just one service. In that case, your options are obviously limited.

Here's a list of the most popular services used to connect users today, as well as a short explanation of how you connect to the service:

- **Fiber**—Some ISPs offer a dedicated fiber-optic connection to residential customers. Using a very small strand of fiber-optic cable, the Internet connection relies on waves of light with very fast and clear connections. A modem is used to convert the light to a digital signal your computer will understand. The modem is typically connected to a router allowing for Ethernet or wireless connections. It is not unusual to have television and phone services available through the same connection.

- **Cable**—Technology companies have learned to piggyback Internet traffic on the cable and hardware that provides cable TV service to their customers. Your ISP, which with this technology is the company that provides your cable TV service, provides you a modem that uses coaxial cable to connect to one of the cable ports in your home.

  The modem is typically connected to a router allowing for Ethernet or wireless connections. You usually do not need a user ID and password to access the Internet with a cable modem, but be sure to ask if one is needed when you have cable modem service installed.

 NOTE Many cable companies provide a choice for speeds of Internet service. Many services start at 3Mbps, which stands for 3 megabits per second, or 3 million bits per second. At 3Mbps, a song available on the Internet would take about 14 seconds to download (assuming the song is 5MB). Cable companies often offer services (at a higher cost) up to 60Mbps, and some fiber services offer speeds of 1,000Mbps or more!

- **Digital subscriber line (DSL)**—A broadband service is DSL, which, because it uses the same lines that support your regular telephone service (if you still have that), is provided exclusively by telephone companies. The ISP provides a small device that splits the signal so that the phone signal goes to the telephone and the Internet signal goes to the modem. The modem is another piece of hardware provided by the ISP.

  You need access to a telephone port close to the location, ideally in the same room, where the modem is installed. Like the cable modem, you connect your computer to the modem with an Ethernet cable. You usually do not need a user ID and password to access the Internet with a DSL modem, but be sure to ask if one is needed when you have the service installed.

- **Satellite**—DirecTV, the largest television and music satellite company, is one of a few companies that provide Internet access through satellite service. The signal is delivered to your home or home office from the satellite dish mounted on a building or based on the ground.

  The signal is then delivered by a cable from the dish that connects to a modem, which is used to convert the signal for use with your computer, as shown in Figure 13.2. You connect your computer to the modem with an Ethernet cable.

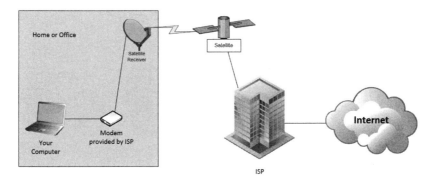

FIGURE 13.2

Satellite service is an option for locations that can't be served by cable or telephone companies.

  The benefit of DirecTV Internet service is its availability where DSL and cable service is not available. You also might save money by bundling satellite enter-tainment service with Internet service. The disadvantage of satellite service for Internet is that overcast skies can cause the satellite signal to be easily lost. The service is also considerably slower than cable service, and you often have a limit on how much data you can use in a month. It's reasonable to say that you should use satellite service only when no other service is available.

- **Dial-up**—Dial-up Internet access is still in use where broadband access is not available. With this service, a dial-up modem is used to send and receive Internet traffic over telephone lines. Some desktop computers have a built-in modem, but these are far less common than they used to be, so it's important to check whether one is installed before you commit to using dial-up service. Dial-up service is slow, but using this technology might be your last resort when other services are unavailable. Your local telephone company can offer dial-up service. If you can get online, you'll find a popular and useful site that lists dial-up services at www.freedomlist.com.

Understanding Routers for Internet Connection Sharing

To extend an Internet connection to several computers in your home or home office, you can use a router. A *router* is a piece of hardware (costing anywhere from $25 to more than $100) that helps share the Internet connection with computers connected to the router. Routers today can provide both wired and wireless access. Higher-end routers can handle more connections from multiple devices and even allow different devices to work at different speeds. A router suitable for home or home office use can usually accommodate 4–10 wired devices. You connect your router to the Internet modem, as shown in Figure 13.3.

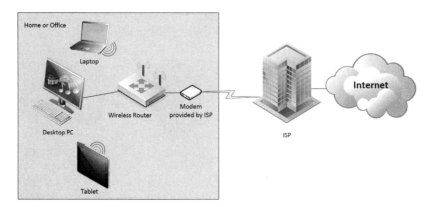

FIGURE 13.3

A router is used to share a single Internet connection with several computers.

 TIP   The modem provided by your ISP might also double as a router by providing support for sharing the connection with multiple computers, including permitting wireless access to the modem.

Understanding the Network Adapter

The *network adapter* is the piece of hardware used to connect your device to a network. Don't worry—it is extremely unlikely that your PC or tablet, if purchased in the past four years, does not have a built-in network adapter. Often these adapters are internal, meaning you can't see them unless you open your computer (which is not recommended), although you can see the port (wired) or sometimes the antenna (wireless).

To view the network adapters set up in Windows so that you can make sure Windows recognizes them and they are functioning, follow these steps:

1. From the taskbar, type **view network connections** into the search box.

2. Select the **View Network Connections** setting, which should appear at the top of the list of results. The Network Connections dialog box shown in Figure 13.4 will open on your Desktop, showing available connections and their current status.

FIGURE 13.4

You can check your connections using the Network Connections dialog box.

Connecting to the Internet

Following are some of the most common Internet connection scenarios. You can follow the step-by-step procedures to connect to the Internet for each scenario in the following list:

- Connecting to a wireless network
- Connecting where free Wi-Fi is advertised
- Connecting where Wi-Fi access can be purchased
- Connecting to a wired network at work or home
- Connecting after you upgrade to Windows 10
- Connecting if you have been forced to restart

Before diving into the individual connection scenarios, it's important to understand that after you install Windows 10 and initially connect to the Internet, you might not need to make any changes to your setup or to even purposely connect to the Internet. Windows automatically connects to the Internet on startup unless you use a manual connection method, such as dial-up.

Unless you want to change how you connect—for instance, if you bring your computer to a new location or if you change your network or connection setup at home (that is, you change your hardware or Internet service provider)—you might not need the information provided in the rest of this section.

 NOTE When connecting to the Internet, you are also connecting to a local network that can have other computers and devices such as printers, game systems, and Internet capable televisions. Interacting with other devices on this local network is examined in more detail in Chapter 20, "Sharing Files and Printers."

Connecting to a Wireless Network

To connect to the Internet through a wireless network, follow these steps:

1. From the Desktop, select the **Network** icon on the taskbar. The wireless networks that are in range will be displayed, as shown in Figure 13.5.

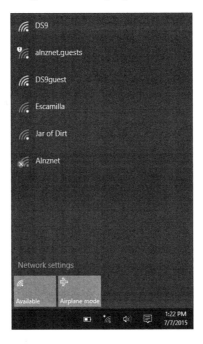

FIGURE 13.5

You can review all the network connections from the taskbar.

2. Select the wireless network you wish to connect to. The wireless network will expand slightly to display options for that network.

3. If this is a network you expect to use again in the future, select the checkbox Connect Automatically, as shown in Figure 13.6. Select **Connect** to initiate the connection.

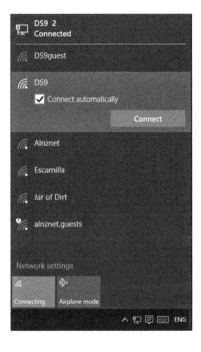

FIGURE 13.6

You are able to easily connect to available networks and retain connection settings for future use.

4. The options for the selected wireless network will expand again, and you will be prompted to enter a password for the network, as shown in Figure 13.7. If you want to confirm that the password has been spelled correctly, select the preview icon that appears in the password field. You can select **Share Network With My Contacts**, which will share this network and password to the remembered networks on their devices if your settings allow this. Enter the wireless network password, and click **Next**.

TIP Most newer routers also have a Wi-Fi Protected Setup (WPS) button that automates the way a computer authenticates with the router and avoids the need for typing in a password. You might need to hold the button for a few seconds to initiate this feature on the router. The router should connect automatically to your Windows 10 device, and it will automatically connect to this router the next time it sees it.

FIGURE 13.7

You type in the password for the wireless network to which you are trying to connect.

5. Windows 10 will now communicate with the router and, if the password is correct, it will show **Connected** for this wireless network. You will also see a connected wireless icon on your taskbar. Hover over this icon with your mouse cursor to see the network name and connection state, as shown in Figure 13.8.

FIGURE 13.8

Once successfully connected, you will see an icon on the Desktop taskbar with bars indicating signal strength.

NOTE   The setting **Share Network With My Contacts** refers to Wi-Fi Sense. Settings related to this feature can be found in the Settings app under Network & Internet>Wi-Fi and then selecting Manage Wi-Fi Settings. If enabled, Wi-Fi Sense shares network passwords with your contacts, and you can receive network passwords from your contacts. This may seem like a security concern, but your shared passwords are not visible, and network settings can disable this sharing of wireless network credentials in a business environment. You can select which networks you share and which types of contacts will have access to the networks you know and use.

TIP   Windows includes a setting to classify wireless networks as *metered connections*. This is intended to prevent a wireless connection from being used for nonessential tasks that could quickly consume a limited data quota, such as would be the case if sharing an Internet connection from a smartphone. Refer to the steps in the following section, and refer to Figure 13.10 to locate this setting.

Connecting Where Free Wi-Fi Is Advertised

There's no doubt that you have come across a store, a coffee shop, a hotel, an airport, or another public location advertising Wi-Fi. If free Wi-Fi is offered, follow the previous steps under "Connecting to a Wireless Network." At step 4, you might need to provide the network passcode, although many public Wi-Fi hotspots are not secured. If a password is required, you might need to ask someone at the location to provide you with it.

NOTE   Some sites do not require a passcode; however, they can require you to read an agreement or watch an advertisement to connect. If you do not seem to be connected, try opening a web browser. Watch for a page to load asking you to agree to terms of use, which you will need to accept before you will actually be connected to the Internet.

When working with a public network, you should exercise caution. You might be prompted when initiating the connection to indicate if this is a private, work, or public network. If you are not prompted, you should make sure that your device knows this is a public network. This will disable sharing and prevent other individuals from having an easy connection to your device and any data. To let Windows know that a wireless network is a public network, follow these steps:

1. From the Desktop, select the **Network** icon on the taskbar and select **Network Settings**. Alternatively, from the Start menu, you can select **Settings** to open the Settings app and then select **Network & Internet**.

2. Select **Wi-Fi** from the left navigation bar, as shown in Figure 13.9.

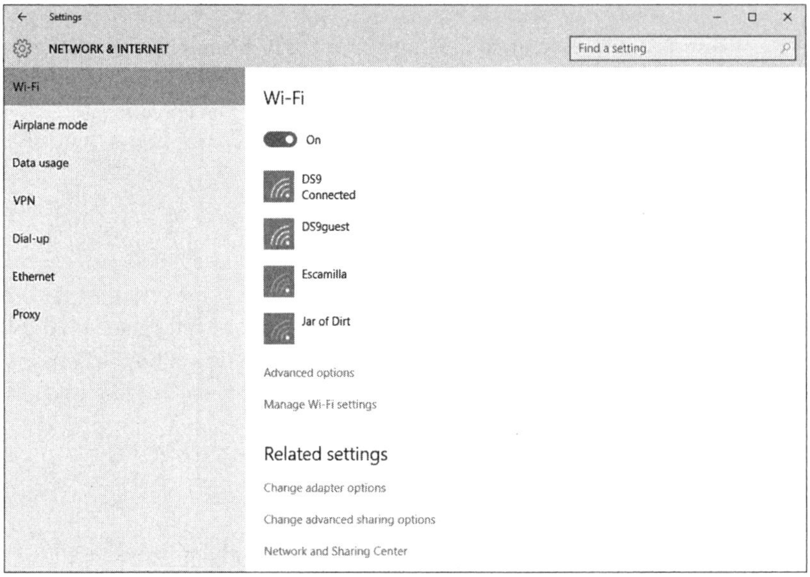

Settings			− □ ×
⚙ NETWORK & INTERNET		Find a setting	🔍

Wi-Fi

Wi-Fi	
Airplane mode	On
Data usage	DS9 Connected
VPN	DS9guest
Dial-up	Escamilla
Ethernet	Jar of Dirt
Proxy	

Advanced options

Manage Wi-Fi settings

Related settings

Change adapter options

Change advanced sharing options

Network and Sharing Center

FIGURE 13.9

Control setting related to privacy using Manage under Network settings.

3. Select **Advanced Options** to open details related to the network to which you are connected. As shown in Figure 13.10, the current properties for the Wi-Fi connection DS9 are shown.

4. Under **Find Devices and Content**, slide the switch to **Off**. The network will now be considered Public as far as Windows is concerned.

The same options are available for Ethernet connections that you may be using in a public place. Network discovery and other advantages to working with a private network connection are examined in more detail in Chapter 20.

 CAUTION Occasionally Windows may automatically and mistakenly classify a home network as a Public network. This will prevent the device from being visible from other devices and disable sharing content. Use the steps above to *enable* **Find Devices and Content**, which will also change the network to Private.

Settings

⚙ WI-FI

Find devices and content

Allow your PC to be discoverable by other PCs and devices on this network. We recommend turning this on for private networks at home or work, but turning it off for public networks to help keep your stuff safe.

◉ On

Metered connection

If you have a limited data plan and want more control over data usage, make this connection a metered network. Some apps might work differently to reduce data usage when you're connected to this network.

Set as metered connection

◉ Off

Properties

SSID:	DS9
Protocol:	802.11g
Security type:	WPA2-Personal
IPv4 address:	192.168.2.25

FIGURE 13.10

Turn discovery settings to Off to protect your device and data when on a public network.

Connecting to Pay-as-You-Go Wi-Fi

Most airports and many small coffee and snack shops offer Wi-Fi, which is almost always provided by a national service. You can usually tell which type of Wi-Fi is offered from advertisements or notices on the walls. Or you can ask someone. Most ISPs charge a fee based on the time you connect, and they might charge based on data consumption with additional fees if you go over your data limit. If you connect from this location frequently, you might consider signing up for a plan that gives you access for a longer period at a reduced price.

If Wi-Fi is offered for a fee, you need to enter credit card information to pay for the access.

Follow these steps to connect to a Wi-Fi hotspot:

1. You need to first connect to the wireless service at your location. This does not provide you access to the Internet yet. You are simply joining the network at your location. Follow the instructions in the previous section, "Connecting to a Wireless Network." Someone working at or supporting your location can identify the network to which you should connect; however, the name of the network (for example, Boingo or _Heathrow Wi-Fi) might make the selection obvious.

2. Open Internet Explorer. You should be brought to the sign-up page for the ISP in use at the location. Enter the information requested. You should connect shortly.

Microsoft has included an app in Windows 10 named Microsoft Wi-Fi. Shown in Figure 13.11, this alerts you to a new Wi-Fi hotspot service that will continue to grow. Microsoft has stated that it intends to expand the service to approximately 10 million locations.

FIGURE 13.11

Microsoft Wi-Fi is designed to be a widely available pay-as-you-go alternative.

Some Office 365 subscriptions include access to Microsoft Wi-Fi, as do some packaged Surface tablet purchases. Transactions are handled through the Windows Store, so if you are set up to make purchases you will have very little hassle using this type of pay-as-you-go Wi-Fi. Chapter 24, "Using Your Microsoft Account for Purchases," considers making purchases through the Windows Store in detail.

Connecting to a LAN/Wired Network

Most corporate and school networks connect to the Internet over a local area network (LAN). This is no different from using a wired network connection in your home.

At an office or a school, look for an unused Ethernet port. There is only one type of port that accommodates the Ethernet plug, so you should be able to determine quickly whether a port is available. At home, simply connect to one of the ports in your modem or router.

After you connect, wait a few seconds and then look at your taskbar to verify you are connected. Hover over the network connection, as shown in Figure 13.12, to verify your connection status. If you are not connected to the LAN, it's a good idea to shut down your computer and restart. After you sign on again, check the taskbar again or open a web browser. If an error message appears, meet with a member of the information technology team or contact the support desk that manages the network at your location.

FIGURE 13.12

Check the status of your Ethernet connection from the taskbar.

Connecting After Upgrading to Windows 10

If you upgraded your computer from Windows 7 or 8 and you could connect to the Internet before you upgraded, you should reconnect without issue in Windows 10. If you installed Windows 10 on a new drive or partition, you were probably prompted to connect to the Internet to complete the setup. You need to connect to the Internet if you want to sign in with a Windows account.

Connecting After You Restart Your Device

Windows automatically reconnects to the wireless network you have been using. If you intentionally disconnected from a network, Windows no longer automatically connects you to that network. Wi-Fi networks always have priority over mobile broadband networks.

THE ABSOLUTE MINIMUM

- You must connect to the Internet to complete the initial configuration and installation of Windows. The connection type you use—wireless, wired, and so on—becomes the default connection type, and Windows attempts to automatically make the same connection each time it starts.

- A number of technologies are in use today to connect people to the Internet. Because in some cases just one ISP serves a neighborhood, you might not have a choice of Internet connection technologies.

- You can specify that Windows should connect automatically if you are using a wireless adapter. Doing so requires you to enter your wireless connection password the first time you connect.

- When using a public network, you should turn off network discovery and sharing to prevent inadvertently sharing your data with strangers.

- Windows supports the use of WPS to automate the connection to a wireless router.

14

BROWSING THE WEB

Surfing the Web probably is the most popular activity in Windows, more so perhaps than checking email, and definitely more so than doing work! If you think the same way, you'll also agree how important it is to like your web-surfing tool.

Microsoft thinks it's important, too—so important that Windows 10 comes with two web browsers. Microsoft Edge is the new default web browser built for Windows 10 and designed for the future of web browsing. Microsoft Edge is slick, modern, and simple to use.

Internet Explorer 11 is the latest version of the familiar Microsoft web browser that first appeared back in 1995. Internet Explorer 11 is included with Windows 10 to provide backward compatibility for websites and web applications that require older rendering methods and features. For most of your browsing needs, Microsoft Edge will be your go-to browser, and you might never use Internet Explorer 11. Microsoft's stated intention is to eventually discontinue support and development of Internet Explorer. For this reason, this chapter focuses on how to use the new Microsoft browser, with some discussion on situations that can require the use of Internet Explorer 11.

Introducing Microsoft Edge

Microsoft Edge is a modern universal Microsoft app that uses a minimal interface to keep the focus on your web browsing experience. Microsoft Edge can be opened directly by selecting its icon from the taskbar. As shown in Figure 14.1, a few essential navigation tools are visible, along with some tools that may look unfamiliar.

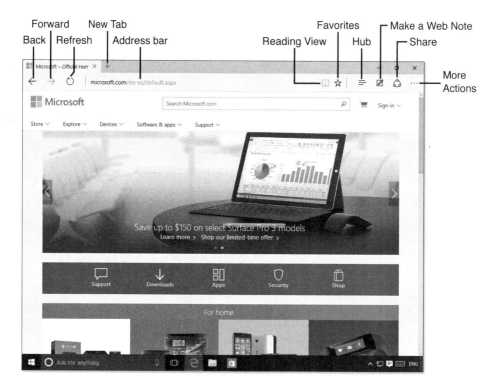

FIGURE 14.1

Microsoft Edge has a nice, clean interface.

Microsoft Edge is not a new version of Internet Explorer. It has been built from the ground up using very little of the older web browser code. Besides stripping away many of the features and code that provided compatibility with older websites, thought was given to how to put Microsoft Edge on the cutting edge of web browsing.

Microsoft Edge uses EdgeHTML for rendering websites. This addresses changes that have occurred on the Internet itself where new and improved codes allow web developers to build better and more interactive websites. Alternative web browsers such as Firefox, Chrome, and Safari have gained popularity based on a number of factors, including a cleaner interface and features such as synchronizing bookmarks and personalizing the browsing experience. Microsoft Edge addresses these issues as well and will be introducing several new features that are only going to improve with time.

Microsoft Edge includes some important improvements:

- Integration with Cortana

- Improved reading experience using Reading View

- New options for input and annotation with Web Notes

- Personalized new tab feature

- Improved security

- Increased speed

Two of the most important improvements brought to Microsoft Edge are Cortana integration and the Reading view. The following sections will look at these and other new features.

Surfing the Web with Cortana

Cortana's integration with Microsoft Edge makes it much easier to retrieve information from the Internet, sometimes without even opening a web page. Similar to the way in which Cortana can retrieve information when you use the search box on the taskbar, Cortana can offer additional information while you use Microsoft Edge. To use Cortana, you must have first enabled Cortana in Windows 10. (Refer to Chapter 9, "Using Search and Cortana.") Cortana is enabled by default within Microsoft Edge, but there is a setting that allows you to disable Cortana integration in the web browser.

Cortana is designed to watch for search queries entered in a new tab or in the address bar, and it can automatically offer information for queries related to temperature, calculations, and other types of simple questions typed into these search fields. If you open a website, Cortana might offer more information about a business or place, as shown in Figure 14.2. Select the Cortana link, and it will open as a pane from the edge of your browser window with information and tools you can use without even leaving the website. Cortana can show directions, phone numbers, maps, hours, reviews, photos, and much more. Cortana also can present tools for flight information, tracking information, and making reservations.

FIGURE 14.2

Cortana can proactively offer to show additional information for locations and businesses in Microsoft Edge.

Another practical way that Cortana can assist you while web browsing is through the Ask Cortana tool when you have selected text on a web page.

To use Ask Cortana in this way, follow these steps:

1. Open Microsoft Edge to a web page containing text such as you might find in a news article.

2. Select a word or phrase you would like to learn more about. (To select a word when using a touchscreen, simply tap a word and then use the control handles to adjust the selection.)

3. Right-click the selection (or tap and hold if using a touchscreen) to view the context menu, as shown in Figure 14.3.

4. Select **Ask Cortana**.

5. Cortana will open in a side pane, as shown in Figure 14.4, with additional information related to your selected text.

Cortana certainly has the potential to change the way we find information and use the web browser. If you feel that you would prefer to turn off Cortana, see the section "Getting to Know Microsoft Edge Settings" later in this chapter.

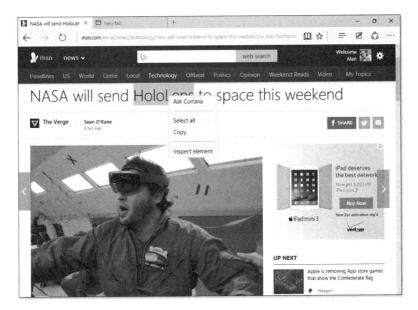

FIGURE 14.3

Cortana can help find information for selected text in Microsoft Edge.

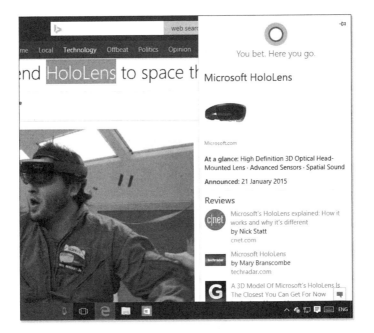

FIGURE 14.4

Cortana can deliver quite a bit of information when you use Ask Cortana.

Using Reading View

Reading View is an awesome feature if you like to get information in a web browser. I am sure you have come to dislike the advertising, videos, and annoying pop-ups that appear if you move your mouse cursor across text in an article. Wouldn't it be great to just strip all the junk away and read in peace? Reading View is the tool you have been waiting for, and it is easy to use.

Follow these steps to use Reading View:

1. Open Microsoft Edge to a web page containing an article (refer to Figure 14.3).

2. Select the **Reading View** icon that appears next to the address bar to enable it (refer to Figure 14.1). The icon will show some animated pages turning as the view is prepared.

3. The page will reappear without the advertising and distractions, as shown in Figure 14.5. (Compare with the same website in Figure 14.3.) Enjoy reading your article in peace!

4. Select the **Reading View** icon again to return to the normal web page.

FIGURE 14.5

Reading View gets rid of the clutter that can frustrate your reading experience.

TIP   The Settings pane of Microsoft Edge includes settings that control the way text is presented in Reading View. This pane can be accessed by selecting the More Actions button (refer to Figure 14.1) to open the Actions menu and then selecting Settings. Select the drop-down menu under Reading View Style to change the background color. The drop-down menu under Reading View Font Size lets you change the font size ranging from Small to Extra Large.

Making Web Notes

Web Notes provide you with Inking tools that enable you to annotate web pages. This is a great way to share your ideas and generate collaboration. You can make notes, draw freehand, highlight, type comments, and then share all these annotations with others.

To add a Web Note, follow these steps:

1.   Open Microsoft Edge to a web page.

2.   Select the **Make a Web Note** icon that appears to the right of the address bar (refer to Figure 14.1). The tab will change color, and the address bar will be replaced with the Web Notes toolbar, as shown in Figure 14.6.

FIGURE 14.6

Web Notes includes several tools for annotating web pages and sharing your ideas.

3.   Start drawing on the page with the Pen tool, or select a different tool to add notes, comments, or highlights.

4.   Select the **Eraser** to remove a few notes just to see how it works. The Eraser tool can clear all notes.

5.   Select the **Pen** or **Highlight** tool a second time to reveal and modify the color and size properties for each tool.

6.   Select **Add a Typed Note**; then select a location on the page to anchor the note. Notice that typed notes are automatically numbered.

7. Type a note.

8. Select the numbered anchor point, and drag it to a different location on the web page.

9. Select the **Clip** tool. Select and drag to create a copy of an area of the web page. This selection is copied to the Windows clipboard and can then be pasted into another application using Paste or Ctrl+V.

10. Select **Exit** to return to the web page and clear all unsaved web notes.

Figure 14.7 shows a web page that was marked up with several web notes while in Reading View. Web notes you have created can be saved by clicking the Save button (as shown in Figure 14.6); your options are to save to Favorites, to the Reading List app for viewing later, or to the OneNote app.

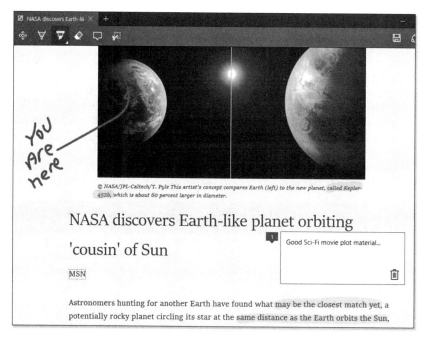

FIGURE 14.7

Web notes can be created in the moment right in the web browser.

Web notes also can be shared. Currently, Microsoft Edge makes a flattened copy of the web page with your annotations and sends this to email recipients you indicate using the Mail app. Microsoft eventually intends Share to send a link that will open the same web page with your annotations present. People you share web notes with can add their own notes for collaboration.

Using the New Tab

Although using tabs is likely not new to you, you will find that Microsoft has thought a bit about what can be done with the tab that is created when selecting New Tab in Microsoft Edge. As shown in Figure 14.8, the New Tab personalizes itself by providing links and shortcuts that reflect your browsing history and favorites that have been noted in other apps that share their data with Microsoft Edge.

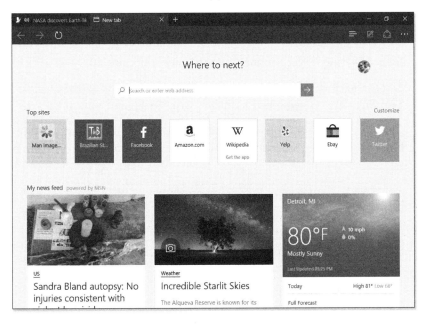

FIGURE 14.8

The New Tab can be a convenient, personalized starting point for your web browsing.

The New Tab includes several features that are worth noting:

- **Customization and Account Settings**—Select the icon with your picture to change account information, customize the New Tab page, or open a new InPrivate window.

- **Search field**—This figures prominently at the top of the page inviting you to start a search or enter a website address.

- **Top Sites**—These are indicated based on your navigating history. The sites you visit most often will appear here.

- **Links**—Links to new stories and other information are presented based on your favorites in MSN apps, such as News, Weather, Sports, Food & Drink, Money, and Health and Fitness.

Occasionally, you might see suggestions appear on the New Tab for apps or other suggestions based on the Windows Spotlight feature. If you decide that you do not benefit from all these suggestions, you can control what appears in the New Tab from the Microsoft Edge settings.

To control what appears on a new tab, follow these steps:

1. Open Microsoft Edge.

2. Select the **More Actions** button (refer to Figure 14.1) to open the Actions menu.

3. Select **Settings**. The Settings pane shown in Figure 14.9 will appear.

4. Select the drop-down menu under **Open New Tabs With**. Choose between **Top Sites and Suggested Content**, **Top Sites**, and **A Blank Page**.

5. Click or tap a place outside of the Settings pane to close it; then select the **New Tab** button. Notice the content has changed based on your selection in step 4.

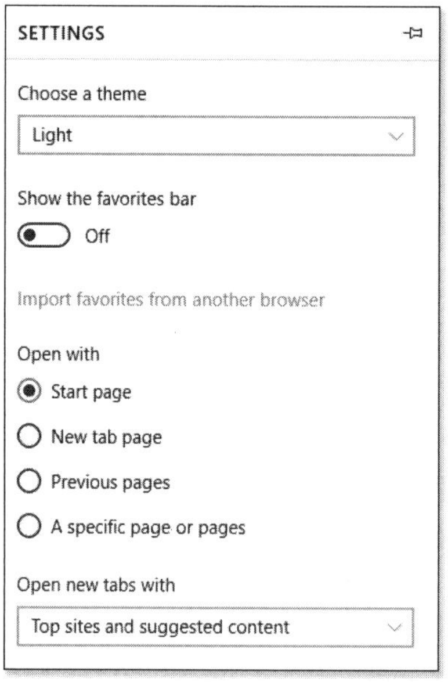

SETTINGS
Choose a theme
Light
Show the favorites bar
● Off
Import favorites from another browser
Open with
◉ Start page
○ New tab page
○ Previous pages
○ A specific page or pages
Open new tabs with
Top sites and suggested content

FIGURE 14.9

You can turn off the suggested content that appears in a new tab from the Microsoft Edge Settings pane.

 NOTE Microsoft Edge also includes a Start tab. This is basically a New Tab that can be selected to open automatically when you open Microsoft Edge.

Browsing the Web with Microsoft Edge

Microsoft Edge has many great features. But none are worth anything if you can't browse the Web and stop at sites you're interested in. The following sections demonstrate a variety of ways you can get to your favorite websites or to websites you never knew existed.

Entering the URL of a Site You Want to Visit

The most direct way to navigate to a site is to type the name of the site you want to go to. Don't worry—you don't have to memorize complicated website addresses. Many times, just the main part of the address will do. For example, to visit Microsoft's website, you don't have to enter http://www.microsoft.com because just **microsoft** would do. Select the address bar and begin entering the name of the site you want to visit.

As you visit more sites, the browser is quick to recognize sites you have visited in the past after you enter just a few characters. As you enter characters into the address bar, the web browser tries to match your input with sites on these lists, as shown in Figure 14.10:

- The most popular sites on the Internet
- Sites you have visited in the past
- Search suggestions

FIGURE 14.10

*Microsoft Edge suggests sites as you enter characters into the address bar. In this example, the characters **y o u t u** are entered, and a number of suggestions appear.*

Searching the Web

Using Microsoft Edge's address bar to perform searches is efficient. Searches can help you find sites on the Internet you probably never knew existed, as well as those you're specifically searching for. Although Microsoft Edge is set up to use Bing as the default search engine, you can switch to other search engines that you prefer or that will provide more targeted searches. Depending on the topic you search for and the engine you want to use, you might see hundreds or even thousands of results returned.

To change the search engine used to perform searches from the address bar, follow these steps:

1. Open Microsoft Edge.

2. Select the **More Actions** button (refer to Figure 14.1) to open the Actions menu.

3. Select **Settings**. The Settings pane opens (refer to Figure 14.9).

4. Scroll down to Advanced Settings, and select **View Advanced Settings**. The Advanced Settings pane is shown.

5. Scroll down to Privacy and Services, as shown in Figure 14.11.

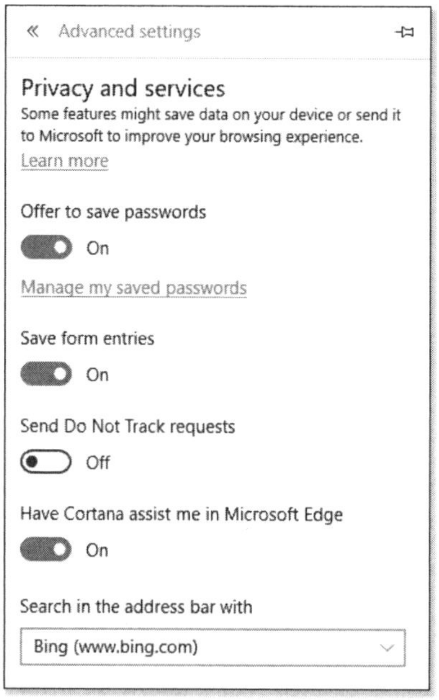

FIGURE 14.11

You can change the search engine used in the address bar of Microsoft Edge.

6. Select the drop-down menu below **Search in the Address Bar With**, and then select **Add New**.

7. Choose from search engines already listed, or follow prompts to add a new one. Select **Add** to add one to your list of search engines in Microsoft Edge.

8. Return to the Advanced Settings pane, and select the drop-down menu again under **Search in the Address Bar With**; then select the search engine you added.

9. Click or tap outside of the Settings pane to close it, and try the new search engine. Type a search word or phrase in the address bar. Figure 14.12 shows search results now are using the YouTube Video Search search engine.

10. Select a search result suggestion to open a web page with results using that search engine.

11. Repeat steps 2–6 to change the search engine that is used in the address bar.

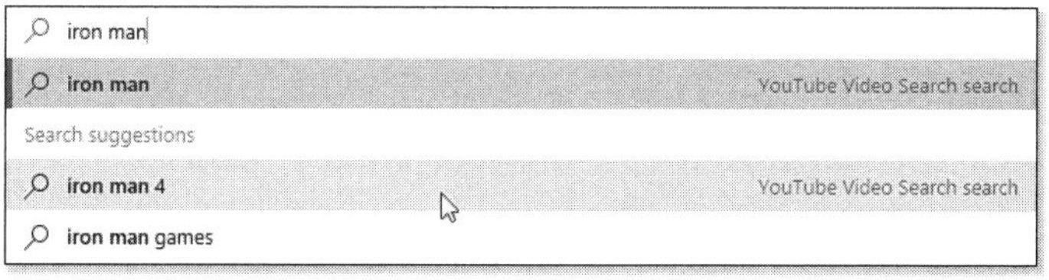

FIGURE 14.12

Microsoft Edge can suggest search results using whichever search engine you indicate.

Following a Hyperlink

It's rare to come across a web page that does not have a link to another page. A link on a web page that brings you to another page is known as a *hyperlink*. A hyperlink normally has a color other than the rest of the text on the page, and often there is a line underneath the words of the hyperlink. A picture or even a word or headline larger than the other text on the pages also can be a hyperlink. On many sites, almost every element on the page links to another page.

Click or tap on a link to open the page targeted by the hyperlink. Whether that page opens in the same window or tab or in a new one depends on the website. If you want control over how it opens, right-click or tap and hold a link. This opens a context menu, as shown in Figure 14.13. From that menu, you can

- Copy the link so that you can use it somewhere else, such as in an email or another web browser.

- Open a new tab containing the page to which the link points.

- Open the page targeted by the hyperlink in a new page for side-by-side viewing.

- Use Ask Cortana to find other web pages related to the hyperlinked page.

- Perform some action based on the type of link you selected, such as saving a picture on the website to your computer.

FIGURE 14.13

The context menu shows you the available options for a hyperlink.

Working with Favorites

Microsoft Edge keeps track of the sites you have visited recently, making it easy for you to revisit any of those sites, you likely will want to save some pages as Favorites. Sites that have been added as favorites will always be remembered even though you might visit them infrequently. You may even have a long list of favorite websites already saved in a browser on a different computer. The good news is that you can import that list of favorites rather than re-create all the work you have done in the past.

To add a website as a favorite, follow these steps:

1. Open Microsoft Edge to a web page you want to save.

2. Select the **Favorites** icon that appears to the right of the address bar (refer to Figure 14.1). A small pane will appear, as shown in Figure 14.14.

3. You might want to change the name of the favorite to something else. If you have many favorites, you should use a folder structure. Select the drop-down menu to change the folder for this link, or select **Create New Folder** to create one. Once everything looks the way you want, select **Add** to add it to the folder indicated. The Favorites icon will now be colored gold.

FIGURE 14.14

Add websites to your list of Favorites with as little as two clicks.

4. To view your Favorites, select the **Hub** icon (refer to Figure 14.1).

5. If it is not already shown, select the **Favorites** hub to see your saved websites, as shown in Figure 14.15.

FIGURE 14.15

Favorite websites are saved to the Favorites hub.

Most modern web browsers allow you to import and export your favorites. Microsoft Edge currently supports only importing favorites from another web browser installed on the same device. In the future you might be able to import bookmarks directly from a file; until then, you should import bookmarks into Internet Explorer 11 first when bringing bookmarks over from a different device.

TIP Importing favorites using a file from a different computer can be a bit of a challenge because this is a task that is not repeated very often. You might have to dig a bit to reveal the Import tool in Internet Explorer 11.

Right-click the title bar in an Internet Explorer window, and select Menu Bar. From the Menu bar, select File, Import and Export; then select Import from a File. Follow the prompts to navigate to a saved bookmark file. I tend to keep a copy of my bookmarks on my One Drive to make it easy to find from other devices.

To import bookmarks from Internet Explorer 11 to Microsoft Edge, follow these steps:

1. Open Microsoft Edge.

2. Select the **More Actions** button (refer to Figure 14.1) to open the Actions menu.

3. Select **Settings**. The Settings pane opens.

4. Select the link **Import Favorites from Another Browser** (refer to Figure 14.9).

5. Select the web browser from which you are importing favorites, and select **Import**. Microsoft Edge imports the bookmarks quickly. Select the **Favorites** hub to view the bookmarks and folders that were imported.

Using the Hub Pane

Microsoft Edge groups together a few important tools under the Hub button. Favorites, which was just discussed, is one of the hubs (refer to Figure 14.15). In addition to Favorites, you'll see three more hubs:

- **Reading List**—You can select a web page for offline reading. The article also can be viewed directly from the Reading List app. When you select a web page as a favorite, you also have the option to add it to your Reading List (refer to Figure 14.14).

- **History**—History lets you backtrack to pages you have visited. This can be helpful to Microsoft Edge when you begin typing a website address that appears in your history. You can clear individual entries that appear in the History hub. Bring your cursor over an entry and select the **X** for any entries you want to remove. If you decide you would rather clear your entire history, select **Clear All History**.

- **Downloads**—If you download a document or an application, it will be found in the Downloads hub. Downloads can be cleared the same way as entries in the History hub. If you right-click a download, you also can report it as unsafe.

The Hub pane can be pinned to keep it visible. Select the thumbtack in the right corner to pin it. Click or tap outside the hub pane to autohide again.

Working with Tabs

A feature known as *tabbed browsing* enables you to have several websites open at one time in the same window, as shown in Figure 14.16. You can easily switch from one tab to another, which is helpful when comparing information or shopping for the same item on different websites. New tabs can be opened by selecting the New Tab button (refer to Figure 14.1) or selecting Open in New Tab from the context menu for hyperlinks (refer to Figure 14.13).

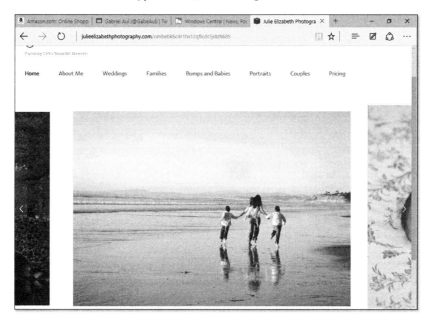

FIGURE 14.16

Microsoft Edge supports tabbed browsing.

Keep the following in mind when using tabbed browsing:

- Select tabs to jump from one tab to another.

- Select a tab and drag it out of position to open the tab in its own window.

- Close a single tab by selecting the X that appears on the right end of the tab.

- When closing Microsoft Edge while several tabs are open, you will be asked if you want to close all tabs. This is intended to prevent you from accidently closing a tab that you are not finished with. You can select Always Close All Tabs to make this a default action.

- Right-click a tab to bring up tab tools, as shown in Figure 14.17. Although some options are obvious, a couple should be pointed out:

  - **Reopen Closed Tab**—Reopens a tab that was recently closed

  - **Close Other Tabs**—Closes all other tabs in that instance of Microsoft Edge

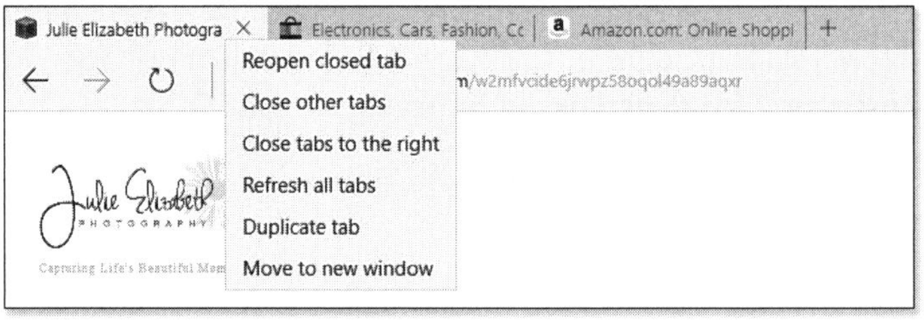

FIGURE 14.17

Right-click a tab to bring up tab tools.

Enhancing Your Browsing Experience

The actions menu provides you with several tools designed to improve your browsing experience and perform basic tasks. Select the More Actions button (refer to Figure 14.1) to open the Actions menu shown in Figure 14.18.

Actions you can perform include

- **New Window**—A new Microsoft Edge window is opened.

- **New InPrivate Window**—A new window is opened that will not leave anything behind after it's closed. Using InPrivate browsing is covered in Bonus Chapter 4, "Keeping Your Computer Healthy."

- **Zoom**—Enlarge or shrink text and images. You also can do this with a mouse by pressing the Ctrl key and then turning the scroll wheel on your mouse.

- **Find on Page**—Perform a search for a word or phrase on a web page. A great keyboard shortcut to remember for this is Ctrl+F.

New window

New InPrivate window

Zoom   — 90% +

Find on page

Print

Pin to Start

F12 Developer Tools

Open with Internet Explorer

Send feedback

Settings

FIGURE 14.18

Use the More Actions menu to perform additional tasks in Microsoft Edge.

- **Print**—Send the web page to the Windows Print pane. You can print to a physical printer or create a PDF file of the web page.

- **Pin to Start**—Add a shortcut to the web page that will appear in the Start menu.

- **F12 Developer Tools**—This is not something you are likely to use. Selecting this opens a new window with tools and visible code intended for individuals who need to work with and examine the actual code for a web page.

- **Open with Internet Explorer**—Use this when a web page is not displaying correctly or when tools are not working as expected. The web page might have older code that requires tools that are included in Internet Explorer 11.

- **Settings**—Select this to make changes to the appearance and behavior of Microsoft Edge.

Most of these options are no doubt familiar to you or are easily understood. The next section looks more closely at some of the settings that have not been considered elsewhere in this chapter.

Getting to Know Microsoft Edge Settings

Microsoft Edge is new, and as a result there are specific settings that might be unfamiliar to you and others located in unfamiliar places.

It is also worth noting that Microsoft is working hard to bring this universal web browser to devices running variations of Windows 10, such as HoloLens, Windows 10 smartphones, and the Xbox One game console. You can therefore expect new settings to appear and be rearranged as Microsoft Edge receives further updates.

Options available in the Settings pane include

- **Choose a Theme**—Microsoft Edge currently enables you to choose between light and dark theme choices (refer to Figure 14.19).

- **Show the Favorites Bar**—Use this switch to enable a toolbar that appears just below the address bar. Favorites added to the Favorites bar will always be visible.

- **Open with**—Choose one of the options to indicate the default content that will open with Microsoft Edge. As shown in Figure 14.19, you can select a specific page or pages to open automatically and use the Custom option to add your own URL to the list. Select the X for any choice you want to remove from this list. You can stick with the Start page or New tab page or have Microsoft Edge open the same tabs that were open in the last browsing session.

FIGURE 14.19

You can configure specific websites to open automatically when you open Microsoft Edge.

- **Open New Tabs with**—This was discussed earlier in this chapter in the section "Using the New Tab."

- **Clear Browsing Data**—You can protect your privacy by clearing your browsing data. Select this button to selectively clear things like your browsing history, passwords, cookies, and much more. See Bonus Chapter 4 for more information on securely browsing the Internet.

- **Reading**—This was discussed earlier in this chapter in the section "Using Reading View."

- **Advanced Settings**—Advanced Settings includes settings that control how your web browser interacts with web pages. Many settings here are covered in other portions of the book, especially those related to privacy and services. Some settings include

    - **Show the Home Button**—Enable this setting and indicate your home web page. This is not enabled by default, though it can be a useful feature.

    - **Offer to Save Passwords**—This is enabled by default, although in some situations it can be wise to turn this setting Off, such as when someone else is sharing your computer.

    - **Save Form Entries**—Enabled by default, this setting can remember common entries such as addresses and phone numbers that will appear as you fill in a form on a website. This makes filling in forms easier, but again you might want to disable this on a device that is shared.

    - **Have Cortana Assist Me in Microsoft Edge**—If Cortana is enabled on your device, you can disable it in Microsoft Edge by sliding the switch to Off.

There are additional settings that you can turn on and off. In some cases, disabling a feature can affect how well web pages work in Microsoft Edge. Other settings can make your device more secure. If you are in doubt about a setting, it is better to leave it as it is.

Using Internet Explorer

Even though Microsoft Edge is the new web browser that most people will use by default, some situations might require the use of Internet Explorer 11 (see Figure 14.20). Microsoft decided to include Internet Explorer 11 to ensure compatibility with websites and web applications that rely on older web technologies such as Silverlight or ActiveX. A business or an organization can even set up its computers to use Internet Explorer by default.

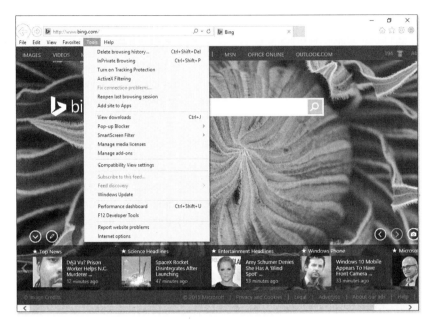

FIGURE 14.20

Internet Explorer 11 provides Windows users with a web browser that can still work with older websites and apps.

TIP Should you use Internet Explorer or Microsoft Edge? Unless you have a specific reason to fall back on Internet Explorer, Microsoft Edge is the browser you should be using. If you need to use Internet Explorer, then there are a few things that are included here to make your life easier. The first thing you may want to do is pin Internet Explorer to the taskbar.

Creating Shortcuts to Websites

You have seen how Microsoft Edge enables you to pin websites to the Start menu using the Actions menu. Internet Explorer also includes a handy tool that allows you to add a website to the list of All Apps. These shortcuts automatically open in the Desktop browser.

To add a website from Internet Explorer to your list of apps, follow these steps:

1. From the search box on your taskbar type **internet explorer**. Select **Internet Explorer** from the search results.

2. Open a website you want to add to your All Apps menu.

3. From the menu bar, select **Tools** to open the Tools menu (refer to Figure 14.20).

4. Select **Add Site to Apps**.

5. In the Internet Explorer dialog box that appears, select the **Add** button.

Websites added as "apps" can be pinned to the Start menu or the taskbar using steps outlined back in Chapter 3, "Optimizing the Start Menu." This shortcut in the Apps screen still lets you easily open websites in the correct browser when working in the modern user interface (UI) environment.

Opening All Links in the Desktop Browser

If you need or prefer to use the Desktop browser exclusively, there is a setting for that. Follow these steps:

1. From the Start menu, select **Settings** to open the Settings app.

2. Select **System** and then **Defaults Apps**.

3. Scroll down to Web Browser and select the current web browser listed.

4. From the drop-down menu, select **Internet Explorer**.

5. Close the Settings app.

Any websites, including ones that were pinned to the Start screen using the modern browser will now open on the Desktop browser. Use the preceding steps to change back if you want to at a later time.

THE ABSOLUTE MINIMUM

- Two Internet browsers are available in Windows 10. Microsoft Edge is designed for a greater user experience with a minimum number of buttons and other onscreen elements. Internet Explorer 11 supports all the traditional browser requirements, such as plug-ins, toolbars, and older technologies like ActiveX.

- There are just a handful of visible controls in the Windows 10 browser. You can select More Actions (...) to reveal additional tasks and settings.

- Cortana can offer assistance while browsing the Web—watch for links that let you know it has additional information or select Ask Cortana from the context menu of selected text or a hyperlink.

- Reading View is a feature you should certainly try when reading articles on websites.

- Annotate websites using Web Notes and then save or share the results.

- Look over Settings in Microsoft Edge that allow you to customize the New Tab features.

- As you navigate to different sites, the sites remain open as tabs. This makes it easy to jump back to any open site you like.

KEEPING UP WITH YOUR CONTACTS IN THE PEOPLE APP

The People app is an essential tool for people on the go. Many of us juggle more than one device and perhaps you use a few different email accounts between your work and personal life. Each of these may include a unique set of contacts. If you find yourself connecting to multiple social networking sites, you may have yet more contacts. The People app brings together all your contacts into a single interface that can be referenced when sending emails or sharing content from your Windows 10 device. While the People app itself is not very complex, it has its own chapter due to its importance. This chapter helps you navigate through the different features of the People app. You will also learn how to link the app to sources of contacts that you may already use, saving you from entering your contacts by hand.

The People app in Windows 10 is a modern universal Windows app that can be upgraded at any time to introduce new features. So do not be alarmed if the interface has some differences from what appears in this chapter. To be sure you can easily follow the instructions in this chapter, consider reviewing some of the content in Chapter 5, "Working with Windows Apps."

Introducing the People App

The People app, shown in Figure 15.1, is the hub for all your web contacts, both professional and personal. This hub allows you to compile names, email addresses, and phone numbers, as well as many other details for all of your contacts. Because the People app is a universal app, your contacts are synced to other Windows 10 devices when using your Microsoft account. From the People app you can initiate an email or phone call, share contact information with others, and manage your contacts.

Additionally, when composing a new email message or sharing something from another app, you can begin typing names of contacts that are saved in the People app. You will see contacts offered based on the characters you have typed.

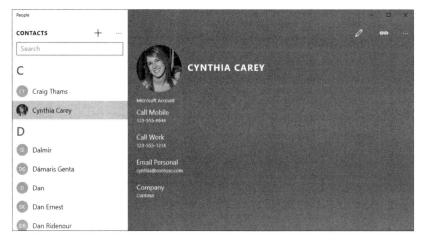

FIGURE 15.1

The People app helps you keep track of your contacts.

The main view in the People app gives you a consolidated list of all the contacts in your personal and professional life in an alphabetized navigation pane on the left. To the right you will see the details for a selected contact. Photos are prominently presented in the People app as circles.

TIP In Windows 10, circles represent people. You will see circles used for people in many places and apps in Windows, including your sign-in image, your account photo on the Start menu, emails, and even the music artists shown in the Groove Music app.

 NOTE While most apps have vastly improved since Windows 8.1, I will admit that the People app has lost some features that made it unique. In the past, the People app allowed you to link to social networking sites like Facebook, Twitter, and LinkedIn, which brought feeds into the People app from your contacts. The latest postings and pictures could be seen right from the People app, and you could comment or post to those social networks from the People app. Making this a universal app, and the fact that many features were underused, has resulted in a much more streamlined app that focuses on keeping track of your contacts. Perhaps additional features will make their way back into this app through future updates.

To start the People app, select it from the Start menu (see Figure 15.2), or search for **people** using the search box on the taskbar. If you have not yet opened the People app or you have signed in with a local account on the computer, you will likely see the invitation to add accounts shown in Figure 15.3.

FIGURE 15.2

The People app can be found under All Apps in the Start menu.

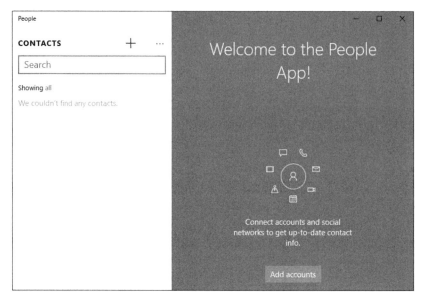

FIGURE 15.3

The People app can only show contacts it knows about.

Adding Contacts to the People App

Adding contacts can be done manually or automatically by adding accounts to the People app. If you are using a Microsoft account to sign into your device, some contacts already may be linked to that account. If you have set up the Mail and Calendar apps, you may see contacts have been added to the People app as a result as well.

To manually add contacts to the People app, follow these steps:

1. Open the People app by selecting it from the Start menu or by searching for **people** in the search field on the taskbar.

2. To add a contact manually, select the **+** button at the top of the Contacts list (refer to Figure 15.3). A new blank contact pane will open, as shown in Figure 15.4.

3. If you have multiple accounts already added to your device, you will see a field labeled **Save To**. Select the drop-down menu to select the account that this new contact will be associated with.

4. Add the appropriate contact information. Name, Phone, Email, and Address fields are indicated.

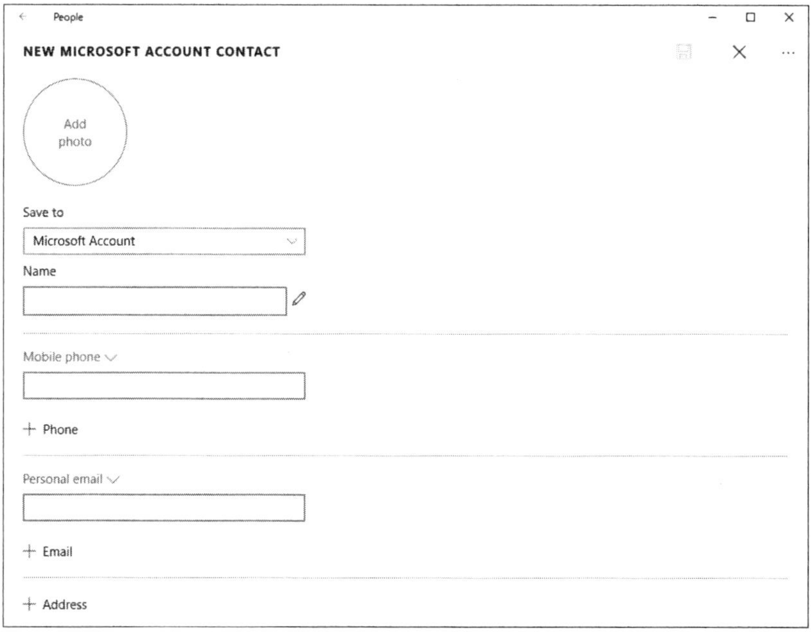

FIGURE 15.4

You can manually add contact information using the appropriate fields in the People app.

5. Select **Other** to add additional information fields to your contact. As shown in Figure 15.5, several fields are available, including company, family, birthday and anniversary, and note fields.

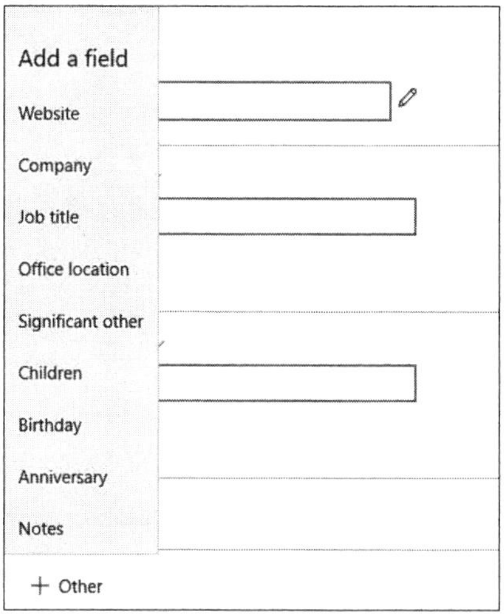

FIGURE 15.5

Select Other to add one of the several additional information fields to a contact.

6. Select **Add Photo** to use an image file that you have saved. The Photo app will open, and you can select an image file that is in your collection. If you do not add an image, the initials for the contact will appear instead.

7. Select **Save** to add the contact to the People app.

 NOTE The People app does not include a way to add groups as contacts at the time of this writing. This is a much requested feature that is expected to appear by means of a future update to the app.

To automatically import contacts to the People app, follow these steps:

1. Open the People app by selecting it from the Start menu or by searching for **people** in the search field on the taskbar.

2. If you have not added accounts to the People app, you can select the **Add Accounts** button (refer to Figure 15.3) and jump to step 4. If you do not see the Add Accounts button, select the See More ellipsis (**…**).

3. Select **Settings**. The Settings pane will appear as shown in Figure 15.6. Any currently linked accounts will appear here. Select **Add Account**.

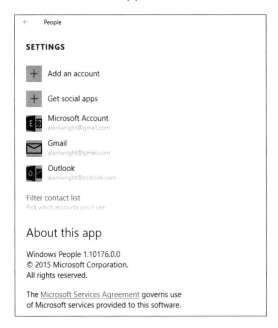

FIGURE 15.6

The Settings pane will display any accounts that are already linked to the People app.

4. The Choose an Account pop-up window appears, as shown in Figure 15.7. Select one of the online account types and follow the prompts to add your credentials. Chapter 16, "Setting Up the Mail App," considers in more detail the steps involved when adding an account.

FIGURE 15.7

You can add several types of online accounts to the People app.

NOTE   The People app includes a link in the Settings pane that invites you to Get Social Apps. The intention is to import contacts from social network apps like Twitter or Facebook. This feature is not working at the time of this writing and will no doubt be fixed by means of an update to the app.

Managing Your Contacts

As you add accounts and perhaps even some manually entered contacts, your list of contacts will quickly grow. Finding your contacts, editing contacts, and even sharing contacts are all basic tasks that you will need to know. Those tasks and others are considered in this section.

Locating Your Contacts

Locating contacts is certainly an important task. Whether it is to check a number, send an email, or just check a note you have added to the contact, locating contacts quickly is important.

To locate a contact, follow one of these methods:

- Type in a first or last name, or a company name into the Search field. As shown in Figure 15.8, you will see matching contacts immediately begin to appear and filter as you add additional characters.

- Select a letter from the alphabetized contact list. The last will show only letters and numbers. Select a letter to jump to that portion of the list. By default the people app lists all contacts by first name—so Alicia Thomber would be listed under *A* and not *T*.

FIGURE 15.8

Use the Search tool to quickly locate specific contacts in the People app.

Modifying or Sharing a Contact

Contacts can be edited, deleted, linked, and shared. All of these tools are available from the contact information pane.

To use tools for modifying a contact, follow these steps:

1. Open the People app by selecting it from the Start menu or by searching for **people** in the search field on the taskbar.

2. Select a contact. The details for that contact will appear to the right.

3. As shown in Figure 15.9, you can select the **Edit**, **Link** or See More (**...**) buttons. When See More has been selected, **Share Contact** and **Delete** also become available.

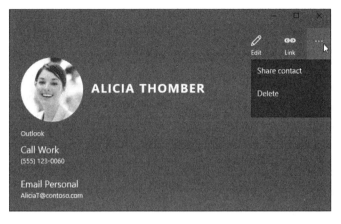

FIGURE 15.9

Choose from tools that allow you to edit, link, share, or delete a contact in the People app.

The tools that you can use with a selected contact are pretty straightforward:

- **Edit**—Edit allows you to modify the contact details. Review the steps considered earlier in the chapter for manually adding a contact for more information on the information fields that can be modified.

- **Link**—Link allows you to combine different instances of the same contact that may have been imported by means of different accounts. Perhaps you have an Outlook account that lists an email, while an iCloud account just gives a phone number. Select Link to combine the two contacts into a single contact in the People app.

- **Share Contact**—Share Contact will take all of the details minus the image and send it as an attached .VCF formatted file by email.

- **Delete**—Delete will ask you to confirm your decision to delete a contact. Besides removing the contact from the People app, the deletion will be synced to the account that provided the contact.

Filtering Contacts

Once an account has been added to the People app, it will by default be added to the Mail and Calendar apps and vice versa. There are actually a couple of ways that you might decide to filter your contacts. Perhaps you do not want to see contacts from an account that has been linked elsewhere to appear in the People app. On the other hand, you may want contact information in the People app, but prefer not to receive synced calendar entries or emails from that account appearing in other apps. This section considers both of those scenarios.

If you do not wish the email or calendars to sync from an online account you can limit the sync to just your contacts by following these steps:

1. Open the People app by selecting it from the Start menu or by searching for **people** in the search field on the taskbar.

2. Select the See More ellipsis (**...**) that appears at the top of the contact list.

3. Select **Settings**. The Settings pane will appear (refer to Figure 15.6). Any currently linked accounts will appear here.

4. Select the account listed in the Settings pane that you wish to limit and then select **Change Mailbox Sync Settings** for the account.

5. Look for **Sync Options**, as shown in Figure 15.10. Turn the features of the online account to **Off** that you do not wish to sync, and make sure that Contacts is switched to **On**.

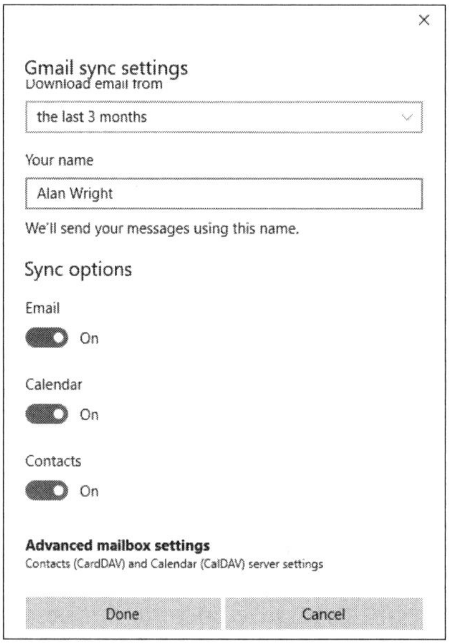

FIGURE 15.10

Turn off the sync options for an online account that you do not wish to be synced to Windows 10.

6. Select **Done** when finished to close the account window. You may see the account listed in the Mail or Calendar apps, but the data from the account will not sync to or from those apps if the Sync option is turned to Off.

If you wish to prevent contacts from appearing in the People app, you can use the Filter Contacts pane by following these steps:

1. Open the People app by selecting it from the Start menu or by searching for **people** in the search field on the taskbar.

2. Select the See More ellipsis (**...**) that appears at the top of the contact list.

3. Select **Settings**. The Settings pane will appear (refer to Figure 15.6).

4. Select **Filter Contact List**. The Filter Contacts pane will appear, as shown in Figure 15.11.

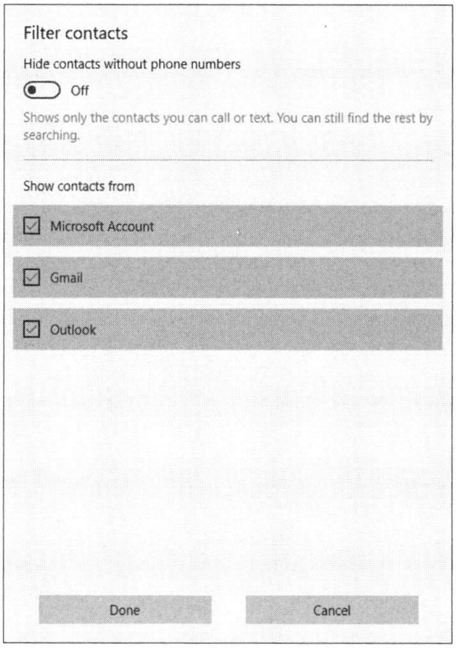

FIGURE 15.11

You can prevent synced accounts in Windows 10 from adding contacts to the People app.

5. Uncheck any accounts that you do not want syncing contacts into the People app.

6. Select **Done** when finished.

THE ABSOLUTE MINIMUM

- The People app links to your online email accounts to show you all your contacts in one place.

- The People app can sync contacts from Google, Exchange servers, Outlook, iCloud, and Yahoo! to name a few online account types.

- You must supply the username (or email address) and password you use to sign in to the online accounts you want to see in People.

16

SETTING UP THE MAIL APP

This chapter considers the initial setup of the Mail app included in Windows 10. The following chapter, "Using the Mail App," considers the everyday ins and outs of using the Mail app to work with your email. The Mail app is a modern Windows app that can be launched directly from the Start menu.

There are certainly many applications that have been designed to help you manage your email. Perhaps you have used Outlook or Outlook Express in the past?

You will find the free Outlook Mail app to be powerful and easy to use with many of the essential features you expect to find in a go-to email application. Although it appears as simply the Mail app on your Start menu, it is actually part of the universal app named Outlook Mail and Outlook Calendar. This explains why you can use buttons to jump between the Mail and Calendar apps.

If your primary need is to exchange email with family and friends, including sending and receiving pictures and other attachments, this app should be perfect for you. It is already integrated with all the important parts of Windows, such as your contacts in the People app. (The People app is covered in detail in Chapter 15, "Keeping Up with Your Contacts in the People App.")

Exploring the Mail App

To start the Mail app, select the Mail tile that is located in the Start menu, as shown in Figure 16.1.

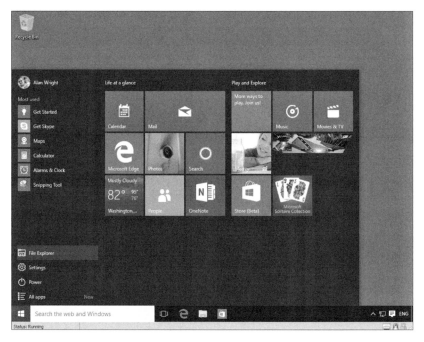

FIGURE 16.1

Select the Mail tile to launch the Mail app.

After starting the Mail app, you see a short bit of animation before the app starts. Depending on how many email accounts are set up in your Mail app, your screen will look more or less like the one shown in Figure 16.2. Your list of accounts and folders appears on the left in the Navigation bar. The middle pane shows a messages list containing the messages in the folder currently selected from the folder list in the hamburger menu. The message selected appears in the message pane on the right.

Hamburger menu
All Accounts   Message list
All Folders   Message pane

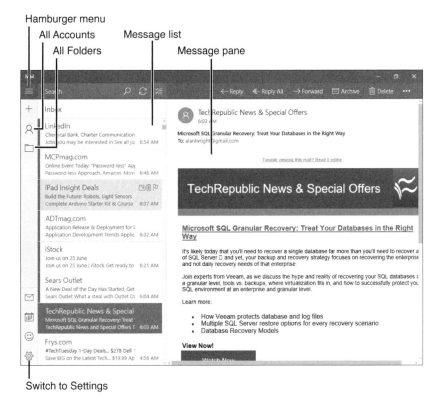

Switch to Settings

FIGURE 16.2

The Mail app shows your accounts and folders, your Inbox, and the selected message.

NOTE   If the account you use to sign in to Windows is a Microsoft account, an email account is set up automatically for you using the same credentials you use to sign in.

Setting Up Your Email Accounts

One of the best features of the Mail app is how it brings together your email from all sources. To see all your email, you need to set up the Mail app to retrieve and send mail from the various email services you use. The Mail app works with the following email providers:

- **Outlook.com**—Microsoft's web email service is known as Outlook.com (previously named Hotmail); you still might see Hotmail.com or Live.com email addresses. Regardless of the name, Outlook.com is Microsoft's primary email service, and the Mail app has been updated with Outlook.com in mind.

- **Exchange**—The Exchange option in the Mail app is for adding email accounts that use Exchange or that are included with an Office 365 subscription. Both of these email types are aimed at corporate customers. The Mail app is one of the first apps that enables users to retrieve their Exchange email without Microsoft Outlook.

- **Google**—Gmail is Google's popular email service. You can learn about Google's email service at www.google.com.

- **Yahoo! Mail**—Yahoo! is a popular email service supported in the Mail app.

- **iCloud**—iCloud email is supported in the Mail app.

- **Other**—You can automatically configure or use manual configuration for email accounts that use IMAP, POP, or Exchange ActiveSync.

You can create as many accounts in the Mail app as you need. If you use just one email service and the service meets your needs, there is no reason to create more accounts. When you're ready to set up the mail account for the first time or add an email account, follow these steps:

1. Start the Mail app by selecting it from the Start menu.

2. If you are greeted by a welcome screen, select **Get Started**. The Accounts screen shown in Figure 16.3 will appear. Jump to step 4.

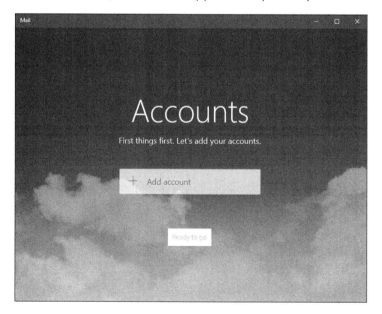

FIGURE 16.3

You are guided through the process of setting up your accounts the first time you open the Mail app.

3. If the Mail app opens to an email account that has been set up previously, select **Switch to Settings** and from the Settings pane select **Accounts** to add additional accounts.

4. Select **Add Account** to get started. A screen like the one shown in Figure 16.4 appears, with a list of the email services you can set up.

From here, check out the following section that applies to the type of email account you want to set up.

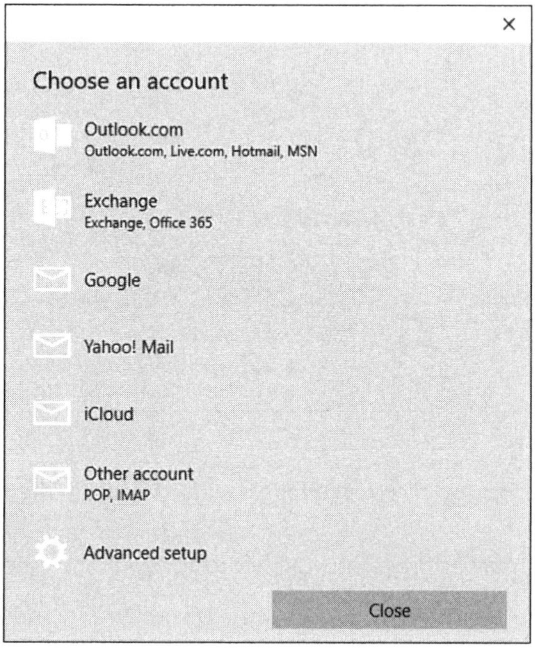

Choose an account

Outlook.com
Outlook.com, Live.com, Hotmail, MSN

Exchange
Exchange, Office 365

Google

Yahoo! Mail

iCloud

Other account
POP, IMAP

Advanced setup

Close

FIGURE 16.4

Select an email service to add to the Mail app.

Setting Up Your Outlook.com, Google, Yahoo!, iCloud, POP, or IMAP Account

These email account types are combined because they all have the same basic steps simply requiring a username and password. To set up your Outlook, Google, Yahoo!, iCloud, POP, or IMAP account with the Mail app, start with the four steps at the end of the preceding "Setting Up Your Email Accounts" section and then continue with the followings steps:

1. Select **Outlook.com, Google, Yahoo!, iCloud,** or **Other Account**. A screen like the one shown in Figure 16.5 appears.

FIGURE 16.5

Google requires just two pieces of information to connect to the server.

2. Enter the email address and password for your account.

   To verify you entered your password correctly, tap and hold or click and hold the **Password Preview** button at the end of the Password box.

3. Select **Sign In**. The Mail app connects to the email provider to complete setting up your account.

4. Depending on the email service, you may see a screen requesting permission to manage various features of the account like the one shown in Figure 16.6. Scroll down if necessary and select **Accept** to finish connecting the account.

5. You will see a message letting you know the connection was successful; you can now select **Done**.

6. In some cases you will be asked for permission to allow Windows to save the account credentials. If you prefer to let Windows sign you in automatically, click **Yes**. Otherwise, click **Skip** and expect to be prompted for your password when you want to access this email account the next time. Your new account appears at the bottom of the list of accounts in the Navigation bar.

FIGURE 16.6

Windows 10 asks for your permission when accessing features in addition to email.

 TIP For some accounts you need to enter your full email address in the Email Address field, including the **@yahoo.com** portion.

Setting Up Your Exchange or Office 365 Account

To set up your Exchange or Office 365 account with the Mail app, start with the four steps at the end of the "Setting Up Your Email Accounts" section and then continue with the followings steps:

1. Select **Exchange**.

2. Enter the email address for your account and select **Next**. The Mail app will attempt to locate your account settings.

3. Once the account settings are verified, you will be prompted to provide your password as shown in Figure 16.7. To verify you entered your password correctly, tap and hold or click and hold the **Password Preview** button at the end of the Password box. Select **Sign In**.

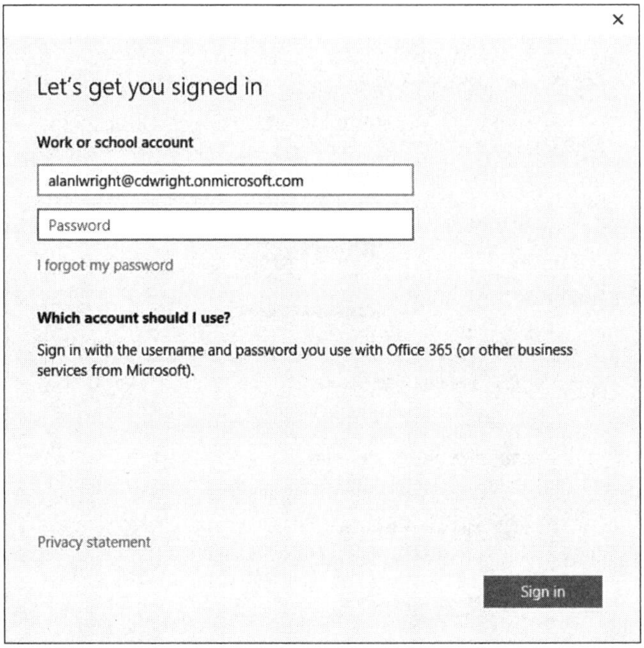

FIGURE 16.7

Exchange and corporate Office 365 accounts will ask for a password after the account has been verified.

4. You might have to enroll your device depending on the settings your orga-nization has put in place, especially when using connecting to an Office 365 account that is managed by an organization. Follow the prompts to enroll your device.

5. You might see a screen notifying you that security settings will need to be changed on your computer to finish connecting this email account, as shown in Figure 16.8. This will appear if your password requirements and settings for logging in to the device are more relaxed than is specified by your organiza-tion. Corporate security settings tend to be more restrictive to protect sensi-tive data that can be accessed by means of the email account contents. You will need to select **Enforce These Policies** to finish setting up the account. The Mail app connects to the Exchange server to complete setting up your account.

6. Select **Done** to close the setup window. Your new account appears at the bot-tom of the list of accounts in the Navigation bar.

FIGURE 16.8

Exchange and Office 365 might require more restrictive security settings to be enforced on your device.

Manually Setting Up an Email Account Using Exchange, EAS, POP, or IMAP

In some cases email accounts are not able to be configured automatically by the Mail app. Perhaps specific information related to server names or ports is required that the Mail app could not retrieve by itself. You will need to check with your email service provider for information related to email client setup. To set up an email account manually with the Mail app, start with the four steps at the end of the "Setting Up Your Email Accounts" section and then continue with the followings steps:

1. Select **Advanced Setup**.

2. Select **Exchange Activesync** (Exchange/EAS) or **Internet Mail** (IMAP or POP), as shown in Figure 16.9. If you're selecting Exchange ActiveSync, continue on to the next step; jump to step 4 if you're selecting Internet email.

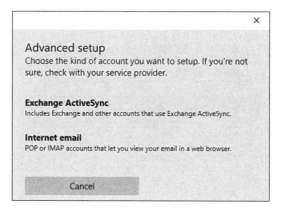

FIGURE 16.9

The Mail app provides an easy-to-use interface for manually configuring web-based email accounts like EAS, POP, and IMAP.

3. To set up Exchange ActiveSync, use the information fields shown in Figure 16.10 to provide the requested account information:

- Enter your **Email Address** and **Password** for your account. To verify you entered your password correctly, tap and hold or click and hold the **Password Preview** button at the end of the Password box.

- Enter the **User Name** for the account.

- Enter your **Domain**.

- Enter your Exchange **Server**.

- Indicate whether SSL is required for the connection.

- Provide the **Account Name** as you would like it to appear in the Mail app.

- Select **Sign In** when finished. Your new account appears at the bottom of the list of accounts in the Mail app.

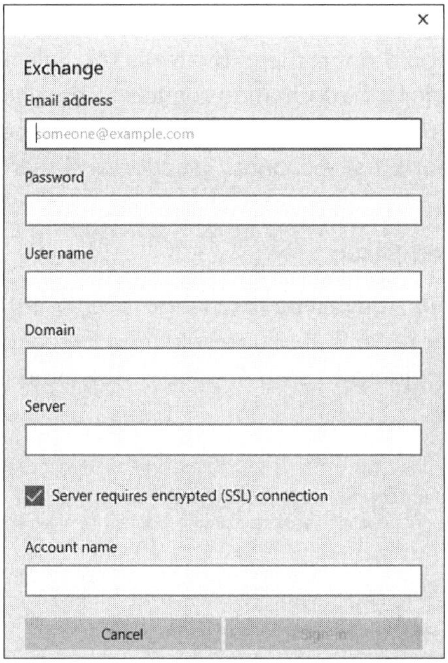

FIGURE 16.10

You can manually indicate settings to connect to an Exchange email account.

4. To set up Internet Mail, use the information fields to provide the requested account information:

- Enter the **Account Name** as you would like it to appear in the Mail app.

- Enter **Your Name** as you would like it to appear on sent messages.

- Indicate the **Account Type** (POP3 or IMAP4).

- Enter your **User Name** and **Password** for your account.

- To verify you entered your password correctly, tap and hold or click and hold the **Password Preview** button at the end of the Password box.

- Indicate the **Incoming** and **Outgoing Email Servers**.

- Use checkboxes to indicate the correct security settings as indicated by your email service provider (see Figure 16.11).

- Select **Sign In** when you're finished. Your new account appears at the bottom of the list of accounts in the Mail app.

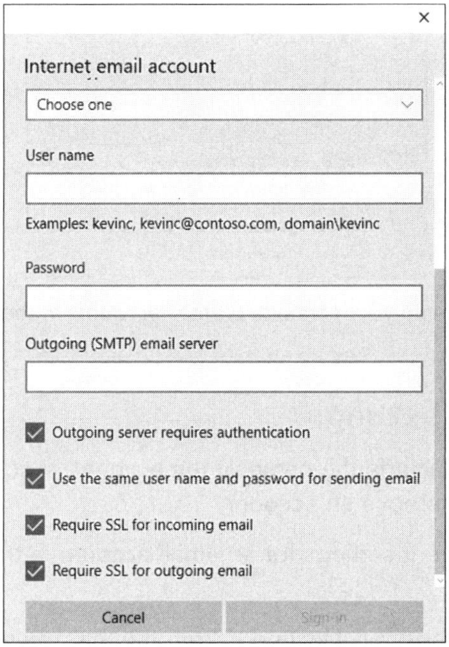

FIGURE 16.11

You can manually indicate settings to connect to an online email account using POP or IMAP.

Managing Your Email Accounts

After you have set up your email accounts, you can jump between your accounts easily by selecting Accounts in the hamburger menu of the Mail, as shown in Figure 16.12. Select an account to view emails and folders from that account. After the initial setup of your accounts, you can easily go back and tweak any settings or options you want. You can change how notifications occur, how long messages are kept locally, whether external images are downloaded, the default email signature, account credentials, and server and port information. Settings you can configure are unique to each email account.

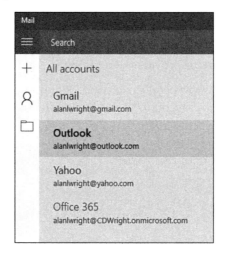

FIGURE 16.12

You can switch between your connected email accounts in the Mail app.

Managing Account Settings

Account Settings include the name of the account, sync and connection settings, and the ability to remove an account.

To modify the current settings for an email account in the Mail app, follow these steps:

1. Start the Mail app by selecting it from the Start menu.

2. From the Mail app, open the Settings pane by selecting **Switch to Settings** (refer to Figure 16.2).

3. From the Settings pane, select **Accounts**. A screen appears with a list of the mail accounts that have been set up so far.

4. Select an account from the list of configured accounts. The account settings pane will appear for that account similar to the one shown in Figure 16.13. From here you can change the name for the account that appears in the Mail app. Additional options appear in this pane as well:

- To manage other details for this account, select **Change Mailbox Sync Settings** and proceed to step 5.

- In some cases you may see the option to select **Change Account Settings**. Selecting this will open a web browser that goes to your online account where you can manage details related to your Microsoft account.

- To remove an account from the Mail app, select **Delete Account**. You will be asked to confirm your decision. Select **Delete** again to remove the account from the Mail app.

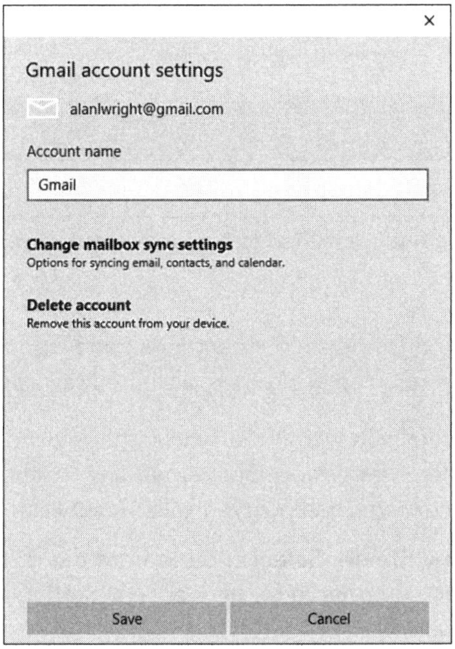

FIGURE 16.13

Adjust settings and customize how an account is configured from the Accounts pane.

5. After selecting Change Mailbox Sync Settings, you will see the available sync settings for that account, as shown in Figure 16.14. Make any changes for that account using the fields in the pane. Click **Done** to keep your changes and close the settings pane for that account, or click **Cancel** to close the pane, disregarding changes.

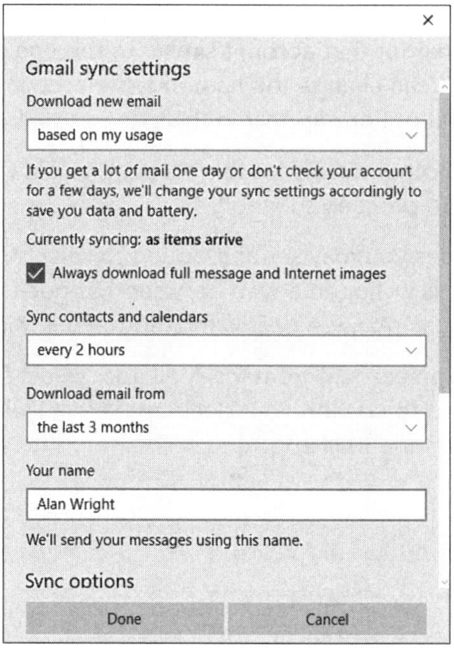

FIGURE 16.14

Manage very specific settings related to how your email is synced to your device in the Mail app.

6. You are returned to the account settings pane from step 4. Select Save to apply any changes. You are returned to the Mail app.

You can tweak several settings in the sync settings pane for each email account. Some accounts offer different options depending on the email service. Here are some of the common sync settings you will encounter:

- **Download New Email**—Select choices from the drop-down menu to control how often checks are made for new emails. Settings range from As Items Arrive to Manually.

- **Always Download Full Message and Internet Images**—Use a checkbox to enable or disable this option. Turn this off if you want to conserve space or data.

- **Download Email From**—Select from the drop-down menu to control how many days of email history will be maintained and displayed for this email account.

- **Sync Options**—Use the switches to select which items are synchronized to this device, You might see only Email, although Contacts and Calendar are also common choices.

- **Your Name**—Indicate the name that will show when emails have been sent from the Mail app for this account.

- **Advanced Mailbox Settings**—Select this to expand the settings that are configured to connect to the account service. Incoming email, outgoing email, contact, and calendar servers as well as the current security settings are listed.

Managing Account Options

Account options include features such as swiping on a touchscreen device, email signatures, and notifications.

To modify the current options for an email account in the Mail app, follow these steps:

1. Start the Mail app by selecting it from the Start menu.

2. From the Mail app, open the Settings pane by selecting **Switch to Settings** (refer to Figure 16.2).

3. From the Settings pane select **Options**.

4. The Options pane, shown in Figure 16.15, includes several features that you can manage:

   - Quick Actions relates to how swipe gestures are used on a touchscreen device. They also control which icons appear on emails in the message list. Quick Actions can be set to Set or Clear a Flag, Mark as Read or Unread, Archive, Delete, or Move. To use a Quick Action, swipe the message to the right or left on a touchscreen or select the Quick Action icon on the message.

   - Signature allows you to enable the insertion of a signature to sent emails using a switch. The Text field allows you to type in a signature.

   - Notifications includes a switch to include notifications in your Actions Center. You can also enable banner notifications or sound notifications using checkboxes.

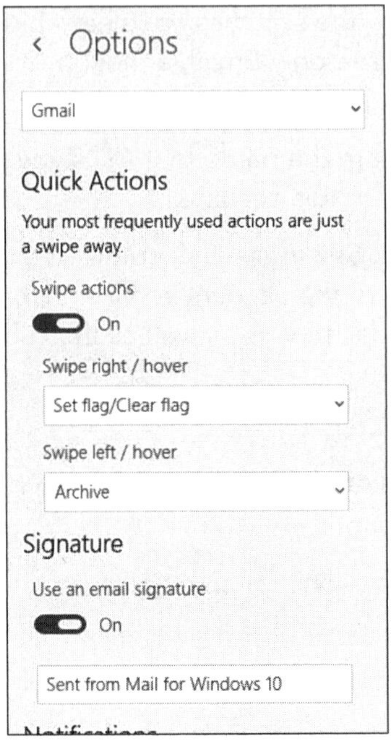

FIGURE 16.15

Manage options for your email accounts using settings for Quick Actions, signatures, and notifications.

Options can be set differently for each account. You can jump between accounts within the Options pane by selecting accounts from the drop-down menu that appears at the top of the Options pane.

THE ABSOLUTE MINIMUM

- The Mail app is provided for free with Windows 10. Although you might find email programs with more functionality, it is hard to justify paying for a program when the Mail app is free.

- With the Mail app, you can bring together your email from many of your accounts and services, including Microsoft Exchange, Google, Yahoo!, and more. This means you can read email from all your accounts in one place but still author and send emails from any account you choose.

- You can tweak many account settings, including how many long messages are retained and whether email is synced for a given account.

- Use the Email Signature to add your own personalized message to all outgoing messages.

- Use settings for notifications to manage how you get alerted to new emails for each account.

- Set up Quick Actions to make often repeated tasks easy to find.

17

USING THE MAIL APP

This chapter builds on the foundation laid in the previous chapter, "Setting Up the Mail App." Refer to Chapter 16 if you have not already set up your email accounts for use in the Windows 10 Mail app. The Mail app has a nice set of features that will meet most of your needs. You will learn how to accomplish the basic tasks associated with email such as writing, replying to, and forwarding messages. You also will learn about some of the methods you can use in the Mail app that will help you manage your email through the use of tools like folders and flags.

Reading Your Email

The Mail app keeps the focus on your email messages. Navigation is simple and intuitive, and by now you are likely familiar with the basic elements of navigation when using a modern app. Because you will be referred to these quite often in this chapter, take just a moment to review the locations of these navigation features in the Mail app. As shown in Figure 17.1, all accounts will display a message list and a prominent message pane. To read a message, select the message from the message list in your Inbox. The message you select appears in the Message pane on the right side of the screen.

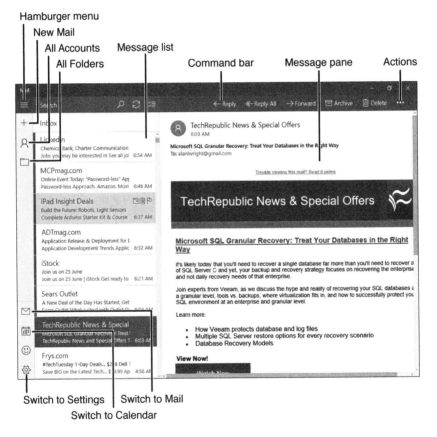

FIGURE 17.1

Navigation is easy if you know these basic features of the modern Mail app.

Your email can be organized using folders, and you can navigate between folders using the hamburger menu off to the left. To see the messages in a different folder, select All Folders from the hamburger menu. Select a folder in that email account and then select the message.

Additional tools can be accessed, and they will open to reveal additional choices as needed by selecting them from the hamburger menu or the upper command bar.

It's easy to read through the email messages you receive. Numbers let you know how many messages in an account or a folder are currently unread. Unread messages are also indicated by a vertical bar of color at the left end of the message in the message list. This bar will disappear after a message has been looked at in the message pane. If you have multiple email accounts set up, they appear as a list when you select the All Accounts icon from the hamburger menu. When you select an account, the folders and options for that account appear.

The Mail app retrieves email from your accounts every few minutes. To force the Mail app to retrieve mail right away, select the Sync This View button that appears above the message list.

 NOTE Depending on the resolution of your screen or the position of your Mail app on the screen, you might not see the Message pane, which is on the right side of the screen. If you are sharing the screen or your resolution is too low, you might see just the Navigation pane and the message list. In this case, selecting a message will slide the message list offscreen to the left, and the message pane will appear. To return to the message list, select the back arrow that appears at the left end of the Command bar.

Replying to a Message

You can send a reply to a message you receive. You can send your reply message just to the author of the message you received or send your message to everyone who received the original message. You can attach documents or pictures to a reply, and you can format your reply however you like.

To reply to an email, follow these steps:

1. In the Message list, select the message to which you want to reply.

2. In the upper-right corner of the Message pane, select either the **Reply**, **Reply All**, or **Forward** button on the command bar, as shown in Figure 17.2.

3. Write your reply message, as shown in Figure 17.3.

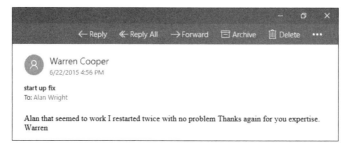

FIGURE 17.2

You can reply to only the sender, reply to everyone on the original email, or forward the message to a new recipient.

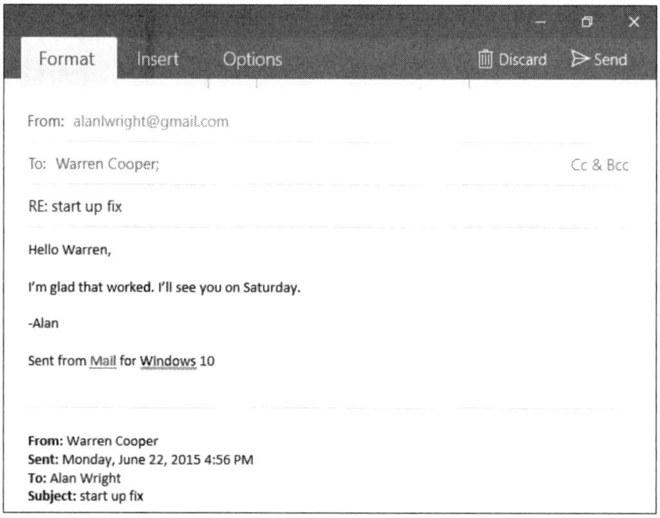

FIGURE 17.3

Type your reply message.

4. Format the message based on the instructions in the "Formatting Your Email Message" section later in this chapter.

5. Address the reply message using the instructions in the "Addressing Your Message" section later in this chapter.

6. To send a file with your message, such as a photo or spreadsheet, follow the instructions in the "Attaching a Photo, File, Table, or Hyperlink to Your Message" section later in this chapter.

7. Select the **Send** button. Your message is sent.

Filing a Message in a Folder

You can reduce the clutter in your Inbox not only by deleting messages that have no value, but also by filing messages that you might want to retrieve at a later date. You can create folders to organize your email. You can usually file your messages into those folders on the email service websites, such as on Google's Gmail page, or with other email services. These folders are visible in the Mail app. Here is how the folders work:

- When you create a folder in your webmail account, the folder appears in the Mail app in that service's list of folders.

- When you file a message in a folder using your webmail account, the message appears in the folder in the Mail app.

- When you file a message in a folder using the Mail app, the message is filed in the folder with the email service.

In Windows 10, you can use drag-and-drop to move messages from your Inbox to a folder, or vice versa. You also can use the Move tool from the Actions menu to file a message in a folder in the Mail app. Here are the steps:

1. In the Message list, locate the message to file.

2. Using drag and drop, select the message, and drag it toward the hamburger menu. The list of folders will expand under the heading Move To, as shown in Figure 17.4. Drag the selected message to the correct folder, and release the message to add it to that folder.

FIGURE 17.4

You can drag and drop a message to any of the folders created with your email service.

3. Right-click a message to reveal actions as shown in Figure 17.5.

4. Select **Move** to display the folders for that email account.

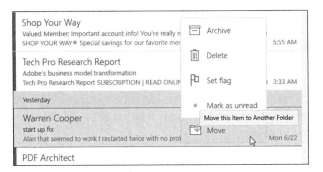

FIGURE 17.5

You can use Move to file a message in any of the folders created with your email service.

4. Select the folder in which you want to store the message. The message is moved to the folder you pick.

 TIP If you have selected Move as one of the Quick Actions for an email account, you can swipe the message to move it or select the Move icon right on the email in the message list. Managing Quick Actions is considered in Chapter 16.

 TIP When working with multiple messages, you can use the Select tool to select messages using checkboxes. The Select tool appears on the Command bar above the message list. After selecting your messages, you can select an action such as Move, Delete, Archive, Flag, or Mark as Read. The action will be applied to all selected messages at once.

Deleting a Message

If you no longer need a message, you can delete it. The message disappears from your Inbox.

To delete an open message, select the Delete button from the Command bar of the Message pane—the button is shaped like a trash can (refer to Figure 17.4). When viewing a message in the message list, hover over the message briefly with a mouse, wait for the trash can icon to appear, and select it as shown in Figure 17.6.

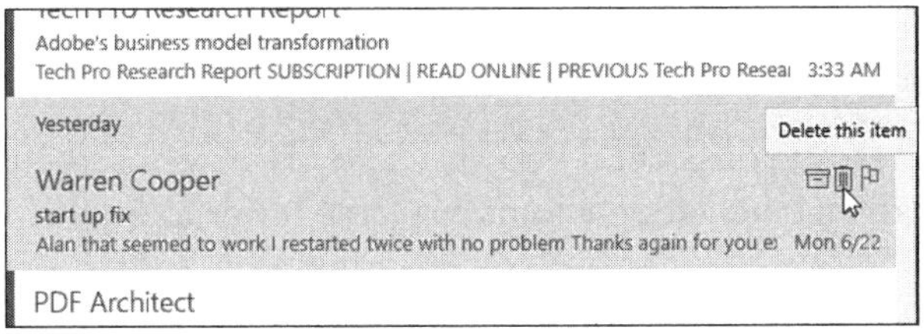

FIGURE 17.6

Delete a message using the Quick Actions icon that appears in the message list.

Forwarding a Message

When you forward a message, you send a message you received to someone else who did not receive it in the first place.

To forward a message, follow these steps:

1. Select the message to forward in the Message list.

2. In the Message pane, select **Forward** from the menu that appears (refer to Figure 17.2).

3. You can add your own text to the message you are forwarding. Your message will appear above the forwarded message. To add your own message to the email you're forwarding, type it just as you would a normal reply. Format your message, if you choose, following the instructions in the "Formatting Your Email Message" section.

4. Address the message to be forwarded using the instructions in the "Addressing Your Message" section.

5. Click the **Send** button.

Marking a Message as Unread

When you select a message by clicking it, tapping it, or moving the focus to the message using the arrow keys, the message appears in the Message pane for viewing. If you don't select another message or if you don't leave the Message pane in five seconds, your message is marked as read (removing its bold format-ting and the colored vertical bar). This system of formatting messages differently for those you have read makes it easy to see quickly what messages are new and deserve your attention. Though some experts suggest that using the read/unread status is a poor method to manage your Inbox, it remains a convenient way to quickly tag messages that have yet to be considered. You can easily switch a message back to unread if you know you want to go back to it later.

To mark a message as unread, tap and hold on a touchscreen or right-click with a mouse to reveal the list of actions available (refer to Figure 17.5). Select **Mark Unread**.

The Mail app also includes settings that determine how the Read / Unread function will work on your device. Select **Switch to Settings** to open the Settings pane. Select **Reading**. As shown in Figure 17.7, there are a few settings you should be aware of:

- **Auto-open Next Item** will simply display the next email in the message list after you have deleted or moved an email message. When disabled, the Mail app just shows your background image.

- **Mark Item As Read** has three possible settings:

  - **When Selection Changes** changes an unread message to read as soon as you select a different message.

  - **Don't Automatically Mark Item As Read** leaves all messages as Unread until you manually mark them as Read.

  - **When Viewed In the Reading Pane** allows you to indicate how many seconds pass before an unread message automatically changes to Unread.

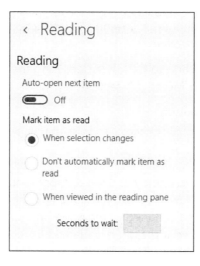

FIGURE 17.7

The Mail app allows you to change how the Read / Unread tool functions.

Writing an Email Message

Writing an email is a simple process. You write your message, format it as you like, address the message, and then click the Send button. There are no restrictions on the type of message you send. You can attach a picture or another document to a message and send it without any text of your own. Or you can write a 20-page letter if you choose. Make sure when sending an email message that you are in the account that you wish to send the message from. Options such as signature and sender name are often configured differently from one account to another. To write a message, follow these steps:

1. From the hamburger menu of the Mail app, select the **New Mail** button (refer to Figure 17.2).

2. A new email message will open, as shown in Figure 17.8.

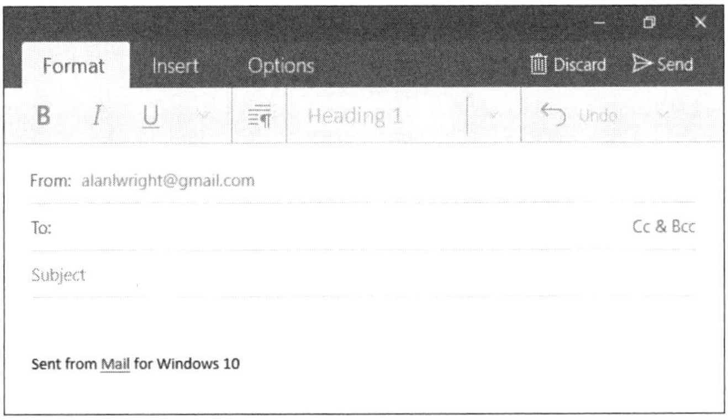

FIGURE 17.8

Select the New button to write a new email message.

3. Address your message using the instructions in the "Addressing Your Message" section.

4. Type your message and subject.

5. You can change the priority by selecting the **Options** tab and selecting **High Importance**, as shown in Figure 17.9, or **Low Importance**. A symbol will also appear on the subject line of your message. Generally, you are best leaving this set to normal. To disable High or Low importance, select the appropriate icon again to disable it.

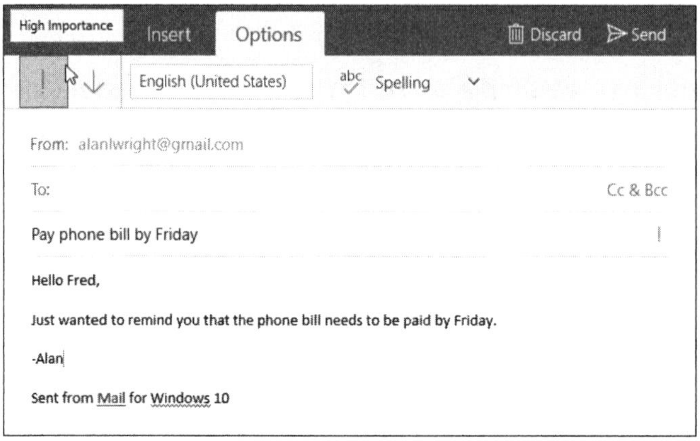

FIGURE 17.9

When addressing a new email message, you can add High Importance to ensure it catches the attention of your recipients.

6. Format your message using the instructions in the "Formatting Your Email Message" section.

7. To send a file, such as a photo or a spreadsheet, with your message, follow the instructions in the "Attaching a Photo, File, Table, or Hyperlink to Your Message" section.

8. If your message is ready to be sent, click the **Send** button.

Addressing Your Message

Addressing a message from the Mail app is a simple process.

1. In the To field, start typing an email address or the first or last name of a contact. As shown in Figure 17.10, a list of possible contacts will appear and will update as you add letters. Select the desired contact. Repeat to add additional contacts in the To field.

2. You can also select or tap **Cc & Bcc** (carbon copy and blind carbon copy) to add these fields to the email.

From: alanlwright@gmail.com

To: cor

Cc & Bcc

Sub

Mike Zimmer
corbz

Kevin Cortina

Sent

FIGURE 17.10

Select contacts quickly by simply typing letters into the recipient fields of your message.

3. Start typing names or email addresses in the Cc field as you did in step 1. This would be for contacts that you would like to be included in an email even though they may not be one of the main recipients of your email.

4. To "secretly" add recipients to the message, select the Bcc field and again choose the recipients you want to include. No one will see any of the Bcc addresses.

NOTE Using Bcc, aside from the obvious benefit of maintaining privacy, can also prevent accidental or unwanted messages from being sent to a contact when someone uses Reply to All, which will not include Bcc contacts.

Formatting Your Email Message

At first glance, the Mail app can appear very simple; however, it has a number of options you can use to format and personalize your email message. You can use colors; different fonts; hyperlinks; and text options, such as bold, italic, and so on. You can also use emoticons to add personality to your message.

Using Text Formatting

To format the text in your message, select the text. To select text, click and drag with the mouse or press and drag with your finger over the characters to format. Select the Format tab in the message pane. Many basic formatting tools are immediately visible. Select the Font Formatting down arrow as shown in Figure 17.11 to reveal additional formatting tools like font colors. Figure 17.12 shows examples of the Styles menu that can be applied to selected text also.

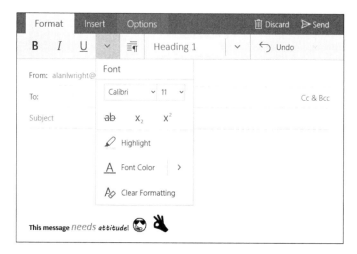

FIGURE 17.11

The Format tab reveals several formatting options.

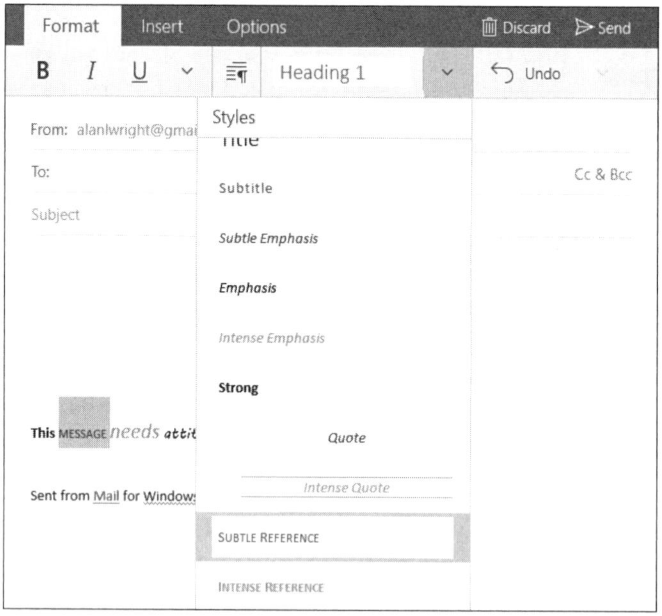

FIGURE 17.12

Drop-down menus like the Styles menu offer many nice formatting choices.

Using Emoticons

Who doesn't like a smiley face or a cheeseburger in messages they write?

In the past the Mail app has included a large library of emoticons to help you add "character" to your emails. You can still easily add emoticons to your messages using the emoticons that are included in the Touch keyboard.

To add an emoticon to your message, do the following:

1. Click, tap, or use the arrow keys to move the cursor to the location in the message where you want the emoticon to appear.

2. Select emoticons from the Windows Touch keyboard. If you are using a keyboard and mouse, you may not see how to use the Touch keyboard while in Desktop mode. Right-click the taskbar and select Show Touch Keyboard Button. Now you can manually select the keyboard when it is needed.

3. Select the category and the symbol you like. You can add as many as you like while the emoticons fly-out panel is on the screen. To select an emoticon, do one of the following:

    *   Click it with your mouse.

    *   Tap it with your finger or stylus.

4. Continue writing your email.

 NOTE   While working with formatting, it can be easy to get carried away. On the Format tab there is a prominent Undo button that can be used to roll back recent changes. You can also select a portion of text and then select the Font Formatting down arrow to reveal additional font tools (refer to Figure 17.11). Select Clear Formatting to return to the default theme font choices.

Attaching a Photo, File, Table, or Hyperlink to Your Message

To send one or more files, such as a photo, with your email, and select the **Insert** tab. As shown in Figure 17.13, you can select from several common attachments:

*   **Attach** will open File Explorer to the Documents folder, which will allow you to navigate to the file you would like to send. File Explorer will be a familiar tool for navigating through the folders on your system and then choosing a file if you have used Windows in the past.

*   **Pictures** will open File Explorer to the Pictures folder, which will allow you to navigate to the file you would like to send.

- **Table** will open a new Table tab with basic tools that allow you to create and format a table on the fly.

- **Link** will open a small dialog box with two text fields: **Text to Display**—the visible text that can be selected to launch the link in your message, and **Address**—the actual link to a website or network resource.

Format	Insert	Options		🗑 Discard ➤ Send

📎 Attach   ⊞ Table   🖼 Pictures   🔗 Link

From: alanlwright@outlook.com

To: Cc & Bcc

Subject

Hello Fred,

You need to see this! I have attached the latest invoice from our client.

-Alan

Sent from Mail for Windows 10

FIGURE 17.13

Select from various attachment types for emails using the Insert tab.

Checking Spelling in Your Message

If you are even mildly embarrassed to have an email you sent appear in your recipient's Inbox with spelling errors or typing mistakes, it makes sense to take advantage of the built-in spell checking in Windows 10. The Mail app will show familiar proofing marks for misspelled words. These marks can be disabled or hidden. You can also trigger suggestions for misspelled words.

To manage Windows spelling features within the Mail app, follow these steps:

1. From the message pane of the Mail app, select the **Options** tab.

2. To start the spellchecker, select the **Spelling** button, as shown in Figure 17.14. The Mail app will start from you cursor and show suggested spellings for unidentified words. Select a word to replace your mistake. You can also add words to the Windows dictionary by selecting **+(your word)**.

3. Select the down arrow next to the Spelling button. Two Proofing and Language settings are available here. Use a checkbox to enable these options: **Hide All Proofing Marks** and **Hide Proofing Marks in Selected Text**.

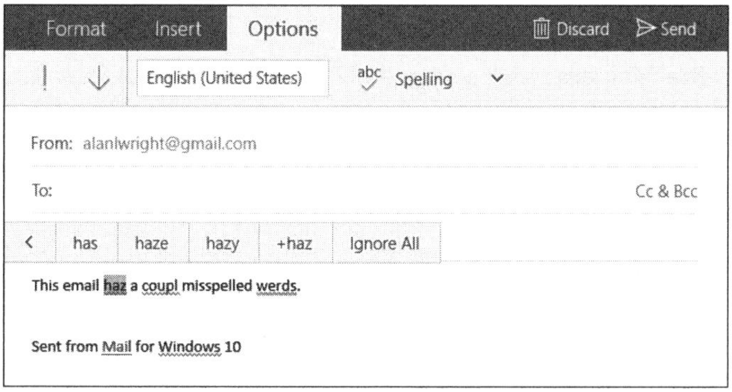

Format   Insert   **Options**   🗑 Discard   ▷ Send

! ↓   English (United States)   abc Spelling   ⌄

From: alanlwright@gmail.com

To: Cc & Bcc

< | has | haze | hazy | +haz | Ignore All

This email haz a coupl misspelled werds.

Sent from Mail for Windows 10

FIGURE 17.14

Let spell checker save you from embarrassing mistakes in the Mail app.

Managing Your Inbox

With the Mail app in Windows 10, you have many practical tools and techniques at your disposal for managing your email.

Pinning Accounts to the Start Menu

The Mail app is a live tile that appears in the Start menu by default in Windows 10. The live tile will show a number for new unread messages and, when using a larger sized tile, the most recent emails will appear in the live tile. While this is a handy way to keep track of new emails, it may not be as useful when you have multiple email accounts. In this case, pinning each individual account, as shown in Figure 17.15, allows the live tile functionality to show each account separately.

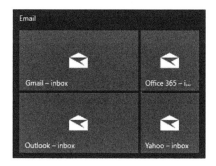

FIGURE 17.15

Pin separate accounts to the Start menu to monitor new emails for each account.

To pin an email account to the Start menu, follow these steps:

1. Open the Mail app and select the **All Accounts** icon from the hamburger menu (refer to Figure 17.1).

2. Press and hold on a touchscreen or right-click with a mouse to bring up the context menu, as shown in Figure 17.16.

3. Select **Pin to Start**. A new tile is added to the bottom of the Start menu.

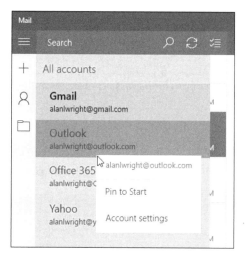

FIGURE 17.16

Select Pin to Start to quickly add an email account to the Start menu.

 TIP Consider grouping tiles for email accounts and positioning the group in a convenient location on the Start menu to benefit from the live tile notifications. Organizing your Start menu is considered in Chapter 3, "Optimizing the Start Menu."

Flagging Messages

Flags can be very useful when you want to make sure you can find an important email again later.

To flag a message, do one of the following three options:

• Hover over a message in the message list using your mouse pointer to select the flag icon.

- Select the flag tool to the right of the subject line in an open email message.

- Open the App Commands bar and insert a flag.

Printing Emails

From time to time, you might need to print emails as part of your management process. Perhaps you want to keep hard copies of receipts or information needs to be filed away in case questions arise later. When you need to print an email, the Mail app hands the particulars off to Windows.

To print an email, follow these steps:

1. Select an email you want to print.

2. Select the Actions button (**...**) on the Commands bar, as shown in Figure 17.17.

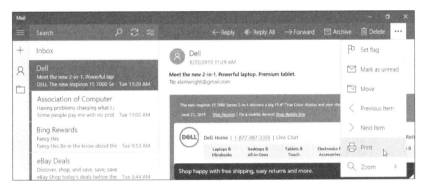

FIGURE 17.17

Select Print from the Actions menu in the Mail app when you need to print an email.

3. Select **Print**. The Windows 10 Print pane will open.

4. From the list of printers, select the printer you want to use. You will see a preview of the print job with options for number of copies, page range, and size (see Figure 17.18).

5. Select **More Settings** to review options that are unique to your printer for paper, color, orientation, and source settings.

6. Make your choices and select **Print**.

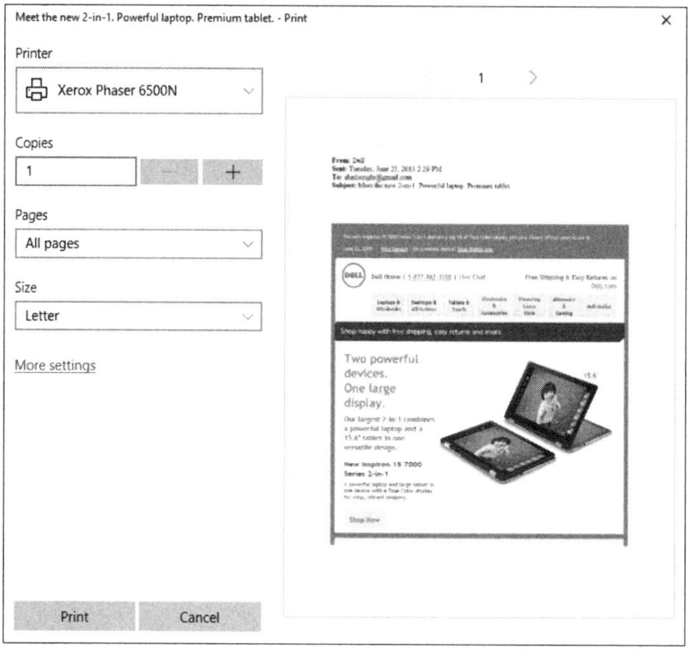

FIGURE 17.18

Make selections to control how your email will print from the Windows 10 Print pane.

Future Improvements

The Mail app will continue to be developed and improved. At the time of this writing, there are anticipated features that are expected to show up in the Mail app through updates. These features will help you to better manage your emails in the Mail app.

Some anticipated updates include

- **Folder creation**—Folders you have created online can be used to organize your email within the Mail app using the Move tool. While the Mail app does not offer the option to create new folders as of the time of this writing, don't be surprised to see this feature return to the Mail app by means of an app update.

- **Group Messages by Conversation**— Group Messages by Conversation is a feature that existed in the Mail app for Windows 8.1. This useful feature allowed you to switch between viewing all emails in chronological order or grouped together when they are part of the same conversation.

- **Flagged emails view**—Flagged emails are useful, but the Mail app does not offer a means of viewing all flagged emails together. This useful way of filtering your email to view messages that had been flagged was included in the Mail app for Windows 8.1, and it would be a surprise to see it not return.

THE ABSOLUTE MINIMUM

- When you're writing an email, the Format, Insert, and Options tabs include multiple formatting and email authoring tools, including colors, attachments, font choices, and hyperlinks.

- Use drag-and-drop to move messages from your Inbox to folders you have set up.

- Pin separate email accounts to the Start menu to keep tabs on each account individually.

- Use flags to keep track of important or time-sensitive emails regardless of which folder they might be in.

- Use the Actions menu to print emails from the Mail app to any of your installed printers.

18

MANAGING YOUR CALENDAR

In today's digital society, people rely on calendars for much more than simply confirming what day it is. We rely on our calendars to make sure we keep appointments, track activity or work, get reminders, lock down scheduling and appointments, and much, much more. All calendars tend to have the same basic functions, and we expect them to be extremely easy to use. The Calendar app included with Windows 10 is no exception, and in this chapter you will learn how to leverage the features built in to it. For example, you can synchronize your calendar with calendars you maintain online. You can create events and respond to invitations in the Calendar app, see those events appear in your online calendar, and invite your contacts listed in the People app.

The Outlook Calendar app in Windows 10 is a modern universal app that is actually linked with the Outlook Mail app. This app can be upgraded at any time to introduce new features. So do not be alarmed if the interface is slightly different from what appears in this chapter due to updates. To be sure you can easily follow the instructions in this chapter, consider reviewing some of the content in Chapter 5, "Working with Windows Apps."

Starting the Calendar App

To start the Calendar app, select the Calendar tile on the Start screen, as shown in Figure 18.1. When the Calendar app opens, the view you last used—daily, weekly, or monthly—appears automatically, as shown in Figure 18.2.

The Calendar app

FIGURE 18.1

You start the Calendar app by selecting the Calendar tile on the Start screen.

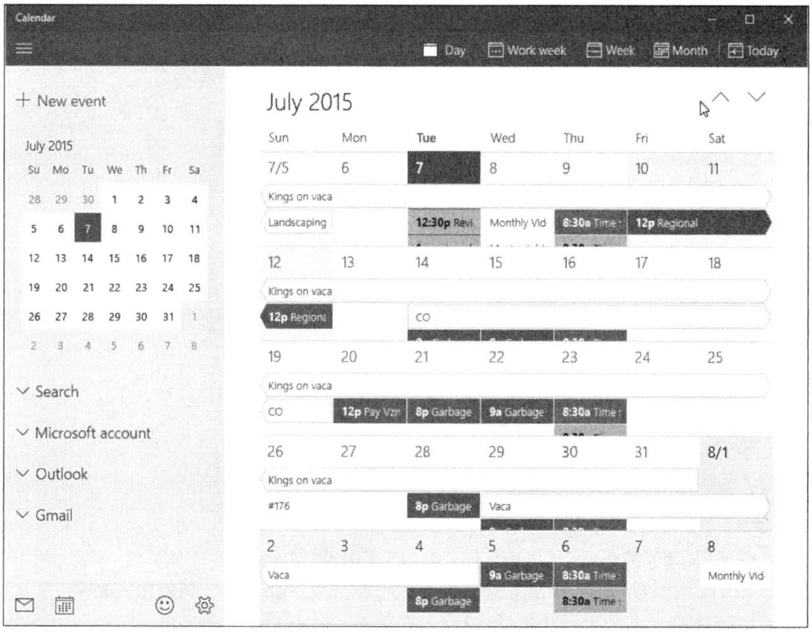

FIGURE 18.2

The monthly view appears automatically because it was the view last used.

Controlling the Calendar View

You can review your calendar in different views: Day and Multi-Day, Work Week, Week, and Month. You can easily change from one view to another. To do so, select the view you prefer, as shown in Figure 18.3.

FIGURE 18.3

You change views by making a choice from the options available.

The Day view includes a drop-down menu to choose from multiday combinations, as shown in Figure 18.4. Select from 2-day up to 6-day views that start with the currently selected day.

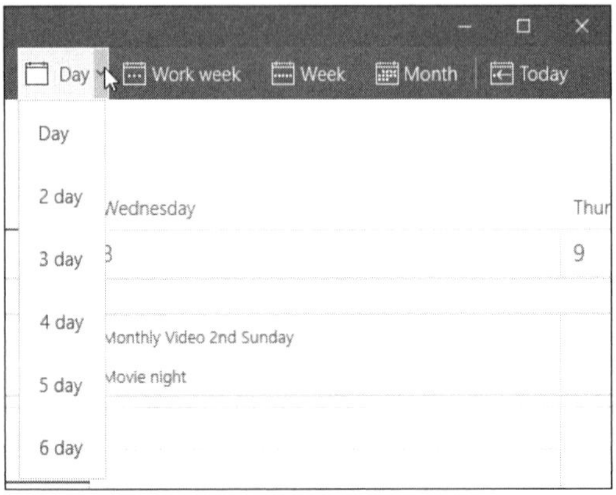

FIGURE 18.4

The Day view includes multiday variations.

The Work Week view displays a traditional Monday through Friday work week with details for each day similar to the Week view. All-day events show at the top, while scheduled events appear below in an area that can be scrolled through. Subtle shading indicates work hours. The Week view shows up to 24 hours in a day and seven days of the week. The default setting uses Sunday as the first day of the week. In the section "Customizing the Calendar View," you learn how to change the day the week starts on, as well as a number of other settings. The Work Week view is shown in Figure 18.5, whereas the Week view is shown in Figure 18.6.

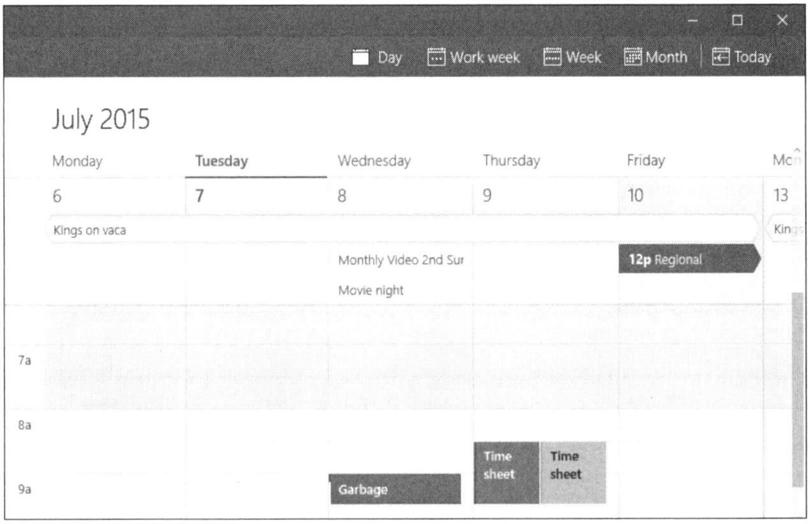

FIGURE 18.5

The Work Week view provides detail for each work day of the week.

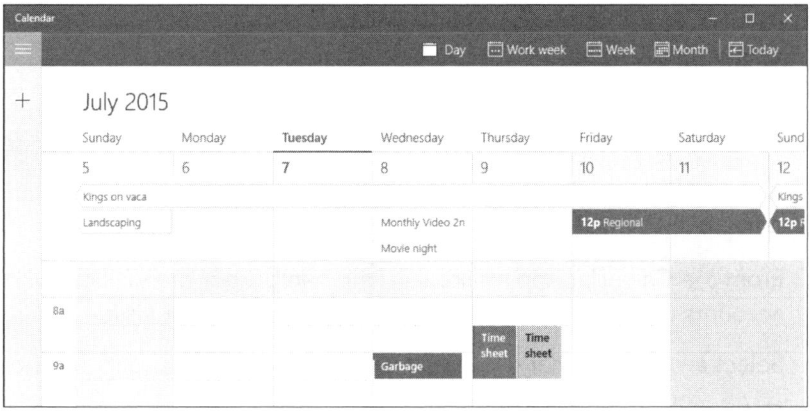

FIGURE 18.6

The Week view shows the current week, plus a portion of the first day of the next week.

You can scroll to a different date from any day, week, or month view by swiping, clicking your mouse, or scrolling with the mouse wheel. When using a mouse, each of these views includes arrow buttons located above the calendar and to the right that will hide until you move your mouse cursor (refer to Figure 18.2). Select these arrows to jump to the next or previous day, week, or month. You can quickly switch to a different date by expanding the hamburger menu to display a monthly calendar. Use this calendar to navigate to a different month and select the date to which you want to switch, as shown in Figure 18.7. At any time you can select the Today button above the calendar view to jump to the present day (refer to Figure 18.3).

FIGURE 18.7

Use the calendar to quickly jump to a different date or to today.

Setting Calendar Colors

The Calendar app uses one color for events related to your account and additional colors for birthdays and holidays related to the account. A different set of colors is used for events from each additional account you set up in the Calendar app.

To change the colors used for each calendar, as well as to hide or show certain calendars, follow these steps:

1. From the Calendar app, make sure the hamburger menu is open. A list of all accounts currently used with the Calendar app will be visible.

2. Select an account that is displayed to expand the calendars for the account.

3. Colored checkboxes indicate the color used to display each calendar. Select a checkbox to disable the color and calendar. Right-click a calendar to choose from a palette of colors to update the color choice, as shown in Figure 18.8.

FIGURE 18.8

You can specify a different color for each calendar you've added to the app.

 TIP The color palette is determined by another setting. Select Settings and then select Calendar Settings. Scroll down to Calendar Color Options to switch between Bright Colors and Light Colors.

Synchronizing with Other Calendars

If you maintain a calendar online, you can synchronize that calendar to the Calendar app. You can synchronize the Calendar app with Microsoft Outlook, Google, iCloud, Microsoft Exchange, Office 365, and others. Events you create in the Calendar app will be synced to online calendars and subsequently to other devices that use those calendars.

When you synchronize multiple calendars, you will see a list of accounts in the hamburger menu of the Calendar app, while the calendars are all merged into the main calendar view. You can see all your appointments booked on all your calendars in one place, including appointments on family members' calendars or work or corporate appointments.

The Calendar and Mail apps are linked, and they share the same tools to add accounts. To add an online calendar to the Calendar app, follow these steps:

1. Select **Settings** from the hamburger menu to open the Settings pane shown in Figure 18.9.

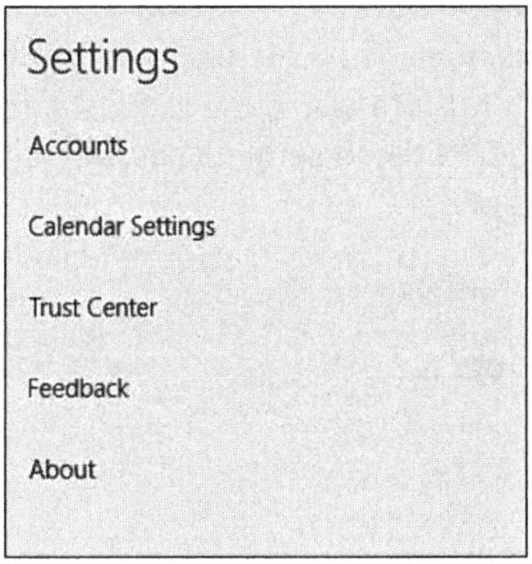

Settings

Accounts

Calendar Settings

Trust Center

Feedback

About

FIGURE 18.9

Add online calendars using Accounts from the Settings pane.

2. Select **Accounts**. A list of connected accounts is shown.

3. Select **Add Account**. A pop-up window, Choose an Account, appears, as shown in Figure 18.10.

4. Select the account type you wish to add and follow prompts to add the credentials for each account. Refer to Chapter 16, "Setting Up the Mail App," for details for adding specific account types to the Mail and Calendar apps.

FIGURE 18.10

Many types of online email and calendar accounts are supported.

After an account is added, you can return to the accounts pane to update any settings and change what is synced. For example, Figure 18.11 shows the Sync options for a Gmail account. The Calendar and Contacts are both set to sync. The advanced account settings are also expanded, showing the calendar server in this case. Knowing how to find these settings can be helpful if troubleshooting sync issues for an online calendar.

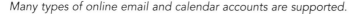

FIGURE 18.11

Manage what gets synced or update settings for online calendars from the Sync Options for an account.

Adding Events to Your Calendar

You can easily enter a new event into your calendar and even generate invites to others for the event. You create your new event by selecting the date of your new event. Then you enter the details about it. You can quickly enter most of the details of your event by choosing from ready-made lists, such as the day, hour, frequency, duration of the event, and if the event recurs. This makes it easy to create new events.

To enter a new event directly into your calendar using the day, week, or month views, follow these steps:

1. Open the Calendar app.

2. From any calendar view, select a blank space on the date of your event in the calendar. A small pane will appear for a new calendar entry on that date. If the event will be multiday or recurring, select the first date. Enter a name for your event. Select the beginning time of your event. Figure 18.12 shows that Subject has been replaced by the event "Drop Kia off."

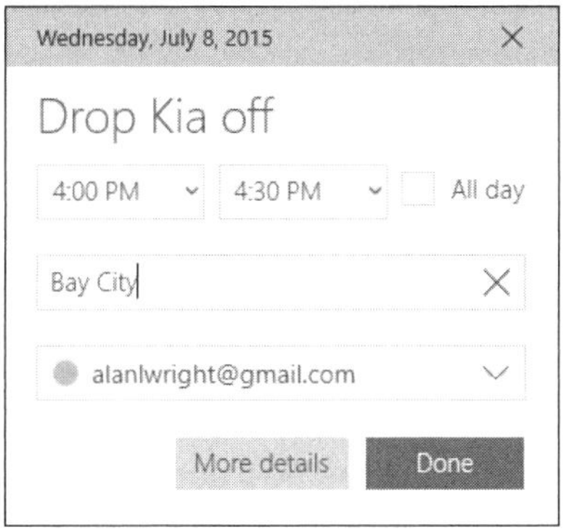

FIGURE 18.12

You can quickly add an event to your calendar with a few basic details.

3. Check the End time for your event and update it if needed. If the event is a general reminder for that day or it is related to an entire day, select the **All Day** checkbox.

4. Select the down arrow to the right of the account to change which calendar this is associated with (see Figure 18.13).

5. For most entries this may be all that is needed, and you can select **Done**. The entry appears on your calendar, and you will receive reminders based on your Notification settings in Windows 10. To add more details, continue to step 6.

6. To add additional options, select **More Details**. The calendar view will switch to the Details view for your calendar event, as shown in Figure 18.13.

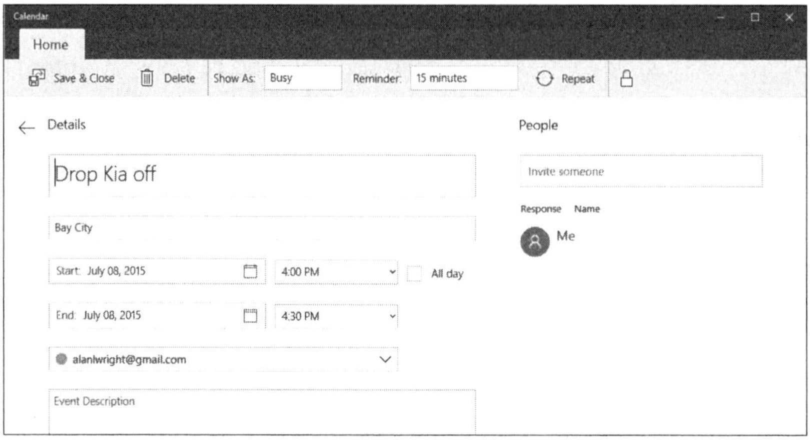

FIGURE 18.13

You can add many more details to a calendar event from the Details view.

7. From the Details view you can

- Change start dates and times and add end dates.

- Use the **Show As** field to choose between Free, Tentative, Busy, or Out of Office.

- Update the **Reminder** field using increments that range from None to 1 Week.

- Enable **Repeat**. You will see additional options appear, as shown in Figure 18.14. Select the **Start** date and then choose a repeat cycle. Weekly is shown, but you can select from many other cycles. Select an **End** date or leave as Never.

- Set the event as **Private** by selecting the padlock.

- Add an **Event Description**.

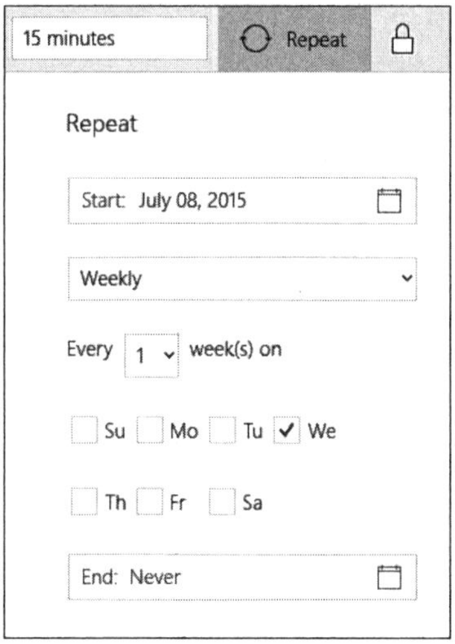

FIGURE 18.14

You can select Repeat details for recurring calendar events.

8. Select **Save & Close** to save changes to your calendar event. If this is an event that involves others, continue to step 9.

9. To invite additional contacts, select the text field under People that is labeled Invite Someone. As you start entering letters, contacts will appear from your list of contacts in the People app. Select contacts to add them to the event. If you are inviting an email address that is not a contact, type in the full address and select Use This Address:*email address*. When finished select **Send**, as shown in Figure 18.15.

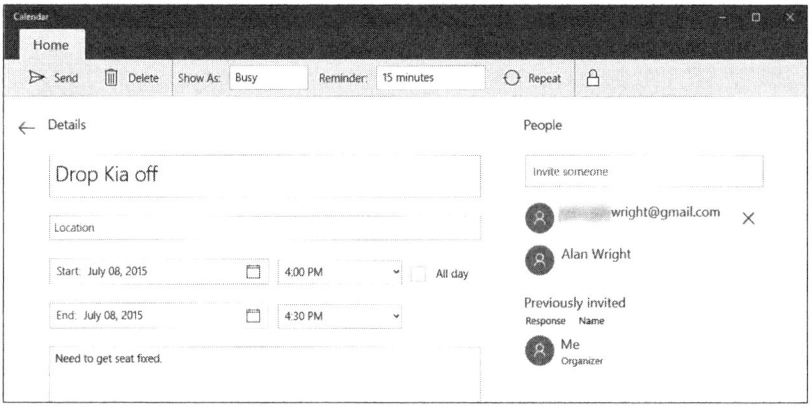

FIGURE 18.15

When creating events that involve others, you can invite your contacts.

10. Invitees will receive an email with the details as shown in Figure 18.16. Invitees can respond by accepting, declining, or indicating tentative or even alternate time responses. Track responses by checking the Details view of the calendar entry.

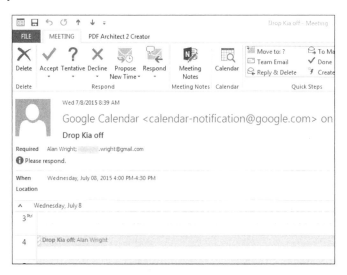

FIGURE 18.16

Invitees will receive a calendar invitation, which enables them to easily update their calendar and indicate their availability.

 NOTE   Don't forget this important point: the event you create will also appear in the calendar on the site of the service whose calendar you choose. So if you select, for example, your Outlook account, the event appears on all devices syncing to your Outlook calendar as well as the calendar at Outlook.com.

To view or modify an existing calendar entry, select the entry to open directly to the Details view (refer to Figure 18.13). At any time you can also create a new entry by selecting New Event from the hamburger menu in the Calendar app to go straight to a blank Details view.

Customizing the Calendar View

The Calendar app gives you control over how your calendar is displayed. Not everyone has the same work week schedule, and many people work different hours than others. Your calendar should take your schedule into account.

To modify the calendar view, follow these steps:

1. Select **Settings** from the hamburger menu.

2. Select **Calendar Settings** from the Settings pane (refer to Figure 18.9).

3. In the Calendar Settings pane, shown in Figure 18.17, update your **First Day of Week** to change how the Week view will appear.

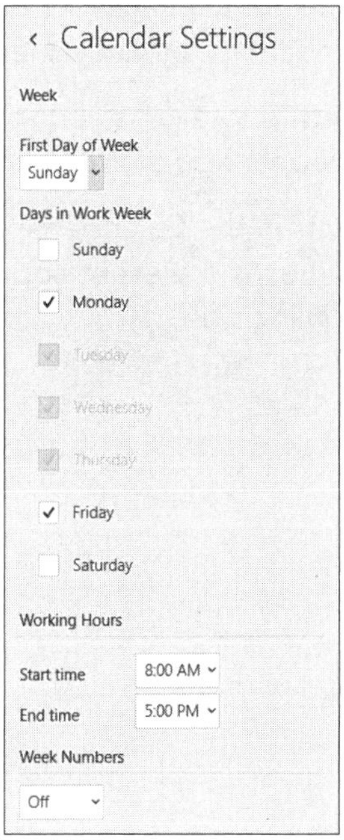

FIGURE 18.17

When using Outlook and Exchange-based calendars, you can invite contacts to an event.

4. Use the checkboxes under **Days in Work Week** to select which days you work. This affects the Work Week view.

5. Under **Working Hours**, select your start and end times. This will affect the shading used on both Week and Work Week views.

6. You can enable **Week Numbers**.

7. Select outside of the Calendar Settings pane to close it. Your new settings are immediately applied to the calendar views.

THE ABSOLUTE MINIMUM

- You can synchronize your Windows 10 calendar with many online calendars including Outlook, Live, Google, iCloud, Office 365, and Microsoft Exchange. This gives you the ability to maintain your online calendars as you always do but bring all your calendars together in one place in Windows 10.

- You select people to invite to events you schedule from the list of persons consolidated in your People app in Windows 10.

- You can schedule events in the Calendar app on the online calendars you synchronize with. This means the event appears on both the calendar in Windows 10 and the online calendar.

19

SHARING YOUR WINDOWS COMPUTER WITH OTHERS

Some people feel the easiest way to share a Windows 10 computer with other users is to provide the username and password they use to whomever they want to share with. Even worse, they might choose to not use a password at all, essentially leaving the device open for anyone to pick up and use. It is increasingly common to see devices used for online purchases and bill paying; you might even have credit card information stored for Windows or Xbox purchases. Additionally, you may have photos, documents, and login access saved for various social networks. Given all these variables, it makes sense to keep your device secure and limit access to individuals you trust. Rather than employing the risky methods mentioned previously, take advantage of some of the built-in security features of Windows 10. Your wallet and online identity may thank you later!

The best way to share your Windows 10 computer is to create a separate account for anyone to whom you want to provide access. The process to create an account is easy, with just a few settings that require some thought. This chapter also shows you how to choose between and configure the various password options available in Windows 10 and how to remove an account and keep your computer secure.

Windows 10 Users and Account Basics

You can give as many persons access to your Windows 10 computer as needed. The portrait for every user account you've configured appears on the Sign-in screen for each new user, as shown in Figure 19.1.

FIGURE 19.1

You might have a number of persons sharing your Windows 10 computer.

A new user in Windows 10 is automatically created as a *standard* user. A standard user contrasts with an *administrator* in that the standard user does not have access to some of the more sensitive settings, including those related to security. This means only an administrator can add new users to Windows 10.

To try out and then put to use the instructions and walk-throughs in this chapter, you must be logged in as an administrator-type user. If you are not sure if your account is an administrator type, select the search box on the taskbar, type "account," and select Manage Your Account. Your account type will be indicated below your name. If you find your account is not an administrator type, try one of these fixes:

- If you were not the person who set up your computer, ask the person who did to change your account to an administrator type. (You cannot promote yourself to an administrator.)

- If you did set up Windows 10, the account you created when you installed Windows is an administrator type. Sign in with that account.

Any person who wants to use Windows 10 must sign in with a valid account and a password. The account can be one of two types. A local account is used only with the computer where it was created. A Microsoft account is tied to an email address and is stored with Microsoft on its servers across the Internet. This means that if you're authorized to log in to the device beforehand by an administrator, you can use a Microsoft account on any Windows 10 device anywhere, including servers, desktops, laptops, phones, and tablets.

If you are the person who installs Windows, you can select which type of account to use to sign in to Windows 10 the first time. If someone creates an account for your use with Windows 10, be sure you understand which type of account is created for you. If you have a choice, it makes sense to use a Microsoft account. Here's why:

- All your Windows 10 preferences and settings, such as the color of the Start screen, a record of all the apps you downloaded, and the tiles pinned to your Start menu, are stored with your Windows 10 account. This means your preferences can be applied to any Windows 10 devices you sign in to. You don't need to spend time setting up any new computer you use. Refer to Chapter 8, "Tweaking Windows to Reflect Your Personality," to learn how to specify which settings and preferences are saved with your account.

- Installing apps from the Windows Store requires a Microsoft account even if they are free. While you can add credentials for a Microsoft account to an app using its settings pane, it generally makes more sense to just log in to the device with a Microsoft account

- Signing in to Windows 10 with a Microsoft account automatically signs you in to any app you downloaded from the Windows Store that requires you to sign in.

- Signing in to Windows 10 with a Microsoft account automatically signs you in to any website that requires a Microsoft account. If you start Internet Explorer and browse to a site such as www.outlook.com, you do not need to sign in to those sites.

- If you forget your password, you can always reset it through Microsoft account services. If you forget the password to a local account and you cannot recall it through one of the reminder features, you might need to create a new local account.

You can create a Microsoft account before you begin to install Windows 10 by visiting *signup.live.com* (see Figure 19.2). If you already have an Outlook.com or Live account, you are ready to sign in to Windows 10. Use the same credentials you use to sign in to those Microsoft online services to sign in to Windows 10. Your account must first be added to the Windows 10 device to which you intend to sign in. This is covered next, in the "Adding a New User" section.

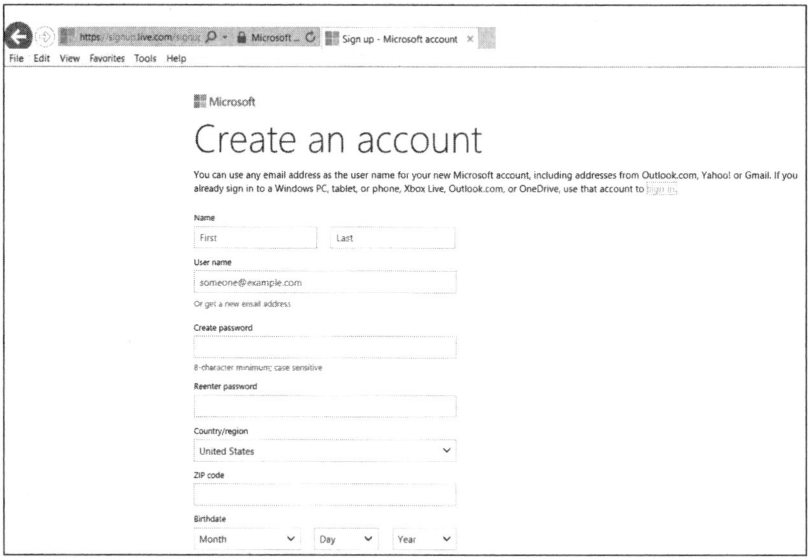

Sign up - Microsoft account
File Edit View Favorites Tools Help
Microsoft
Create an account
You can use any email address as the user name for your new Microsoft account, including addresses from Outlook.com, Yahoo! or Gmail. If you already sign in to a Windows PC, tablet, or phone, Xbox Live, Outlook.com, or OneDrive, use that account to sign in.
Name
First
Last
User name
someone@example.com
Or get a new email address
Create password
8-character minimum; case sensitive
Reenter password
Country/region
United States
ZIP code
Birthdate
Month
Day
Year

FIGURE 19.2

You can create a Microsoft account before you add the account to your Windows 10 device.

NOTE If you installed Windows 10, you are granted administrator rights, which means Windows 10 enables you to do anything with the software. Most relevant with administrator rights is that you can add new accounts, thereby giving other people access to Windows 10.

Adding a New User

Before you start the process of adding a new user to Windows 10, you should keep a few things in mind:

- You must be signed in with an administrator-type account. For information about administrator-type accounts, see the "Changing a User's Type" section later in this chapter.

- You must select whether the new user has a Microsoft account or a local account. You can find information about account types earlier in the "Windows 10 Users and Account Basics" section.

Because there are differences in the process to create a local account versus a Windows 10 account, there are separate walk-throughs for each in the next two sections.

Adding a New User with a Local Account

To add a new user account that will be recognized only on a single Windows 10 device, create a local account by following these steps:

1. From the Start menu, select **Settings** to open the Settings app.

2. Select **Accounts** from the settings categories.

3. Select **Family & Other Users**. As shown in Figure 19.3, you will see two groups of users: Your Family and Other Users.

FIGURE 19.3

Adding new local accounts to your device starts with adding someone under Other Users in the Settings app.

4. Under Other Users select **Add Someone Else to This PC**.

5. Under How Will This Person Sign In, you will be asked for an email address of the new user. Since this is a local account, select the text below that says: **The Person I Want to Add Doesn't Have an Email Address**.

6. Under Let's Create Your Account, you are invited to set up a new email address. Instead, select the **Add a User Without a Microsoft Account** link at the bottom of the screen, as shown in Figure 19.4. Although Microsoft does not recommend this, it is not dangerous, and in some situations a local account is actually required.

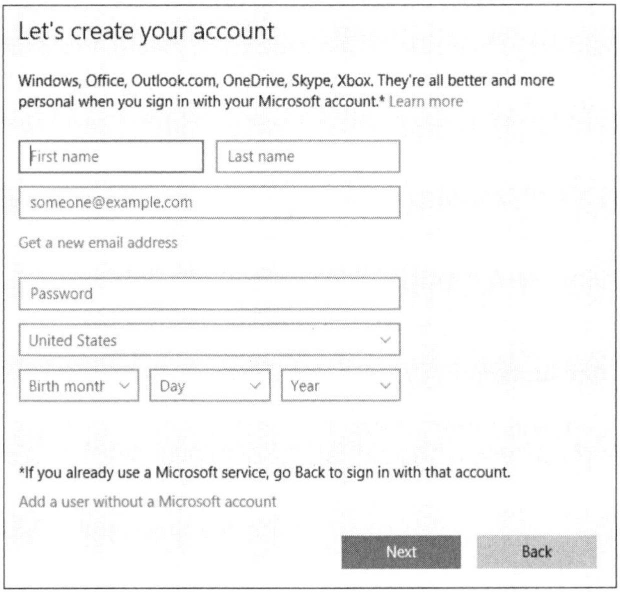

Let's create your account

Windows, Office, Outlook.com, OneDrive, Skype, Xbox. They're all better and more personal when you sign in with your Microsoft account.* Learn more

| First name | Last name |

someone@example.com

Get a new email address

Password

United States

Birth month | Day | Year

*If you already use a Microsoft service, go Back to sign in with that account.

Add a user without a Microsoft account

Next   Back

FIGURE 19.4

You might feel like you are living dangerously when choosing to log in without using a Microsoft account.

7. As shown in Figure 19.5, enter a username (20 characters max; any combination of numbers and letters, including spaces; no /\[]":;|<>+=,?*%@), a password (any characters, including numbers, letters, spaces, and symbols), and a password hint into the fields provided. Select **Next**.

8. You return to the Family & Other Users screen that appeared with step 3. The listing should now include your new user.

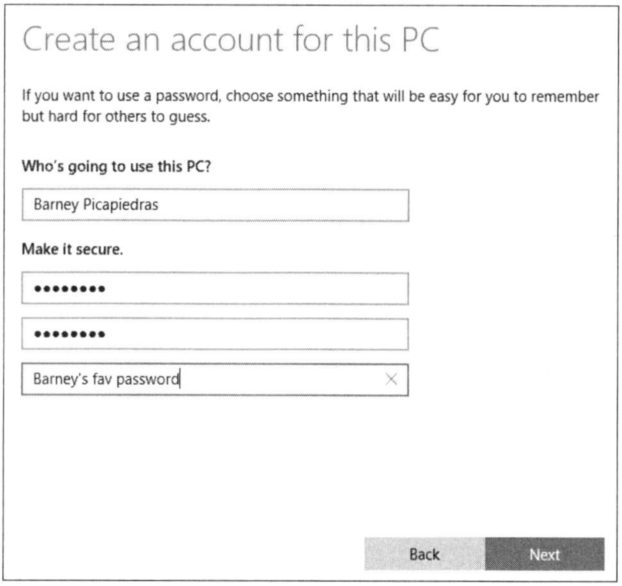

FIGURE 19.5

You need to supply a username, password, and password hint to create a local account.

Adding a New User with a Microsoft Account

There are two scenarios in which you add a new user to your Windows 10 computer with a Microsoft account. You can add an account that already has been created, or you can add a user and create the user's Microsoft account at the same time. Both scenarios are covered in this walk-through.

To add an account that can be used with any Windows 10 device, follow these steps to create a Microsoft account:

1. From the Start menu, select **Settings** to open the Settings app.

2. Select **Accounts** from the settings categories.

3. Select **Family & Other Users**. You will see two groups of users: Family and Other Users. If you have added a local user following the steps in the previous section, your screen should look something like the one shown in Figure 19.6.

4. Under Other Users, select **Add Someone Else to This PC**.

FIGURE 19.6

The Family & Other Users screen enables you to manage most aspects of the accounts authorized to use your Windows 10 device.

5. Under How Will This Person Sign In, you will be asked for an email address of the new user. If the user you want to add does not have a Microsoft account and you would like to create one, select **The Person I Want to Add Doesn't Have an Email Address**. Then skip to step 7.

If the user already has a Microsoft account, type the email address associated with that account into the Email address box. Then click **Next**. Windows attempts to verify the email address you entered.

6. If Windows does not recognize the email you entered, you are prompted to create a new Microsoft account. If you want to create a Microsoft account with this email address, skip to step 7. If you want to change or correct the email address you entered, click **Cancel**. You will be returned to the screen described in step 3.

If the email address is verified, the screen shown in Figure 19.7 appears. Select **Finish**; then skip to step 11.

7. To create a new Microsoft account, you are prompted to provide your name, email, and password (see Figure 19.8). The email can be an existing email account that is not currently linked to a Microsoft account, or you can create a new Outlook.com account. You must provide a birth date, which is used to determine age appropriate content for the user. Click **Next**.

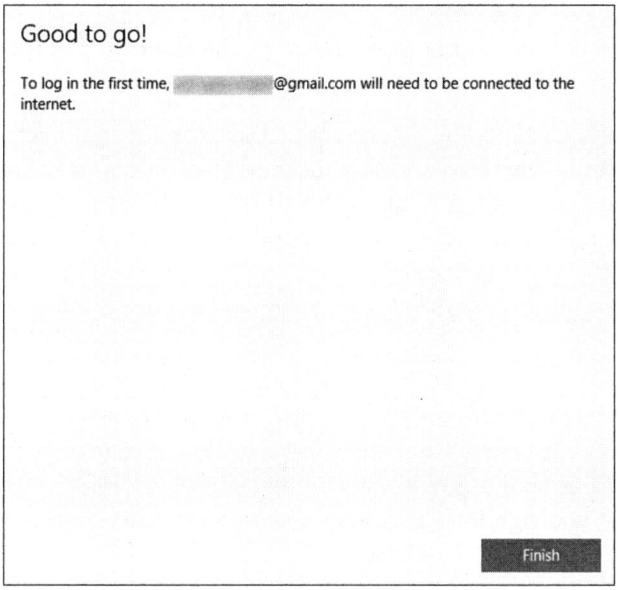

Good to go!

To log in the first time, ███████@gmail.com will need to be connected to the internet.

Finish

FIGURE 19.7

Your work is done if you enter an email address associated with a working Microsoft account.

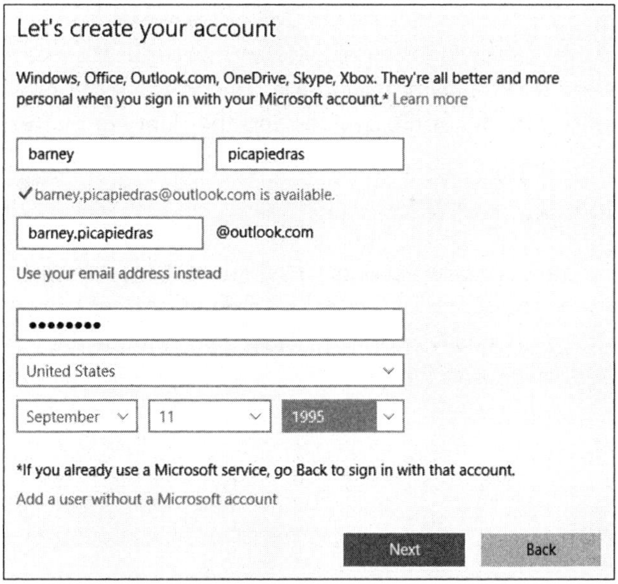

Let's create your account

Windows, Office, Outlook.com, OneDrive, Skype, Xbox. They're all better and more personal when you sign in with your Microsoft account.* Learn more

| barney | picapiedras |

✓ barney.picapiedras@outlook.com is available.

| barney.picapiedras | @outlook.com |

Use your email address instead

| •••••••• |

| United States ⌄ |

| September ⌄ | 11 ⌄ | 1995 ⌄ |

*If you already use a Microsoft service, go Back to sign in with that account.

Add a user without a Microsoft account

Next   Back

FIGURE 19.8

You can create a new Microsoft account from scratch.

8. You are prompted to add security info. This can be a phone number or alternate email that can be used to verify your identity. This is used for account security—at least one alternative contact option is required. Click **Next**.

9. You are asked to allow Microsoft to use your account information to provide enhanced advertising and to subscribe to promotional offers from Microsoft. Leave these selected to allow this or uncheck the boxes to avoid extra emails and targeted advertising. Select **Next** to agree to Microsoft's terms of use and create the new Microsoft account.

10. You are returned to the screen where you started at step 3. You should see the new account you created in the Other Users list.

When adding new accounts to your device, you can also use the category of Family. Accounts created as Family users will be linked to your Microsoft account, and they will appear automatically in the list of Family users on other Windows devices that you sign into. Enabling access is a simple matter of selecting their account and then clicking **Allow**.

Family users can also be created as Child accounts. Child accounts are designed to have restricted permissions on the device, and you can configure settings for child accounts that are managed by your Microsoft account when accessing your online Microsoft account. Settings include blocking inappropriate websites, blocking specific websites, blocking inappropriate apps and games based on their age, setting limits on screen time for each day of the week, and getting weekly reports sent to your email showing their activity and websites they have visited. This can be an excellent tool for parents who are concerned about how much time their children spend with electronic devices and the dangers that exist on the Internet.

Creating a PIN or Picture Password

When you create your new account in Windows 10, you need to supply a password, but you can use one of two newer sign-in options, replacing the use of the password after you initially supply it. These two options are PIN and picture password. Besides saving you the repetitive stress of entering your password often, these two new options are impressive, and you'll want to use them to impress your friends!

 NOTE In some cases you might not see the options to use a PIN or picture password. This generally is caused by a stricter password policy required for using Exchange or Office 365 accounts. This is intentional because complex passwords are considered more secure and harder to guess. In other cases you may have been invited to create a PIN when first signing into a new device.

Adding a PIN to Your Account

A PIN is a 4-digit number you use to identify yourself when you sign in to Windows. Any 4-digit combination of numerals is acceptable, including repeats such as 9999. A PIN is particularly useful to tablet users who normally don't have a physical keyboard. On a tablet, a virtual keyboard appears on the screen as you sign in to Windows, enabling you to enter just your PIN to access Windows.

To add a PIN to your account, follow these steps:

1. From the Start menu, select **Settings** to open the Settings app.

2. Select **Accounts** from the settings categories.

3. Select **Sign-In Options**.

4. Select **Add** under PIN.

5. You first must verify your password. Enter your password and click OK. The Set Up a PIN screen appears, as shown in Figure 19.9.

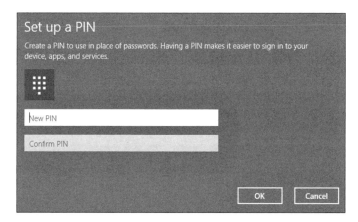

Set up a PIN

Create a PIN to use in place of passwords. Having a PIN makes it easier to sign in to your device, apps, and services.

New PIN

Confirm PIN

OK   Cancel

FIGURE 19.9

You can enter a PIN (and confirm it) to use as a substitute for your password.

6. Enter your PIN, and then enter it again in the Confirm PIN box.

7. Select **Finish**.

Adding a Picture Password to Your Account

If you enjoy drawing mustaches and other funny shapes on pictures of your friends, family, and pets, this is the password option for you. A picture password is a combination of a picture and touch gestures. To set up a picture password, you choose a picture from your Pictures folder and then make three gestures, which can be your choice of tapping or drawing a line or circle. Windows records the position of the gestures, as well as the order in which you made them. This combination creates the picture password.

TIP It's helpful if you have a picture in mind to use as your picture password. If you don't, you should locate or take a new photo and then load it onto your computer before you start this process. A good candidate photo has a number of recognizable items, as opposed to a broad, landscape photo. This way, it's easier to remember the objects on which you drew the required symbols.

To use a picture password with your Windows 10 account, follow these steps:

1. From the Start menu, select **Settings** to open the Settings app.

2. Select **Accounts** from the settings categories.

3. Select **Sign-In Options**.

4. Under Picture Password, select **Add**.

5. You first must verify your password, as shown in Figure 19.10. Enter your password and click **OK**.

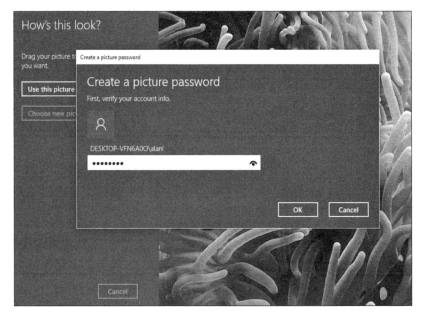

FIGURE 19.10

The first step in creating a picture password is to verify you are the owner of the account.

6. Select **Choose New Picture**.

7. Your screen displays the photos in your Picture folders. Look through the photos to find one to use as your picture password. Select the photo to use, and then select **Open**.

8. The picture you selected should be on the screen. The picture password screen uses only about three-quarters of the picture you chose. Click and drag or touch and drag the picture directly on the screen to a position you like. Select **Use This Picture**.

9. The Set Up Your Gesture screen should be visible. This is the screen where you draw the three gestures. Windows asks you to draw them twice to be sure you can recall what they are and where they are drawn. Draw the three gestures. The large number highlights itself with each gesture you draw. Figure 19.11 shows the second gesture is being confirmed.

   Select **Start Over** if you want to redraw all the gestures. If you want to save creating a picture password for another time, click **Cancel**.

10. After you confirm the three gestures for the picture password, you will see a Congratulations screen. Click **Finish**, and you are then returned to your account setting screen. You can sign out to try your new picture password.

FIGURE 19.11

You can see the gestures on the screen when you redraw each as part of the verification step.

Making Changes to User Accounts

After you've created an account and a user has used the account to sign in to Windows 10, you can still make changes to it. You can change the account to an administrator from a standard type, or vice versa. You can also remove an account.

Changing a User's Type

You might want to give certain users administrative access to Windows 10 so they can install software or change security settings. Closely related, you might want to remove an individual's administrator rights and instead give them standard user capabilities. Making either change is easy.

 TIP Best practice is to leave new users as standard users. This prevents someone from making changes to the way your computer behaves and can avoid accidently exposing your device to malware or viruses that depend on an unwary user with administrator-type access clicking OK to install something you will regret. Standard users also cannot snoop into data that belongs to other users.

To change a user's type, follow these steps:

1. From the Start menu, select **Settings** to open the Settings app.

2. Select **Accounts** from the Settings categories.

3. Select **Family & Other Users**. Users who can sign into your device will be listed (refer to Figure 19.6).

4. Select the account to change, which will expand the account to reveal a Change Account Type button and a Remove button, as shown in Figure 19.12. Select **Change Account Type**.

5. A Change Account Type user window will appear. Select the current User Type to reveal a drop-down menu, as shown in Figure 19.13. You can select between **Administrator** or **Standard User**. Make your choice and then select **OK**.

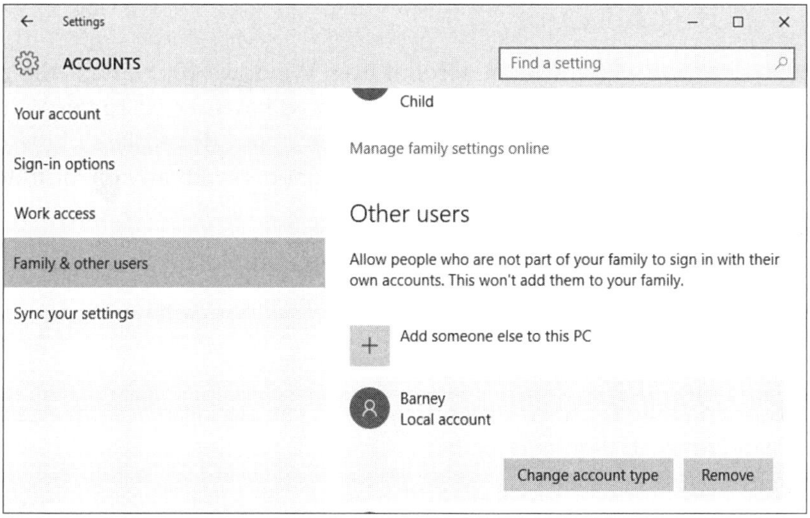

FIGURE 19.12

You can change important aspects of an account by selecting an account in the Family & Other Users screen.

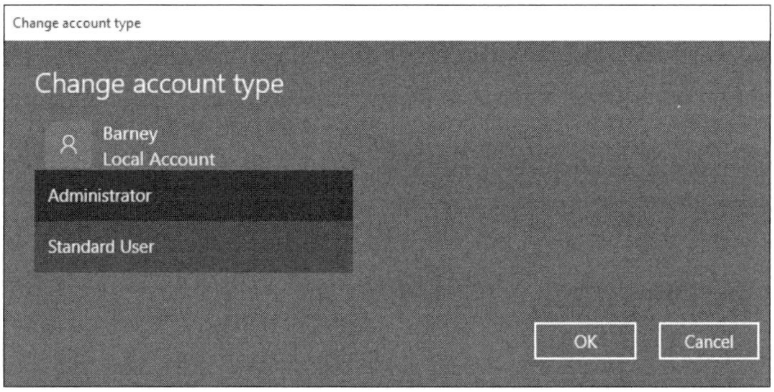

FIGURE 19.13

Assign the appropriate account type to a user using the Settings app.

6. You are returned to the screen where you started at step 3. You should see the account with its new account type displayed in the Other Accounts list.

Removing a User Account

You might need to remove an account from Windows 10. Perhaps the person who is associated with the account no longer should have access to this Windows 10 device, or perhaps the account was created in error. Regardless of the reason, it is easy to remove the account. You must be signed in with an administrator account to remove an account.

To remove a user account and the associated data, follow these steps:

1. From the Start menu, select **Settings** to open the Settings app.

2. Select **Accounts** from the settings categories.

3. Select **Family & Other Users**. Users who can sign into your device will be listed (refer to Figure 19.6).

4. Select the account to delete, which will expand the account to reveal a Change Account Type button and a Remove button (refer to Figure 19.12).

5. Select **Remove**.

6. The Delete Account and Data window appears, as shown in Figure 19.14. In this case, you are not offered a way to retain any data associated with the account besides what might have been backed up by the user. To delete the account and all the account files, click **Delete Account and Data**.

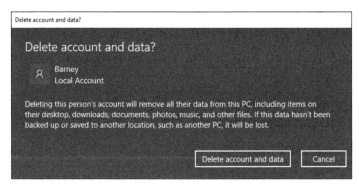

FIGURE 19.14

You have few options related to user data when removing an account in the Settings app.

7. You are returned to the screen where you started at step 3. You will no longer see the account displayed in the Other Accounts list.

If you are concerned about losing all the data that might have belonged to an account that needs to be removed from your device, there is another method you could use to remove the account that will enable you to save the data. Removing the account using the Control Panel applet for User Accounts provides more settings related to user accounts, and many of the steps in this chapter for creating or changing accounts can also be managed using this applet.

To remove an account using the User Accounts applet, follow these steps:

1. From the taskbar, start typing **user account** in the Search field. Select **User Accounts** from the search results, as shown in Figure 19.15.

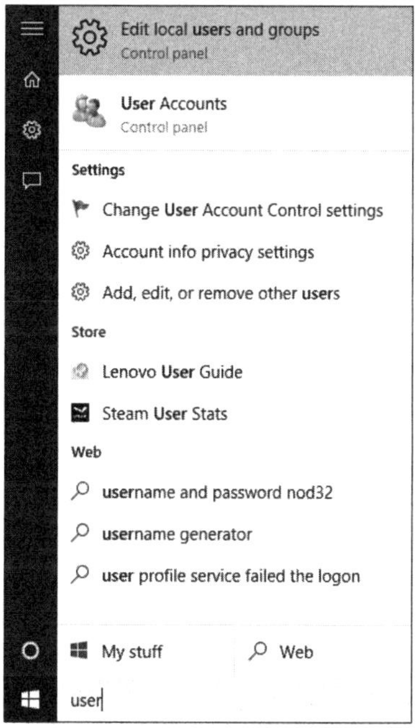

FIGURE 19.15

For greater control when removing an account, search for the User Accounts applet that is located in the Control Panel.

2. The User Accounts window opens. Under the main title of Make Changes to Your User Account, select the link **Manage Another Account**.

3. All user accounts for this Windows 10 device will be listed in Manage Accounts, as shown in Figure 19.16. Select the account you want to remove.

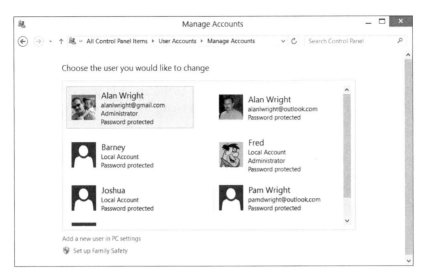

FIGURE 19.16

Manage Accounts provides you with another way to take control of user accounts on your device.

4. The Change an Account window appears. Select **Delete the Account** from the list of options for this account.

5. As shown in Figure 19.17, the Delete Account window appears. Select **Keep Files** to copy the files from the user account desktop, Documents, Favorites, Music, Pictures and Video folders. (To delete everything, click **Delete Files**.)

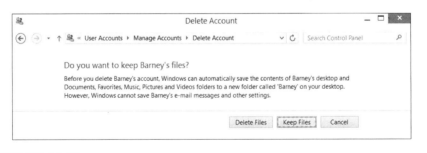

FIGURE 19.17

You have options related to user data when removing an account using the User Accounts applet.

6. Windows asks you to confirm your choice. Click **Delete Account**. To keep the account, click **Cancel**.

7. You are returned to the Manage Accounts window. You can close the window if you choose. If the user actually had any data on the device, on the desktop you will now find a new folder containing the data files from the user who was just removed. You can copy the data to give to that person or go through the files to ensure nothing needs to be saved before deleting the data files.

Maintaining Security

This section focuses on user account security. Perhaps you use a laptop or tablet away from home on occasion. If a curious workmate or acquaintance were to open or wake up your device, would it be secure, or would it reveal unwanted details? If your device is lost, will it reveal sensitive information to others?

Windows 10 is the most secure operating system to date, encrypting your data by default. All the built-in security is useless, however, if you unwittingly leave your device open or reveal the password needed to unlock it. It is surprising how often data and identities are stolen because users themselves granted access to their information.

Consider a few practical suggestions to help you maintain security on your Windows 10 device. Obviously, it is not a good practice to write a password on a sticky note stuck to the side of your Windows 10 device. PIN numbers and even the picture passwords might not be practical in public places where social engineers can watch over your shoulder as you log in to your device. And never—ever—should you reply to an email, no matter who it appears to be from, requesting your system's login credentials.

Windows Hello

With Windows 10, Microsoft has integrated a new set of biometric tools that allow you to use fingerprints, facial recognition, or iris scans to sign into your device and even complete purchases.

The capability to use these alternate sign-in methods will depend on the hardware available to your device. Although inexpensive fingerprint scanners that use a USB connection to connect to your device can be purchased, the facial recognition requires special cameras that manufacturers have only recently started to offer. If these devices are not present, you will not be able to set them up.

Follow these steps when setting up a fingerprint scanner with Windows Hello:

1. From the Start menu, select **Settings** to open the Settings app.

2. Select **Accounts** from the settings categories.

3. Select **Sign-In Options**.

4. To set up your fingerprint scanner, select **Setup** under Fingerprint. Follow the prompts to swipe the same finger over the scanner a few times until a good scan has been compiled. When finished, you can enroll other fingers by selecting **Add Another** and then following the same procedure.

5. Select **Remove** if you need to delete fingerprint scans.

After you have enrolled a fingerprint, you will see that option available when signing into Windows. Swipe your finger the same way you did during setup, and you will be signed in. When Windows needs to authenticate you for administrative tasks or purchases, you will be prompted to swipe your finger on the fingerprint reader.

Using the Screensaver to Add Security

In the Desktop environment, you can enable and adjust a setting to engage a screensaver and require a password to wake up a device after a time interval you establish. To use this setting, follow these steps:

1. From the Start menu, start typing **screen saver** in the Search field. Select **Change Screen Saver** from the search results.

2. The Screen Saver Settings dialog box opens on your Desktop (see Figure 19.18). You can also navigate here using the Control Panel.

3. Select a screensaver from the drop-down menu and a wait time. Enable the check box **On Resume, Display Logon Screen**.

4. Click **OK**.

 NOTE Some devices might not have these settings. Some tablets, for example, do not use a screensaver.

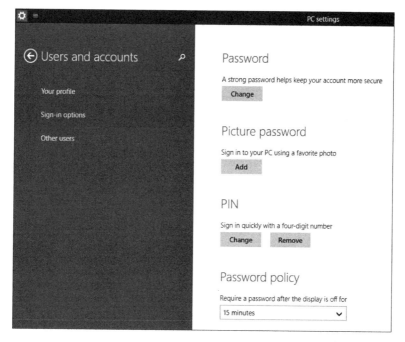

FIGURE 19.18

Enable the screensaver settings to require a login with password to increase security.

Two-Step Verification

A newer security feature Microsoft has introduced provides an added layer of security for Microsoft accounts. In addition to the password you will have set up for your Microsoft account, you are prompted for a code that can be generated and supplied using email, SMS, or an authenticator app on your smart phone that is paired with your Microsoft account. The number generated will expire, which makes it very difficult for a hacker who knows your password to also know the code. As an example, the Microsoft Authenticator app for Windows Phone generates a new six-digit code every 60 seconds.

Setting this up is managed from your online Microsoft account profile. You can log in to this account using the link https://account.live.com/proofs/Manage. After logging in, you will find the option to enable two-step verification under the security settings for your account.

Once enabled, you will be prompted to supply a code in addition to your password the first time you use a new device, use a new app, or log in to a Microsoft website using your Microsoft account. Figure 19.19 shows a request for a code when signing into a new device for the first time.

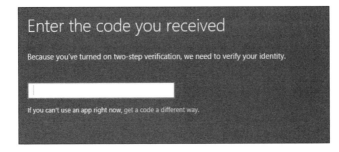

FIGURE 19.19

Enabling two-step verification provides you with additional security for your Microsoft account.

THE ABSOLUTE MINIMUM

Keep these points in mind as you wrap up this chapter:

- To give others access to your Windows 10 device, you should add an additional account to Windows 10. This is also known as "adding a user" in Windows 10. Best practice is to create this new user as a standard user to avoid the possibility of unwanted changes to your device.

- There are many practical reasons to use a Microsoft account when adding the new account. A Microsoft account includes information about your settings and preferences. If you sign in to Windows 10 running on a computer other than your own, all your settings and preferences are applied to this new computer. This won't happen if you create a local account instead.

- A picture password replaces the standard password. To sign in with a picture password, swipe or tap three times on a picture you choose. Windows checks your gestures against what it recorded when you created the picture password.

- You can also use a PIN to substitute for a password.

- Set up Windows Hello if you have a fingerprint scanner or a Windows Hello compatible camera.

- Consider using a two-step verification with your Microsoft account to provide additional security.

20

SHARING FILES AND PRINTERS

Say the word *network* to a novice Windows user, and you're sure to notice a look of fear mixed with confusion. But for the person who simply wants to share some pictures or music, or perhaps all the family's important files, among the computers in their home, there shouldn't be too much panic. Windows makes sharing easy with a function called homegroups. Homegroups provide exactly what you want from a small network: to provide easy sharing without introducing complexity. It strips away most of the tough network concepts and procedures and lets you focus on what sorts of files, folders, printers, and other stuff you want to share. This chapter helps you understand what you need to know about home networks and walks you through the easy process to set up sharing.

Setting up homegroup sharing is easy, although you need to leverage some information presented in other chapters. In particular, you might find it helpful to review the "Navigating Through Your Folders" section in Chapter 21, "File and Folder Basics."

Networking with Homegroup

This section eases you into the idea of creating a small network. A *network* is just a term that refers to multiple computers or devices that are connected and can share data. These devices can be connected by cables or wirelessly. And yes! You can boast to your friends that you know how to implement a computer network! The education begins with a brief review of the benefits of a small home network.

 NOTE Homegroup is appropriate for smaller networks, but how small is small? There is no reason why 10 or more computers can't be set up in a homegroup, or even 20 or more. But most homes have between 5 and 10 networked devices to share (everything from PCs and tablets to DVRs and game consoles), and a small home office can have a similar number of computers and devices.

If you have more than one computer in your home or home office, it might make sense to connect the computers into a small network. Consider some of the benefits to setting up a small sharing network at home:

- Consolidate all the files of a certain type, such as music or pictures, on one computer. This way, it's easy to find a particular song or photo if they are all stored in one place.

- Avoid running between devices in your home or office looking for a file. With two computers that are in the same homegroup, you can access files that are on another computer as if they were saved to your device.

- Set up one computer as a home theater PC (HTPC), storing all your movies and music, and also having all your audio equipment attached to it. You can stream music and video to other devices from your HTPC.

- Buy just one printer and connect it to one of your homegroup computers, and then share it with the rest of the homegroup.

There are usually a few settings to adjust, and possibly some hardware to acquire for a small group of computers to form a network. If all the Windows computers that you want to join to a network can already connect to the Internet from your home (refer to Chapter 13, "Connecting to Networks and the Internet"), then very likely they are already joined to a network. It's as easy as that.

Using the Windows Homegroup

The homegroup is an incredibly helpful feature in Windows 10 that enables you to share files with other computers that belong to the homegroup. As a member of a homegroup, you can see all the files that other members of the homegroup make available for sharing, and vice versa, as if the files were on your computer. You usually can open and edit the shared files, make copies of them, and delete them as if they were your own. Figure 20.1 shows Windows Explorer displaying some shared photos on other homegroup computers.

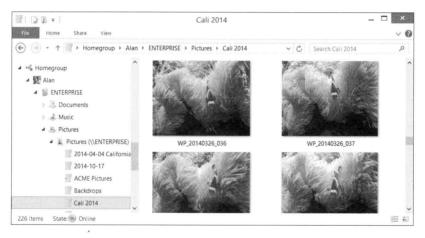

FIGURE 20.1

You can access shared files and folders as easily as files and folders on your computer's hard drive. In this example, you can see pictures that are shared from a different computer named Enterprise.

Here are a few facts about homegroups and networks:

- Each computer whose files you want to share must join the homegroup; see the section "Joining a Homegroup."

- There can be only one homegroup on your network.

- If one computer on the network has created a homegroup, any computer on the network from which you want to share must join *that* homegroup.

- To create a new homegroup, all computers must leave the homegroup, including the computer that started it.

- One computer creates a homegroup, and all other computers then join it. This does not give ownership or responsibility for the homegroup to the computer that created it. All computers in a homegroup are on par with one another. None have any more responsibility or capabilities than any other.

- It might sound daunting to navigate through all your files and folders to find, discover, or identify what you might share. Windows 10 makes it easy to specify and organize the files you might share by using common folders you already use, such as Documents, Pictures, and Music. You simply specify which folders to share with your homegroup.

 NOTE To make things even easier, you can use a feature called a *library* to further organize your folders. Libraries, which are special folders that "point" to several other folders, are a convenient way to bring together all the files that share a particular use or function no matter where folders are located. The files and folders that reside in a folder specified by a library become members of that library. For a discussion of libraries, look ahead to Chapter 21.

Although these folders are set up for you, homegroups are not. You must create one as the first step toward sharing on your home network.

Follow these three steps to set up a homegroup in Windows:

1. Create a homegroup.

2. Join a homegroup.

3. Set up homegroup sharing.

Each of these steps is covered in detail in the following sections.

Creating a Homegroup

Creating a homegroup is a simple matter of clicking a few buttons and then making a password. Before you can start, however, you need to get to the homegroup screen. Here's how:

1. From the **Start** menu, select the **Settings** app.

2. Select **Network & Internet** from the Settings categories.

3. Select **Ethernet** or **WIFI** depending on the choices you see listed.

4. Select **HomeGroup** from the list of Related Settings (refer to Figure 20.2).

5. You should see a screen like the one in Figure 20.2, Figure 20.3, or Figure 20.4.

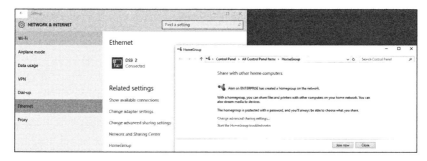

FIGURE 20.2

This screen indicates that a homegroup already is set up on your network but you haven't joined it yet.

FIGURE 20.3

This screen indicates a homegroup has not been set up on your network.

 NOTE If your device is already connected to an existing homegroup but you want to create a new one anyway, skip to the section "Leaving a Homegroup."

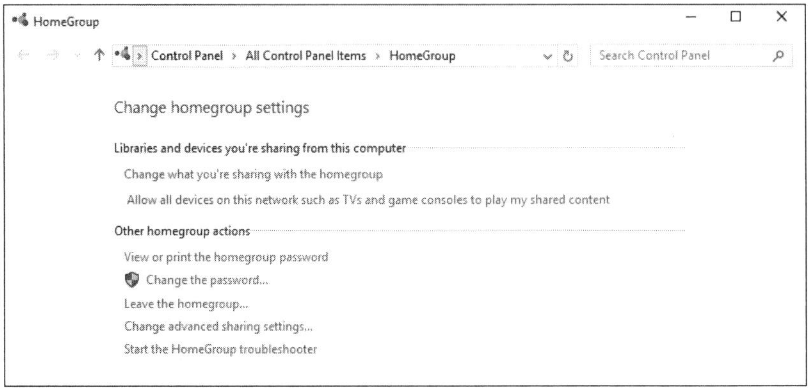

FIGURE 20.4

This screen indicates that you belong to a homegroup but have not shared anything yet.

For now, we're interested only in Figure 20.3, which gives you the opportunity to create a homegroup. We'll get to the other two figures in a little bit. Follow these steps to create a homegroup:

1. Select **Create a Homegroup**. A small Create a Homegroup pop-up window appears explaining the purpose of a homegroup. Select **Next**.

2. The screen you see in Figure 20.5 appears. Select the drop-down menus to change Permissions to **Shared** or **Not Shared**. Select **Next** when finished.

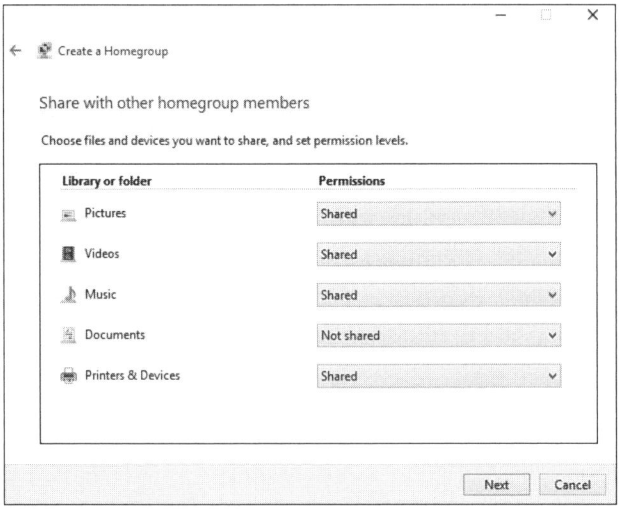

FIGURE 20.5

When creating a new homegroup, you can select what you will share with other devices.

3. The next screen provides a password of 10 characters for the homegroup. Carefully make a note of the password shown in the box under Write Down This Password. Note the case used for letters. (7abc8 is not the same as 7ABC8.) You need this password so that other computers can join in the homegroup. Select **Finish** when done. Your homegroup has been created, and the computer you've been using is a member of it.

At this point, your computer has created and joined the homegroup. The homegroup, though, is a quiet one with just this computer as a member. In the next section, you learn how other computers in the network can join the homegroup.

Joining a Homegroup

You can join a homegroup as long as one computer that belongs to the homegroup is signed on. Even if the computer that was used to create the homegroup is turned off, you do not need to wait for *that* computer to be signed in to join.

To join a homegroup, follow these steps:

1. Get the homegroup password. That password can be retrieved easily from another homegroup computer by bringing up the screen shown earlier and selecting **View or Print the Homegroup Password** (refer to Figure 20.4).

2. From the **Start** menu, select the **Settings** app.

3. Select **Network & Internet** from the settings categories.

4. Select **Ethernet** or **WIFI** depending on the choices you see listed.

5. Select **HomeGroup** from the list of Related Settings (refer to Figure 20.2).

6. Select **Join Now**. A small Create a Homegroup pop-up window appears explaining the purpose of a homegroup. Select **Next**.

7. The sharing options become available (refer to Figure 20.5). You can set the sharing options immediately. For guidance, however, read the section, "Setting Up Sharing," later in this chapter. Select **Next** to continue.

8. You are prompted for the homegroup password. Enter the password into the box. If the password is accepted, your device becomes part of the homegroup and you can access resources shared to the homegroup from other devices on your network. Select **Finish** to close the window. If the password did not work, check the password and make sure you are entering the password exactly as shown in step 1.

Leaving a Homegroup

You read earlier that all computers must leave a homegroup before a new homegroup can be created. To leave a homegroup, follow these steps:

1. From the **Start** menu, select the **Settings** app.

2. Select **Network & Internet** from the settings categories.

3. Select **Ethernet** or **WIFI** depending on the choices you see listed.

4. Select **HomeGroup** from the list of Related Settings (refer to Figure 20.2).

5. Select the link that says **Leave The Homegroup**. (You can see this link in Figure 20.4.)

6. You will be warned that you will lose access to shared homegroup resources if you leave. Select **Leave The Homegroup** and then select **Finish** to close this window.

Troubleshooting Homegroup Connections

If you experience difficulty either joining a homegroup or leaving one, try using the troubleshooting tool included in Windows. To run the HomeGroup troubleshooter, follow these steps.

1. From the search box on the taskbar, start typing the word *homegroup*. Select **Find and Fix Problems With Homegroup** from the search results.

2. The HomeGroup Troubleshooting tool will open, as shown in Figure 20.6. Select **Next**.

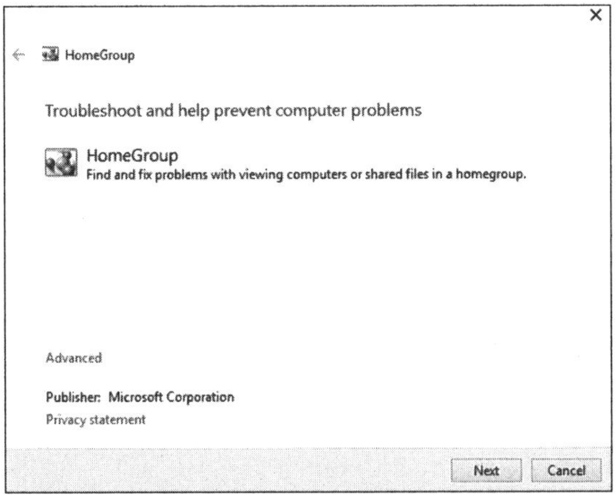

FIGURE 20.6

Try using the HomeGroup troubleshooter to automatically detect and correct problems on your computer.

3. Follow the prompts as the troubleshooting tool automatically compares set-tings to common issues for this category. You will be presented with sugges-tions, and it might recommend that you run related troubleshooters, such as the network problems troubleshooter.

Her are a few other tips to consider if you're experiencing trouble accessing a homegroup:

- You can experience difficulties joining a homegroup if you use a third-party (non-Microsoft) antivirus program. If you don't mind disabling your antivirus program for a short time, you can attempt to join or leave the homegroup again after temporarily disabling the software.

- You can experience difficulties joining a homegroup if you use an all-in-one Internet privacy or protection software suite. If so, disable the protection tem-porarily before trying to join the homegroup again. If you can connect, you can create an exception for Windows 10, enabling you to join a homegroup.

 CAUTION If you disable your antivirus or other Internet protection software, it's not a bad idea to disconnect from the Internet (but not your network) before you do.

- Windows networks are of a specific type: home, office, or public. The type defines the level of security for each. For example, a private home network enables more computer-to-computer communication than a public network. A homegroup is allowed only on a private network.

If you are still unable to resolve your problem, you might need to resort to con-sulting a computer expert or taking advantage of technical support that might well be included with your Windows 10 device purchase.

Setting Up Sharing

Windows 10 organizes everything you might share into five categories:

- Documents
- Music
- Pictures
- Videos
- Printers and Devices

At any time you can review what you are sharing with your homegroup by opening the homegroup control panel, as shown in Figure 20.7. To change sharing for any of these items, select the link **Change What You're Sharing With The Homegroup**. The sharing tool shown back in Figure 20.4 will open again, and you can update your choices.

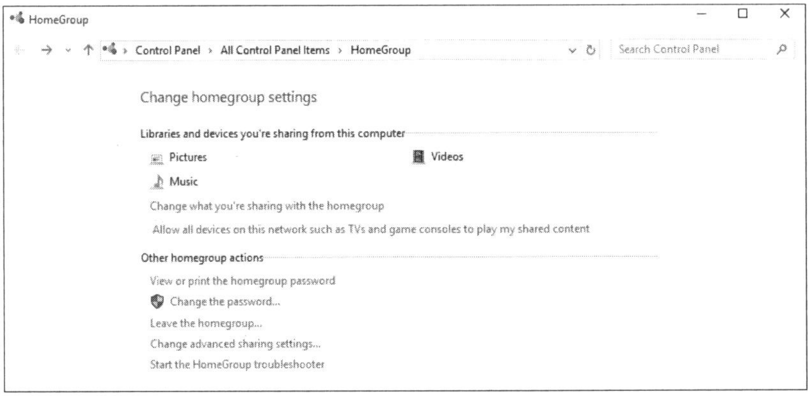

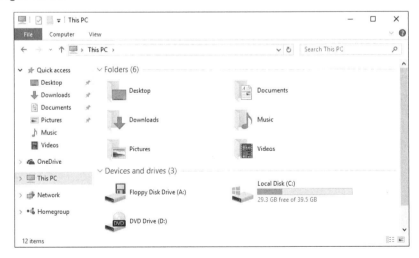

FIGURE 20.7

Music, Pictures, and Videos have been shared on this device.

You might recognize some of these names from elsewhere. They appear when you browse for files using File Explorer as the names for some of the default folders when you're looking at content on This PC. An example of this is shown in Figure 20.8.

FIGURE 20.8

When viewing This PC, you will see folders that point to your most commonly shared resources.

Before you share everything on your device, here are some things you need to know about sharing:

- By default, every file in a folder is shared with every computer in the home-group (when you turn on sharing for that folder, of course).

- You can prevent one or more folders from being shared.

- You can prevent one or more files in a folder from being shared even if the folder is being shared.

- You can prevent one or more files in a folder or one or more entire folders from being shared with certain users in your homegroup.

The following sections show you how to deal with each of these cases.

Disabling Sharing for Specific Files or Folders

To prevent one or more files or folders from being shared, follow these steps:

1. Open **File Explorer**. You can do this by clicking the File Explorer icon on the Desktop taskbar.

2. Navigate to the folder where the file or folder you want to restrict from sharing is located. You can find assistance with navigating in Chapter 21.

3. Select the files or folders. You can use the multiselect approach (also described in Chapter 21) to select all the files or folders at once, select them in small batches, or set sharing for each file or folder one at a time.

4. Under the Share tab in the Share With group, click **Stop Sharing**, as shown in Figure 20.9. (The same options can also be found by right-clicking and select-ing **Share with** from the context menu.)

5. You might have to repeat these steps a few times.

NOTE   Although you might not see any change in the file that is readily apparent, Windows removes access for the *HomeUsers* group to the file or folder when you stop sharing it in this manner. This group is what allows other homegroup users to see files and folders that have been shared.

FIGURE 20.9

You can stop sharing selected folders or files with your homegroup.

Sharing Files and Folders Only with Specific Users

To share certain files or folders only with specific persons, follow these steps:

1. Open **File Explorer**. You can do this by clicking the File Explorer icon on the Desktop taskbar.

2. Navigate to the folder where the file or folder you want to share with only certain people is located.

3. Select the files or folders. You can use the multiselect approach (refer to Chapter 21) to select all the files or folders at once, do them in small batches, or set each file or folder one at a time.

4. Under the Share tab in the Share With group, expand the list of groups and individuals by clicking the More arrow button on the right side of the box (see Figure 20.10). You will see a list of the persons with whom you can share.

5. Click **Specific People**. The dialog box shown in Figure 20.11 appears.

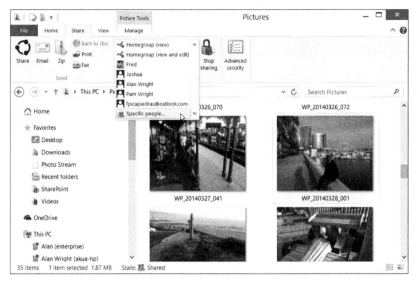

FIGURE 20.10

Click Specific People to display the list of users.

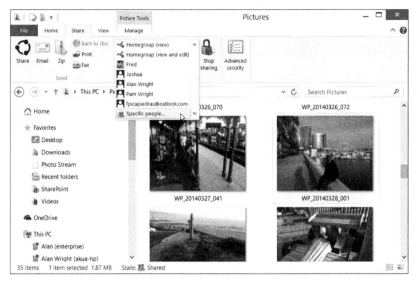

FIGURE 20.11

Select persons to filter sharing.

6. Enter the email address or the username that the person uses to log in to his computer; then click **Add**. Under Permission Level, you can select **Read**, **Read/Write**, or **Remove** access.

7. Repeat the last step if needed to select more persons with whom to share the files you selected.

8. To allow all the users you selected to access the files and folders with the permissions you have indicated, click **Share**.

9. You might be asked to confirm the access you are granting if write permission is given and this permission level can affect the entire folder. Click **Next**.

 NOTE When working with steps 6–8, refer to Figure 20.11. To allow users you selected to only be able to read (and copy) the file you're sharing and not change the original file, select Read from the Permission Level column to prevent changes to the files you're sharing. (This is the default setting Windows uses when sharing to a homegroup.) Change the setting in the Permission Level column to Read/Write to allow the person to edit, change, and even delete the original. Choose wisely. To save your changes, click Share.

Sharing Your Printer

Sharing all printers you have installed on your device to your homegroup is as easy as sharing files and folders. When you turn on sharing for Printers (refer to Figure 20.6), each of your printers potentially becomes available to all computers in the homegroup. You might decide not to enable sharing of printers to your homegroup—perhaps to protect the ink supplies in your precious color printer. You can still share a specific printer using a couple of methods that involve a few simple steps.

Here is how to share specific printers to your homegroup:

1. From the **Start** menu, start typing the word *printers*. Select the **Devices and Printers** applet that appears in the search results. The Devices and Printers applet of the Control Panel opens.

2. Locate the printer you want to share. Right-click or tap and hold the printer, and from the menu that appears, select **Printer Properties**.

3. Select the **Security** tab.

4. Click **Add**.

5. The Select Users or Groups dialog box opens, as shown in Figure 20.12. In the box **Enter the Object Names to Select**, type in the group name *homeusers*; then click **Check Names**. The name will be updated based on the correct name for that group on this computer.

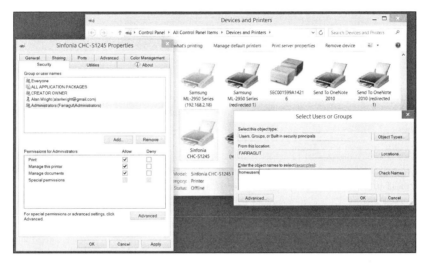

FIGURE 20.12

Use the Security tab of the Printer Properties dialog box to specifically share a printer.

5. Click **OK**. You will notice in the printer properties Security tab the new HomeUsers group appears with default permissions to Print. Click **OK**.

6. Close the Devices and Printers window by clicking the Close button in the upper-right corner of the window.

This printer will now be available to other computers and devices in your home-group. However, it might not appear automatically. To check for new devices such as printers in a homegroup, open the HomeGroup applet by typing **homegroup** into the Search field from the Start menu. Select the HomeGroup applet. (Look for the icon with four globes.) Figure 20.13 shows that on this computer a new shared printer has been found. Click Install Printer to install the drivers and use this printer from this computer. You will likely be asked to trust the printer, and you will also likely be asked to verify you want changes to be made to your computer by install-ing these drivers. Confirm both choices to add this printer to your local list of printers. After the drivers have been installed, you can print to a shared printer as long as that printer and the computer sharing it are online and awake.

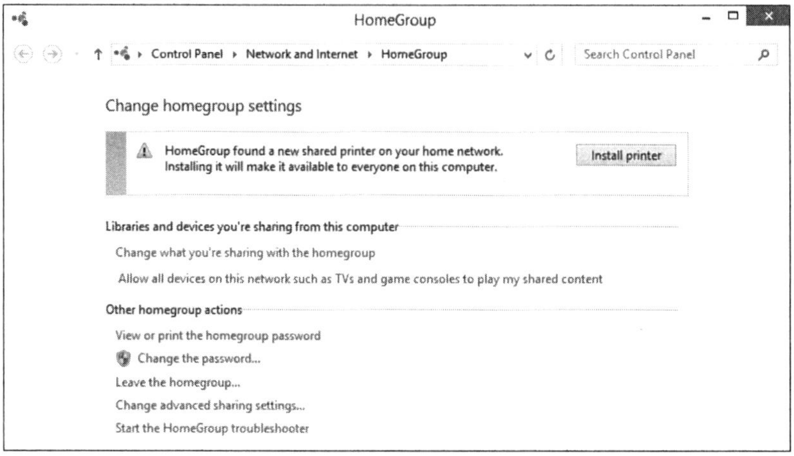

FIGURE 20.13

Newly shared printers might first appear in the HomeGroup applet, or you might be notified that a new homegroup printer is available.

In some cases you might not have a homegroup. Can you still share printers to other computers on your network? Yes, you can. Here is how to share specific printers without using a homegroup:

1. From the **Start** menu, start typing the word *printers*. Select the **Devices and Printers** applet that appears in the search results. The Devices and Printers applet of the Control Panel opens.

2. Locate the printer you want to share. Right-click or tap and hold the printer, and from the menu that appears, select **Printer Properties**.

3. Click the **Sharing** tab.

4. Select the **Share This Printer** check box (see Figure 20.14). You'll notice a name for your printer is automatically filled in for you. This is the name everyone will see on the network. You can change it if you like.

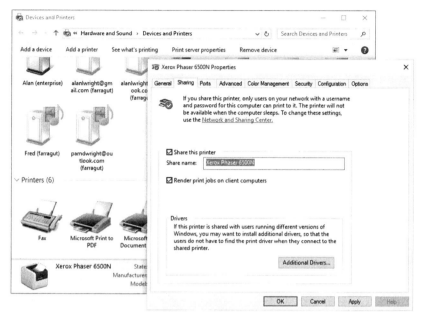

FIGURE 20.14

Use the Printer Properties dialog box to specifically share a printer.

5. Click **OK**. You will notice a small shared badge appears on your printer now in the Devices and Printers window.

6. Close the Devices and Printers window by clicking the Close button in the upper-right corner of the window.

This printer will appear to other computers on your network as a shared resource on your computer. Figure 20.15 shows that a different computer on the same network has browsed to the Network in File Explorer and selected the computer that just shared the printer in the previous steps. Double-clicking the printer can prompt a request as shown here to trust the printer before installing the correct drivers. After the drivers have been installed, you can print to a shared printer as long as that printer and the computer sharing it are online and awake.

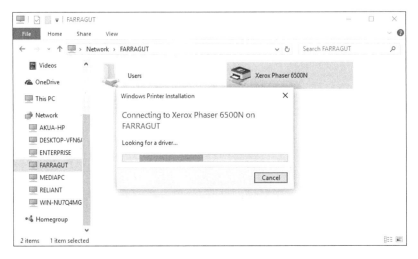

FIGURE 20.15

Specific printers can be shared to your network without using the homegroup.

Seeing Stuff Shared by Others

Although it's good to share, it's also really good to receive. Whatever your homegroup partners decide to share you can access very easily via the File Explorer. Follow these steps to access shared content:

1. From the Desktop taskbar, open File Explorer. If you are unclear how to open File Explorer, see Chapter 21.

2. In the Navigation pane, scroll down to the Homegroup group. It should show Homegroup at the top entry in the tree. Select the small arrow beside the word Homegroup to reveal homegroup users and their computers, as shown in Figure 20.16.

3. Select the computer whose shared files you want to see. Then navigate through the folders in the Content pane as you would if browsing through files on your own computer.

Navigation pane   Shared files

Homegroup computers (including yours)

FIGURE 20.16

Browse through the folders shared on a homegroup computer as if the folders are on your own computer.

THE ABSOLUTE MINIMUM

- Homegroups are a feature in Windows 10 that makes it extremely easy to share resources, such as pictures, music, and other files, with other nearby computers. Homegroups also enable you to share printers.

- Computers and tablets that connect to the Internet at your home or home office are already part of a network and can be in the same homegroup.

- There can be just one homegroup in a network.

- Use libraries to simplify which files get shared. When you turn on sharing, all the files in that library are shared. You must use the settings available through File Explorer to restrict sharing.

- The printers connected to your computer are automatically shared with all other computers in the homegroup as soon as you turn on sharing for printers on the Homegroup screen. You can choose to share all your printers or select only a specific printer(s) to share.

- Printers can be shared on a network even without using a homegroup.

21

FILE AND FOLDER BASICS

The exciting new Windows 10 environment, with its broad palette of active tiles, gives the perception that everything you do in Windows can be accomplished through the immersive, colorful screens you see on the Start screen, as well as on the Web in advertisements, videos, and reviews.

The reality is that although you'll certainly work with the Windows 10 apps and features, you'll also spend a lot of time just managing your files and folders as you might have done with the previous version of Windows. This chapter helps you understand the basics about files and folders and how to keep them all under control using File Explorer.

Files and Folder Basics

Before diving into the methods of managing your files and folders, you should have a firm grasp of the basics. The following sections offer an overview of both and look at how you can use a somewhat hidden feature called libraries to manage them all.

Understanding Files

At their absolute simplest, files store data. Different types of files serve different purposes. But for this discussion, it's best to categorize all files in two ways:

- System files
- User files

System files are the parts of the Windows 10 engine. Windows 10 uses these files to do its job, from connecting to the Internet to recognizing a mouse-click from a finger tap on the screen to figuring how much time you have before your battery runs out. These system files are important, and Windows 10 expects not only that they remain located on your computer, but also that they are in a specific location. You generally do not need to worry about accidentally erasing a system file and causing Windows to stop working. System files are stored in system folders, and these folders are in a location generally difficult to access unless you are an administrator. Even so, it's best to avoid these folders and all their subfolders:

> \Windows
>
> \Program Files
>
> \Program Files (x86)

Many programs enable you to select the folders into which the system files for the program are installed. Unless you know better, it's best to use the default folder option the programs offer and remove them only via the Windows Uninstall a Program feature. The steps for uninstalling Desktop applications are discussed in Chapter 7, "Working with Windows Desktop Applications."

These system files contrast with user files. *User files* are the files you use and create every day, such as text documents, spreadsheets, music, photos, and so on. Software programs define the format of the user files that work with their program. You usually cannot use one of these files in a program other than the one that created it, although there are exceptions. For example, you can't open a file created by your tax preparation tool in your photo editing program, but you can open a Notepad text file in Microsoft Word.

User files are normally stored in a person's own folders. As you read next, all users in Windows 10 have their own set of folders that other users usually cannot access.

Understanding Folders

Whereas files are containers for data, folders are containers for files. It's as simple as that. A folder can contain other folders, and those folders can contain yet other folders, and so on. A folder in Windows is represented by, no surprise here, the Folder icon, as shown in Figure 21.1.

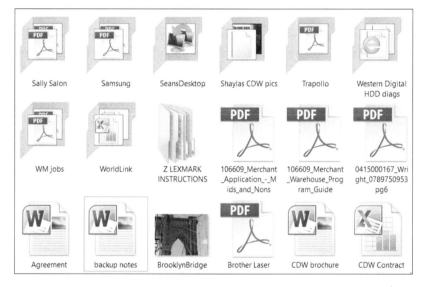

FIGURE 21.1

You can easily tell which of the items in Windows are files or folders.

Adding new users to Windows by creating an account for them also creates a set of unique user folders. Windows creates these folders in a parent folder. The folder is named after the user's first name if the account is a Microsoft account. If the account is a local account, the folder name is the same as the username you provided when you created the account. This folder is known as the user's *home folder*, and you can see an example of it in Figure 21.2. (To learn more about creating accounts and the difference between account types, see Chapter 19, "Sharing Your Windows Computer with Others.")

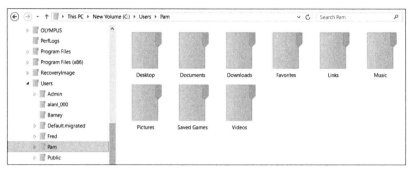

FIGURE 21.2

A set of folders is created for each Windows user.

You can store files anywhere you like in your own home folder and subfolders. You can create as many folders and subfolders as you like in your home folder. It makes sense to store certain special files, such as music files, in the folders specially designed for them. You cannot save or create files in any other folder in Windows, including the home folders of other users, unless you are a system administrator—and even then, it's generally not a great idea.

With some planning, you can create a hierarchy of folders to help organize all the files related to a task, subject, project, hobby, and so on. Figure 21.3 shows an example of a folder tree used to store photos. As you'll soon see, you do not need to be a Windows expert to stay organized.

 CAUTION   Software programs you purchase also leverage folders to organize their files. When you install programs, they often create their own folders. You should never move, rename, or delete program folders, even if you know you will never use the program again. Sometimes these folders contain files that are used by other programs. When you manually delete a folder that contains files, all the files are deleted along with the containing folder, which can cause unintended consequences.

FIGURE 21.3

You can design a folder system for specific needs.

Exploring with File Explorer

You use File Explorer to manage your files and folders. Although Microsoft keeps changing the name—it was previously known as Windows Explorer and before that File Manager—File Explorer has been around for many years, and the version that comes with Windows 10 has been further refined to make it even easier to use.

You can launch File Explorer from the Desktop, and its icon appears on the taskbar by default. If you use a keyboard, it is worth remembering that the keyboard shortcut for opening File Explorer is the Windows key + E.

 TIP You can also add a File Explorer tile to the Start menu by using the Search tool to locate an app named "explorer." When File Explorer appears in the list of results, right-click the icon and select Pin to Start from the menu that appears.

After opening File Explorer, you'll see a new window like the one in Figure 21.4.

The Navigation pane, as shown here, drives almost all the activity in File Explorer. Whatever you select in the Navigation pane determines what appears in the Content pane.

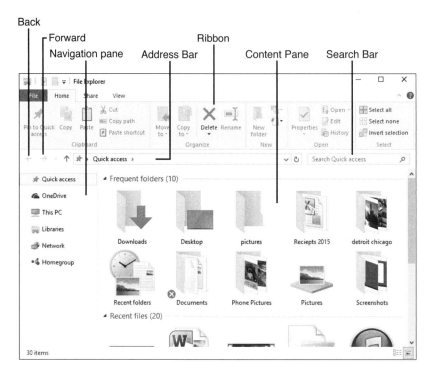

FIGURE 21.4

File Explorer includes a number of controls to enable you to navigate through your file system.

Working with Quick Access

Quick Access is a twist on the recently used folder and file lists that you would see in previous versions of Windows. Now when you open File Explorer, you land in Quick Access, where you see two sections: frequently used folders and below that a list of recently opened files (refer to Figure 21.4). Quick Access also appears when you open or save a file from another application using File Explorer.

One way to make Quick Access work for you is to pin folders to Quick Access so they will be front and center anytime you open File Explorer. To do this, simply right-click or select and hold on a touch screen to bring up the context menu, as shown in Figure 21.5. Select Pin to Quick Access, and you will see this folder appear in Quick Access with a small thumbtack to remind you it is pinned there.

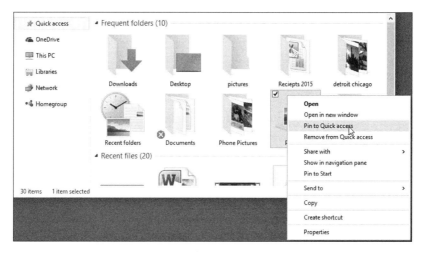

FIGURE 21.5

Pin folders to Quick Access using the context menu so you can find them easily.

 TIP If you do not like Quick Access keeping track of your recent files and folders you can disable this feature. Right-click Quick Access to bring up the context menu and select Options. The Folder Options dialog box will open to the General tab. Under Privacy uncheck the boxes Show Recently Used Files In Quick Access and Show Frequently Used Folder In Quick Access. In addition, you can clear the File Explorer history in this same section by selecting the Clear button.

Working with Libraries

The *library*, introduced in Windows 7, is an extremely useful tool to organize your files. Windows 10 continues to use libraries even if you do not notice their presence right away. A library usually appears as a themed folder in File Explorer that contains folders that can actually be located anywhere on your device, on attached media, or even on separate computers.

When you select a library, all the folders designated by the library appear as if they were in the same place. A library does not store a file the way a folder does; it does not actually move your files and folders. As an example of how you might use a library, you can add folders that have pictures that are saved on your Desktop, external storage device, and another computer that is always connected to the same network. When you open your Pictures library, you will see all these folders in one place. This provides you with a very powerful way to organize with a minimum of effort.

 NOTE Libraries are already used by Windows 10 even if they have not been made visible in File Explorer. When you open the modern Video, Photos, or Music apps, they display the contents of your corresponding library and not merely the folder of that same name in your user profile. Because libraries are often confusing to new users, they have been hidden by default in Windows 10.

Windows creates a number of libraries automatically, including one for pictures, one for documents, one for videos, and another for music files. You can create additional libraries yourself. You might create a library to organize all the files related to your career, or you might consolidate all the folders for all the projects you're working on.

To work with libraries, you first need to make sure they are visible in File Explorer. To do this, follow these steps:

1. Open File Explorer using the icon on the Desktop taskbar. In the Navigation pane to the left, you will see clusters of folders labeled Quick Access, This PC, Network, and likely Homegroup and OneDrive.

2. Select the **View** tab and then select the Navigation pane button, as shown in Figure 21.6. Select **Show Libraries**.

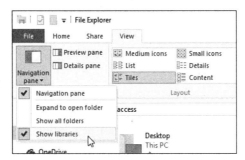

FIGURE 21.6

File Explorer does not show libraries by default.

3. You will see that a group of default libraries is now visible in the Navigation pane of File Explorer. Select one of your Library folders to view its contents, as shown in Figure 21.7.

4. When you have a library selected, File Explorer will show a **Library Tools** tab. Select this tab.

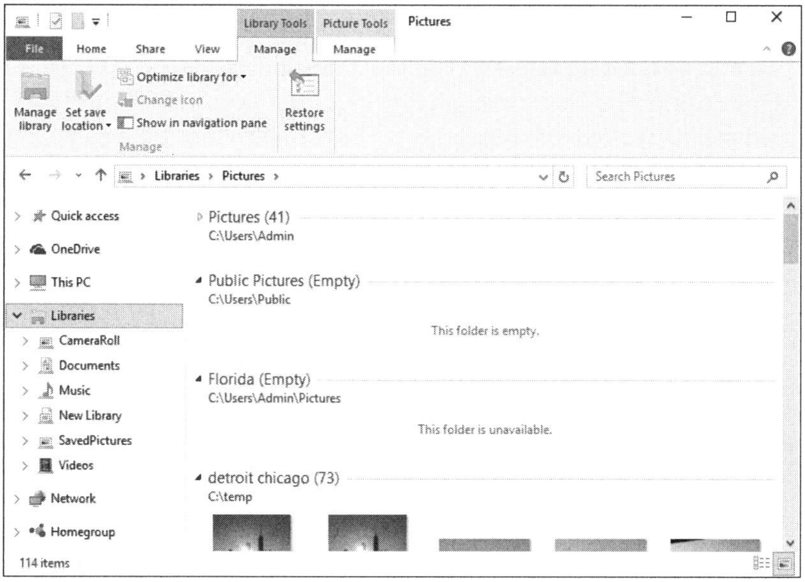

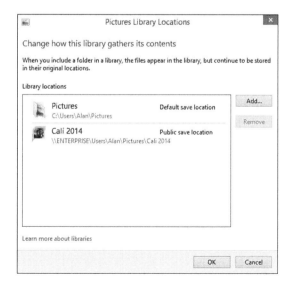

FIGURE 21.7

After you have enabled Show Libraries, you will see them in your Navigation pane as a cluster of folders.

5. Click **Manage Library** to open the Library Locations dialog box for that library, as shown in Figure 21.8.

FIGURE 21.8

Edit a library's location settings to add folders to include in the library.

There are a few basic ways you can manage a library:

- To add a folder to a library, use the steps in this section to open the Library Locations dialog box shown in Figure 21.8. Click Add. A small File Explorer type window appears. Navigate to the folder to include and then click **Include Folder**. In this example, the second folder is actually located on a different computer in the homegroup. You can read how to navigate in File Explorer later in this chapter.

- To remove a folder from the library, select the folder and then click **Remove**.

- To define where files are stored when you save to a library, close the Library Locations dialog box. With the library still selected in the Navigation pane, under Library Tools, select the **Manage** tab; then select **Set Save Location** (refer to Figure 21.7). Finally, select the library folder to which you would prefer to save files by default.

- When navigating in File Explorer, you can right-click a folder to open the context menu, select Include in Library, and then select the library. This is the easiest way to add folders to your libraries.

- To create a new library, right-click/press-and-hold on **Libraries** in the Navigation pane. Then select **New**, and select **Library**. An empty library appears in the list of libraries. Enter a name for the new library and click Enter. Next, add folders to the library.

Navigating the Folder Tree

The center of attention of the Navigation pane is the folder tree. The folder tree shows all your computer's drives, folders, libraries, and other content as hierarchal directories that let you easily see how everything is related. Think of your computer as the main trunk of the tree, and think of those leftmost-positioned items as the primary branches growing from the trunk. In many cases, those branches have other branches growing from them.

Each of the five primary branches in the Navigation pane folder tree contains related kinds of items.

- **Quick Access**—Just as you can specify websites as Favorites, making it easy to reach these sites by choosing from the Favorites menu of your web browser, you can pin folders to Quick Access. Folders that have been pinned appear with a thumbtack in Quick Access. You might find it easier to think of these as shortcuts because the folders have not moved; they are simply easier to navigate to when pinned.

- **Libraries**—As you read earlier in this chapter, a library organizes related folders, making it easy for you to see and work with all the related files and folders. The Libraries branch contains all your libraries. Once it's enabled, you will see this branch below the library name showing all of a library's folders.

- **Homegroup**—This node shows all the content shared with the homegroup to which your Windows 10 device belongs. The tree is organized by the user that joined the computer to the workgroup. Under each user are the computers to which the user has access. You will not see anything in this branch until you join or start a homegroup.

- **This PC**—This PC is the branch that contains all the computer's physical objects, such as hard drives and removable drives. You will also find your principle user folders and network locations your device can see on the network.

- **Network**—The Network branch shows all the computers on the network to which the computer connects.

You can tell if an item in the Navigation pane has concealed directories (or branches) by the appearance of a small triangle symbol besides its name. That triangle icon is black or white, as shown in Figure 21.9. If it is black, the branches growing from it are visible. When the triangle is white, the branch's sub-branches are hidden.

To display more branches in the tree, select the white, triangle-shaped icon. To hide the branches growing from a main branch, select the black, triangle-shaped icon.

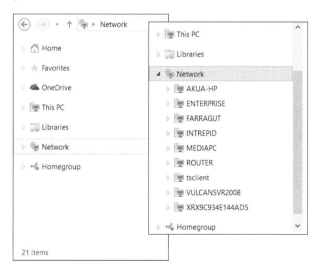

FIGURE 21.9

Show and hide branches in the folder tree by selecting the triangle-shaped icon.

Following are a few options to help you organize the Navigation pane. Each of the following, with the exception of the Navigation pane width, can be set by accessing the Navigation pane options menu. Under the View tab in the ribbon's Panes group, select the **Navigation** pane down arrow (see Figure 21.10):

- **Show/hide the Navigation pane**—After you navigate to the folder with which you want to work, you can close the Navigation pane to maximize your screen real estate.

  To show or hide the Navigation pane, on the View tab in the Panes group, select the **Navigation** pane down arrow (see Figure 21.10). Then select the **Navigation** pane to toggle the appearance of the pane on and off.

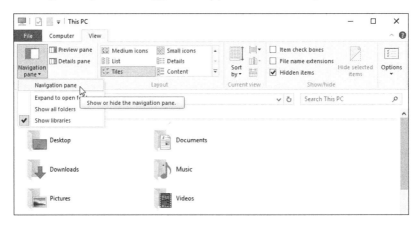

FIGURE 21.10

Show and hide the Navigation pane to suit your needs.

- **Change the width of the Navigation pane**—If your folder names are particularly long, or if you have several levels of folders in your file system, you can increase the width of the Navigation pane. You can also decrease the width of the Navigation pane to see more of the Explorer pane.

  To change the width of the Navigation pane, point to or tap-and-hold on the right edge of the slider bar that separates the Navigation pane from the Content pane. When the pointer becomes a double-headed arrow, drag the bar to change the width of the Navigation pane.

- **Showing/hiding Favorites**—If you tend to work with some folders more than others, even temporarily as you work on a project, you can add a folder to the list of Favorites. Keeping a folder on the Favorites list makes it easier to access the folder than having to navigate through your file system each time you want to work with it. If you just do not use Favorites, you can hide Favorites in the Navigation pane.

To show or hide Favorites in the Navigation tree, on the View tab in the Panes group, select the **Navigation** pane down arrow (refer to Figure 21.10). Then select **Show Favorites** to toggle the appearance of the Favorites on and off.

- **Showing/hiding all folders**—A few objects in the Navigation pane are a bit different from files, folders, drives, or libraries, and they are generally not displayed by default. The Control Panel, Recycle Bin, and user profile are actually special folders. The Control Panel contains small programs used to configure different aspects of Windows 10. Recycle Bin stores files and folders you have deleted. Your user profile folder contains many more folders than the six displayed in the This PC directory. You can enable these folders if you like, although you might find the Navigation pane to be more cluttered by doing so.

  To show or hide these special folders in the Navigation tree, on the View tab in the Panes group, select the **Navigation** pane down arrow. Then select **Show All Folders** to toggle on and off the appearance of the Control Panel, your user profile folder, and Recycle Bin. Notice that Desktop appears also as a higher-level container in the Navigation pane when this is enabled.

- **Automatically expand to current folder**—If you open a folder without using the Navigation pane, you can configure the folder tree in the Navigation pane to expand automatically to that folder. You can also turn off this feature.

  To update the folder tree in the Navigation pane when the address is entered, under the View tab in the Panes group, select the **Navigation** pane down arrow. Then select **Expand to Open Folder** to toggle this feature on or off.

Customizing the Content Pane

The Content pane is the main attraction of File Explorer. It shows you the contents of the folder, drive, branch, or computer selected in the Navigation pane (see Figure 21.11). Think of the Content pane as your workbench. It's the place where you maintain and organize your computer's folder and files, such as copying, renaming, moving, deleting, burning, and so on.

Selecting items in the Content pane is important because the commands you execute, such as Copy, Share, Delete, and all the others, affect the items selected in the Content pane. To learn more about selecting files and folders, refer to the section "Selecting Files and Folders" in the next chapter.

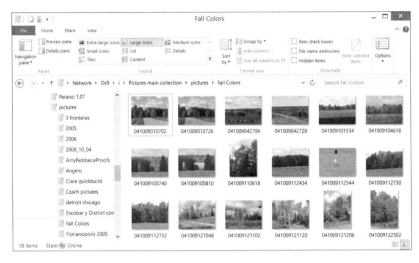

FIGURE 21.11

The Content pane shows the contents of the folder selected in the Navigation pane.

You can change the appearance of the icons listed on the Content pane by choosing the size or layout you want from the ribbon under the View tab in the Layout group. The Current view group contains commands to change the order in which objects appear:

- The choice of icon size (small, medium, large, and extra large) is a matter of personal choice and the size of your display. If you have a large display (perhaps greater than 24") and a high resolution (greater than 1024×768), you can fit more of the large icons on the screen.

- The List view is helpful when you must select items, especially when you need to make a noncontiguous selection, as shown in Figure 21.12.

- The Content and Details views are useful if you need to see (and sort by) the size, the type, and the date the items were last modified. Click the name of the column to sort by that field. Click it again to change the sort order. Select **Add Columns** in the Current view group on the View tab to add more information in columns to the view.

- Experiment with the various options on the View tab. As the name of the tab indicates, the commands change only the appearance of the icons on the screen. It is impossible to mistakenly delete anything by making a selection from the View tab.

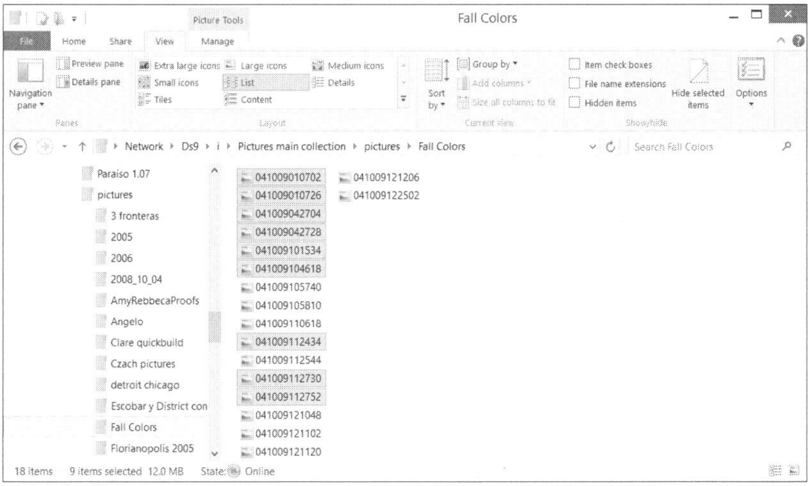

FIGURE 21.12

The List view is extremely helpful when you need to select items that do not appear next to one another.

Exploring the Preview and Details Pane

The rightmost area of File Explorer is also capable of displaying one of two bonus panes: the Preview pane and the Details pane. Only one of these panes can be visible at a time. Select the view you want from the ribbon's View tab by selecting **Preview pane** or **Details pane** from the Panes group, as shown in Figure 21.13.

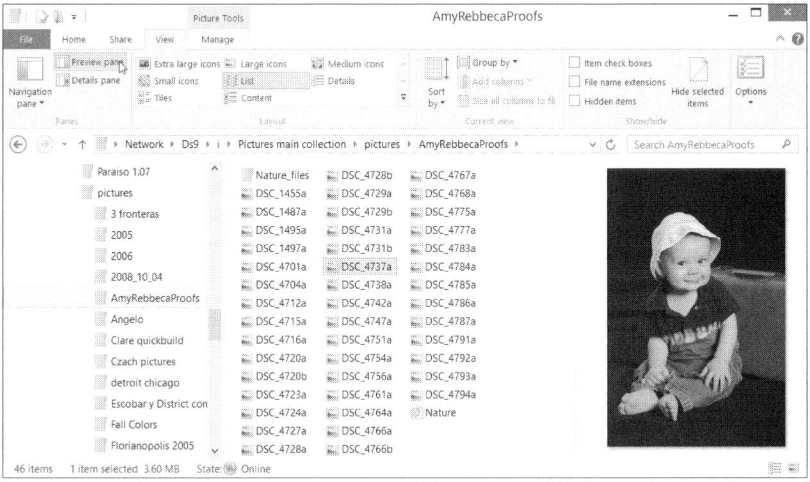

FIGURE 21.13

You can select one of two views to show in the Preview/Details pane.

Where possible, the Preview pane shows a snapshot of the object selected in the Content pane. If the software used to create the file is installed in Windows 10, or if the file is of a common type, you see a snapshot, such as the one shown in Figure 21.13.

The Details pane shows information about the file and enables you to input some personalized information. The data in the fields you see might have been entered manually by persons who have worked with the file, whereas other fields might have been filled by the software when the file was created. The file shown in Figure 21.14 displays size, rating, author, title, and tags fields. The specific fields displayed will differ depending on the file type selected. Modifying these values can prove useful later when searching for data you have added to tags, authors, and title fields.

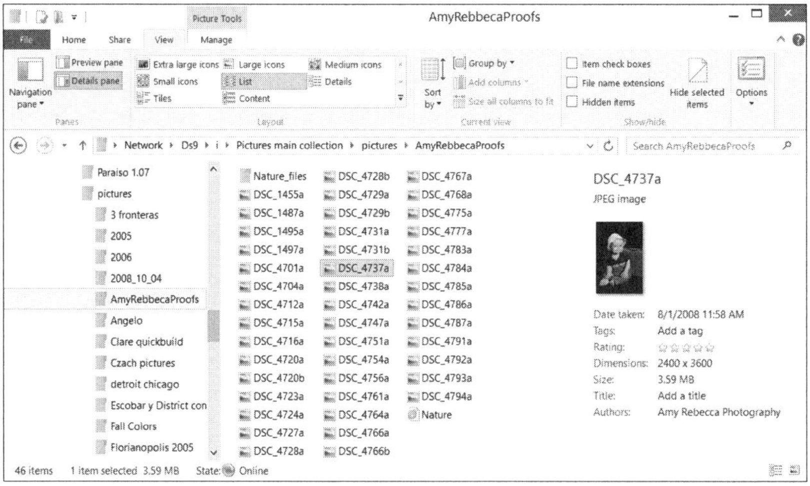

FIGURE 21.14

The Details pane displays information about the item selected in the Content pane.

NOTE If you want to see a preview of how the Preview pane will appear using any of the icon views shown in the Layout section under the View tab, just pass the mouse cursor over each choice without clicking. The Preview pane changes to the view you hover over.

TIP When using the Details pane, you can select multiple files at once and indicate a common rating as well as add tag and author information that will be applied to all selected files at once. Depending on the selected files, you might be able to add other data as well, such as comments or categories.

Folder Options

A number of configurable options affect how folders work and appear. Occasionally you might need to change a setting here when troubleshooting an issue or to find something that is hidden. Just remember that many of these settings are set as they are by default to protect you from accidently altering or deleting system files and folders your computer uses to operate correctly. To change one or more of these settings, follow these steps in an open File Explorer window:

1. On the ribbon, under the View tab, look for a button labeled Options on the far right of the ribbon (refer to Figure 21.14). Select **Options**. If you select the down arrow under Options, you will get the same results if you select **Change Folder and Search Options**. The Folder Options dialog box appears.

2. Select the **View** tab, as shown in Figure 21.15.

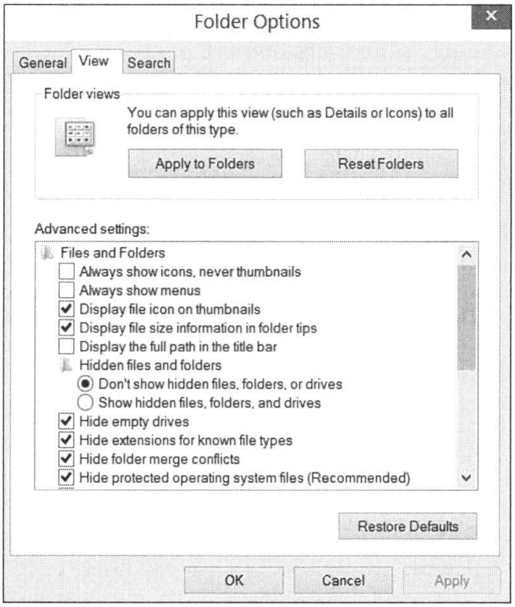

FIGURE 21.15

Nearly 20 options help you control exactly how folders work in File Explorer.

3. Adjust the options you're interested in.

4. Click **OK**.

You can review the most useful of these options in Table 21.1.

TABLE 21.1 Folder Options

Option	Description
Always Show Icons, Never Thumbnails	Displaying thumbnails requires extra computing power. You can help Windows run faster by clearing this option.
Always Show Menus	The ribbon provides much of the same functionality as provided by the menus and the commands on them in File Explorer. This option ensures the menus are always available because certain processes in Windows hide the File Explorer menus.
Display the Full Path in the Title Bar	This option displays the full path to the content displayed in the Explorer pane.
Hidden Files and Folders	Show Hidden files, folders, and drives. Some files and folders are hidden automatically in Windows. This option displays these hidden files and folders.
Hide Empty Drives	In addition to the main hard drive installed into your computer, you might have additional drives plugged into your computer, such as small, removable USB drives (known as *thumb* drives) or flash memory card readers. This option hides these drives if no device is plugged in.
Hide Extensions for Known File Types	As you learned earlier in this chapter, some file extensions are associated with a software program. For example, files with an XLS extension are almost always associated with Microsoft Excel. This option saves a little space by hiding the extension for a file when the filename displays and when the file's extension has an association with a program.
Restore Previous Folder Windows at Logon	When you sign on to Windows and start File Explorer, this option automatically opens folders just as you left them when you signed off. This is a useful option if you routinely work with the same set of folders or are working on a special project that requires you to work with several folders.
Show Status Bar	This option displays the status bar at the bottom of the File Explorer window.
Use Check Boxes to Select Items	This option creates a small checkbox with each file's icon, making it simple to select the file.
Use Sharing Wizard	Sharing files and folders with members of your family at home can be tricky. There are a few settings that must be just right for the information you've intended to share to be accessible by the other party. Using the wizard ensures that you will see each setting necessary for sharing to work. There is no reason a beginning user would have this option cleared.
When Typing into List View	This option is driven by personal preference. If you routinely work with long lists of files or folders, a quick method to moving to a file you want to work with is to type its name. If this option is set to Select the Typed Item, the cursor moves to that file. If you prefer to search for the files whose name you entered, select the Automatically Type into the Search Box option.

THE ABSOLUTE MINIMUM

- The raw materials of your Windows 10 system are files and the folders that store and organize them. Files are categorized as either system files, which are used by Windows 10 and the programs that run in Windows 10, or user files, which are the files you work with every day. You normally do not directly interact with system files.

- File Explorer is the tool used to manage your user files. You can start File Explorer from an icon on the desktop taskbar. If you find it a hassle to go to the desktop, you should locate the tile and then pin it to the Start menu if you anticipate using File Explorer often on a touchscreen device.

- Consider pinning folders to your Quick Access directory in File Explorer.

- Libraries are often misunderstood. Take time to consider how you can use their dynamic nature to simplify your life.

- Invest in your sanity by organizing your folders and files. Think about a folder structure that will help you find your files easily.

- You must first select those files that you need to interact with, such as when you plan to copy or move the files.

WORKING WITH ONEDRIVE

Cloud storage is by no means unique to Windows 10. You can choose from many cloud storage services and many websites—and even apps in the Windows Store—to manage their use from inside Windows. Microsoft created OneDrive (formerly known as SkyDrive) to provide a valuable alternative to traditional storage methods. It has become an integral part of Windows 10, which makes it incomparable for ease of use and availability. If you have never used OneDrive before, you will certainly have questions about what it is, how to use it, and why it will become increasingly important to you. If you have used OneDrive in the past, you might be surprised by how integrated it is in Windows 10. This chapter helps you understand how to manage OneDrive.

NOTE In the exercises, this chapter relies on basic file and folder navigation skills using File Explorer that were considered in Chapter 21, "File and Folder Basics."

Introducing OneDrive

It's amazing how much content, files, and data users have access to today. You can have several gigabytes (if not terabytes!) of pictures, video, and music. Documents may be small, but they add up. Many people find that they work with several devices between home, work, and when traveling. It isn't practical to carry all your important data with you. That's where the cloud comes in. OneDrive is an Internet-based (cloud) storage area in which you can put files such as pictures and documents and have access to them from virtually any Internet-enabled device. Synchronization even enables you to keep local copies that you can take with you when you're not connected to the Internet.

If you are skeptical about "free stuff," be assured that OneDrive is the real thing. You automatically get 15GB of free cloud-based storage with your Microsoft account. Additional free storage is often offered through promotions, and you can pay a fee to add further storage to your OneDrive.

If you have an Office 365 subscription, OneDrive or OneDrive for Business is included, which generally means you have 1TB of OneDrive space by default. OneDrive for Business is really a similar product to the personal OneDrive with a few additional tools aimed at collaboration and security that are more important for managing a business.

Besides file storage, OneDrive provides tools that care for synchronizing your settings between multiple devices so that your color choices, wallpaper, apps, music playlists, and many other features will behave the same way on any Windows 10 device. As you read through this chapter, it's important to keep in mind that I'm assuming that you are logged in to a device with a Microsoft account and that you have an Internet connection. Both are needed to access OneDrive.

OneDrive can be accessed using File Explorer, but you also can jump straight to your OneDrive by selecting the OneDrive tile from the Start menu. To open OneDrive, select the OneDrive tile, shown in Figure 22.1. You might find it practical to right-click OneDrive and select Pin to Start to keep OneDrive highly available.

ANTICIPATED ONEDRIVE IMPROVEMENTS

OneDrive is an important service for Microsoft. This can be seen by looking at the many planned improvements Microsoft has revealed as of this writing.

While a OneDrive app existed for Windows 8.1, Windows 10 does not include an app upon its official release. A universal Windows 10 app is planned for release toward the end of 2015, which will make it easier for touch-driven devices to manage their OneDrive content as well as include additional tools to manage files and folders in OneDrive without visiting a website. Apps are already available for Android and iOS, making management and access to files stored in OneDrive a breeze from most any mobile device you might be using.

Although OneDrive and OneDrive for Business are two different products, there will continue to be tighter integration—for example, both can already be managed from the same app if you are using a mobile device.

Further expected improvements include greater control over which files and folders are synced, improvements to managing user permissions when sharing files and folders, usage reporting, offline file editing, PDF annotation tools, expiring share links, larger file support, increased storage, and control over quotas for shared OneDrives.

FIGURE 22.1

OneDrive is available from the Start menu.

As you can tell from Figure 22.2, OneDrive looks like a normal set of folders on your device with one big difference—OneDrive folders include a sync indicator that provides you with sync status information.

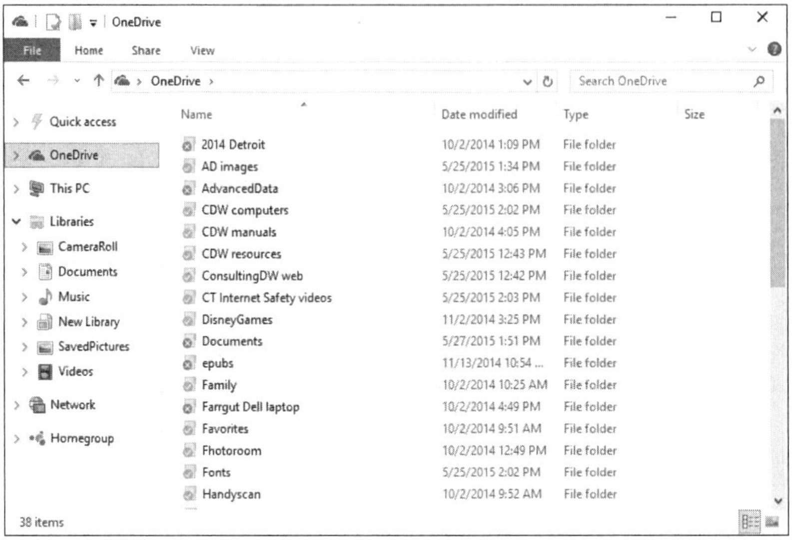

FIGURE 22.2

OneDrive opens to your folders and shows you their sync status with your device.

There are many practical reasons to use this new form of storage. Consider some of these common uses:

- If you work with the same document on a number of computers, such as your work computer and your home computer, or if you also work on a tablet, use the OneDrive account to store the documents. This saves you from emailing the document to yourself. You can even access your OneDrive from most smartphones.

- If you have a tablet, you might be faced with the reality of having limited storage space on the device itself. OneDrive provides a flexible storage solution to hardware limitations on your device.

- OneDrive enables you to easily share with others. You can specify by email address those people who have access to one or more of your OneDrive folders.

- OneDrive stores your data on servers that are maintained, backed up, and kept highly available. This provides a lot more protection from disaster than most people are in a position to provide when it comes to important personal data like pictures and documents. Theft, hard drive failure, alien invasion… they're pretty much all covered.

- If you work with a small team, all the documents can be stored in a folder of a OneDrive account. Instead of emailing files around the group, you can use the OneDrive folders as the source for all team or project documents.

NOTE OneDrive and OneDrive for Business are both cloud-based storage tools that will provide you with the most complete and robust controls while accessed using the web browser. This chapter focuses on OneDrive features that are built in to the Windows 10 operating system.

Setting Up OneDrive

Unless you set up your OneDrive when initially signing in to your device, the first time you actually open OneDrive on a device you will need to set up the way OneDrive will be used on that device. Follow these steps when prompted to set up OneDrive:

1. Open the OneDrive shortcut from the Start menu (refer to Figure 22.1).

2. If OneDrive has not been set up, you will see a Welcome to OneDrive window, as shown in Figure 22.3. If OneDrive opens to your OneDrive folders, then you are already set up and you can skip the following steps.

FIGURE 22.3

If OneDrive has yet to be configured, you will be prompted to set it up the first time you use it.

3. Select the **Get Started** button.

4. Sign in to your Microsoft account, as shown in Figure 22.4, and select **Sign In**. If you do not have a Microsoft account, you can create one from here by selecting **Sign Up Now**. (Setting up a new Microsoft account is covered in Chapter 19, "Sharing Your Windows Computer with Others.")

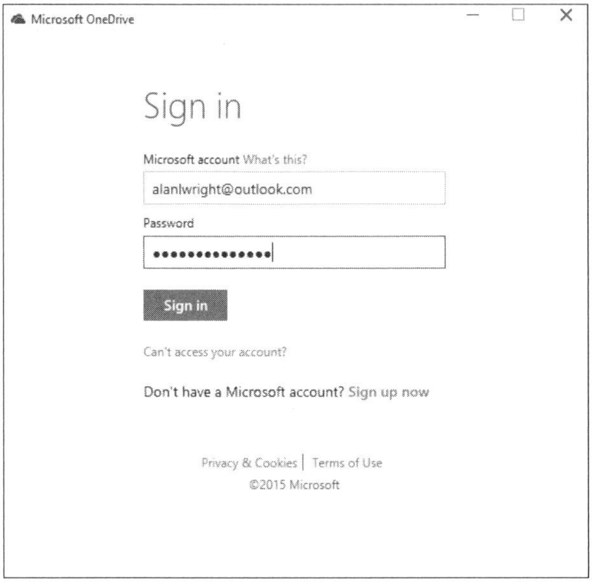

FIGURE 22.4

You can sign in to OneDrive with an existing Microsoft account or create one.

5. You will see the Introducing Your OneDrive Folder screen. A location is indicated where a local copy of your OneDrive will be saved on this device. You can modify the location by selecting **Change** if you need to; however, it is generally best to leave it where it is. Select **Next**.

6. The next screen is one of the more important choices you will face. Choose what you want to sync. As shown in Figure 22.5, you have two choices: Sync All Files and Folders in My OneDrive or Sync Only These Folders. When using Sync Only These Folders, use check boxes to indicate the folders you want to copy to your local drive. After making your choices, select **Next**.

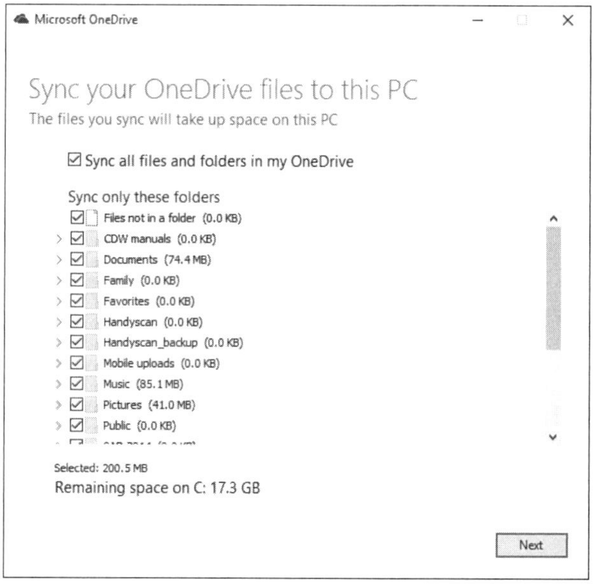

![Microsoft OneDrive dialog box showing "Sync your OneDrive files to this PC"]

Microsoft OneDrive — ☐ ✕

Sync your OneDrive files to this PC
The files you sync will take up space on this PC

☑ Sync all files and folders in my OneDrive

Sync only these folders
☑ Files not in a folder (0.0 KB)
> ☑ CDW manuals (0.0 KB)
> ☑ Documents (74.4 MB)
> ☑ Family (0.0 KB)
> ☑ Favorites (0.0 KB)
> ☑ Handyscan (0.0 KB)
> ☑ Handyscan_backup (0.0 KB)
> ☑ Mobile uploads (0.0 KB)
> ☑ Music (85.1 MB)
> ☑ Pictures (41.0 MB)
> ☑ Public (0.0 KB)

Selected: 200.5 MB
Remaining space on C: 17.3 GB

Next

FIGURE 22.5

Use selective syncing to select just the folders you want to sync to your device.

7. Fetch Your Files from Anywhere enables you to access files on your device remotely from OneDrive when accessing it through a web browser. This can be a useful feature if you frequently work with more than one Windows computer. Select the checkbox to enable this feature, and then select **Done**.

After OneDrive is enabled and set up, you will see the folders you have elected to sync when opening OneDrive from your device.

TIP   If your tablet has limited storage, you might find it advantageous to change your OneDrive storage to an SD card. Your tablet will not lose valuable storage space, and you will have more control over the size of SD card used for this type of roll-over storage space.

CAUTION   I recommend you select folders you want to sync. You might have more storage space on OneDrive than your device can handle, so storage is a factor. Sync itself can be a factor because OneDrive will verify and update any files that have changed in the folders you sync locally.

NOTE Enabling the Fetch Your Files from Anywhere option while setting up OneDrive will create a tile for your computer in the online OneDrive web page. To access files remotely, make sure the computer is powered up and connected to the Internet. Additionally, as a security measure you will need to generate and input a security code through the phone or email contacts of your Microsoft account to actually gain access to the computer.

Adding Files to Your OneDrive

The process to load your files to OneDrive is pretty straightforward and is identical to the way you would copy or move files and folders between folders and drives on your device. To add files and folders to OneDrive, follow these steps:

1. Open File Explorer and navigate to the folder or file you want to add to your OneDrive.

2. Copy the file or folder to create a second copy and retain the original, or use Cut to remove the original and paste it into a new location. Tap and hold or right-click to reveal these choices in a context menu.

3. Open the OneDrive shortcut (refer to Figure 22.1), or from File Explorer select OneDrive in the navigation pane.

4. Navigate to the folder within your OneDrive where you want to paste the file or folder you have copied, and then paste. Your file or folder will appear with a small blue sync icon showing synchronization is pending.

5. After a few seconds, the icon should change to a green checkmark letting you know that the item is synced.

NOTE It might take some time to upload especially large files. Status messages appear near the notifications area. You also can select these status messages or select the OneDrive icon in the notifications area to view details regarding sync progress.

Managing Your OneDrive Files

You have as many options for managing your OneDrive files as you do for your local drives. You can create folders and subfolders, select multiple files, delete files, and see thumbnails of a file's contents. Another useful tool for managing your OneDrive is located in your notifications area. From here, you can change settings that might have been selected when setting up OneDrive for the device as well as find links to your online OneDrive.

To access OneDrive settings, follow these steps:

1. Select the **Show Hidden Icons** button from the notifications area of the task-bar. Locate and right-click the OneDrive icon, as shown in Figure 22.6. From here, you could select **Go to OneDrive.com** or **Manage Storage** to jump to your online OneDrive account; instead, we will focus on settings related to your device.

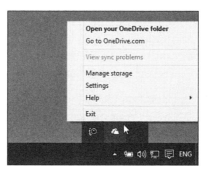

FIGURE 22.6

You can access settings from the OneDrive icon in the notifications area.

2. Select **Settings**. The Microsoft OneDrive window will appear, as shown in Figure 22.7.

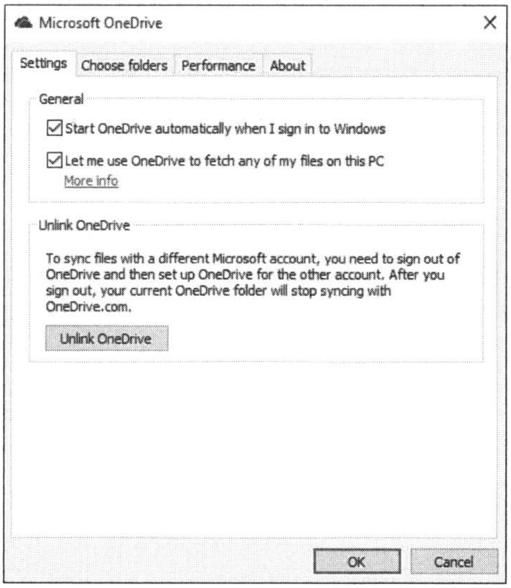

FIGURE 22.7

You can make changes to how OneDrive works on a device after setup or unlink a device from your OneDrive.

3. From the Settings tab, you can make changes using a few checkboxes:

- **Start OneDrive Automatically When I Sign In to Windows**—This should be enabled unless you simply do not use OneDrive.

- **Let Me Use OneDrive to Fetch Any of My Files on This PC**—You should enable this only if you expect to remotely access files on this device from the web-based OneDrive.

- **Use Office to Sync Files Faster...**—This is fine to leave enabled. It permits the OneDrive integration available in Office 2013 and Office 2016 as well as collaboration tools that exist in these Office products. If you do not have Office products installed you will not see this option.

4. At the bottom of the Settings tab is the option to **Unlink OneDrive**. This tool will cut the cords between your device and OneDrive. To reconnect OneDrive, you will need to go through the setup process all over again outlined earlier in this chapter.

5. A common task with OneDrive is to change which folders are synced with a device. In the Choose Folders tab, select the button **Choose Folders** to open the same selection window shown back in Figure 22.5.

6. From the Performance tab, you can enable the **Improve Upload Speed by Uploading Files in Batches** checkbox. This can negatively impact other activities like video streaming when OneDrive is syncing. Otherwise, this is a good feature to leave enabled.

7. Select **OK** to save any changes and close the Microsoft OneDrive window.

Sharing a File on Your OneDrive

Sharing a file as a link rather than an email has many advantages. Email can be rejected by servers when attachments are too large, and even when a large email makes it to your recipient, the recipient might not thank you for having another attachment in her mailbox. OneDrive makes it easy to share a link to a file that can then be sent by email, posted to a social network site, or sent as a text message.

To generate a link for a file on your OneDrive, follow these steps:

1. Open OneDrive by selecting it from the Start menu or by opening File Explorer and navigating to OneDrive. Locate the folder or file you want to share.

2. Right-click the file or folder to reveal the context menu, as shown in Figure 22.8. Select **Share a OneDrive Link**.

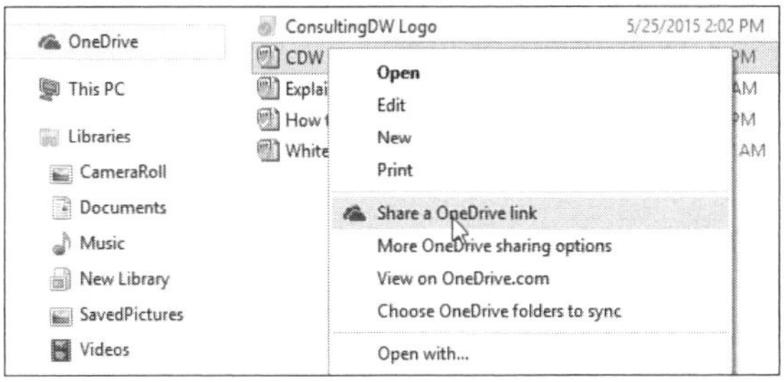

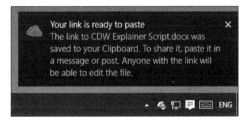

FIGURE 22.8

The context menu includes a tool for generating links to share OneDrive files and folders.

3. After a few seconds a notification will appear letting you know that a link has been prepared (refer to Figure 22.9).

FIGURE 22.9

Windows prepares a link for sharing and stores it in the Windows clipboard ready to paste.

4. Paste the link into an email or a text message to share it.

Figure 22.10 shows an example of what the link would look like. Even though this link grants access to only the document or folder it was generated for, there is nothing to identify who used the link, and it could be shared with anyone. Nothing prevents downloading or editing the files shared in this way. For greater control, you might want to share from the web interface, which will allow you to share with specific email addresses and grant limited access to the file to prevent changes to the original.

NOTE   The yet-to-be-released universal OneDrive app will include sharing tools that will enable you to generate links for sharing limited to specific emails and with limitations on their permissions, such as read-only access.

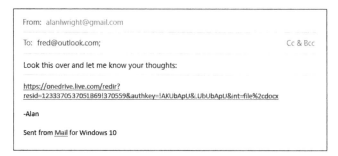

From: alanlwright@gmail.com

To: fred@outlook.com;   Cc & Bcc

Look this over and let me know your thoughts:

https://onedrive.live.com/redir?
resid=1233370537051B69!370559&authkey=!AKUbApU&.UbUbApU&int=file%2cdocx

-Alan

Sent from Mail for Windows 10

FIGURE 22.10

Sharing a OneDrive link is fast but does not provide access controls.

Viewing OneDrive Status

Storage space is limited on OneDrive. To see how much space you have available, follow these steps:

1. Select the **Show Hidden Icons** button from the notifications area of the taskbar. Locate and right-click the OneDrive icon (refer to Figure 22.5).

2. Select **Manage Storage**. Your web browser will open a web page to your online account, as shown in Figure 22.11.

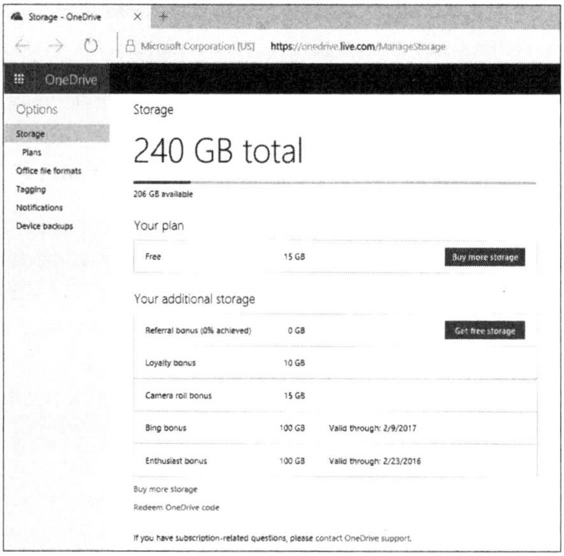

FIGURE 22.11

Check your storage space status using the Manage Storage setting from the OneDrive icon in the notifications area.

3. Your current total storage is indicated, as well as promotions and expiration dates that might be connected to promotional storage space.

4. If you need more space, there is a convenient **Buy More Storage** button. Select this to see current offers, as shown in Figure 22.12, which include incremental storage plans with monthly rates indicated. You will also see an option for an Office 365 subscription that includes a hefty 1TB of OneDrive storage.

5. Press the **Select** button for a plan to get more details and confirm payment methods. Select **Confirm** to proceed or **Cancel** to stay with your current storage level.

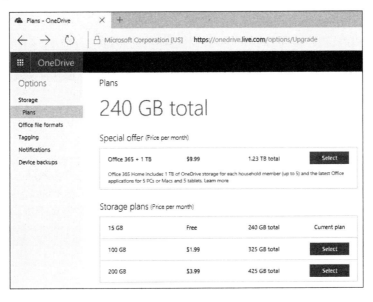

FIGURE 22.12

You can buy additional OneDrive space for a monthly subscription price.

You might hesitate to purchase additional space. Consider a few factors that perhaps will put things into perspective:

- **Ease of use**—You do not need to carry a flash drive around, and it will be there any time you log in to a computer with your Microsoft account—even if you choose to log in to your Microsoft account from a web browser on someone else's computer.

- **Security**—What happens if you lose a flash drive or, worse yet, your laptop? Will you get your data back if your hard drive fails? OneDrive space is encrypted and is backed up on Microsoft servers, so you do not have to worry if a hard drive fails.

- **Convenience**—By sharing files with other people, you can simplify collaboration and avoid issues with email attachments.

 TIP Before buying additional space, make sure you are wisely using the space you already have. Just because you *can* save all your music and videos to your OneDrive does not mean it is practical or even a good idea. Things that you share or that need to be highly available should get priority.

Configuring OneDrive Preferences

There are a few settings that enable you to customize how your device uses OneDrive storage; many of these are found in apps that are capable of using OneDrive. You learn about some of these setting in this and the following sections.

Sync Settings with OneDrive

Perhaps the most obvious setting related to OneDrive preferences is how your device preferences can be synced to other Windows 10 devices using OneDrive. This provides many advantages, but there might be times that you do not want changes to one device to influence or change other devices. Although OneDrive is not mentioned in the Settings app in the steps that follow, the mechanism for transferring settings is actually using OneDrive.

To disable this feature, follow these steps:

1. Open the Settings app from the Start menu.

2. Select **Accounts**.

3. Select **Sync Your Settings** from the vertical navigation menu, as shown in Figure 22.13.

4. Turn Sync Settings to **Off** to disable this feature entirely. You can leave Sync Settings **On** and just turn off individual settings if there is a specific change you are trying to avoid.

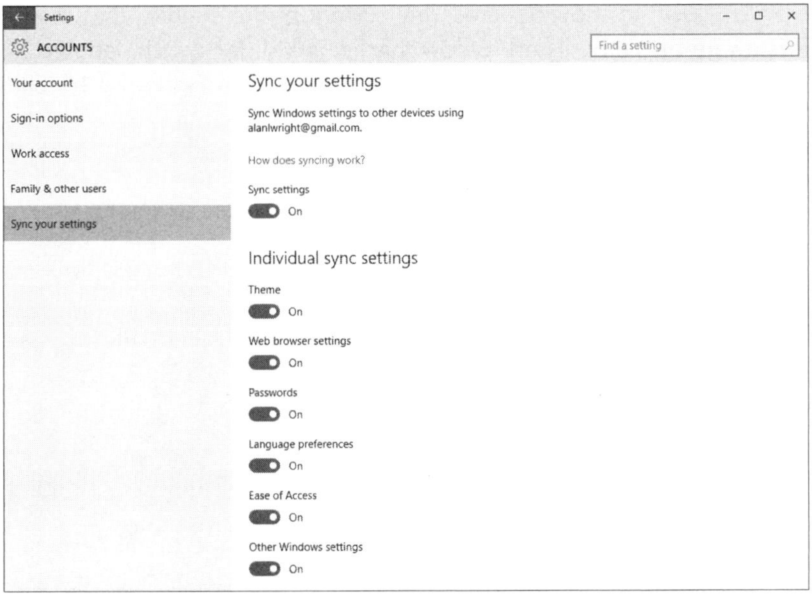

FIGURE 22.13

Disable the synchronization of device settings through OneDrive in the Settings app.

Using OneDrive in the Photo App

The Photo app is a great app for viewing, editing, and managing your photos. The Photo app is considered in detail in Chapter 26, "Working with Photos in Windows," but there is a setting related to OneDrive you should be aware of. If you have an Android or iOS device, you might want to install the OneDrive app. You will be able to auto-upload photos from that device to your OneDrive, gaining an extra 15GB of free storage in the bargain, which now gives you a total of 30GB of free storage! The Photo app will look for photos in your OneDrive by default, which automates the process of seeing pictures from your phone on your Windows 10 device.

To manage whether your device looks for pictures on your OneDrive, follow these steps:

1. Open the Photos app from the Start menu.

2. Select the gear-shaped **Settings** icon to open the Settings pane.

3. Scroll down to show Sources; any current photo sources that the photo app is aware of will be listed. Below this list is a slider switch, labeled **Show My Photos and Videos from OneDrive**, as shown in Figure 22.14. Slide the switch to **Off** to disable this feature.

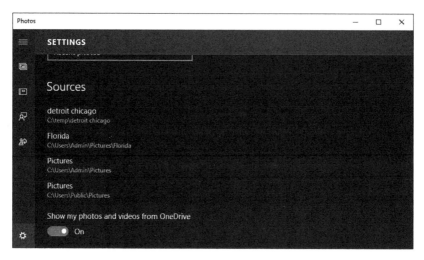

FIGURE 22.14

You can control whether the Photos app sees photos in your OneDrive.

Using OneDrive with the Music App

OneDrive integration in the Groove Music app is a new feature and one that is sure to see improvements with time. OneDrive now includes a special Music folder by default designed to accommodate MP3, M4A (AAC), and unprotected WMA-formatted music files as of the time of this writing. Copy music files to this folder in your OneDrive using the web browser, and it will be seen automatically by the Music app. Songs can then be streamed without downloading them to your Windows 10 device using the Music app.

TIP You might find that the Music folder is also set to sync to your device. If you do not want to sacrifice local storage space because of a large music collection saved to your OneDrive, remove this folder from the folders that are synced using the steps outlined in the section "Managing Your OneDrive Files," found earlier in this chapter. You will still be able to stream your music using an Internet connection.

To stream music from your OneDrive music folder, follow these steps:

1. Open the Music app from the Start menu.

2. Select **Albums**, **Artists**, or **Songs** from the hamburger menu to display your music. Select the current **Filter** option above your music to reveal the drop-down list shown in Figure 22.15. Select **On OneDrive** to see only music that is in your OneDrive Music folder. You will see a small icon indicating this song or album is available for streaming.

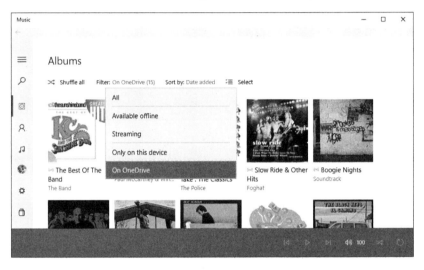

FIGURE 22.15

From the Music app you can stream music that is saved to your OneDrive.

3. To download a song or album from OneDrive to your device for times when you might be offline, right-click the song or album and select **Download**. The selection will be download to the *Music>Xbox Music>OneDrive Cache* folder on your device.

4. To hide duplicate songs from your Music collection that are in the OneDrive Music folder, select the gear-shaped **Settings** icon. Scroll down to the switch under OneDrive and make sure the switch is **On** for Automatically Clean Up Duplicate Tracks, as shown in Figure 22.16.

There are many other features and settings that you can use in the Music app. The Music app is covered in detail in Chapter 26, "Enjoying Music."

 TIP You can save music to any folder in your OneDrive and then add it to the locations that the Music app monitors for your music.

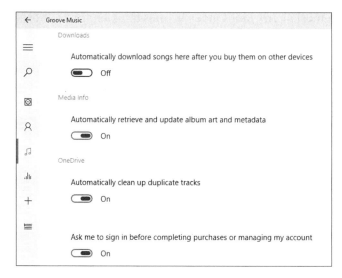

FIGURE 22.16

The Music app can hide duplicate songs when you already have a copy in your OneDrive Music folder.

CAUTION   If you delete a song from your collection in the Music app that is in your OneDrive Music folder, that song is also deleted from the Music folder and placed in the OneDrive recycle bin where it will remain for 90 days before disappearing.

Managing Metered Connections Considerations

Occasionally, I am out on the road and I will share the Internet from my smartphone. This enables me to use a process called *tethering* to connect to the Internet with my laptop and tablet using the same cellular Internet connection my smartphone uses. This is handy, but depending on your plan, it could quickly suck up your monthly data allotment. I exceeded my quota for the month the first time I used it because my older Windows laptop downloaded a bunch of updates, and I didn't notice what was happening in the background until it was too late. This illustrates why it's important that you protect your more costly connections to the Internet from unnecessary data consumption. OneDrive is certainly another factor that can increase your data consumption with updates and syncing taking place behind the scenes.

Another factor could be bandwidth. Hotels can be terribly slow and stingy with "free Wi-Fi," and I have friends who still live with dial-up connections. If you have a slow connection, you might need to consider what type of data gets priority when you connect to the Internet.

Microsoft uses the term *metered Internet connection* to refer to a connection that has restrictions on data, especially related to quotas or limits. Fortunately, Windows enables you to categorize a connection as metered, which in turn lets Windows know that lower-priority data such as updates and some OneDrive tasks should be postponed until using a nonmetered connection. Some apps that use OneDrive can indicate that you are on a Limited Network while you work from a metered connection.

To mark a Wi-Fi network connection as metered, follow these steps. (You must be connected to the Wi-Fi connection to indicate that it is metered.)

1. From the Start menu, select the Settings app, and then select **Network & Internet**.

2. Under Wi-Fi, make sure that you are connected to the network connection you intend to modify. Select **Advanced Options** from the bottom of the Wi-Fi list.

3. Above the properties for the current network you will see a switch for Metered Connection, as shown in Figure 22.17. Slide the switch to **On** to mark it as a metered connection.

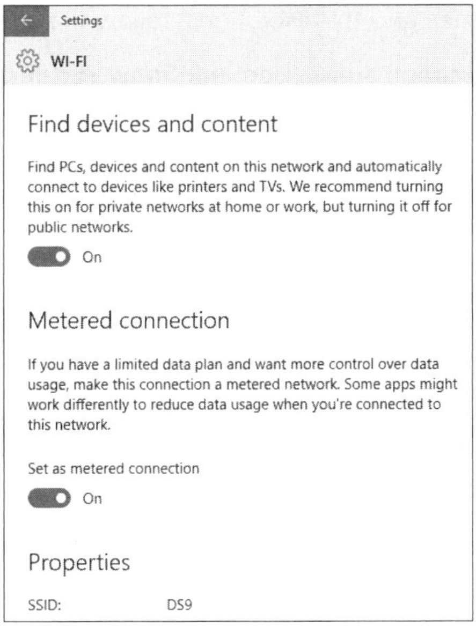

FIGURE 22.17

Make sure you identify a network as metered if you are concerned about data consumption.

Troubleshooting OneDrive Issues

OneDrive is so integrated into Windows 10 that you might forget you are connected to cloud-based storage until things go wrong. Most OneDrive issues are related to what happens to files on your device while you are offline or when the same file is being accessed in two places at once. Perhaps a filename has changed or you have moved or modified a file. Syncing may have been interrupted. All these factors can contribute to an alert that appears in the notifications area letting you know that there is a problem with a file (see Figure 22.18).

FIGURE 22.18

The OneDrive icon in the notifications area can alert you to sync problems and help you resolve them.

To look at sync issues and try resolutions, follow these steps:

1. From the notification area, select the **Show Hidden Icons** button and then right-click the OneDrive icon (refer to Figure 22.5).

2. Select **View Sync Problems**. If this option is grayed out, then good news—you have no sync problems to resolve.

3. The Microsoft OneDrive window will open, as shown in Figure 22.19, with file-names and folder names, error messages, and proposed resolutions.

4. Select the entry to open File Explorer, where you can implement the proposed resolution.

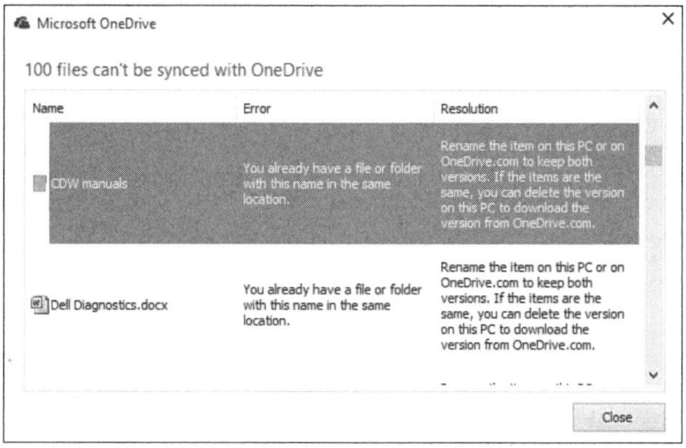

FIGURE 22.19

OneDrive will propose solutions and help you troubleshoot sync issues.

Other factors that could cause problems include

- OneDrive currently has a file size limit of 10GB.

- When updates are not appearing, check to see whether you are using a metered connection that is preventing sync.

- The filename may be an issue if it contains certain characters. Change the name of the file so that it doesn't begin or end with a space, end with a period, or include any of these characters: / \ < > : * " ? |

- The file path might be too long. The entire path, including the filename, must contain fewer than 255 characters.

- Missing files can be the result of accidental deletion by you or someone sharing a folder. Check the Recycle Bin and restore the file if it is there. Files are retained up to 90 days.

- Verify that you have the latest Windows updates installed.

THE ABSOLUTE MINIMUM

- OneDrive is an integral part of Windows 10. Take some time to open your OneDrive and add files and folders.

- You can check your available drive space and even purchase additional OneDrive space by opening OneDrive in your web browser.

- Using the OneDrive app, you can add files, create and manage folders, and delete files.

- Use selective sync to control which folders are available offline and to control how much space your OneDrive files take up on your local device.

- Look for settings in Windows apps that manage how OneDrive is used.

- Check your settings for metered connections, and tag connections as metered if data consumption is a concern.

23

WORKING WITH PHOTOS IN WINDOWS

It's nearly impossible to find people who take photos with film anymore. The moment it became cheaper and easier to snap shots on a digital camera, store pictures on a computer, make excellent prints on affordable consumer printers, and share photos on the Internet, film cameras were obsolete. Windows 10 makes it easy to view and edit pictures you have shot and even share photos by email or to other apps. The Photos app has been designed to do more than showcase your photos; it includes tools for managing your photos and editing tools that are noteworthy and worth exploring. This chapter covers the basics of the app, how to access editing tools, and how to manage your photo collection.

We will also look at the Camera app included with Windows 10. Even though this app is pretty straightforward, it adds an important element to devices equipped with a webcam or camera.

You might find it useful to understand Libraries and how to control what is included in a Library by reviewing Chapter 21, "File and Folder Basics."

Using the Photos App

Everyone likes to look at their digital photos and share their pictures with others. For many, it's a race to get home from an event to load photos onto a computer and then upload them to a website for others to enjoy. Those with smartphones can upload photos right away so that the entire world can get instant visual updates of what happens. The Photos app provides an easy-to-use hub for your digital pictures and videos with features designed to enhance your photo viewing experience. Keeping with design principles found throughout Windows 10, the focus remains on your photos; tools and menus are hidden or minimized until needed.

To open the Photos app, select the **Photos** tile from your Start menu. If you cannot locate that tile, start entering the word "**photos**" into the Search bar next to the Start button. Select the **Photos** tile from the list of results. After you do so, the Photos app will open, as shown in Figure 23.1. It quickly analyzes your device for any new photos that have been added since it was last used.

FIGURE 23.1

The Photos app enables you to view your pictures stored in the Pictures library.

The capabilities and features in the Photos app might seem limited compared to some of the applications available in the Windows Store; you can find applications that create fancier slideshows or ones with professional tools for editing photos. However, the ease of use of the Photos app can't be challenged. If you're more dedicated to photography and working with photos, the app can still be used as a streamlined, simple, central library for your photos, enabling you to leverage other applications to do the interesting work.

Viewing Your Collection

The Photos app presents you initially with a collection of large thumbnails of photos and videos that are located in your Pictures library. You can either import or add pictures to your Pictures folder or add folders to your Picture library so the Photos app will see them. If you are logged in to your device with a Microsoft account, you also might see pictures from your OneDrive, which are included by default. All pictures are grouped by date to help you easily navigate through all your pictures with no reference to folder.

To look at a specific photo, simply select it from the **Collection**. The photo will fill the window, as shown in Figure 23.2. A toolbar will be visible across the top with tools that can be used when viewing a photo.

FIGURE 23.2

Selecting a photo in the Photos app lets you view the photo with no screen clutter.

Navigation is intuitive within the Photos app. Scroll using a mouse, swipe left or right with a touchscreen, or select the arrows that appear at the middle of the left or right edges of the photo. To reveal additional options available for a photo, select the ellipsis (…), as shown in Figure 23.3, to expand the upper toolbar. Return to the initial Collection view of the Photos app by selecting the back arrow located to the far left on the title bar or down on the taskbar if using a touch-screen device.

FIGURE 23.3

Essential tools are revealed when selecting the ellipsis on the toolbar while viewing a specific photo.

When you are looking at a photo, several tools are available on the toolbar:

- **Share**—Share opens a Share pane that will offer apps designed to accept photos. Figure 23.4 shows the Share pane for a photo that offers to open the photo in several apps, including a few social media apps.

- **Slide Show**—Slide show will initiate a full-screen slideshow starting with the current photo that will run until interrupted by selecting somewhere on the screen.

- **Edit**—Edit opens the photo in the edit interface surrounded by a number of tools that enable you to tweak the current image properties. Edit is discussed in more detail later in this chapter.

FIGURE 23.4

You can select Share to send your photos to other apps for a variety of reasons.

- **Rotate**—Rotate will rotate a photo 90° clockwise each time it is selected.

- **Delete**—Delete asks you to confirm a deletion if it's selected. Select Delete to remove a picture from your device or Cancel to change your mind.

- **Open With**—Select Open With to open this photo in another application that can work with images. A pop-up window will appear with a list of applications to choose from.

- **Copy**—Select Copy to add the picture to the Windows Clipboard. You can then paste the picture into another application.

- **Print**—Select Print to hand the picture over to Windows to print. A print window will open and allow you to control how the picture is printed, as shown in Figure 23.5.

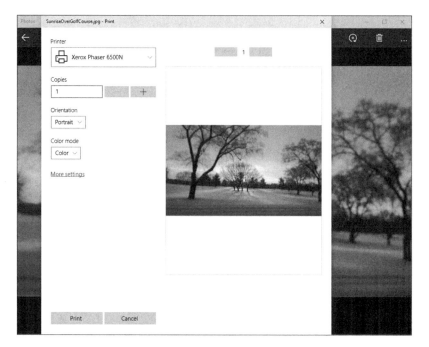

FIGURE 23.5

Send pictures to your printer by selecting Print from the Photos app.

- **Set as Lock Screen**—Set as Lock Screen will replace the current choice your device has for an image that is displayed when the device is not in use. Lock screen options are considered in more detail in Chapter 8, "Tweaking Windows to Reflect Your Personality."

- **File Info**—As shown in Figure 23.6, File Info will show details regarding the photo, including size, resolution, and even the device that took the photo. Scroll up or press Esc to return to the photo.

FIGURE 23.6

File information can be viewed when looking at photos in the Photos app.

THE WINDOWS PHOTO VIEWER

The Windows Photo Viewer has been around for years (a version was included with Windows XP), and it is still a handy way to quickly view an image file, browse through images in a folder, or even run a quick slideshow for a folder full of images. By default, if you are viewing image files in File Explorer, the Photos app is used to open the image file when double-clicking or using the Open command from the context menu for an image file. If you would rather use the Windows Photo Viewer to view images from File Explorer, just right-click (tap and hold on a touchscreen) and select Open With from the context menu; then select Windows Photo Viewer to open the image with the Windows Photo Viewer application.

Using Albums

Albums is a new feature that provides a way of grouping your photos (and videos) in an attractive way; Windows will actually analyze your photos and create albums for you automatically. Photos are dynamically enhanced when viewing. To view the albums currently available on your device, select **Albums** from the hamburger menu. As shown in Figure 23.7, photos that share common dates appear grouped together into albums with the date as a title.

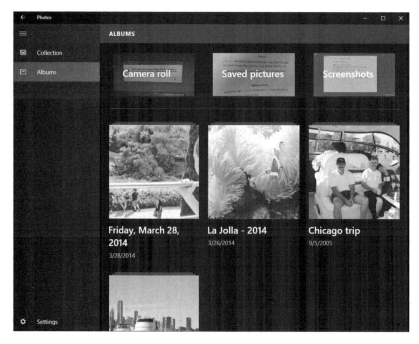

FIGURE 23.7

Select Albums to view grouped photos available on your device.

To view an album, simply select it, and the album is displayed as shown in Figure 23.8. A cover photo is shown, sometimes referred to as a *hero* image, which is used to represent the album with smaller thumbnails of other photos that are currently in the album shown below. Select a photo in the album, and the photo will fill the window. While you're viewing individual photos in your album, the same tools are available that you would see when viewing a photo from the collection (refer to Figure 23.3)—the exception being that the Slide Show will show only pictures from the album.

FIGURE 23.8

Albums provide a new and attractive way to organize and present your photos.

Albums can be edited in a couple of ways, allowing you to change the photos that are included or to change the cover photo and title for the album. To edit an album, follow these steps:

1. To simply edit the photos included in an album, you can scroll to the bottom of the album and select the box **Add or Remove Photos**. (This choice is also available in step 3 when selecting **Edit**.)

2. A mosaic of available photos will be shown, and photos that are currently included in the album will be outlined and marked with a checkmark. Add or remove photos from the album by simply selecting them. When finished, select the checkmark to make the changes or select the **X** to cancel any changes (see Figure 23.9). You are returned to the album view.

FIGURE 23.9

Adding photos to or removing photos from an album is easy.

3. To change the title or cover photo, select the **Edit** tool from the upper menu bar of the Photo app (represented by a pencil). The edit options in Figure 23.10 will be shown.

4. Select the text box of the current title to make changes to the title. After making your changes, select the checkmark to make the changes or select the **X** to cancel any changes

5. To change the cover photo, select the **Change Cover** button. The images of the current album are displayed, and whichever photo is selected is the cover photo. Make any changes here; then select the checkmark to apply the change, or select the **X** to cancel any change. You are returned to the edit options from step 3.

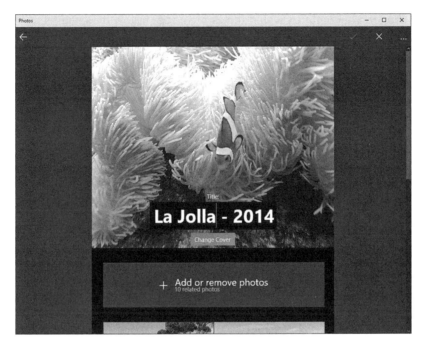

FIGURE 23.10

Customize the appearance of albums by changing the Title and Cover photo.

6. When finished, select the checkmark to make the changes or select the **X** to cancel any changes. You are returned to the album view.

 NOTE Albums is a new feature that is intended to sync across your devices using the power of OneDrive. The Photos app can create albums from OneDrive photos, and these albums will be seen by other Windows 10 devices such as a Windows phone or Xbox One. This creates a nice sense of continuity and can make it more rewarding when taking the time to customize your albums.

Tweaking the Photos App with Settings

The Photos app has a few important settings you should be aware of. Most casual photographers should appreciate the auto-enhance feature that can straighten and correct photos for viewing. Some individuals such as professional photographers might not want subtle changes being applied to their work. This is just one of the settings you can control in the Photos app.

To change your settings within the Photos app, follow these steps:

1. Select **Settings** from the hamburger menu of the Photos app. The app opens to Settings, as shown in Figure 23.11.

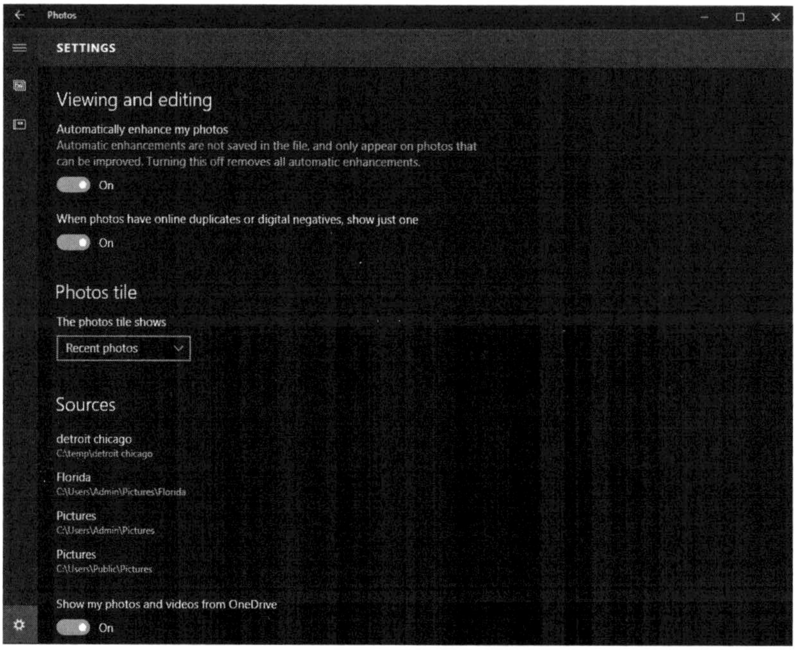

FIGURE 23.11

The Photos app has its very own Settings tools you can tweak.

2. Under Viewing and Editing, slide the switch for **Automatically Enhance My Photos** to **Off** if you do not want any enhancements to be applied.

3. I recommend that you leave the next switch enabled. The Photos app will try to filter out duplicate photos that might have been added over time to a large collection of photos. To prevent this default action, slide the switch **When Photos Have Online Duplicates or Digital Negatives, Show Just One** to **Off**.

4. Under Photos Tile, select the drop-down menu to change how your Photos app tile appears in the Start menu. By default, the live tile will flip through **Recent Photos**. You can assign a specific photo to appear on the tile by selecting **A Single Photo**. A Choose Photo option appears, and you can select a photo using File Explorer. (If you wish to disable Live tile, right-click the actual tile in the Start menu and select **Turn Live Tile Off**).

5. Under Sources, information is provided regarding the current photos, sources that the Photos app is monitoring. Any folders that have been added to your Pictures library on the device will appear here. To change the folders that the Photos app sees, add them to your Pictures library. Adding folders to libraries is examined in Chapter 21.

6. The last setting shown here is a switch labeled **Show My Photos and Videos from OneDrive**. This is enabled by default and will work at adding everything that is in your OneDrive camera roll to the Collection and Albums. Although this is generally a nice feature, you might prefer to not include OneDrive photos for a variety of reasons. If this is the case, simply slide this switch to **Off**.

 NOTE OneDrive options are available only when using a Microsoft account.

Editing Your Photos

Besides viewing and managing your photos, it is important to have a reliable way to edit photos. The Photos app has you covered. Some powerful tools are built in to the Photos app and are sure to please the casual photographer. This is certainly no replacement for high-end photo editing software, and it is unfair to compare it to more expensive (and complicated) applications dedicated to photo editing. When considering the ease of use and the fact that it is included in Windows 10, you might not ever need to install additional apps for working with your photos. Several categories of tools are included in the Photos app, including Basic Fixes, Filters, Light, Color, and Effects.

Let's take a closer look at the tools included in the Photos app for editing.

To edit a photo in the Photos app, follow these steps:

1. With a photo open in the Photos app, select **Edit** from the upper toolbar (refer to Figure 23.3). The app opens the original unenhanced photo in the Edit workspace, as shown in Figure 23.12.

2. Take a moment to familiarize yourself with available tools shown here. Editing tool categories are located to the left of the photo, while individual tools belonging to the selected tool category are shown to the right. There is an upper toolbar with several more icons. Selecting the ellipsis (...) on the upper toolbar reveals the names for the icons: **Undo**, **Redo**, **Compare**, **Save a Copy**, **Save**, and **Cancel**. In the lower-right corner of the photo, zoom controls are available using the – and + symbols. The zoom controls will autohide until moving the cursor or selecting the photo.

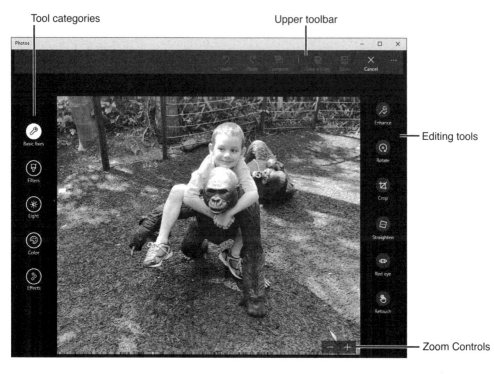

Tool categories   Upper toolbar   Editing tools   Zoom Controls

FIGURE 23.12

The Photos app includes a nice variety of basic editing tools.

3. Select the **Basic Fixes** category to access the most commonly used tools for correcting a photo:

- Select **Enhance** to allow the Photo app to determine which set of adjustments to apply to a picture.

- Select **Rotate** to rotate the photo 90° in a clockwise rotation with each click.

- Select **Crop** to zoom into the photo with touch-friendly controls so that you can select and drag the corners of the area to crop. A grid is provided to give you a sense of proportions. From the upper toolbar, while using the Crop tool, you can also select from preset crop sizes (see Figure 23.13).

- **Straighten** enables you to rotate a photo gradually using a radial control. A useful grid is overlaid that helps you to orient objects such as the horizon in the photo.

FIGURE 23.13

Crop tools in the Photo app are easy to use and take all guesswork out of getting the correct size.

- The **Red Eye** tool presents a small shaded area that follows the cursor. This lets you see the area to which it will be applied. To better control the area of application, zoom into the photo using the zoom control to the bottom right of the photo.

- The **Retouch** tool is easy to use. A shaded area will follow the cursor until you select a spot in the photo. The Photo app will magically remove blemishes and spots that might mar an otherwise perfect photo. Again, you will have better control when zooming into the photo. This tool works very well.

4. Select the **Filters** category and use the filters that appear to the right of the photo to apply the filters to your photo. These will adjust the saturation of colors and even convert the photo to black and white. This is where the Compare tool comes in handy. You can select **Compare** in the upper toolbar to toggle the filter effect on and off when evaluating a filter effect.

5. Select the **Light** category, and then select **Brightness**, **Contrast**, **Highlights**, or **Shadows** from the tools that appear to the right of the photo. Each tool uses a touch-friendly radial slider to increase or decrease each property by values ranging from 100 to –100.

6. Select the **Color** category, and then select **Temperature**, **Tint**, or **Saturation** from the tools that appear to the right of the photo. Each tool uses a touch-friendly radial slider tool to increase or decrease each property by values ranging from 100 to −100.

7. To exaggerate or remove a color, use the **Color Boost** tool also located in the Color category. Select and drag the Color Boost tool into the photo, or simply select a spot on the photo to have the tool jump to that location. As it moves, you will see the color picker display the color currently selected in the photo. After you have selected the color you would like to boost, use the radial slider control to heighten or diminish the color from all areas of the photo, as shown in Figure 23.14. This tool also works very well.

FIGURE 23.14

Color Boost is an easy-to-use tool to increase or remove a color from a photo, adding that dramatic look.

8. Select the **Effects** category to apply a couple professional effects to your photos. Select **Vignette** to darken or lighten the outer area of the photo using a radial slider control.

9. To apply a tilt shift focus effect, select the **Effects** category and then **Selective Focus**. As shown in Figure 23.15, an area of focus is overlaid on the photo with touch-friendly control points. Drag the focus area to the desired location and shape. From the upper toolbar, while using the Selective Focus tool, you can select the **Blur** tool to manage the strength of the blur effect outside of your focus area.

FIGURE 23.15

Selective Focus makes it easy to add a tilt shift effect to your photos.

 TIP If you get carried away when editing your photos, remember that the tools located in the upper toolbar let you easily **Undo** changes that perhaps are undesirable. You can also use **Cancel** to back out of the editing workspace without making any permanent changes.

 CAUTION Consider using **Save a Copy** when creating radical changes to a photo. If you select **Save**, you will overwrite the original photo, and changes cannot be undone.

Using the Camera App

Most portable devices running Windows 10 include at least one camera or webcam, and many have both rear- and front-facing cameras. You also can inexpensively add a USB-powered webcam for videoconferencing or Skype to a desktop computer; thus, the Camera app is a standard app included in Windows 10.

The options you see will be affected by your hardware, and if you open the camera app on a device without a camera, it will prompt you to connect a camera. Figure 23.16 shows the Camera app open on a tablet that has two cameras. The Camera app has basic settings related to photo and video properties, which you can configure if needed.

Photos app   Toggle front facing camera   More: Self Timer / Settings

Video button
Camera button

FIGURE 23.16

The Camera app has a pretty basic interface.

To use the Camera app, follow these steps:

1. To take a picture, make sure the device is in Camera mode. Aim the device and press the camera key. Some devices might include focus tools allowing you to tap or select a region of the display to target the autofocus; however, this is not very common on computer hardware.

 TIP You can also enable the Self Timer from the More ellipsis (...) menu. Select a delay for the shutter, and you can enable a continuous mode that takes a photo every 5 seconds until you press the camera button again. This is a great way to make sure you get at least one perfect group shot.

2. To record a video, you actually have two methods from which to choose:

   • Position your device and select the video key to switch to Video mode. A timer will appear at the bottom of the Camera app. To begin recording, select the video key once. The camera will begin recording using the current settings for video, and the timer will begin to display the length of the recording. To stop recording, select the video key again. The timer will reset to 00:00.

   • While in Camera mode, press and hold the camera key. A timer will appear, and the camera will begin recording video using High Quality settings.

3. To view a picture or video that was taken using the Camera app, select the Photos app icon from the upper-left corner of the Camera app to open the Photos app to the last image taken. (This icon might not appear until after a picture has been taken.) New pictures are saved by default to the Camera Roll folder located in the Pictures library of your device.

4. To modify your preferences, select the More ellipsis (**...**) and then **Settings** (refer to Figure 23.16). The Settings view will open, as shown in Figure 23.17.

   • **Press and Hold Camera Button** allows you to change what happens when you select and hold the camera key button. The default is **Video**, but you can select **Photo Burst** or **Disabled**.

   • Under Photos you can select your **Aspect Ratio**. The drop-down lets you toggle **16:9** (widescreen) or **4:3**.

   • Use onscreen guides by enabling a **Framing Grid**. The drop-down menu offers a variety of framing grids, such as **Rule of Thirds** and **Golden Ratio**. You can also keep it simple and select **Crosshairs** or **Square**.

   • Settings for Videos includes a setting for **Resolution**. The drop-down menu offers a list of video resolutions possible with the camera hardware. Choices are presented with pixel size and frame rate. A higher resolution provides a much sharper image; a higher fps (frames per second) results in smoother playback.

   • **Flicker Reduction** allows you to choose between 50 and 60 Hz. This adjusts the frame rate of video to work with the electrical current where you are that may make artificial lighting appear to flicker in a video.

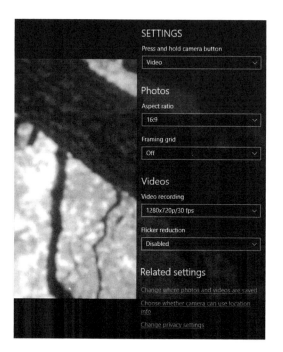

FIGURE 23.17

Make changes to your preferences for the Camera app using Settings.

5. Make adjustments in the Settings section or select **Use Default Settings** to undo your changes. Select the back arrow to return to the Camera app.

 NOTE When making changes to your video settings, bigger is not always better. 30fps is very smooth, while 15fps would seem a bit choppy to the eye. Lower rates would naturally be even lower quality. The higher numbers selected for both pixel resolution and fps will result in larger file sizes in the final video file. Your final preferences here will be determined by your purpose in recording the video.

Controlling Camera Security

Webcams are useful tools that let us video chat and videoconference with people across the Internet. They also can be exploited to create an unexpected window into our environment by skilled individuals, which is why some people place tape over their webcams "just in case." Windows 10 works with apps by allowing the app to access hardware resources and system information in a controllable manner. This means that hardware such as webcams can be made unavailable to apps to prevent misuse. It also means that apps can unexpectedly fail to work correctly when a resource is not available.

To allow apps to access your webcam, or to remove this access, follow these steps:

1. From the Start menu, select **Settings**. The Settings app will open.

2. Select **Privacy**. From the vertical menu to the left, select **Camera**, as shown in Figure 23.18.

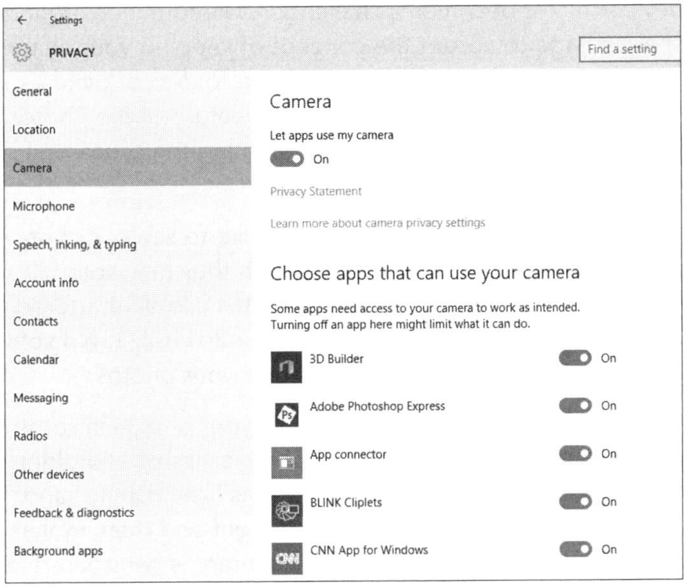

FIGURE 23.18

Windows 10 lets you control which apps have access to your webcam using the Settings app.

3. If you never use your webcam, access can be disabled with a single action by changing the first switch, Let Apps Use My Camera, to **Off**. This list can become quite long, and apps by default are generally granted access when they are installed if the app indicates it needs this access.

4. Access for individual apps can be granted under Choose Apps That Can Use Your Camera by switching access to either **On** or **Off**.

5. Review the apps listed, and make any changes you feel are appropriate. Close the Settings app.

NOTE Most modern webcams include an indicator light that lets you know when they are in use. This is true of built-in and external webcams. If the light is on, it is wise to act under the assumption that whatever is in the camera's line of sight is visible to someone or something.

Organizing the Pictures Library

Digital photography has made it so easy to take pictures and make them available on our devices that it becomes a challenge to keep things organized. You will find it to your advantage to accept the concept of keeping your pictures in the Pictures library or on your OneDrive rather than saving folders of pictures to a desktop or another location. Tools like the new Albums feature of the Photos app considered earlier in this chapter help us by automating the process of grouping photos together by date.

Even so, when viewing our photos we often like to see our photos grouped together based on other criteria, even though they may span many dates or locations. For example, family, friend, or pet photos can be scattered throughout our digital camera roll with names like Image23 or 20110321. No software exists that can anticipate how you might like to organize your photos.

It is a good practice to periodically organize your photos in some way using folders. You might simply create folders with years and subfolders with months, or you could create folders that use categories like "Family" and "Flowers." I encourage you to give the matter some thought and then implement your plan. Creating folders and then managing their content is considered in greater detail in Chapter 21.

The methods you use to organize your folders will ultimately depend on what makes sense to you and is the easiest to maintain. It takes time to keep pictures organized into folders, but it is well worth the effort. Otherwise, you will find that things spiral out of control, and trying to find a particular picture becomes a time-consuming effort when you can least afford it.

Renaming Your Pictures

One last detail that will help you keep things organized is to rename important pictures you want to find later. You can use the powerful search assistant Cortana to quickly locate photos you have named. To try this, follow these steps:

1. From the Start menu, select **File Explorer** and navigate to a folder containing photos.

2. Right-click (or tap and hold using a touchscreen) a picture to open the context menu. Select **Rename**. Type a name for the picture, and then press **Enter**.

3. Next to the Start button, select the search field and type all or part of the name of the photo you renamed in step 2, as shown in Figure 23.19. (Do not press Enter.) A list of web and store search results will appear. Select **Search My Stuff** to direct the search to your device.

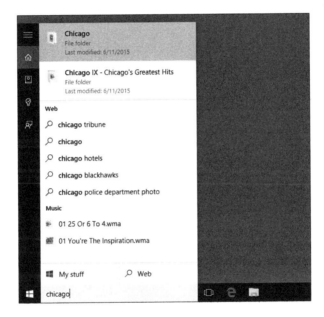

FIGURE 23.19

You can search for pictures on your device by searching for their names and then selecting Search My Stuff.

4. Your search results will now offer documents, photos, and anything else that might be on your device and match your search. To filter the search even further, select the drop-down menu next to Show and select **Photos**, as shown in Figure 23.20. Your photo will be included in the search results.

FIGURE 23.20

Filter search results by using Photos to quickly locate photos.

Taking the time to rename all your photos is probably unrealistic. Select pictures you really like. In some cases, it may be enough to name a couple of key pictures in a folder because right-clicking the search item allows you to jump to the folder in File Explorer by selecting Open File Location.

THE ABSOLUTE MINIMUM

- The Photos app uses Albums to organize your photos in an attractive way. Take the time to customize the title and cover photos to further polish this manner of presentation.

- OneDrive is integrated into your Photos app, which makes it a good choice for saving pictures. Weigh the benefits against the possibility of not having access to OneDrive if traveling and not having an Internet connection.

- Take time to familiarize yourself with the tools available in edit mode. You might not use some tools as often, but knowing how to use Selective Focus or Vignette to enhance a picture can make you even prouder of your great pictures.

- If you are having trouble with an app that does not work correctly when attempting to use the camera, check the Settings app under Privacy to ensure that the app has permission to use the camera.

- Organize your pictures using folders, and keep them in the Pictures library. Consider how renaming pictures will make it easier for you to locate them later using Search.

USING YOUR MICROSOFT ACCOUNT FOR PURCHASES

If you watch movies, listen to music, or play videogames on your computer, you will want to know how to use your Microsoft account to make purchases in the Windows Store and elsewhere. Microsoft has gathered several services together and tied them all to the Microsoft account. So even if a person has used separate services in the past like Xbox Live or Xbox Music, these are now managed by your Microsoft account. Having a Microsoft account allows you to sync content, preferences, and gaming achievements across several devices. A Microsoft account is required to purchase and subscribe to additional content that is offered in the entertainment apps that use Xbox services. In this short chapter you will see how to set up and manage your Microsoft account for purchases. The various entertainment apps are themselves discussed in separate chapters.

What Are Xbox Services?

If you don't even own an Xbox, you might be wondering what Xbox services are. Xbox Live is Microsoft's digital online entertainment service and has actually been around since 2002. This entertainment service offers gaming, music, and video content through subscriptions or purchases. Xbox services (sometimes referred to as Xbox Live services) require an Xbox Live account membership profile that is linked to an email account. An Internet connection is required to use the service. Games, music, and videos you have purchased through Xbox services are linked to your Xbox Live account, and they can be accessed from other devices as long as you use your credentials. Payment information can be entered and stored with your account to make purchases a simple process.

Although it can seem confusing to talk about two different accounts, what is really happening is that your Xbox account membership is being added to your Microsoft account. You can think of it as an enhancement or added feature for an automobile. In the end, your Microsoft account will be used to manage any services or memberships that have been added to it.

If you created a Microsoft account with your Windows 10 device, then you will find that your Microsoft account includes access to Xbox services automatically. Because Xbox services have been around longer than Microsoft accounts have, you may have had an Xbox Live account in the past. If that is the case, it's a good idea to use the same email account for your Microsoft account so your Xbox account can be added to your Microsoft account. Because these two accounts are linked, you might never even see a reference to Xbox or Xbox Live on your device unless you are working with the Xbox gaming system.

When using a Microsoft account with the Xbox app or with an Xbox device, you will see a username has been associated with your account profile known as a *gamertag*. Although the Music and Video apps do not display a gamertag, they do attempt to sign in to the Xbox services automatically when you open the app using the Microsoft account used to log in to the Windows 10 device. Any purchases or subscriptions made with the Xbox account used when signing in will be available.

If you open an entertainment app using a local account and no Microsoft account has been used in the past, you will be able to use the app; however, features related to Xbox services will not be available. In the upper-right corner of the app will be a prompt to sign in, as shown in Figure 24.1.

FIGURE 24.1

You will be directed to sign in if you do not have an account with Xbox Live.

 NOTE If you have trouble syncing an Xbox account, or if you have an Xbox Live ID already but it's not connected to your Microsoft account, you can find more details about joining the two, as well as support for other issues, at www.xbox.com.

Purchasing with Your Microsoft Account

Although your Microsoft account has access to Xbox services, you will still need to add payment methods to ensure that you can make hassle-free purchases. Setting up a Microsoft account for purchasing is an easy process. Purchases can be expected in the following scenarios:

- You want to purchase music or listen to streamed music through the Music app.

- You want to purchase or rent videos through the Movies & TV app.

- You want to purchase an app in the Windows Store.

- You want to purchase additional cloud storage for your OneDrive.

In the first three cases, you will be working with your payment methods through the Windows Store. For other purchases or upgrades, you will complete purchases online using the same payment methods that are tied to your Microsoft account. If the Microsoft account does not currently have any methods of payment associated with it, you will be prompted to add a new payment method, as shown in Figure 24.2. Setting up a payment method only needs to be done once, and then you will see that method listed as your default for future purchases.

FIGURE 24.2

You might need to add a method of payment to your Microsoft account.

Let's look at the steps required to add a payment method when making a purchase through the Windows Store:

1. Open the Store app and locate an app, song, or video that you would like to purchase.

2. Select the button with the price to start the purchase process. (You may be asked to provide your Microsoft password as a security measure when making purchases.) A window will pop up showing the amount to be charged to your current default payment method. You can select **Buy** to proceed with your purchase. To add a new method, select **Change** and then proceed to step 3.

3. Select **Add a New Payment Method** (refer to Figure 24.2).

4. Under Add a New Way to Pay, you will see several fields for entering information related to a credit or debit card, as shown in Figure 24.3. Enter your card holder name as it appears on the card, card number, CVV number, expiration month and year, billing address, city, state, postal code, and country/region. Select **Next** when finished.

5. Under Check Your Info, you will see the information you just entered. Confirm that it is correct. To make changes, select **Edit**. If everything looks good, select **Save This Info**.

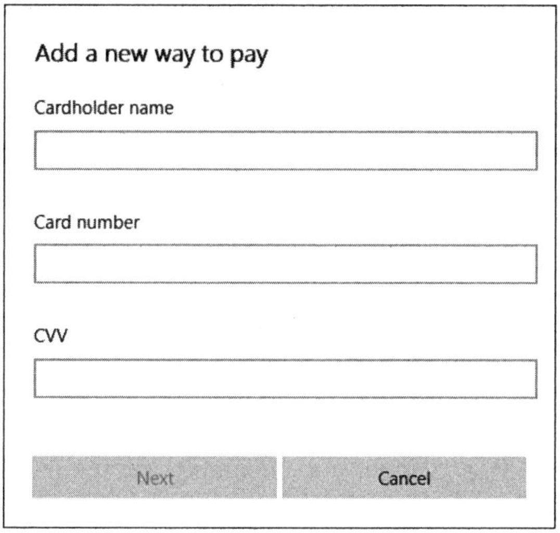

Add a new way to pay

Cardholder name

Card number

CVV

Next   Cancel

FIGURE 24.3

Add credit card information to create a new payment method when making a purchase in the Windows Store.

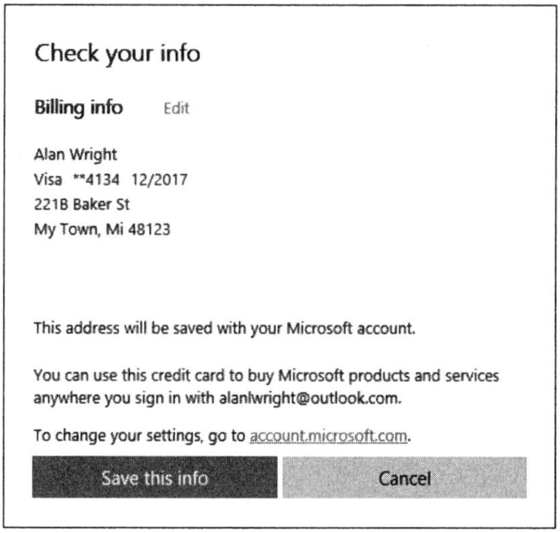

Check your info

Billing info   Edit

Alan Wright
Visa **4134 12/2017
221B Baker St
My Town, Mi 48123

This address will be saved with your Microsoft account.

You can use this credit card to buy Microsoft products and services anywhere you sign in with alanlwright@outlook.com.

To change your settings, go to account.microsoft.com.

Save this info   Cancel

FIGURE 24.4

Confirm your payment information is correct when adding a method of payment.

6. Your Microsoft account is updated and the purchase information from step 2 will be regenerated, this time showing the amount to be charged using the method of payment that you just added.

This method works fine for adding standard methods of payment. However, you may wish to perform basic tasks related to your billing information, such as update existing payment methods or add other types of payment information to your Microsoft account.

Managing Your Microsoft Account

The Microsoft account has many details associated with a membership profile. Many tasks related to your Microsoft account are best handled online, and you will find helpful links in various apps that help you to jump to your online account (refer to Figure 24.4). To go to your account profile manually, you can use this link: https://commerce.microsoft.com.

To manage or review billing information for your Microsoft account, follow these steps:

1. Open the Store app. Select your account picture to open the account drop-down menu, as shown in Figure 24.5.

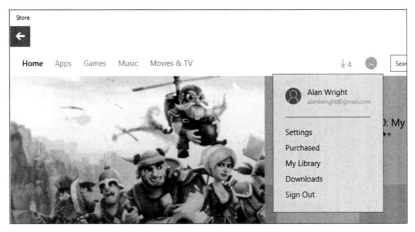

FIGURE 24.5

Access your online Microsoft account profile from links in apps like the Windows Store.

2. Select **Purchased**, and your web browser will open to the Billing Overview for your Microsoft account. (You will likely be prompted to sign in to the website as a security measure.) Recent purchases and current payment options are shown, as you can see in Figure 24.6. Notice that you can add funds to your Microsoft account by redeeming gift cards or using Bitcoins.

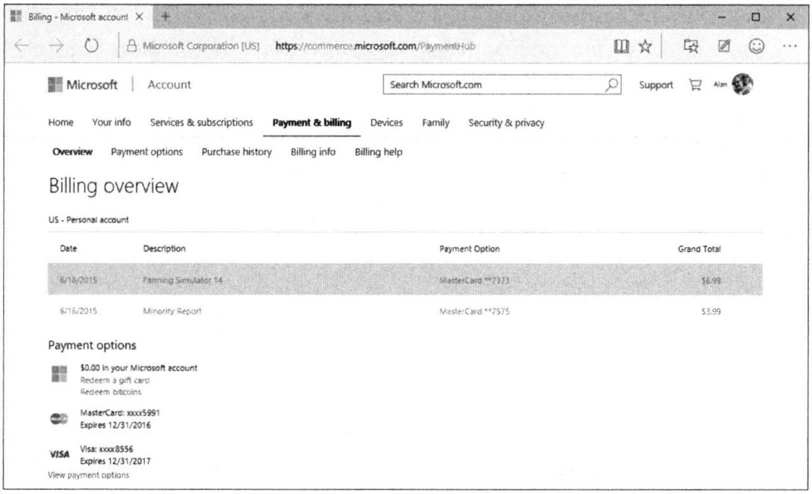

FIGURE 24.6

Go online to view your billing information and recent purchases for your Microsoft account.

3. Select **Payment Options**. As a security measure you will again have to provide your password. Payment Options will be shown under Manage Your Payment Options, as shown in Figure 24.7.

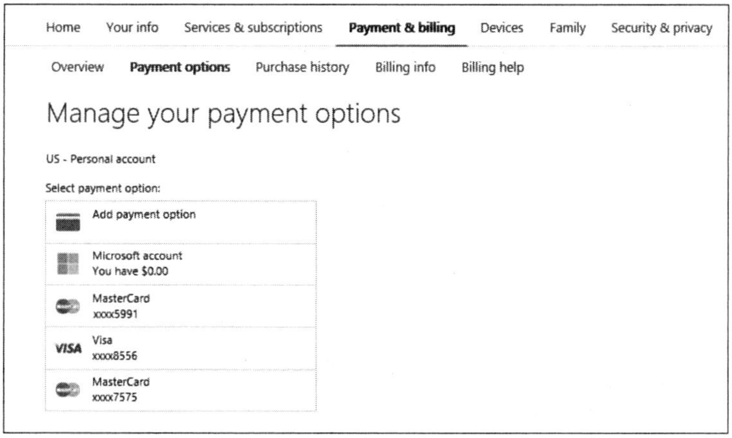

FIGURE 24.7

From online you can manage your payment options that are linked to your Microsoft account.

4. Select an existing method of payment to edit or remove it from your Microsoft account.

5. Select **Add Payment Option** to add a new credit or debit card or to add other options that may be listed here, such as PayPal (see Figure 24.8).

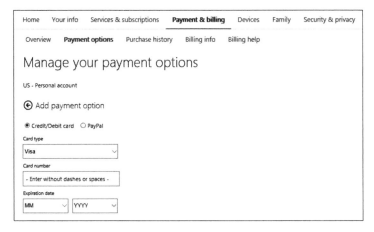

FIGURE 24.8

You can add additional types of payment to your Microsoft account using online tools.

6. Follow the prompts to finish entering information required for your method of payment.

Accepted payment methods can vary depending on the country or region you are in, and they can be found listed under Billing Help. Credit and debit cards, PayPal, as well as a few prepaid methods can be added, which should cover most situations that are likely to face a computer user.

From the online Microsoft account dashboard, you can manage several vital elements of your profile, including the following:

- Purchase subscriptions for Xbox Live, Xbox Music Pass, or EA Access.

- Redeem codes from gift cards, prepaid cards, or promotional codes.

- Review transactions made using your Microsoft account.

- Manage payment information, including credit card and PayPal accounts, as well as update your billing address.

- Manage devices associated with your Microsoft account.

- Review and change privacy settings for you and any family members managed by your Microsoft account profile.

- Connect directly to your Xbox profile to handle tasks such as editing your gamertag or avatar.

THE ABSOLUTE MINIMUM

Keep the following points in mind after you've completed reading this chapter:

- Xbox Live membership is added to your Microsoft account.

- If you plan to purchase games, music, or videos in Windows 10, you will need a Microsoft account that has at least one linked method of payment. It can save some work by doing it upfront.

- If you have different IDs for your Microsoft account and an existing Xbox Live account, look into merging these two accounts. You can find information about merging accounts on www.xbox.com.

- To manage billing issues for your Microsoft account, use links from the Store, Video, Movies & TV, or Xbox apps to quickly jump into your online account profile.

25

HAVING FUN WITH MOVIES AND TV SHOWS

If you watch movies or TV shows on your computer, you should begin a friendship with the Movies & TV app that uses Microsoft's Xbox Video service. The app is easy to use, yet it has enough new features and capabilities to meet many of your needs. Certainly some folks with a bit more experience in integrating digital media with personal computers might bellyache at the lack of interesting features in the app, but you cannot argue with the price (free) or the ease of adding your content to the library. This chapter covers all the basics, from navigating through all the movies and TV shows offered in the marketplace to renting or purchasing a selection that interests you.

Getting Started with the Movies & TV App

The Movies & TV app is an easy-to-use modern Windows app that enables you to watch videos from both your private collection and the enormous selection available in the Windows Store. If you are looking to add to your collection, you can purchase videos offered in the Windows Store. If you don't want to make a purchase commitment, you can rent one or more of the videos offered. If you don't have the time to watch a full movie, you can always occupy a few minutes by watching the many movie trailers that are available.

To start the Movies & TV app, select the tile, as shown in Figure 25.1. If you cannot locate the tile, select the search box on the taskbar. Type **tv** or **movie**, and then select the Movies & TV app from the list of results.

FIGURE 25.1

Launch the Movies & TV app from the tile on the Start menu.

 NOTE The Movies & TV app is a universal Windows app. As such, it can be updated at any time, and its appearance and features can be altered from what is shown in this chapter through automatic updates in the Windows Store.

Navigating the Movies & TV App

Moving around in the Movies & TV app is accomplished using the prominent hamburger menu and the back arrow that are always visible on the title bar. (The back arrow appears next to the Start button on touchscreen devices in tablet mode.) The hamburger menu, shown in Figure 25.2, lets you jump between three sections of your collection: Movies, TV, and Videos. As you purchase movies and TV programs, they will appear in those sections of your collection; videos saved to the Videos folder of your device will appear in the Videos section.

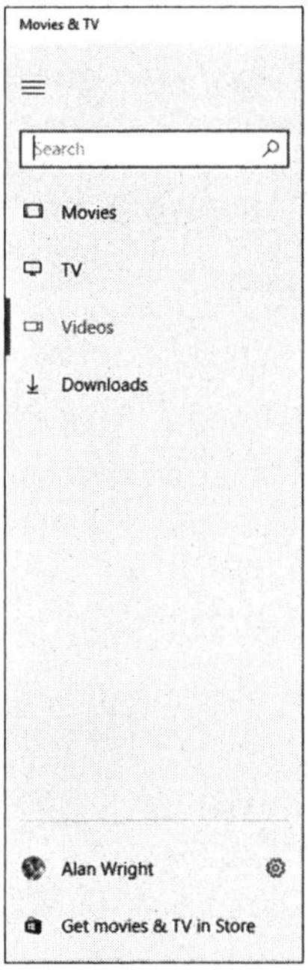

FIGURE 25.2

Navigate your collection using the hamburger menu of the Movies & TV app.

Use the search tool in the hamburger menu to quickly locate videos in your collection. As shown in Figure 25.3, links also are available to continue your search in the Windows Store.

FIGURE 25.3

Search for videos in your video collection.

The Movies & TV app includes some basic settings and links to manage your purchases. You can set a default download quality as well as manage devices that can view video purchases and rentals.

Follow these steps to view and manage your settings:

1. Open the Movies & TV app.

2. Select **Settings** from the hamburger menu. Settings will appear, as shown in Figure 25.4.

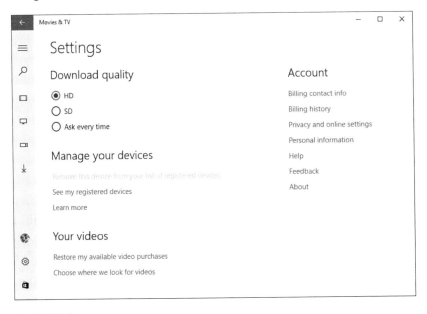

FIGURE 25.4

Manage settings for the Movies & TV app.

3. Under Download Quality, choose between **HD** and **SD** as your default video quality or leave the default setting as **Ask Every Time**. Choosing HD or SD enables you to save a step when downloading video you have already purchased.

4. If you are signed in to your device with a Microsoft account, you will see a section named Manage Your Devices. Select **See My Registered Devices** to manage multiple devices that you can work with using your Microsoft account.

5. If you are signed in to your device with a Microsoft account, you will see links under Account that take you to your online Microsoft account. From there, you can manage settings related to purchases and methods of payment.

Chapter 24, "Using Your Microsoft Account for Purchases," covers in more detail the process of setting up your Microsoft account for purchases. If you are using a local account, you will see links for the app itself, such as Help and About.

NOTE   You might wonder how much difference there is between SD and HD video quality. SD video playback is 480p resolution, while HD is 720p. This can make a big difference on a large high-def flatscreen television. If you are playing your movie on a tablet or smaller display, then the SD quality will display pretty well. Another factor that may affect your decision is that streaming HD will require more bandwidth and will involve more data being downloaded than would streaming in SD quality.

Adding Your Videos to the Videos Library

You can add your previously acquired movies, TV shows, and videos to the Videos Library. You also can load videos you've recorded into Windows 10. By loading all your video content into Windows 10, you can access all your onscreen digital content from one place. Until you add your own content to the Movies & TV app, the screen shown in Figure 25.5 appears.

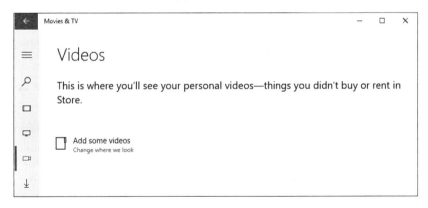

FIGURE 25.5

This message almost begs you to get some videos on your device!

If you have no digital videos—that is, you have never purchased videos online and have never imported videos into your computer—you can skip this section. If you do own movies, TV shows, home movies, and other videos, you can link their locations to the Videos folder in Windows 10. The Xbox Movies & TV app uses that folder—which is actually a special folder sometimes referred to as a *library*—as its source for your videos. You can learn about libraries in Chapter 21, "File and Folder Basics."

CAUTION You must maintain the link to your video collection's location, such as across your home network or to a removable hard drive, for your videos to be available. If your Windows 10 computer is a laptop, it's likely you'll move that computer to a location away from the network or drive where those videos are located. If your computer stays in one place, of course, you won't have this problem. In addition, Windows must be able to index the folder. If indexing is not possible, the Movies & TV app will not add external folders to the video collection.

TIP To find your personal videos easily, you should name them. A name like "WIN_20130818_190138" is much harder to remember than "Joshua's first bike ride." Earlier in this chapter, you saw how to use search in the Movies & TV app. The easiest way to rename files is to use File Explorer, which we covered back in Chapter 21.

Follow these steps to link your collection of videos to Windows 10 and the Movies & TV app:

1. Open the Movies & TV app and select **Settings**—the small gear next to your name—from the hamburger menu (refer to Figure 25.2).

2. Select the link shown in Figure 25.4, labeled **Choose Where We Look for Videos**.

3. A pop-up screen, shown in Figure 25.6, appears that invites you to build your collection. It points to the Videos library and contains the same folder list that appears if you were to open the Videos folder in File Explorer. To add a new folder containing videos, select the button with a large plus sign (+). This opens File Explorer, which enables you to choose locations on your hard device, OneDrive, or your network. Find a folder and select it; then select **Add This Folder to Videos** to add it to your folder list. If you have videos scattered in different locations, either consolidate all the content to one place or repeat these steps for each location where videos are stored.

FIGURE 25.6

Add the location of your videos to the Windows 10 Video library.

4. Select **Videos** to verify that your videos are present.

5. To remove a video file, select it and then select **Delete**. The video file is deleted—not just from your collection, but from the folder as well.

 CAUTION   Exercise caution when deleting videos from the Movies & TV app. Videos deleted in this way normally go to the Recycle bin, from which they can be recovered or restored, but large files such as movie files might be permanently deleted due to their size.

After adding new folders to the Videos library, it can take a minute or two for these videos to appear in your videos collection, especially when there is a lot of content to sort through. After videos are added to the Videos library, they appear alphabetized as folders or videos (see Figure 25.7).

 TIP   You will likely find that personal videos taken with tablets and smartphones are placed in a camera roll and saved with your photos. These files tend to appear only in the Photos app—which is able to play videos as well. If you do want to see them in your Movies & TV app, you will need to do some housework and either: 1) move your video files from your Photos library to the Videos library; or 2) add your folder containing photos mixed with videos to the Videos library, too. The Movies & TV app will ignore any photos and see the video files.

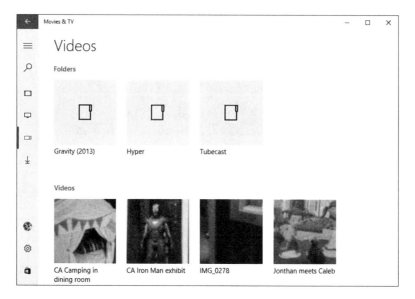

FIGURE 25.7

Video files appear alphabetized as folders and videos in the Movies & TV app.

NOTE There are many different video formats, each offering certain advantages. Windows 10 and the Movies & TV app include support for the most common formats, including WMV, AVI, MOV, MP4, and MKV. If you experience problems with playback for videos you have in a less common format, try some of the alternative video apps mentioned in Bonus Chapter 1, "These Are a Few of My Favorite Apps."

Playing Videos in the Movies & TV App

Playing a video is pretty intuitive in the Movies & TV app. Select a video file, and video play begins automatically. Controls appear briefly, as shown in Figure 25.8, and then they hide from view. Select the video to make the controls reappear.

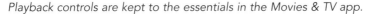

Timeline | Cast to Device | Play/Pause | Full Screen

Playhead   Aspect Ratio Volume   Loop

FIGURE 25.8

Playback controls are kept to the essentials in the Movies & TV app.

Video controls include

- **Timeline**—The timeline lets you see how far you are into a video and how much time is remaining. A touch-friendly control handle enables you to select and drag the playhead to a different point on the timeline.

- **Cast to Device**—This button searches your network and other possible connections for devices that could display your video, as shown in Figure 25.9. Select a device to start playing the video to that device. In some cases, the video format may prevent casting to that device.

FIGURE 25.9

Connecting to a device.

- **Aspect Ratio**—Select this button to toggle between a letterbox 16:9 format and a 4:3 display. Depending on the video file, you might see black bars or have to sacrifice the left and right edges of a video when changing the aspect ratio.

- **Play/Pause**—Select once to pause; select again to resume playback.

- **Volume**—Select the volume button and then use a slider to adjust the volume level.

- **Full Screen**—Select the Full Screen button to fill your display with video playback goodness; select it again to exit full-screen display.

- **Loop**—Loop will simply keep playing the current video in a loop. Select the button once to enable looped playback and again to disable.

NOTE You might be wondering about devices that are compatible with Cast to Device. Cast to Device includes connected screens using traditional video cables, wireless devices that can use Bluetooth and Miracast, as well as devices on your network that support DLNA. Common devices that can be used include the Xbox One and Chromecast.

Shopping for Videos

You can browse through the movies and TV shows in the Windows Store with an eye toward buying or renting. You usually have a choice between standard-definition (SD) and high-definition (HD) versions of a video, and you can generally choose to download or stream either selection.

NOTE As of this writing, you cannot rent TV shows. Only movies are available as online rentals.

If you are unfamiliar with the idea of renting or purchasing a digital movie or TV show, this section explains how that works. Purchases will require that you have a Microsoft account and that you have a method of payment associated with your account. Keep in mind that the screens and options used to process your purchase or rental certainly can change, so what you see here may have some variation compared to your own experience.

Making a Purchase

The Movies & TV app makes it easy to browse for movies and TV programs. With the release of Windows 10, Microsoft has combined many types of media into the Windows Store, making it a one-stop place for shopping from your device. Movies and TV programs are new additions to the Windows Store. You will find prices clearly indicated for both purchases and rentals.

To purchase a movie or TV show in the Windows Store, follow these steps:

1. From the Movies & TV app, select **Get Movies & TV in Store** from the hamburger menu. The Windows Store will open to the Movies & TV section, as shown in Figure 25.10.

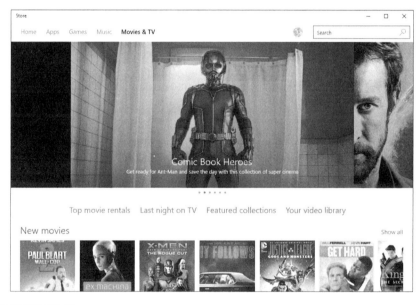

FIGURE 25.10

Browse for movies and television shows to purchase in the Windows Store.

2. Below the prominent sliding viewer of featured movies and TV shows, four links are provided to help you with navigation:

- **Top Movie Rentals**—Provides a long list of movies ranked by current rentals, as shown in Figure 25.11. Under Refine, you can filter the results. Under Chart, select the drop-down menu to view New Movies, Top Rentals, Top-Rated Movies, or Top-Selling Movies. Genre is another intuitive way to filter your results. Finally, under Refine, a list of movie studios listed under Studio can be used to filter results.

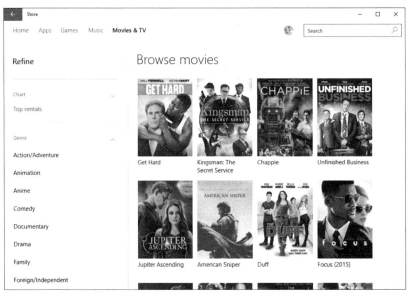

FIGURE 25.11

Use filters and categories to find movies or television shows to watch.

- **Last Night on TV**—Opens a list of current television programs. Select a TV show to view episodes and air dates. Episodes can be purchased, or you can purchase a season pass for the show, which will include future episodes as they are released.

- **Featured Collections**—Presents you with themed collections of movies or television programs. Use this to get your fix of categories like Bond, James Bond; Top Gear; Family TV; or videos that feature Xbox SmartGlass.

- **Your Video Library**—Returns you to the Movies & TV app.

3. From the home page of the Movies & TV section of the Windows Store, you can browse featured selections or scroll down to view lists of new, top-selling, or featured movies and TV shows.

4. Select a movie or TV show to learn more about it. Ratings and runtimes are shown. You can read a synopsis about it, and in some cases trailers can be available to watch. Episodes are listed for television shows, and reviews are provided for movies. Other information is also provided, such as similar movies or TV shows and other shows from a specific television studio.

5. Select the video quality—**SD** or **HD**—and then select **Buy** to start a purchase. You will most likely be prompted to reenter your Microsoft account password and select **Sign In** as a security feature. You will see a summary of the amount,

and the default linked method of payment for your Microsoft account will be indicated, as shown in Figure 25.12. If everything looks correct, select **Buy** to complete the transaction. You can now play the movie or television show. Purchased items will no longer show a price; instead, you can select **Play** to stream the purchase.

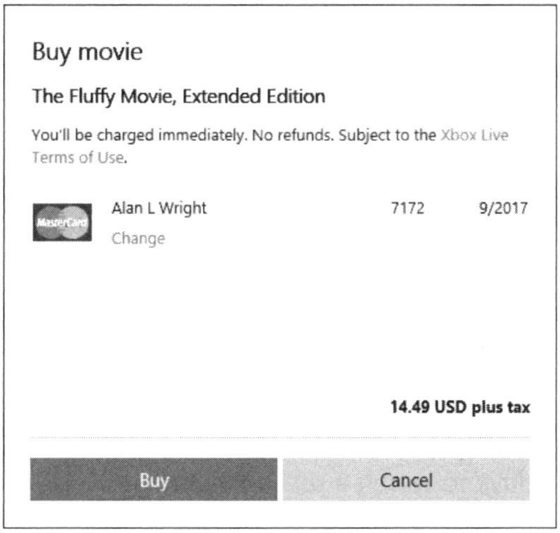

Buy movie

The Fluffy Movie, Extended Edition

You'll be charged immediately. No refunds. Subject to the Xbox Live Terms of Use.

Alan L Wright   7172   9/2017
Change

14.49 USD plus tax

Buy   Cancel

FIGURE 25.12

Purchasing a movie takes just a couple clicks in the Windows Store.

6. Return to the Movies & TV app, and then select Movies or TV to view your purchase. As shown in Figure 25.13, purchases can be streamed or downloaded for viewing later.

FIGURE 25.13

Purchases can be streamed or downloaded to a device in the Movies & TV app.

If you know what you are looking for, then the search tool in the Windows Store is your friend. Searches within the Windows Store will give relevant results from the apps, music, and video categories. Purchases made in the Windows Store can be downloaded to up to five other Windows 10 devices you use with your Microsoft account.

Renting a Selection

If you prefer not to make your purchase permanent, you can rent most movie titles. The process for renting is very similar to the steps outlined in the preceding section for purchasing a video. The only minor difference is that in step 5, instead of selecting Buy, select **Rent**.

Terms tend to change on an unannounced basis, so you should certainly read the terms indicated for your rental before confirming your purchase (refer to Figure 25.14). Read the terms carefully because you are charged immediately, and no refunds are given. Following are other details regarding rentals that you should consider:

- You have 14 days to watch a rented video.

- Downloading the video for playback offline might not be offered. You will see this whether this option is available as soon as you select Rent.

- After you start playback of a rental, you must complete watching it in 24 hours before the rental becomes nonfunctional.

- Renting is much cheaper than purchasing a movie, especially one you only expect to watch once.

- During the 24-hour rental period, you can watch the movie as many times as you like.

 NOTE Currently, the Xbox Video policy on www.xboxlive.com regarding video rentals includes a viewing period of 14 days from the time of your order or 48 hours from the time you start to watch, whichever comes first. However, as you can see in Figure 25.14, the rental terms for this HD download of a movie allow only 24 hours for viewing, and this is consistently the policy stated at the time of rental.

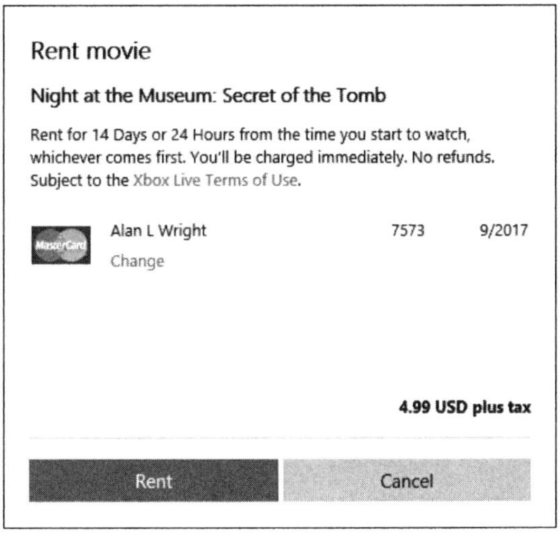

FIGURE 25.14

Read the terms carefully when renting or purchasing video content before confirming a rental.

THE ABSOLUTE MINIMUM

- Move your existing videos to the Videos folder on your Windows 10 device so that they can be integrated into the video collection. Doing so also enables you to watch your videos whenever you choose.

- You can also consider linking to the existing location of your videos by adding the physical folder location of your videos to the Videos library by letting the Movies & TV app know where to watch for videos. This is an easier option than moving your videos, but you can't access this content if you move your computer to a place where it can no longer connect with your video library's location.

- If you plan to purchase or rent a video in the Windows 10 Movies & TV app, be sure to set up your Microsoft account for purchasing before you start. It can save you some time by doing it upfront.

26

ENJOYING MUSIC

The Groove Music app in Windows 10 is fun to use, attractive to look at, and generally does everything you'd expect it to do. You can play music you've purchased in the past, and you can buy new music. The Groove Music app isn't full-featured, though. You might want to play music that resides on a CD, or someone else in your home might want to play tunes on your computer. These and a few other features are not available in the Groove Music app; however, other tools in Windows can substitute for the Music app for these tasks. In this chapter, you learn the basics—playing music, setting up and looking through your library, shopping for music online—and learn when you must use another tool.

Getting Started with the Groove Music App

You can use the Groove Music app to play and manage your music in Windows 10. You can bring into the Music app the music you've already purchased online or imported from CDs, listen to music that is stored on your OneDrive, and purchase new music.

 NOTE The Groove Music app has experienced some name changes, including Xbox Music and simply the Music app. Microsoft explains that this latest name for the Music app uses Groove because this describes what people feel and do with music and is more intuitive for Windows 10 customers on what they'll find with the app. Because of the name changes and the fact that Xbox Music service has been around for many years, do not be confused if you still see references to Xbox Music—especially if you use links that take you online to websites from the Groove Music app.

To start the Groove Music app, select the tile, as shown in Figure 26.1. If you cannot locate the tile, open the search box on the Desktop taskbar and enter **music** into the search box. Select the **Groove Music** tile from the list of results.

FIGURE 26.1

Select the Groove Music app from the Start menu.

 NOTE The Groove Music app is a universal Windows app. As such, it can be updated at any time, and its appearance and features can be altered from what is shown in this chapter through updates in the Windows Store.

Learning What's Where in the Groove Music App

When you first open the Groove Music app, it will invite you to start setting things up right away, as shown in Figure 26.2. As you add music to your collection, the Music app lets you view your collection using three groupings: Albums, Artists, and Songs. Each way of viewing your collection allows you to sort and filter your collection.

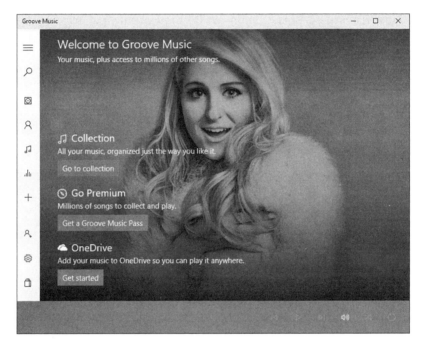

FIGURE 26.2

The Groove Music app can start out pretty barren until you begin adding music.

The hamburger menu of the Music app contains all the navigation tools you will need for moving around within the Music app (see Figure 26.3):

- **Search**—Allows you to search for music within your collection. Use artist, album, or song queries.

- **Albums**—Shows whole or partial albums you have added to your collection. Albums can be sorted by date added, release year, alphabetically, genre, or artist.

- **Artists**—Lets you arrange your collection alphabetically.

- **Songs**—Lists every song in your collections; you can sort by date added, alphabetically, genre, artist, or album.

- **Radio**—Only visible if you have a Groove Music subscription, Radio allows you to stream online music from Microsoft's Groove Music service.

- **Explore**—Only visible if you have a Groove Music subscription, Explore allows you to find new artists from Microsoft's Groove Music online catalog.

- **Now Playing**—Displays album art for the currently playing song track, which can be used as an impromptu screensaver by selecting the full screen icon that appears on the album art.

- **Playlists**—These are listed as well as an icon to create a new playlist. Depending on a few factors, some playlists will sync with other devices that you use running Windows 10 as well.

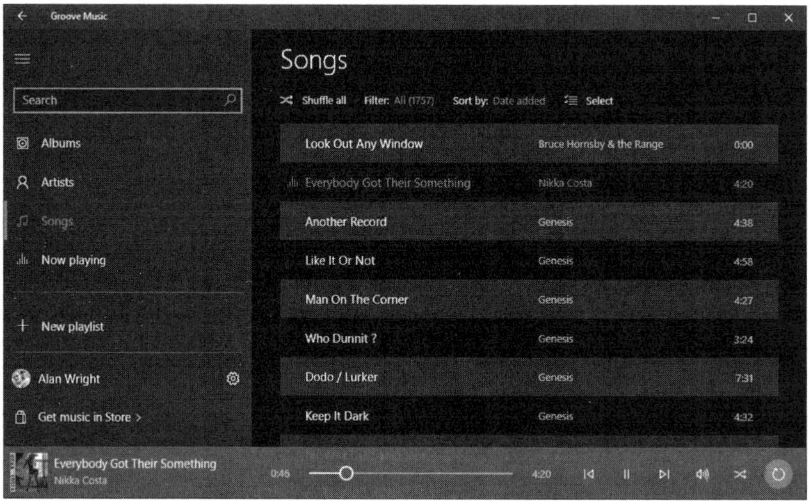

FIGURE 26.3

The hamburger menu of the Groove Music app, shown here with the dark theme, enables you to view your collection in different ways.

While you're playing music, the Groove Music app displays a music player bar across the bottom that is always visible and presents the exact commands you need, no matter what you're doing in the app. For example, as shown in Figure 26.4, when you play music, the music player bar presents commands to play the next song, repeat the current song, control volume, and more. Select the album portrait to jump to the album view.

FIGURE 26.4

The music player bar gives you access to commands you would see on an MP3 player as you play music in the Groove Music app.

 TIP The Groove Music app includes two color themes: light and dark. To switch between these themes, select Settings and scroll to the bottom of the Settings pane. Under Background select the drop-down menu to select Light or Dark.

Adding Music to the Groove Music App

When you first open the Groove Music app, your collection can appear rather empty, as shown in Figure 26.5. The whole point of the Music app is to listen to your music, right? Before doing so, you need to bring your music into the Groove Music app collection. Digital music includes music you have purchased online or imported from CDs onto your computer. Thankfully, the Groove Music app makes it incredibly easy to buy new music.

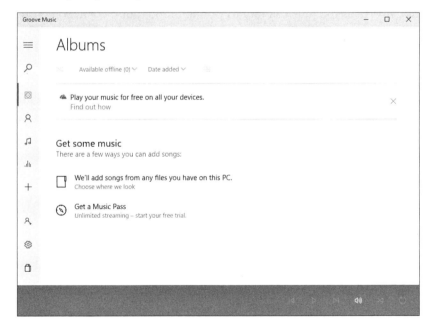

FIGURE 26.5

You might start with very little to listen to in the Music app on a new device.

The Groove Music app does a lot with a little. The app presents an attractive, well-laid-out, informative, and well-organized library of music. The Groove Music app is very flexible when adding music, allowing you to specify where your music collection is located rather than moving your music to a specific directory.

You have two basic options to bring your existing music into the Groove Music app:

- You can link to your existing collection of music, even if it's on another computer, a removable drive, or OneDrive.

- You can either copy or move your entire collection from a different system to the device running Windows 10.

The following two sections explain how to connect your music to Windows 10 using these approaches.

How to Link Your Music

Linking to your music takes advantage of the libraries function in File Explorer. A *library* is a special folder type that consolidates folders from different locations on your computer to make all the folders appear to be in the same location. The Music folder is actually one of several built-in libraries in Windows 10. The Groove Music app uses the music library to populate the music collection. You can find detailed information in Chapter 21, "File and Folder Basics," for instructions on working with libraries.

To manage the music in your collection, follow these steps:

1. Open the Groove Music app. If you see a link inviting you to add music to your PC (refer to Figure 26.5), select the link **Choose Where We Look**, and jump to step 4.

2. Select **Settings** from the hamburger menu to open to the Settings pane of the Groove Music app, as shown in Figure 26.6.

3. Under Your Music, select the link **Choose Where We Look for Music on This PC**.

4. The pop-up shown in Figure 26.7 will appear. Locations that the Groove Music app is aware of that should contain music files will be included (your Windows Music library). You might also see a folder from your OneDrive included.

FIGURE 26.6

The Settings pane of the Groove Music app provides you with ways to add music.

Build your collection from your local music files
Right now, we're watching these folders:

⊕	**Music** ✕ \\ds9\Music
Music ✕ C:\Users\Public\Music	**Music** ✕ C:\Users\Admin\Music

Done

FIGURE 26.7

The Groove Music app collection uses the Music library of Windows and even allows you to update the library from within the Music app.

5. To add a new folder containing music, select the first folder placeholder (+). File Explorer will open. Navigate to the folder you want to add to your collection, and select it. Select the button **Add This Folder to Music**. The folder will now be included in the Music library and will appear as a separate folder in the list shown in step 4.

6. To remove a folder, select the X that appears on the folder (refer to Figure 26.7). A pop-up will appear, as shown in Figure 26.8. Select **Remove Folder** to confirm or **Cancel** to leave it. If you select Remove Folder, the folder is removed from the library container but continues to exist as a normal folder—nothing is deleted.

7. Select **Done** when you are finished to return to the Groove Music app.

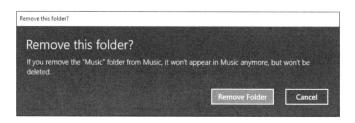

Remove this folder?

Remove this folder?

If you remove the "Music" folder from Music, it won't appear in Music anymore, but won't be deleted.

Remove Folder   Cancel

FIGURE 26.8

Remove folders that you no longer want the Groove Music app to monitor.

 CAUTION Keep in mind that if you cannot reach the network or cannot travel with your removable drive, you will not have access to your entire collection of music. Also, network locations that Windows 10 cannot index for one reason or another are not added to your Music library.

Another unique way to link music with Windows 10 is from the cloud, as indicated by the invitation to add your music to OneDrive (refer to Figure 26.2). OneDrive contains a Music folder designed for music files, and this folder is automatically included in the Groove Music app as a folder that is watched (see Figure 26.9). Although uploading your music collection to OneDrive has many advantages for those who live with easy Internet access, it does include some caveats.

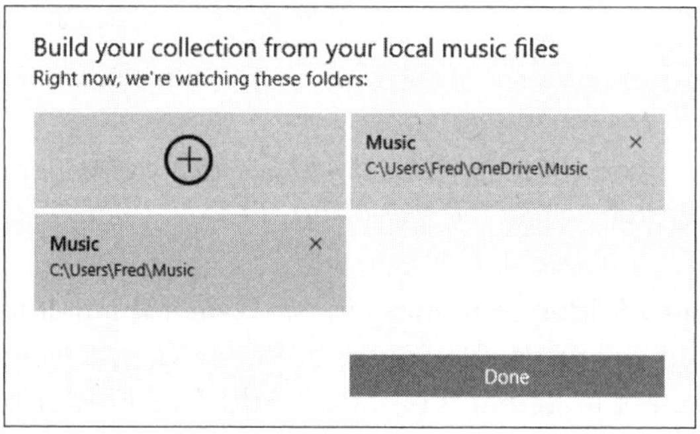

Build your collection from your local music files
Right now, we're watching these folders:

(+)

Music
C:\Users\Fred\OneDrive\Music   ×

Music
C:\Users\Fred\Music   ×

Done

FIGURE 26.9

The Groove Music app works very well with music saved to your OneDrive.

Currently, OneDrive reserves local hard drive space to sync OneDrive content to your device. This can be an issue for devices with limited hard drive space. Chapter 22, "Working with OneDrive," covers how to use OneDrive with the Groove Music app in more detail.

You might notice that some songs have an icon next to the song title. Icons indicate one of the following when they appear next to a song or an album:

((•)) This icon indicates that a song is available for streaming only while connected to the Internet. It cannot be played while offline unless downloaded to the device.

(i) This icon indicates that information is available; select it to reveal information. In the Groove Music app, this generally appears when a song is located on a different device that you use and cannot be played from this device. This icon sometimes appears in playlists that have been synced when you do not have the same music on each device.

How to Move Your Music

If linking folders and cloud options are not for you, follow these steps to move your music to the computer running Windows 10:

1. The first step is to prepare your music. It will be easier, but not required, to move your music if all your music is in a single folder or grouped in subfolders within a single folder.

2. Check that your Windows 10 computer has enough free disk space to accommodate your music. Ensure that you have more than 10% of the total drive capacity available after copying your library.

    For example, suppose your music takes up 10GB, you have a 250GB hard drive, and 50GB is free. When you add your music to your hard drive, you have just 40GB free space remaining, but 40GB is greater than 10%, so in this example, you are okay.

3. Move or copy your music folder to the Music folder on the Windows 10 computer. You might need to use a removable drive to move the folder, or you can use a homegroup network to complete it.

4. Open the Groove Music app. Inspect your collection to verify that your music is present.

Using Album View

Album view provides a few important tools that you should be aware of when working with your music. Some of these tools are available in other views; others are available only in Album view.

To use Album view tools, follow these steps:

1. Select an album in the Groove Music app.

2. To play all tracks of an album, select the upper **Play** icon.

3. To add all tracks of an album to a playlist or to create a new playlist with this album, select **Add To**. A drop-down menu will open, as shown in Figure 26.10, with existing playlists. Select **New Playlist** to create a new playlist. Type in a name for the playlist, and then select **Save**.

FIGURE 26.10

Create playlists or add music to an existing playlist in the Groove Music app.

4. Select **Explore Artist** to jump to Artist view. You might have other albums by that artist that can be accessed easily from Artist view.

5. Select **More** to reveal additional tools, as shown in Figure 26.11.

- **Pin to Start**—Allows you to add a tile for that album to the Start menu. Selecting the pinned album opens the Groove Music app, and that album will begin playing.

- **Delete**—Presents a pop-up asking you to confirm that you want to permanently delete the album from your library. Select **Delete** to proceed or **Cancel** to keep the album.

- **Find Album Info**—Does an impressive job of updating metadata for unidentified or poorly tagged albums and songs. The Groove Music app compares the album and songs to online sources, and possible albums are presented with checkmarks indicating tracks that can have their metadata automatically updated. Song names, album art, genre, and artist are all fields that are corrected if you find the right album. Select **Finish** to update metadata tags for the album and selected songs.

FIGURE 26.11

Use tools from Album view within the Groove Music app to pin albums to the Start menu or update metadata for songs.

6. Select the **Select** tool located above the songs, and then select a song if you're using a touchscreen (refer to Figure 26.13). With a mouse, just right-click a song within the album to open the context menu and select **Properties**. Detailed information for a song is revealed, as shown in Figure 26.12. File location and streaming status are useful details if you will be without Internet access or if you need to locate the actual song file.

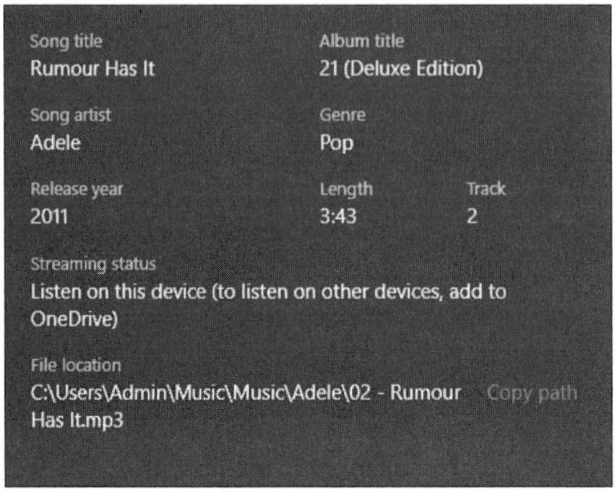

Song title
Rumour Has It

Album title
21 (Deluxe Edition)

Song artist
Adele

Genre
Pop

Release year
2011

Length
3:43

Track
2

Streaming status
Listen on this device (to listen on other devices, add to OneDrive)

File location
C:\Users\Admin\Music\Music\Adele\02 - Rumour Has It.mp3   Copy path

FIGURE 26.12

Review details about song files by selecting Properties for the song in the Groove Music app.

Most of these tools are available when right-clicking a song, an album, or an artist within the Groove Music app. On a touchscreen you need to use the Select tool to enter selection mode. Selected items bring up a lower app bar from the bottom of the app, as shown in Figure 26.13. Select **Cancel** to exit selection mode.

	Now playing				
					Cancel
+	New playlist	☐	1 Rolling In the Deep	Adele	3:48
☰	Driving Music	✓	2 Rumour Has It	Adele	3:43
		☐	3 Turning Tables	Adele	4:10
⊘	Can't sign in ⚙	☐	4 Don't You Remember	Adele	4:03
☐	Get music in Store ›	☐	5 Set Fire to the Rain	Adele	4:03

▷ Play   + Add to   ⧎ Explore artist   🗑 Delete   ⇥ Pin to start   ☰ Properties

FIGURE 26.13

Using the Select tool will reveal actions for selected artists, albums, or songs.

 TIP *Metadata* refers to additional information that can be added to media files such as music and is sometimes referred to as *tagging*. This metadata can be critical when trying to keep a music collection organized. Different formats can be used, and editing tags is not always easy. The Music app updates metadata used by the Music app, but this is not always visible in other music players. If you are looking for a good tool for this, MP3TAG is a free application that can be downloaded and used to tag your music files.

CAUTION   Deleting music from your library also deletes the music files that are stored on your device. The files will be placed in the Recycle bin. Deleting songs stored on your OneDrive results in those music files being deleted from OneDrive and placed in the OneDrive Recycle bin.

Creating Playlists

A big part of playing music is the *playlist*. If you've used a previous version of iTunes or Windows Media Player, you probably know about creating playlists. Playlists are custom song selections that you pick to play together. Maybe it's a "best of" Tom Petty mix or a selection of your favorite classical music. The Groove Music app has made it much easier to create and manage playlists. To create a playlist from your collection or add a song to an existing one, select the + sign when a song is selected; then choose an existing playlist or select **New Playlist** (see Figure 26.14). Playlists that are created on other Windows 10 devices you use are synced by default.

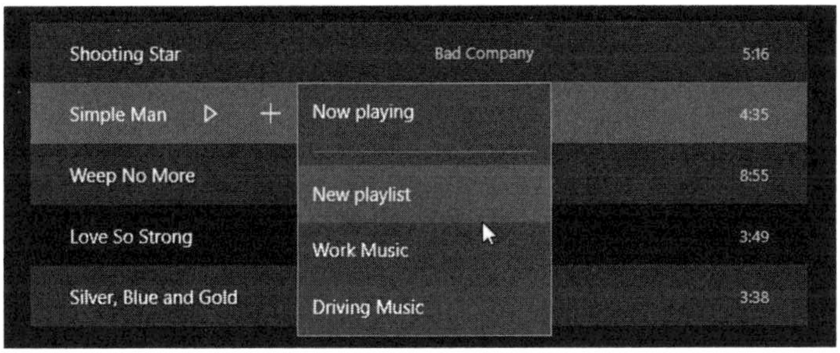

FIGURE 26.14

Add songs to an existing playlist or create new ones on-the-fly.

NOTE   Currently, there is no tool available to import playlists created using other applications. Hopefully, this feature will make its way into the Groove Music app by means of a future update.

Purchasing Music

There are two ways to purchase music through the Groove Music app. You can purchase a music streaming subscription, or you can purchase digital music through the Windows Store. Both choices are explained in the following sections.

Using Groove Music Pass

There are many competitors in the streaming music service industry. Microsoft continues to promote the Groove Music Pass streaming service that contains millions of songs, no ads, and smooth integration into the Groove Music app; this is an attractive option to anyone owning a Windows 10 device. Music Pass has long been associated with Xbox services, so you might see it referred to as Xbox Music occasionally. Activating a Groove Music Pass subscription adds Radio and Explore features to the Groove Music app, as shown in Figure 26.15.

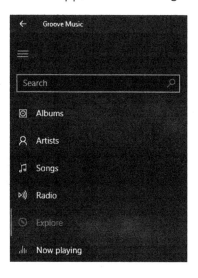

FIGURE 26.15

Activating a Groove Music Pass subscription unlocks additional features of the Groove Music app.

Although Groove Music Pass no longer offers a free ad-driven subscription as it had in the past, there is a free 30-day trial that lets you get an idea if this service is worth the current subscription rate of $9.99 per month. A Groove Music Pass code can be purchased at retailers and redeemed later, or you can activate a subscription with a few clicks. You should have billing information in place with your Microsoft account. Chapter 24, "Using Your Microsoft Account for Purchases," discusses how to ensure that your Microsoft account is ready for making purchases.

To activate a Groove Music Pass subscription, follow these steps:

1. Open the Groove Music app and select **Settings** from the hamburger menu.

2. From the Groove Music Pass section of Settings, select **Get a Groove Music Pass** or **Redeem a Code** (refer to Figure 26.6).

3. When selecting Get a Groove Music Pass, you will see a few payment options, as shown in Figure 26.16. Select one of the pass options presented. Unless you are purchasing the discounted annual subscription, select the **Free Music Pass Trial** if offered—no need to throw away 30 free days. (Just be sure to cancel the subscription before the trial ends, *then* purchase the discounted 12-month music pass.)

FIGURE 26.16

Choose a Groove Music Pass option to start enjoying streamed music in the Groove Music app.

4. You will be prompted to enable or disable password prompts for purchases. I recommend you leave this **On**. Select **Next** to continue.

5. A summary of your purchase will be presented showing the amount to be charged to your default payment method that is linked to your Microsoft account. Select **Confirm** to make the purchase.

6. The Groove Music app is updated, enabling new features associated with Groove Music Pass.

With a Groove Music Pass subscription, you can enjoy radio stations based on artists you enjoy. Select **Radio** from the hamburger menu, select **Start a Station**, and then indicate an artist. The Groove Music app will remember radio stations you have created, and music will be streamed by a variety of artists that fit into the same genre as the artist you indicated.

Other benefits of Groove Music Pass include

- Search now includes artist, album, and song choices from your collection as well as the deep Groove Music Pass library.

- Selecting songs playing in the radio includes links to purchase the album in the Windows Store.

- Explore Artist reveals other albums by the artist, related artists, top songs, and bio information.

- Songs added to playlists from Groove Music Pass content are automatically downloaded locally for playing when not connected to the Internet.

Purchasing Music in the Windows Store

Windows 10 has combined many types of media into the Windows Store, making it a one-stop place for shopping from your device. Music is a very new addition to the Windows Store. You will find prices clearly indicated for both albums and songs. Purchases in the Windows Store require that billing information be linked to your Microsoft account.

To purchase music in the Windows Store, follow these steps:

1. From the Groove Music app, select **Get Music in Store** from the hamburger menu. The Windows Store will open to the Music section, as shown in Figure 26.17.

2. Below the prominent sliding viewer of featured albums, three links are provided to help you with navigation:

    - **Top Songs**—Provides a long list of hundreds of songs ranked by sales. Select from genres to filter the list when looking for top-selling songs.

    - **Genres**—Opens a list of genres from which to choose. Select a genre and further filter your browsing by selecting **New Albums** or **Top Albums** from the Chart filter.

    - **Your Music Library**—Returns you to your music collection in the Music app.

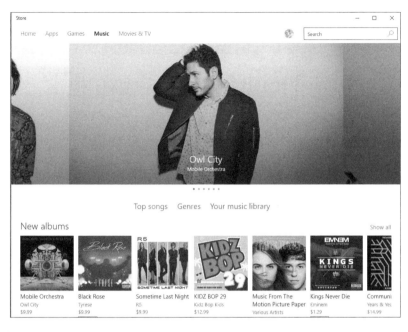

FIGURE 26.17

Browse for new music and make purchases in the Windows Store.

3. From the home page of the Music section of the Windows Store, you can browse featured albums or scroll down to view lists of top-selling albums, songs, and artists.

4. Select an album or artist to learn more about it. When viewing an album, you can read information about the album, listen to short previews of songs, find additional music from the artist, and check out related artists. Artist pages include bios, latest albums and singles, top-selling songs, and related artists.

5. Select the price button for a song or an album to start a purchase. You will most likely be prompted to reenter your Microsoft account password and select **Sign In** as a security feature. You will see a summary of the amount, and the default linked method of payment for your Microsoft account will be indicated, as shown in Figure 26.18. If everything looks correct, select **Buy** to complete the transaction. The Groove Music app will begin downloading your purchase. Purchased music will not show a price; instead, you can select the link **View in My Music** to jump back to the Groove Music app.

If you know what you are looking for, then the search tool in the Windows Store is your friend. Searches within the Windows Store will give relevant results from apps, music, and video categories. Purchases made in the Windows Store can be downloaded to other Windows 10 devices you use with your Microsoft account.

FIGURE 26.18

Purchasing music requires a couple steps to confirm a transaction, which should avoid accidental charges.

Importing Music and Creating Music CDs

So far in this chapter, you've read about managing digital music stored on your computers and hard drives, as well as streamed music and music purchased through the Windows Store. With all the great music in your library, you might want to create a music CD of your own design. It's also a good bet that you'll purchase new CDs or come across CDs in your home or office whose music you want to add to your library. These two likely scenarios are the focus of this section.

As mentioned in the beginning of this chapter, the Groove Music app isn't up to the task of addressing all your music enjoyment needs. To import a new CD into your library or to create a new CD, use the desktop application Windows Media Player. Users of past Windows versions probably know the Windows Media Player, which is a handy tool that can also be used to manage all your music.

Importing Music from a CD

Windows Media Player is included with Windows 10. Besides listening to music, you also can import songs from music CDs using Windows Media Player. The music you import becomes part of your music library. In almost all cases—and as long as you have an active Internet connection—Windows can identify the CD. The name of the artist, the name of the album, and the name of each selection are automatically loaded into the library. If not, you must enter that information manually.

 TIP If you find that you need to use Windows Media Player often, it's not a bad idea to pin it to your Start screen. Just search for Windows Media Player using the Windows taskbar Search box, right-click (or tap and hold) it in the search results, and select **Pin to Start**.

Follow these steps to import music from a CD:

1. Open the Windows Media Player. You might find it easiest to use the Windows search box on the taskbar to quickly locate it by name.

2. Load your CD and wait for Windows to recognize it. Do not press any buttons for a few moments.

3. The CD's tracks plus a snapshot of the cover artwork associated with the CD appear, as shown in Figure 26.19.

FIGURE 26.19

The CD's contents appear, enabling you to use the checkbox to deselect songs you do not want to import.

4. Select **Rip Settings** from the menu bar if you want to adjust any quality settings; otherwise, select **Rip CD** to begin.

5. Wait for each track's Rip Status to become Ripped to Library. You can eject the CD when complete.

Creating a Music CD

Burning a CD using Windows Media Player is just an extension of creating a playlist, although any playlists you create in the Music app don't appear in Windows Media Player. So, to burn a CD, you first need to create a playlist. Follow these steps to create a music CD based on a playlist you've created:

1. Open Windows Media Player. Note the tree structure of your media on your computer on the left side of the screen (refer to Figure 26.19). This is known as the Navigation Tree.

2. Select the **Burn** tab located toward the upper-right corner of the application window (refer to Figure 26.19). The area below the tabs displays a blank burn list.

3. Under Music in the Navigation Tree, click **Artist**, **Album**, or **Genre** to choose music to burn to the CD. Drag songs to the burn list. If you have a playlist you want to burn to a CD, you can drag the playlist to the burn list; the individual songs will appear in the list.

4. To remove any songs from the burn list, right-click them and select **Remove from List**.

5. Insert a blank, writable CD into a drive on your computer capable of burning CDs.

6. From the top of the Burn tab, select **Start Burn**.

7. Remove the CD when Windows Media Player reports that the CD is complete.

THE ABSOLUTE MINIMUM

- You can play existing music in the Groove Music app either by moving the music directly into the Music folder on your Windows 10 device or by indicating where the music is located within the Music app.

- You also can connect to a music source over a home network, but this solution will fail when you move your computer out of range of the network or if the network location cannot be indexed by Windows.

- Have a method of payment linked to your Microsoft account for Groove Music Pass subscriptions or to purchase music in the Windows Store.

- You need to use Windows Media Player if you want to import music into your library from a CD or want to burn music to a CD.

27

HAVING FUN AND PLAYING GAMES

Microsoft has long recognized that the computer is more than a tool for productivity. Games like Solitaire and Minesweeper were standard features of Windows for decades, and high-end graphics and processing power brought bigger and better games to the PC.

With Windows 10, things have come full circle. Windows 10 now powers the Xbox One game console, and the high-end hardware on the Xbox lets you stream your games from the Xbox to your Windows 10 devices. The Windows Store includes a huge catalog of games; you might have noticed that Solitaire is back in Windows 10 celebrating its 25th anniversary.

This short chapter focuses on the ways you can get the most out of games on your Windows 10 computer or tablet. We will explore the Xbox app and examine some features that work when you have an Xbox One on your network. Although the Xbox One is yet to be upgraded to Windows 10, at the time of this writing, the features and capabilities described in this chapter will be available for Xbox One owners.

Gaming with Windows 10

Windows 10 has been designed to run on many devices and for many different purposes. Windows 10 users are a diverse group of individuals who range from business persons who may do some casual gaming to the hardcore gamer who wants to play everything on his gaming rig. The hardware that is on each device is an unknown factor that will influence how well some games perform, but Microsoft has included some features in Windows 10 that will improve your gaming experience on any device.

Gamers love eye candy, and some of today's games look astonishingly realistic. Even casual gamers appreciate high resolution and smooth animation. For those familiar with DirectX, DirectX 12 is the latest version of the application programming interface (API) that enables a computer's central processing unit (CPU) to communicate with the graphics processing unit (GPU). Technical jargon aside, just know that because this is handled much more efficiently in DirectX 12 than in past versions, Microsoft is promoting this as a big deal for gamers. The hardware on your device still plays a big factor, but you will see better graphics on a device running Windows 10 than the same device running Windows 7 or 8/8.1.

Windows 10 includes drivers for the Xbox One game controller. Just plug it in using a microUSB cable, and drivers are installed automatically. A wireless adaptor can be purchased that will allow your wireless adaptor to work with your computer without the need for a USB cable.

Microsoft Solitaire Collection is included in Windows 10. As shown in Figure 27.1, popular variations of this addictive game can be selected. Play a challenge or play a few minutes of your favorite version of solitaire when you need to get away from those spreadsheets.

The Xbox app is included in Windows 10. This serves as a game hub that enables you to track your activity and achievements as well as keep up with your friends. The Xbox app is covered in detail later in this chapter. First, though, you might want to know more about Xbox Live services.

FIGURE 27.1

Microsoft Solitaire celebrates 25 years of bringing serenity to the workplace.

Understanding Xbox Live Services

Although you can install a variety of quality games from the Windows Store or download and install gaming applications from trusted sources, you will quickly notice that some games in the Windows Store have an Xbox tag that sets them apart from other games. What is the difference?

Xbox Live is Microsoft's online gaming and digital media service. Games that have gone through the extra steps to be certified with Microsoft Studios can feature Xbox Live. This lets you know that a game offers additional features that leverage Xbox Live services.

Here are some of the features Xbox Live offers to gamers:

- **Gamertag identity**—Your activity and achievements are linked to your Xbox Live username, or *gamertag*, which can help sync your play across multiple devices.

- **Achievements**—Achievements are awarded as you progress through a game. These achievements automatically show up for your friends in their Activity Feeds.

- **Gamerscore**—Your Gamerscore is simply an overall total from your achievement points that you build up gradually when playing any Xbox Live game. It allows you some bragging rights and a way to evaluate how serious a gamer is.

- **Content sharing**—Members can share screenshots and video clips.

> **NOTE** To benefit from games that offer Xbox Live, you will need an Xbox account, which should be the same account used to sign in to your device. If you are using a local account, you will be encouraged to upgrade this to a Microsoft account. You might be able to play a game; however, you will not be signed in, and your achievements may not be saved. Refer to Chapter 24, "Using Your Microsoft Account for Purchases," to learn more about using a Microsoft account with Xbox Live services.

To see some of the features included in a game that features Xbox Live, follow these steps:

1. Install a game from the Windows Store that features Xbox Live. (There are many free choices.)

2. Open the newly installed game app. You might be prompted to grant permission to access your Xbox Live info, as shown in Figure 27.2. Select **Yes** to continue.

FIGURE 27.2

Games that feature Xbox Live need permission to update your Xbox Live info.

3. After the game has loaded and signed you in to Xbox Live services, notice
    your gamertag. The gamertag may be located in different places; how-
    ever, it usually appears in one of the upper corners of the app, as shown in
    Figure 27.3.

FIGURE 27.3

Your gamertag appears when you have signed in to an Xbox app successfully.

4. Games featuring Xbox Live include a special toolbar. Press Windows+G to
    reveal the Game bar shown in Figure 27.4. Notice that it quickly hides if the
    cursor is not located over a button.

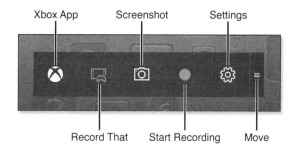

FIGURE 27.4

Xbox games include a hidden Game bar.

The Game bar is a new feature with Windows 10, including

*   **Xbox**—This button opens the Xbox app.

*   **Record That**—You can use the game DVR to save the last 30 seconds of
    gameplay. Some devices might not be able to use this feature. A compatible
    video card is required, which will require a higher-end desktop or laptop.

*   **Screenshot**—You can save a screenshot from the game by selecting this but-
    ton or pressing Win+Alt+PrtScr. Images are saved to the Videos>Captures
    folder.

- **Start Recording**—Start a manual recording of gameplay. As with Record That, your hardware must be compatible with this feature.

- **Settings**—Select this button to reveal settings related to Xbox Live features for this device. As shown in Figure 27.5, some settings related to recording clips can be configured here.

- **Move**—Select Move to drag the Game bar to a different location to avoid obstructing your view during gameplay.

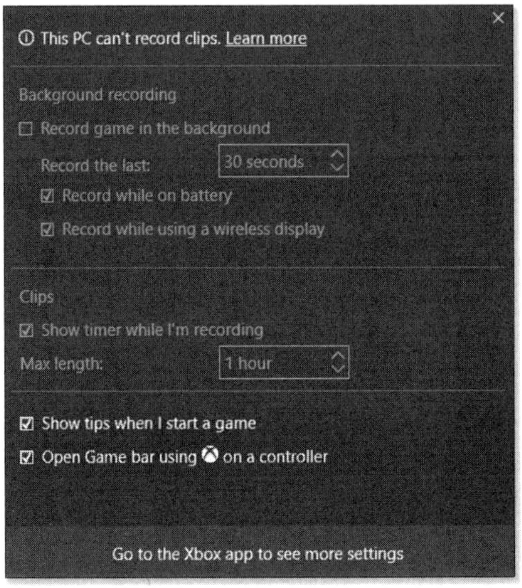

![Settings panel screenshot showing recording options. Top shows "This PC can't record clips. Learn more" with a close X button. Background recording section with "Record game in the background" unchecked, "Record the last: 30 seconds", "Record while on battery" checked, "Record while using a wireless display" checked. Clips section with "Show timer while I'm recording" checked, "Max length: 1 hour". Below: "Show tips when I start a game" checked, "Open Game bar using Xbox button on a controller" checked. Bottom link: "Go to the Xbox app to see more settings".]

FIGURE 27.5

This device is not able to record clips according to Settings opened from the Game bar.

NOTE   Currently, Microsoft has indicated that Game DVR requires videocards that match the following requirements: AMD: Radeon HD 7000 series, HD 7000M series, HD 8000 series, HD 8000M series, R9 series, and R7 series.

NVIDIA: GeForce 600 series or later, GeForce 800M series or later, and Quadro Kxxx series or later. Intel: Intel HD Graphics 4000 or later.

Using the Xbox App

Windows 10 includes the Xbox app. This app is a hub that lets you track your activity and achievements as well as that of your friends. You will know when they are online and can chat with them through the Xbox app. You also can connect to an Xbox One console on your network and enjoy many additional features, including the ability to stream games that are played using the hardware on the game console to render the game rather than the hardware on your Windows 10 device. This is a great feature if you're using a device with inferior hardware to the Xbox One. The Xbox app, shown in Figure 27.6, is organized into a few sections.

FIGURE 27.6

The Xbox app can help you manage all your gaming activities from your Windows 10 device.

Sections of the Xbox app include the following:

- **Activity Feed**—Keep up with achievements and events of your friends. You can like, make comments, and share activities that show up here.

- **Recently Played**—Recently Played lists the Xbox Live games you have played lately.

- **Featured Games**—Discover new games here that may interest you.

- **Friends**—The Xbox app makes it easy to keep track of your friends and even find new ones. You can invite friends to play online, message them, and make them a favorite.

The hamburger menu of the Xbox app, shown in Figure 27.7, has many areas of focus. You can review aspects of your profile and activity, start games, jump to the store to look for new games, and even connect to and manage your Xbox One.

FIGURE 27.7

The hamburger menu of the Xbox app allows you to jump into games or keep up with friends, among other tasks.

The hamburger menu of the Xbox app includes

- **Profile**—Select your avatar in the hamburger menu to open the pane shown in Figure 27.8. You can customize your avatar, appear offline, and allow your real name to appear along with your gamertag. In addition, you can review your activity, achievements, captures, and the people you are following.

- **Home**—Home returns you to the initial view you had when opening the app (refer to Figure 27.6).

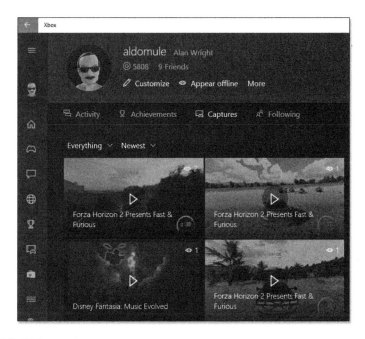

FIGURE 27.8

Customize your avatar or check out some of your own gaming activities in the Xbox app.

- **My Games**—My Games displays all the game apps on your device. Select a game to open the Game Hub. You can manually add games that were not automatically included here by selecting Add a Game from Your PC and then selecting the applications to include here. Games can be launched from this list by selecting Play without opening the Game Hub.

  Game Hubs allow you to select Play to launch games, including Xbox One games that appear here. Additionally, you can look up information about the game in the Windows Store and look for players to follow for a specific game.

- **Messages**—Messages show your messages. Select New Message to pick a contact you want to message.

- **Activity Alerts**—Focuses on any activity related to your favorites.

- **Achievements**—Lets you view and filter your gaming achievements.

- **Game DVR**—Here you can look at clips and screenshots you have taken on this PC, select Shared to view clips you might have generated on other devices, or select Community to view clips that have been shared to everyone by other Xbox Live members.

- **Store**—Select Store to open the Windows Store.

- **OneGuide**—OneGuide enables you to manage your TV listings using the Xbox One. You can review listings add favorite channels and even start playing a program through the Xbox One console from the Xbox app on your device. You must be connected to an Xbox One to use this feature.

- **Connect**—If you are not yet connected to an Xbox One, you can select Connect to look for an Xbox One console on your network. After you are connected, this changes to Connected. When connected to an Xbox One console, you can enable a virtual controller or remote control to control the Xbox. In this way you can add an impromptu controller from a touchscreen tablet.

- **Settings**—There are a few settings categories you can configure:

  - Account settings allow you to sign out of Xbox Live Services or sign in with a different account. You can also create an account from here.

  - Notification settings enable you to get notifications when favorite friends are online, when favorite friends start a twitch broadcast, and allow pop-up notifications when you receive a message.

  - Game DVR settings, shown in Figure 27.9, include keyboard shortcuts and settings related to video and audio quality.

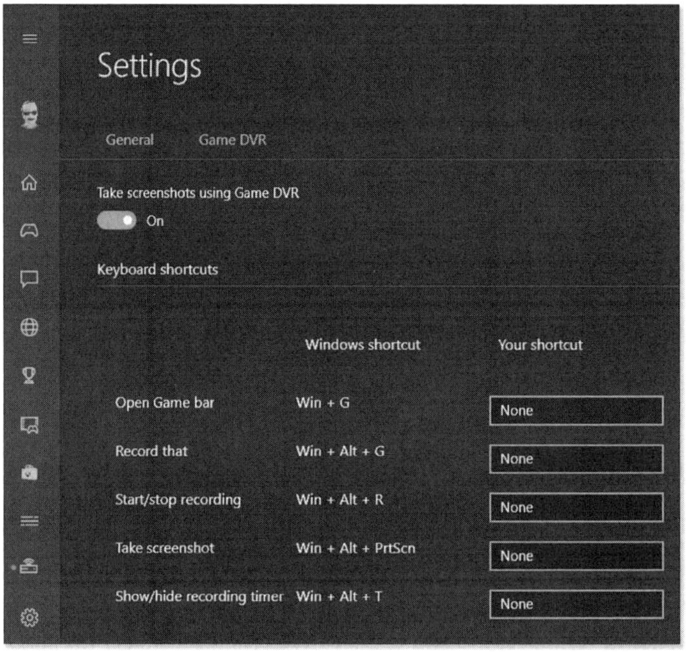

FIGURE 27.9

You can create your own keyboard shortcuts for Xbox Live features in the Xbox app.

The Xbox app unlocks a lot of features when paired with an Xbox One gaming console on the same network and when signed on with the same gamertag. Streaming games from an Xbox (Game Streaming must be enabled in Settings) is a feature that is not fully available at the time of this writing because Xbox One game consoles must be running a special preview of Windows 10 to use the feature. Although game streaming is a great feature that creates new ways to enjoy your console games, there are limitations that can damper some of your excitement:

- When streaming from an Xbox, the console cannot be used for other activities.

- You cannot stream video or TV from the Xbox One to your computer. The exception is if you own an Xbox One Digital TV Tuner (sold in Europe and Australia) or purchase a device like an Hauppauge 955Q TV Tuner ($79) that reportedly will allow you to stream TV to your Windows 10 devices.

 NOTE Microsoft has indicated the following recommended requirements for streaming a game from your Xbox One gaming console:

Best Performance: Wired Ethernet connection

Good Performance: Wireless—5 GHz 802.11 N or 802.11 AC wireless access point

Limited Performance: Wireless—2.4 GHz 802.11 N or 802.11 AC wireless access point

It is also recommended that your Windows 10 PC have at least 2 GB of RAM and a 1.5-GHz CPU or faster.

THE ABSOLUTE MINIMUM

- Setting up your Xbox account includes a gamertag and an avatar.

- Xbox Live services bring a lot of extra features to gaming, such as friends and messaging.

- Use the Xbox app to find friends you can play with, watch clips, and follow skilled players you can learn from.

- Use the Xbox app to play Xbox One games on your Windows 10 device.

Index